Let the Record Show

To my wife, Carolyn, for enduring all the loud frustrations brought on by my own ineptitude with the word processor.

LET THE RECORD SHOW

Medical Malpractice—The Lawsuit Nobody Wins

J. Kelley Avery, MD

STATE VOLUNTEER MUTUAL INSURANCE COMPANY
BRENTWOOD, TENNESSEE

First Edition published January, 2000

Published in 2000 by State Volunteer Mutual Insurance Company, PO Box,
1065, Brentwood, Tennessee 37024-1065.

The cases contained herein were originally published in the *Journal of the
Tennessee Medical Association* and are used by permission.

Cover photograph of author by Dee Dee Evans.

Editorial and production services by Word Weavers, Inc., PO Box 1151,
Franklin, Tennessee 37065.

ISBN: 0-9665454-1-9

Printed in the United Sates of America.

Contents

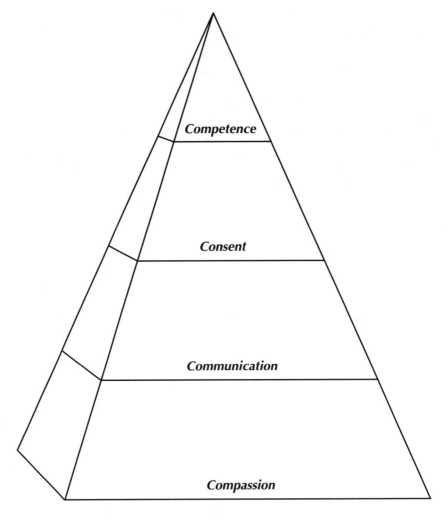

The pyramid of the doctor-patient relationship.

Preface

Tennessee physicians are fortunate to practice in a state where the primary medical liability insurance carrier is truly devoted to the interests of its policyholders. They are doubly fortunate to enjoy and benefit from the expertise of J. Kelley Avery, MD. Dr. Avery is indeed one of the pioneers in medical liability risk management.

In the early days of State Volunteer Mutual Insurance Company (SVMIC), I had the distinct honor and privilege of being invited to speak to Tennessee physicians on medical liability risk management topics on more than one occasion. Dr. Avery refers to that program in his introduction to this volume.

In Colorado we had been attempting similar risk management seminars, and we were industriously seeking more productive methods. Dr. Avery, even in those days, had devised what were called "vignettes." Webster describes vignette as "a short descriptive literary sketch" or "a brief incident or scene." Briefly, these were stories of medical incidents that had led to "malpractice lawsuits" and loss. It was of importance that Dr. Avery selected cases where there were lessons to be learned. Of greater importance, however, was his having the insight and expertise to present them in a way that held the attention of the audience (Tennessee physicians) and to do it in a way that, insofar as possible, avoided pointing fingers at an individual practitioner. Dr. Avery and his associates had accomplished this to near perfection.

Dr. Avery has gathered cases, similar to the original vignettes, and placed them in this volume. I have had the pleasure of reviewing a few of them. The messages they demonstrate are universal. Any medical practitioner could benefit by giving personal attention to these lessons and could substantially reduce his or her exposure.

There is one facet of medical practice that does not lend itself quite as well to the method of vignettes. That is the personal relationship of the doctor and patient. The long unexplained wait; the "talking down" to; the failure to discuss (in advance) the potential

1

magnitude of the bills; the unconscionable treatment of nurses, staff, and others by the practitioner; the inadequate explanation of risks; the repeated failure to communicate with the families of critical care patients, etc. These habits, if avoided, can go a long way toward preventing the initial family trip to the malpractice lawyer. If practitioners can increase the "humanity and humility" of their practice and learn the lessons contained in this volume, they should experience a leveling and perhaps a decrease in their liability losses.

ROBERT S. BRITTAIN, MD*

*Private practice, surgery, Denver 1963-72; Risk Manager for the Colorado Medical Society Medical Liability Insurance Program 1973-82; COPIC 1983-99; Risk Manger for Arizona Medical Liability Insurance Program MICA, 1983-90.

Introduction

The cases in this book are actual cases from the files of State Volunteer Mutual Insurance Company (SVMIC), the physician-owned medical malpractice insurance carrier in Tennessee, serving a large part of that market along with physicians in Arkansas, Mississippi, Alabama, Georgia, Virginia, and Kentucky. I am grateful to the company for its support in this effort. I am grateful as well to the Tennessee Medical Association, in whose journal all these cases have been published. I appreciate TMA giving me permission to use these cases in the creation of this book.

This effort began in the middle 1980s when I was the Medical Director of SVMIC as an adjunct to a program of loss prevention education. The program was started in a rudimentary fashion in 1976, the year in which SVMIC sold its first medical malpractice insurance policy. The company, chartered in 1975, realized that in light of the explosion of lawsuits against physicians, a structured educational effort was essential. We began by speaking to local medical societies on their invitation, and we received a lot of invitations. It quickly became apparent that SVMIC, as a physician-owned company, had to take ownership of the educational effort. We began with seminars that lasted all day. This was too long, so we reduced the time of the seminars to three hours with a break that took half the day.

As we experimented with this program, it became apparent that with a two-hour seminar without a break the same amount of material could be covered as in the three-hour program. The seminars continue today with the staff, the moderator, and panelists conducting three two-hour sessions each day.

The company made the decision in the middle to later 1980s to give a 10 percent premium discount for attendance to the seminars and, of course, attendance grew. That program continues today and reaches about 75 percent of the members, who, in a mutual company, are the owners.

The publishing of a "Case of the Month" in the *Journal of the Tennessee Medical Association* paralleled the seminar effort and also continues today. The cases are closed and have been fictionalized in order that the physicians involved not be identifiable. Some of the published cases are very close to the actual facts while others are edited and amended in order to make the point that is, we believe, most valuable from the standpoint of preventing lawsuits against physicians. Very few of these cases have been recognized by the physicians involved. And in those instances where there was recognition of the case, the physicians have recognized that the story is told to help physician colleagues.

Having served on the Claims Review Committee since the founding of the company, I have had access to the cases coming through and have been able to glean from them those that seem to embody the facts and the lessons that are important to the doctor members of our company. I am told that the "Case of the Month," is the most widely read item in the journal, so I know that physicians are interested in doing their part in this educational effort, and they do take it seriously.

There has been a perceptible change in the claims and lawsuits in the last twenty years. Early in the malpractice explosion, the majority of claims and lawsuits involved surgical or procedural misadventures by a factor of three to one. As time has gone on, we have seen the claims and lawsuits change to involve more of the non-proceduralist physicians, i.e., Family Practice, Internal Medicine, Pediatrics, etc. In the case of radiologists, as their practice has become more invasive, the numbers of claims and lawsuits has increased accordingly. Now the ratio between the proceduralist and the non-proceduralist lawsuits approach one to one. As far as the non-proceduralist is concerned, the claim usually has to do with a delay in diagnosis or treatment or failure to diagnose and treat according to the prevailing standard of care.

Just as the physicians have become more and more educated to the threat of legal action against them, lawyers have become more educated in the art of litigation, whether representing the physician on the defense or the patient as the plaintiff. The cost of the process has matched, or exceeded, the economy. The settlements and awards have also matched the economics of the times. There have been more "shock" verdicts, those exceeding $1 million, and this fact has produced for both the physician and the company an extremely cautious atmosphere surrounding the litigation. With all of this, however, only about half the claims evolve into lawsuits and of those that go to trail, the physician wins about 80 percent of the time. The number of dollars involved in the expense of the litigation from filing to resolution is staggering, and this has to be reflected in the cost of coverage borne by the physician.

There is another element of cost that must not be ignored, and that is the emotional and psychological devastation that frequently occurs following the filing of a lawsuit against a physician. Many doctors feel that their entire life is somehow being attacked. Of course the complaint itself contains language that attacks the physician's care of the plaintiff in every conceivable way. He or she is accused of negligence in each and every aspect of the patient's care. The reason for the unexpected outcome is solely due, it is claimed, to the physician's actions or inaction, which are said to be outside the acceptable standard of care. The physician's family feels this assault as well. Significant depression is always present. Divorce occurs more often than would be expected. Suicide has rarely occurred. Most physician-owned malpractice carriers have support groups organized consisting of both physicians and the spouses to help in these situations.

There is also the cost related to the enormous amount of time required for the doctor to prepare the case for the lawyer: studying the medical record, every aspect of it; doing research on the clinical nature of the case; and attending all the pretrial depositions that are taken. The depositions involve experts who support the doctor as well as those who accuse the doctor of wrongdoing. All this time is non-productive as far as the physician's income is concerned. This cost alone can run into the thousands of dollars.

As we look at these cases, what do they tell us? The over-powering lesson is that the reasons for the patient becoming angry enough to sue the doctor lie in the physician-patient relationship. These reasons are not, in the main, scientific or related to substandard care; they are behavioral.

In the late 1980s, we asked our defense lawyers to examine their experience with medical malpractice defense and tell us the most common reasons that patients become litigious. The findings were interesting, and we have no reason to believe that there has been a significant change since that time. Seventy percent of the lawsuits were related to the communication in the relationship between the caregiver and his or her patient. Within that large majority of the reasons were physician attitude, i.e., too rushed to talk, an air of superiority, a lack of perceived caring and concern for the patient's problems, etc. Lesser but important roles were the cost of care, the media coverage of the huge damages claimed in the lawsuits, which are almost never realized, and the criticism by a doctor of care previously rendered by another physician. The physician-owned company of Colorado, COPIC, recently reviewed their claims and found that only 7 percent were related to care below an acceptable level.

The cases that are described in this publication will demonstrate why in my opinion the claim/lawsuit developed, and I will offer some suggestions about preventing future claims/lawsuits from arising. It is my hope that the facts related here will prevent at least some legal action against physicians.

J. Kelley Avery, MD

I

Anesthesiology

Anesthesia is one of the few specialties that has enjoyed a reduction in class and premiums since the onset of the physician-owned medical malpractice insurance movement. It has made an enormous difference in the number, cost, and character of claims. The change came about with the development of the technology allowing the measuring the oxygen saturation of the blood by simply placing a sensor over the pad of a finger. Results were available instantaneously. A little later there was developed the technology enabling the physician to measure the carbon dioxide in expired air by incorporating in the endotracheal tube a CO_2 sensor. Again, this critical measurement was available to the anesthesiologist in real time.

The American Society of Anesthesiologists led the crusade for hospitals to make this technology a standard in all their operating rooms. The physician-owned companies were active in this effort as well.

The cases that are now brought are generally less serious for the anesthesiologist. They are nevertheless reason for us to remain alert for means that will further reduce exposure in this very critical specialty. A clear communication with the surgeon before, during, and after the procedure is essential. Before the case, the anesthesiologist needs to recognize a unique responsibility for a true informed consent relative to the risks and benefits of the anesthesia itself apart from the surgical case. He/she should not attempt to protect the surgeon by documenting informed consent for the operation. During the case the surgeon must be made aware of all intraoperative events that might affect the outcome of the case. After the case, the anesthesiologist must be very careful to put his/her training and experience to work in recovery. All these duties are complicated, but are not rendered impossible, by the movement of procedures from the operating room suite to the outpatient setting.

It is hoped that the cases presented here will be a reminder of ways that can, and do, reduce bad or surprising outcomes that can lead to legal action.

1.   LET THE RECORD SHOW . . .

Allegation—Patient injury remote from operative site
Physician Issue—Failure to protect patient
Patient Issue—Nerve injury
Outcome—Decision for physician

CASE STUDY

A 50-year-old construction company owner was admitted for surgery for a detached retina. Preoperative examination conducted by the anesthesiologist revealed no contraindications for the use of general anesthesia. A review of the patient's chart revealed a normal electrocardiogram, normal chest x-ray, and normal laboratory work. The next morning, the patient was taken to the operating room for a scleral buckling procedure with encircling band of the right eye.

The anesthesiologist did the induction and intubation, as well as the positioning of the patient for the procedure, after which maintenance of the anesthesia was turned over to his certified registered nurse anesthetist. The surgery lasted approximately three hours and twenty minutes. Several months later, the patient complained to the anesthesiologist about paresthesia of his left arm. "Exercise and warm compresses" were prescribed by the anesthesiologist.

Because of continuing arm pain, the patient sought the services of an orthopedic surgeon, whose x-rays revealed a small spur over the ulnar epicondyle. An electromyelogram revealed rather mild atrophy, but good motor strength.

The pain and paresthesia persisted and the patient filed suit alleging that the anesthesiologist was negligent in positioning his arm. The patient also alleged that the anesthesiologist was negligent in failing to use the proper padding over pressure point areas.

Even though this injury was relatively insignificant and affected a wealthy plaintiff, the case was vigorously pursued. The ultimate result was a jury verdict for the defendant.

LOSS PREVENTION COMMENTS

The anesthesiologist was successfully defended largely on the strength of his records. At deposition and at trial the anesthesiologist was able to testify and show by his records that the risks, benefits, and any alternative to general anesthesia had been discussed with the patient. The anesthesia record reflected that elbow pads as well as padded arm boards were utilized. In addition, the preoperative history and physical examination conducted by the anesthesiologist showed that the patient himself made reference to an old elbow injury. Finally, there were no complaints of arm pain found in the hospital chart during the entire hospital stay.

It is important to realize that if a lawsuit is filed, the medical record is a physician's absolute "best friend." It is the most important evidence that will be presented in the courtroom. Just as a sloppy record equals sloppy care in the minds of the jury, so does a carefully documented, complete record reflect careful and complete patient care.

2.   COMPLICATION DURING ARTHROSCOPY

Allegation—Failure to monitor
Physician Issue— Failure to communicate (physician to physician)
Patient Issues—Paraplegia; anterior spinal artery thrombosis
Outcome—Spinal cord injury; six-figure settlement

CASE STUDY

A 56-year-old truck driver with a long history of pain in his knees had previously had arthroscopic surgery on his right knee for osteochondritis with fair results. Now the left knee was so painful that it interfered with his work. The pain was aggravated by long periods of walking and lifting. Driving his truck caused aching in his knee to the degree that he would have to stop his truck, get out, and walk around to get some relief, only to have the same problem recur when he resumed driving. These symptoms were the same that he had experienced with his right knee, and the surgery four years earlier had helped considerably. His physician recommended the same approach to his left knee, with the caveat that it would probably delay the inevitable arthroplasty for a few years.

For years the obese patient had experienced moderately severe hypertension that was difficult to control. His treatment had been Atenolol, Vasotec, and Catapres. He was admitted to the outpatient surgery area, where the note by the anesthesiologist indicated that he had been informed of the risks and benefits of the knee operation by the orthopedic surgeon and had agreed to the arthroscopic surgery for debridement of the joint. Pre-operative medication was given about 12:45 PM. At 1:00 PM an epidural was administered. The procedure went smoothly and without incident through the use of xylocaine and epinephrine, along with good analgesia. The surgery began about 2:00 PM and ended about an hour later. He was transferred to the postanesthesia care unit in good condition but still unable to move his lower extremities.

It is significant to note that the operating room clinical record did not mention a blood pressure reading during the procedure. However, after transfer to the postanethesia care unit, about one and a half hours after the epidural had been given, the blood pressure was reported to be 148/90 mm Hg.

The anesthesia record indicated that the blood pressure was tracked at 80-90 mm Hg systolic during the one-hour operation. Intravenous fluids were running with the patient receiving about 2,000 cc preoperatively and intraoperatively.

The patient remained unable to move his lower extremities while in the postanesthesia care unit. Three hours after the anesthesia had been given the patient was transferred to a bed on the floor, still unable to move his legs. Thirty minutes later the surgeon was called about the patient's condition. He asked that a resident see and evaluate the patient. The patient then was transferred to a 23-hour observation bed. At 10:15 PM the blood pressure was recorded at 160/100 mm Hg, and throughout the night and early morning hours it remained at about this level or higher, on one occasion reaching 206/110 mm Hg.

At 8:00 AM the morning after the surgery the patient was seen for the first time by his anesthesiologist and his surgeon. At this time a consultation was asked of a neurologist, who found the patient still unable to move his legs, but with some ability to flex at his hips. The circulation seemed intact in his legs, and he had some perception of touch but no pain on pinprick. CT and MRI were both negative. EMG showed no motor function in the lower extremities, indicating a lesion at the L2-3 level. The diagnosis was occlusion of the anterior spinal artery, presumably brought about by the prolonged hypotension (one hour) during surgery. The patient did not recover significant function and remains paraplegic.

A lawsuit was filed charging the surgeon and the anesthesiologist with negligence in not treating the intraoperative hypotension, which was presumed to be the causative factor in the diagnosis. The complaint further charged that there was no informed consent for the anesthesia.

LOSS PREVENTION COMMENTS

Again the record condemns us! There is no record of an informed consent that discussed the epidural anesthetic itself. The rather prolonged period of hypotension during the operation was not treated. It is certainly open to question whether or not one hour of systolic pressure readings of 80-90 mm Hg would contribute to the occlusion of the anterior spinal artery, but this patient had been hypertensive for years and was taking treatment for his hypertension preoperatively. Then there was the prolonged interval between the time the surgeon became aware that the patient could not move his legs and his personal appearance at the patient's bedside. Neither the surgeon nor the anesthesiologist came to see the patient until the next morning, some 18 hours after the anesthetic had been given. While this could not have contributed to the result, it probably did contribute to the anger felt by the patient toward the operating team.

Expert witnesses stated unequivocally that the period of hypotension could have contributed to the final outcome and indicated that prompt intervention by the anesthesiologist could have prevented or mitigated the resulting paralysis.

The doctors had no expert witness support, and the patient had been a productive working man prior to his operation. Thus trying this case was out of the question, and a very large settlement was required to close this case.

3.   INFORMED CONSENT—SUBSTANDARD CARE

Allegation—Procedure not indicated
Physician Issue—Clinical error
Patient Issues—Spinal cord injury; impotence; weakness;
     continued pain
Outcome—Failed treatment; six-figure settlement

CASE STUDY

A 48-year-old man, who had sustained severe injuries in a motor vehicle accident some eight years previously, was admitted to a psychiatric hospital for treatment of substance abuse/addiction of about five years' duration. Following the accident, in which the patient sustained a fracture of the lumbar spine with cord injury, the patient had undergone years of therapy and had improved to the degree that crutch-walking was possible. He had bowel and bladder control, and he was able to have sexual intercourse.

The residual disabilities of the injuries were further complicated by severe pain in the area of the right hip and leg, requiring daily narcotics for relief. His drug dependency was thought to have been precipitated by the injudicious use of narcotics following the injury and during the long period of rehabilitation.

After admission, the attending psychiatrist consulted an anesthesiologist who was associated with a "pain clinic." In the hope that dependency on narcotics could be somewhat ameliorated by epidural injections, the anesthesiologist gave an epidural morphine block, affording several days of significant relief of pain.

At this point the patient was transferred to a general hospital, where epidural injections of alcohol were planned. By this time the severe right hip pain had recurred, unchanged from the past history.

The patient was fully informed of the possible side effects of the alcohol injections, including loss of bladder/bowel control and impotence. Consent was given since the narcotic requirements had increased at least to the level of pre-epidural needs. The patient had repeatedly said that he was willing to have "anything" done to relieve the intractable pain and help him recover from his drug dependency.

A series of three alcohol epidural injections was given. The result was loss of bladder/bowel control, impotence, and residual severe pain in the low back.

LOSS PREVENTION COMMENTS

Although this patient represents a situation in which both the physician and patient were willing to accept unusual risks in pursuing a satisfactory resolution of the problem, there was one fundamental principle that was ignored. Epidural alcohol injections are an acceptable mode of therapy for severe and incapacitating pain of this kind under certain circumstances. However, expert testimony was produced in this case that stated that this particular method of treatment was acceptable only in terminal patients, because loss of bowel/bladder control and impotence almost always resulted to some degree. The most important consideration in any treatment plan is that the treatment be within an acceptable standard. Good informed consent offers no protection in litigating cases where the treatment is bad!

4.   UNANSWERED QUESTIONS—SOMEBODY PAYS

Allegation—Failure to monitor
Physician Issue—Failure to attend

Patient Issue—Death
Outcome—Patient death; large settlement

CASE STUDY

A 45-lb 5-year-old boy had had recurrent bouts of tonsillitis and otitis media virtually all of his life and in the preceding year had been ill on six separate occasions, requiring antibiotics and absence from kindergarten with each episode. His physician had observed the progressive hypertrophy of the tonsils and adenoids and, because of the enlargement and the recurrent febrile bouts of tonsillitis and otitis media, had discussed with the mother the need to consider surgery. The decision was made and the surgery scheduled.

Tonsillectomy was to be done as an outpatient procedure, and after appropriate education of the parents as to its risks and benefits, the child was admitted. After clearance by the anesthesiologist, routine preoperative medication was given, and the procedure was done without incident. The operative note by the surgeon noted some "excessive" bleeding, which was "easily" controlled by pressure and fulguration. Postoperative orders included Demerol 25 mg every three hours as needed, Phenergan suppository 25 mg every three hours as needed for nausea/vomiting, and other supportive measures. In the recovery room, an IV of 500 ml D5 1/4 NS was running. Orders were written by the anesthesiologist for IVs to follow, 500 ml D5 1/4 NS, 500 ml D5 1/4 NS, and another 500 ml D5 1/4 NS.

On arrival in the recovery room the patient was described as unresponsive, breathing shallow, color good, lying on the right side. Ten minutes later 15 mg Demerol was given IM, and 50 minutes later this was followed by another 10 mg Demerol IV and a 12.5 mg Phenergan suppository. He voided normally 250 ml clear urine, was reacting appropriately, and was discharged from the recovery room about two hours after the operation.

The patient vomited a small amount of bile-colored emesis on three occasions about three hours postoperative and was given another 12.5 mg Phenergan suppository. Six hours postoperative the child was still having small amounts of bile-colored emesis, and the anesthesiologist was consulted. Reglan 2 mg and droperidol 0.25 mg IV were ordered as needed for nausea and vomiting, and it was given. The order was not timed, the medication was not charted, and the physician did not see and examine the child prior to ordering the medication. Some time later, perhaps an hour, another 5 mg Demerol was given IV. About one hour after the last medication was given the child was described as "resting comfortably," but very soon after this observation the mother called the nurse and reported that her child had suddenly gripped her hand very tightly and begun to breathe very heavily. Respirations were described as "moist" and a "large amount of frothy bloody secretion" was aspirated from the throat. About eight minutes later, intubation was attempted by the respiratory technician, but was not successful, and the patient was immediately transferred to the operating suite. The attending physician and the anesthesiologist arrived about 30 minutes afterward. The child was being given 100 percent O_2 by bag. Pupils were "dilated" and the patient was "cyanotic." Intubation was accomplished immediately by the anesthesiologist. Color and vital signs improved. At time of intubation the O_2 saturation was recorded at 21 percent, becoming 88 percent in a matter of seconds. Chest x-ray revealed bilateral infiltrates. A sodium of 122 became 124 over the next hour with fluid resuscitation. O saturation was 78 percent just prior to transfer to the intensive care unit and deteriorated despite ventilatory support. Ventricular fibrillation occurred, which was thought to be central in origin, and the patient was declared brain dead 24 hours after the operation.

A lawsuit was filed alleging negligence on the part of the attending physician, the anesthesiologist, and the institution.

LOSS PREVENTION COMMENTS

After a tragedy of this kind, everybody involved with the care of this patient suffers along with the family. Many facets of the post-operative care of this patient can be questioned. Were the postoperative orders for narcotics excessive, and was the staff too aggressive in its use? Did the combined use of the antiemetic, Phenergan, which is known to have some potentiating interaction with the narcotic, play a role in this death? Did the untimed order for the droperidol, which was not recorded as having been given, throw enough doubt as to the activities of the nursing staff and the anesthesiologist to be damaging to them in the lawsuit? Was the 2,000 ml of D5 in 1/4 NS enough to produce some fluid overload, driving the sodium down to dangerous levels? Should there have been more capacity in the hospital to get this patient intubated in a timely manner?

Almost certainly the death was due to massive pulmonary aspiration of gastric contents. When did this occur? Did medication cause or contribute to this complication? There can be no absolute answer to any of these questions, but all of them can certainly be seen to have had some adverse effect. While this is all speculation and subject to differing opinions, the fact that the anesthesiologist did not examine this child after he had been consulted by the nurse and before ordering the additional medication is not in dispute! Had he come and examined the patient, would his orders have been any different or could he have intervened at that time and prevented this tragic outcome? There remains the possibility that, under those circumstances, the outcome could have been different. A large settlement charged to the anesthesiologist's corporation was negotiated, ending this very unhappy situation.

5.   SURGEON OR SYSTEM—MALPRACTICE

Allegation—Esophageal intubation; lack of appropriate
  monitoring devices
Physician Issue—Failure to recognize hypoxia; left room
  during CPR
Patient Issue—Severe brain damage
Outcome—Death; six-figure settlement

CASE STUDY

A 62-year-old woman came to the emergency department (ED) shortly after midnight with severe right flank pain that radiated anteriorly and inferiorly into the area of the right groin. Her blood pressure was 180/110 mm Hg, she had tenderness to percussion over the right flank, and her urine showed a 2+ protein. On the basis of the typical history and physical findings, the urologist on call ordered a STAT IVP, which showed a slight hydroureter on the right and what appeared to be a calculus in the region of the right ureterovesical (UV) junction.

Narcotics by injection gave some relief from her pain, and she was sent home, with instructions to see the urologist the following morning in his office. She kept the appointment, and on cystoscopy a calculus was found at the UV junction. A conservative approach was tried in hopes that the stone would pass without intervention, but five days later the stone had not moved, and the patient was experiencing intermittent severe right flank pain. She was therefore scheduled as an outpatient to have a cystoscopy and attempted extraction of the calculus.

The anesthesiologist requested by the urologist was scheduled to give the anesthesia, but he was occupied with another case at the time, and another anesthesiologist was assigned to manage her case. She was assessed by the anesthesiologist in the holding area, who noted the history of hypertension and recorded the blood pressure as 180/100 mm Hg. A history of allergy to chloramphenicol was noted, along with loose teeth, poor oral hygiene, and exogenous obesity. Her weight was 178 lb that morning and her estimated height was about 60 in. No notation was made about her neck, nor was there any history of previous problems with anesthesia. On the basis of these findings, an ASA classification of 2 was assigned.

Anesthesia was started and the patient was intubated at about 11:50 AM. Almost immediately her blood pressure began to rise to 220/100, 248/114, and 230/105 mm Hg. Bradycardia occurred within a minute or two. The code team was called to the operating room five minutes after the intubation, arriving five minutes later. The anesthesiologist checked the endotracheal tube (ET) and, hearing breath sounds over both sides of the chest, concluded that the tube was in place. The first blood gas analysis was done 15 minutes into the procedure and showed a PO_2 of 19, with severe acidosis. About 22 minutes into the case the patient was reintubated and was given 100 percent O_2 by AMBU bag. Another 20 minutes elapsed before the PO_2 was recorded as above 60. Active CPR was begun approximately 15 minutes into the procedure and continued for 30 minutes before an adequate heart rate was obtained and the blood pressure was about 110/70 mm Hg.

She had sustained a devastating period of hypoxia, which resulted in severe brain damage. After three days in the SICU, a bedside EEG reported no brain activity. She was declared brain dead, and all supportive measures were stopped. She died a few minutes later. A lawsuit was filed charging both the urologist and the anesthesiologist with negligence in failing to identify esophageal intubation in a timely manner. The suit also requested punitive damages because the anesthesiologist left the room during resuscitation, showing a "callous disregard for his patient's welfare."

LOSS PREVENTION COMMENTS

There is a risk to general anesthesia that is not proportional to the severity of the procedure for which the anesthesia is given. The devastating effects of esophageal intubation are well known, and before we had the ability to continuously monitor CO_2 and O_2, it was more common than it is today.

This case occurred after such monitoring of gases had become the standard of care, and had, in fact, resulted in a gradual reduction in the premiums for the anesthesiologist's professional liability insurance. In the examination of this case, it was found that CO_2 was not being monitored, and the ET tube was not equipped with the device that would have immediately warned the anesthesiologist of trouble. Investigation revealed that the device was defective and was being repaired.

Surely in the absence of such a monitoring device the physician could have been expected to more closely observe his patient and more quickly react to signs of trouble. Inflaming the surviving family's anger at the caregivers was the impression that neither the urologist nor the anesthesiologist was actively involved in the effort to protect their patient either by the earlier recognition of trouble immediately after intubation or during CPR once the cause of the trouble had been discovered. There was testimony that the anesthesiologist left the room during CPR.

The anesthesiologist relied on the questionable observation of breath sounds on both sides of the chest to delay his attempts to reintubate. It was not until about 20 minutes into the case that the patient was adequately oxygenated. There was also the significant obesity and a long history of hypertension that made the patient a less than ideal anesthesia risk.

The absence of the necessary monitoring device was evidence of system laxity, which contributed to the constellation of difficulties that contributed to this anesthesia death. Why was the monitoring device not functional? Why did not the physicians delay the case until appropriate monitoring was available? Questions related to these system problems went without satisfactory answers, and a very large settlement was required to protect against the possibility of a much larger ward by the jury for punitive damages.

6.   QUESTIONABLE APPROPRIATENESS OF/ CONSENT FOR PROCEDURE

Allegation—Lacking informed consent; procedure not indicated
Physician Issue—Failure to warn of nerve damage; patient, a diabetic, at increased risk
Patient Issues—Incontinence of bladder and bowel; loss of libido; divorce and mental anguish
Outcome—Six-figure settlement

CASE STUDY

A 42-year-old employed woman who had had previous surgery for coronary artery disease (CABG-6), a herniated nucleus pulposus (HNP) at L5, S1, and who had been treated for chronic depression, went to her primary care physician (PCP) after stumbling over a cart at work. This resulted in pain in her low back for about 24 hours. Having previously had surgery for HNP, she was examined carefully and found to have marked paravertebral muscle spasm in the lumbar area with inability to straighten her back, and she walked with about 20 degrees flexion at the lumbar level. She exhibited good motor strength, no loss of sensation to pinprick, and positive SLR of the left at about 40 degrees. Because of the possibility of a recurrent herniated disk she was admitted to the hospital for pain relief and appropriate evaluation and management.

She was treated conservatively, and the neurologist consulted on the fourth hospital day suggested that observation and physical therapy be continued unless the symptoms increased. On the fifth hospital day, still with some pain, the patient was seen in consultation by an orthopedic surgeon. A CT scan of the spine showed only some minimal bulging at the L4-5 level, and continued conservative treatment was suggested. While in the hospital under physical therapy she regained a full range of motion in the lumbar spine and was able to walk without difficulty. She was discharged home on the eighth hospital day. About a week later she again saw the surgeon for continuing back pain, with some paresthesia along the posterior aspect of the right leg. Further study with a myelogram was suggested, as the need for repeat HNP surgery was thought possible at this time. Two weeks later a CT scan of the lumbar spine done with contrast was reported to show minimal central bulging at L5, with no pressure on the thecal sac. The L4 disk was normal. Her PCP began treatment with an NSAID, and noted some improvement over the next two weeks. During this time she had an acute anxiety episode, and her PCP began treatment with Prozac.

The patient continued to complain of back and leg pain but improved on conservative management. She was encouraged to continue her exercise program, which was not described in the record, but compliance with the exercise program was thought not to be good.

After about nine months, she was again admitted to her consultant's hospital in a major city. MRI was done but did not add to the picture, and epidural block was suggested. Initially she did not go through with this, but on a subsequent visit about two weeks later a caudal and lumbar epidural block was done with Marcaine and steroids for possible postlaminectomy scarring. Immediately following the block, the patient began to have difficulty emptying and controlling her bladder. Numerous studies of bladder function were done, and further consultation by a neurosurgeon was obtained. Two and a half years after her initial fall, the prevailing diagnosis was cauda equina syndrome secondary to the epidural block.

A lawsuit was filed alleging negligence on the part of the anesthesiologist in performing the block and lack of informed consent to do the procedure. It was alleged that the block had rendered her unable to control her bladder and occasionally bowel continence as well. She lost sexual capacity and was divorced after 20 years of marriage. No experts were found that would support the use of the epidural block in this case, and there were qualified experts who criticized the procedure both as to appropriateness and technique. A six-figure settlement was thought to be the best way to close this claim, as the chance of trial was thought to be too risky.

LOSS PREVENTION COMMENTS

Epidural injection is not totally innocuous! Injury to the cord, infection, and bleeding into the canal all are possibilities. It is true that these complications are rare, but they do occur. One would expect that the anesthesiologist did discuss with this patient some of the risks of this procedure, but there was no documentation substantiating that he did. The record did state that after the patient refused to allow the block the first time it was recommended, she remembered little of the prior discussion. Without a record of the discussion and with the patient denying that she understood the procedure, the contest was decided in the patient's favor, as it almost always is in such cases.

The "conservative treatment" was mentioned many times in the record, but there was no clear description of the treatment or the patient's compliance with the program.

The block was done purely on subjective findings. All of the tests for disk rupture were negative or equivocal at best. Low back pain is not an easy condition to treat even though it is one of the most common patient complaints. The treatment is noninvasive unless there is objective evidence of organic disease. As systematic studies of the condition of low back pain continue, it becomes more and more evident that any invasive treatment is rarely indicated.

This patient had been treated for chronic depression in the past and had been given Prozac for an anxiety attack she had experienced only a short time before the block was done. With this history and no objective findings indicating disk disease, a psychiatric evaluation was in order before other modalities were chosen.

On reading this record, one gets the impression that much of the pertinent information is not available. Documentation is always important, but with a patient of this kind with this kind of complaint, more than ordinary care must be taken with the record. Had that been done, the probabilities are that this lawsuit would not have been filed or that the legal outcome would have been more favorable for our physician.

7.   MEDICINE—A BUSINESS OR PROFESSION?

Lack of physician-to-physician courtesy
No legal action
Unfortunate lack of professionalism

This case is a departure from the usual in that I will present a case where no litigation was or will be involved. I believe, however, that it epitomizes the basic reason that the public, our patients, are increasingly prone to file medical malpractice lawsuits.

Following one of SVMIC's Loss Prevention Seminars, a youngish doctor approached me rather angrily with the statement that, "The practice of medicine is a business and you try to make it something else." I admitted to "trying to make it something else," but agreed that in the practice of medicine one had to apply good business principles. It was this insistence that our work was strictly a business that caused me to remember the experience when I got a letter from a colleague that will be the basis for this "Case of the Month."

CASE STUDY

My colleague, whom I had not seen for several years, wrote of his own experience. I will not describe the contribution that I believe this retired physician has made to the health of Tennesseans over the years for fear of breaking the confidentiality that my friend expected when he wrote:

> *Recently I had a herniorrhaphy at a local major hospital. An anesthesiologist, whom I did not know, was assigned to my case. Since I have had seven previous generals, I wanted to discuss the possibility of a spinal.*
> *He did not visit my room preoperatively. After receiving preoperative medications in my private room, he did greet me on entering the operating room. The operating room was set up for general, so I said nothing.*
> *The general must have been excellent for I awoke promptly, well oriented and hungry.*
> *He did not visit me postoperatively to see that I did well.*
> *Less than a week later, I received a bill with a statement that full payment was expected now and that Medicare and Blue Cross would not be filed until after the full payment was received.*
> *About two months later, a notice from Blue Cross arrived*

stating that it had paid the anesthesiologist the difference between the charge and the Medicare reimbursement. I called the anesthesiologist's office asking for a refund. It came promptly, signed by the doctor, with no attached note.

I did receive an excellent anesthetic but had I been a layman and anything gone wrong in the operating room, or later, the anesthesiologist had opened the door widely to anger (the way the bill had been presented), to medical doubt (no preoperative or postoperative visit), and to disappointment (no discussion of the route of the anesthesia).

In other words, if anything had gone wrong whether or not due to poor medical practice (we doctors know the unexpected after all does happen), it would have required a most forgiving soul to have passed up the opportunity for a juicy lawsuit.

My plea is that doctors always treat patients as people and not as machines in our repair shop.

LOSS PREVENTION COMMENTS

In our discussion of this case, let's try to forget that the patient is one of the most respected physicians in the area of the state where he practiced. Let's assume that we are dealing with an ordinary patient. Let us also allow some latitude for the anesthesiologist who does have great difficulty in this day and time trying to adequately evaluate his patient preoperatively and to establish any kind of rapport or relationship with him. But for the conscientious, caring physician, regardless of the specialty, this evaluation and rapport are absolutely essential.

Let's think primarily about the financial obligation owed by the patient to the doctor. This side of the physician-patient relationship is becoming increasingly difficult for most of our patients to meet. The surprise of a bill that is impossible to pay causes many patients to become plaintiffs. Just as our patients have a right to understand and consent to the procedure, they have a right to know something of the financial obligation that they are assuming. Without either, if anything should go wrong with the experience, litigation is almost assured.

In this particular case there was good insurance coverage. This patient had both Medicare and Blue Cross. Payment of all the allowable charges was virtually a given! Why demand payment before filing the claim and receiving payment from the carriers? It is difficult to imagine in a specialty with as high a risk for litigation as anesthesiology, that a physician or group of physicians would demand payment before filing the assured insurance coverage. This is literally holding the patient's funds hostage and is a practice to be condemned if, indeed, it is not illegal in the first place! I believe the anesthesiologist in this case would have refunded this patient's Medicare-Blue Cross payment, but it is interesting that the refund came so promptly after the patient called the doctor's office and requested it. This paints a picture of a highly trained serviceman who believes the money derived from his work is the only important element in the transaction.

Are we engaged in a profession or a business? "Both," you answer, and you are right. But, strictly speaking, we are still considered professionals by the public and under the law, and we had better understand the difference before we lose the privilege! As professionals, we are given the privilege and responsibility of controlling access to our profession. Our license is granted under conditions largely developed and controlled by our peers. Although we have not done an adequate job in the past of policing our ranks, our peer review activities can have the weight of law and are protected by it. Whether or not we do a good job in our practice is judged by a standard that is established by the way we do things as doctors, not by legislative act. These privileges are granted us by a society that values our services to that society above the level at which it places the services of the ordinary business, which has to be licensed. We have lost a lot of the public respect that goes with being members of a profession. Why?

Could some of the deterioration in our image be due to our acting without regard to the public demands for a service only we are able to provide? How can we allow a person like the anesthesiologist in our case to become one of us? It is only because somewhere along the road to becoming a physician, he never got the message that our first obligation is to perform a service for the patient who trusts us and that rewards can only be the result of those obligations, fulfilled in a manner that values first the whole person, including the responsibility to be fair in our financial dealings with that person. In this case, bill collecting appears to have been the most important aspect of this doctor's business.

8.   OPERATING ROOM INJURIES—NOT ALWAYS A SLIP OF THE KNIFE

Allegation—Negligence in failure to protect patient from injury remote from the site of the operation
Patient Issue—Postoperative blindness right eye

Physician Issue—Loss of vision right eye
Outcome—Six-figure settlement

Case Study

A 33-year-old male employee of a lumber company was injured while cutting down a tree. The tree fell, striking the man across the neck and shoulders and causing immediate neurologic impairment. He was taken to the emergency room (ER), where neurologic examination revealed paraplegia with diminished use of his arms; x-rays revealed a fracture of the sixth cervical vertebra. The man was placed in halo-type skull traction and evaluated for about five days. There was no improvement, and it was decided that the patient should undergo cervical fusion.

The patient was taken to the operating room and positioned by the surgeon and the anesthesiologist on the operating table in the prone position with his head in a horseshoe-shaped headrest. He was then prepared and draped in the usual manner, and the operation proceeded routinely. Late in the procedure the surgeon requested elevation of the headrest to obtain adequate x-ray visualization of the fusion. The surgeon held the patient's head while the anesthesia team raised the headrest. The intraoperative x-rays were then taken, and it was determined that the fusion was satisfactory.

When the patient awakened from the anesthesia, it was noted that he had a dilated right pupil. An ophthalmology consultant diagnosed retinal infarction, probably secondary to pressure on the eye during the operation.

On review of the records, it was noted that the surgeon indicated in his operative note that the injury was probably caused by pressure on the face during the procedure. It was determined that both the surgeon and the anesthesia team were jointly liable. The case resulted in a large settlement.

Loss Prevention Comments

Increasingly, claims occur because of injuries to the patient arising out of operating room situations where the injury is primarily related to the patient position required by the surgical procedure. The patient injury sustained is remote from the operative site and usually results from some alleged failure to properly protect the patient by either careful preparation before surgery or adequate monitoring during the procedure.

Consider the large loss sustained when an ace bandage applied to a patient's leg was not watched carefully enough, resulting in skin loss and nerve damage to an extremity. This occurred during some reconstructive surgery on the breast.

Consider also the alleged damage resulting from improperly padded stirrups during a vaginal operation, or ulnar palsy said to come from an arm board not being properly positioned during chest surgery lasting for hours.

The case presented here is one of serious patient injury occurring because of positions required during surgery. If the operating team of which you are a part does not keep in mind what can happen in an area remote from the operative site, this could happen to your patient and to you.

We do function as a "team" many times in medicine, whether in the operating room or not. When we do, the members of the team need to be sure that all the "basics" are covered so that injuries of this type can be reduced to an absolute minimum.

9.   PATIENT WALKS IN—PATIENT WALKS OUT

Allegation—No lawsuit filed
Physician Issue—Responsible anesthesiologist at risk
Patient Issue—Frightened by description of surgery
Outcome—No legal issue; prolonged pain and disability, but
    no settlement

CASE STUDY

A 60-year-old woman experienced increasing pain in the right hand for six months, and for the past six weeks she had also noticed some difficulty with picking up small objects. Since her job was in a factory making clothes, which required good dexterity, she was rapidly losing her ability to make production schedules after having exceeded her goals for many years.

She was referred to a neurosurgeon by her primary care physician with a diagnosis of carpal tunnel syndrome. The specialist confirmed the diagnosis and suggested that the release of the pressure on the nerve in her wrist would probably relieve her pain and that she could expect a gradual return of function of her hand. The neurosurgeon stressed that without surgery her symptoms would continue and that the loss of function in her hand would get worse.

The patient was scheduled for surgery in the hospital's outpatient department, but because of a minor scheduling error, the patient was hurried from place to place in the outpatient center in order to get the preoperative orders accomplished. The personnel in the center were abrupt and critical of the patient because of the scheduling error. The technicians talked to each other as if the patient were not there, complaining of the scheduling, the early morning hours, and other things that were not related to their work.

The patient was very concerned about what she interpreted as disinterest and preoccupation by the personnel, and by the time she saw the certified registered nurse anesthetist (CRNA) for her preanesthetic visit, she was extremely apprehensive and anxious.

The anesthetic procedure was described quickly and without pausing to inquire if the patient had any questions. When asked by the patient what anesthetic agent would be used, the CRNA replied with irritation, "I had to get here so early for your case that I didn't have time to look at the board." The patient then asked if it would be possible to discuss the matter with the anesthesiologist. The CRNA replied, "Your case is scheduled for eight o'clock and it is already 7:50. I don't even know which one of our doctors is scheduled to do you. I will see what I can do." And with that the CRNA, obviously angry, left the room. The patient was terrified at the experience. She was so frightened that she put on her clothes and left the center.

Three months later, having become so disabled in her right hand that she had been forced to quit her job, she returned to see her family physician. With some difficulty the FP persuaded the patient to return to the neurosurgeon and to have her surgery. The neuropathy had progressed since her initial visit to the hospital, and it was months before she could return to work after successful surgery.

LOSS PREVENTION COMMENTS

Although no suit was filed in this case, the negligence involved is apparent. All the elements of a successful lawsuit were present:

The doctor-patient relationship legally existed between the anesthesiologist and the patient, although only the CRNA was involved in the preoperative discussion; the duty under that relationship was breached when the approach to the patient was so frightening that she could make no rational decision; the breach of the duty caused damage to the patient; and that damage could be measured by a jury in monetary terms.

In this particular case we were lucky!

II

Emergency Medicine

Perhaps one of the most stressful and difficult areas of medical practice is in the emergency department. The diversity of presentations of injury and disease requires the broadest possible application of knowledge and procedural skills. Consequently, claims charging malpractice can and do involve all the general and specialty areas of practice.

A patient's history must be taken under the most adverse circumstances. The physical examination must at times be limited to the presenting complaint because of the urgency of the presentation. Privacy is at a premium, and crowds of family and friends sometimes tax the physical facilities. Yet by and large the physician in charge of the emergency department does a remarkable job.

The areas critical to preventing litigation and prevailing in a lawsuit, if filed, are most likely to be from the record. This does not mean that these areas are not covered by the staff. But when the documentation of the patient history is lacking or illegible, when the physical examination in sufficient detail to cover the differential diagnoses considered is not recorded, or when the appropriate laboratory/x-ray studies are not given the attention due them in the record, a bad or unexpected outcome can and sometimes does lead to litigation.

When it is apparent from the record that the physician has followed a logical and sound pattern of reasoning, even a wrong conclusion or action can be defended successfully most of the time. This can be considered a truism in the whole arena of medical malpractice.

10.   WHO'S IN CHARGE HERE?

Allegation—Oversedation; traumatic intubation
Physician Issue—Failure to communicate physician to physician

Patient Issues—Cardiac arrest; prolonged hospitalization;
tracheal tear
Outcome—Six-figure settlement

CASE STUDY

A 29-year-old man was brought to the emergency room of a metropolitan hospital where the nurse obtained a history from family members that the patient had ingested "three beers and some pretzels" one hour earlier. Thirty minutes later he began to complain of cramping abdominal pain, the pain so severe that the patient "writhed on the floor in agony." The past history was entirely negative. No history of recent illness was obtained, and alcohol and drug use was denied.

Dr. A, an emergency room physician, saw the patient and observed that he was breathing deeply and rapidly and was unable to speak. His color was good, and because of his obvious difficulty with respiration, Dr. A quickly did a Heimlich maneuver without benefit. Shortly thereafter, the patient completely lost control, began to thrash about wildly, assaulting everyone present, and appeared to be hysterical. The loud commotion brought Dr. B into the room to be of assistance.

Dr. B told a nurse to "draw up 10 mg of Valium and give 5 mg now" in an effort to sedate this noncommunicative and combative patient and to prevent self-injury. In the confusion, the nurse did not hear the "give 5 mg now" and gave the full dosage. A few minutes later Dr. A, not realizing what Dr. B had ordered, told another nurse to give Demerol 50 mg and Vistaril 25 mg IV. Sedation was now accomplished and both doctors left the patient in the care of the emergency room nurse, with Dr. A planning to order laboratory work and x-rays as preliminary studies of the patient.

Within 10 to 15 minutes, both doctors were summoned STAT because of respiratory arrest; Dr. A did an emergency tracheal intubation. Dr. A discovered that the patient had received the medication ordered by each of them and Narcan was immediately given. The arrest was successfully treated although the patient required mechanical ventilator support for several hours. Later it was learned that the trachea had been torn by the emergency intubation requiring surgical treatment and prolonged hospitalization.

LOSS PREVENTION COMMENTS

In every case there must be a "chief" to coordinate all aspects of management. Subordinate members of the team must recognize this and accommodate their participation in the case to the physician in charge. Dr. B deviated from the standard of care in failing to recognize Dr. A's role as the physician in charge and in ordering the medication without his knowledge and approval.

Dr. A's order of Vistaril IV was contraindicated according to the *PDR*, which indicates that it is intended only for IM administration.

11.   A GOOD HISTORY USUALLY GIVES A DIAGNOSIS

Allegation—Failure to do adequate history and physical;
*   failure to perform the necessary testing*
Physician Issue—Failure to recognize signs of intestinal
*   obstruction*
Patient Issues—Severe pain; emergency surgery; death
Outcome—Large settlement

CASE STUDY

At 3:00 AM abdominal pain and vomiting began. At 4:30 AM she was seen by the emergency department physician, who discharged her at 6:30 AM. Thirty hours later she was returned to the ED in cardiorespiratory arrest and died following an emergency laparotomy. She was 22 years of age!

When the patient was seen on admission to the ED the history was recorded by the ED physician: "Abdominal pain since 3:00 AM. Vomited two times. Normal BM yesterday. No flatus since onset. Menstrual history normal." Examination: "22-year-old woman appears in pain. VS normal. Chest, heart, lungs OK. Abdominal tenderness, lower abdomen, but no guarding or rebound. Less tenderness mid-abdomen. Bowel sounds positive." Laboratory studies were unremarkable except for a blood glucose of 194 mg/dl.

Nursing note at 4:30 AM: "Alert and oriented. Appears in pain. Rolling around on the stretcher. Medicated for pain. Sleeping since." The record indicates that she was given "Talwin 30 mg and Phenergan 25 mg by injection at 5:50 AM. Discharged home with instructions at 6:35 AM." She was given an antacid/antispasmodic and Phenergan suppositories for use at home. She was told to return to ED if further problems occurred "this weekend."

The narrative is blank until she returned "this weekend" 30 hours after leaving the ED. CPR was in progress when the patient arrived She was resuscitated, hydrated, acidosis corrected, and taken to the OR, where the strangulated, infarcted small bowel was found to have herniated through a defect in the mesentery. The dead bowel was resected, but despite vigorous and heroic efforts, the patient died about 6:00 PM, four hours after surgery.

In the lawsuit that followed, the physician was charged with failure to take an adequate history and do a thorough physical examination, failure to monitor adequately in the ED, and failure to use appropriate testing to determine the true nature of her complaints. Going to trial with a record as incomplete as this one was considered unwise, and the case was settled.

LOSS PREVENTION COMMENTS

The loss prevention lesson to be learned here can be derived from the charges filed against this ED physician. There was ample evidence that the doctor did not get a good history. He missed the significance of the sudden onset of severe pain and the prompt vomiting that followed. He made no comment as to the apparent severity of the pain. He recorded, "No flatus since onset." The nurse, in her note two hours before the patient was discharged from the ED, noted that the patient was in pain severe enough to cause her to roll around on the table and to need the side rails to keep her on the stretcher. There was no note that the patient was re-evaluated by the ED physician in view of these findings. In fact, there was no evidence in the record that the patient was checked at all from the time of her initial examination to the time of her discharge except to administer the injection. This gave validity to the charge of failure to adequately monitor the patient in the ED.

The initial examination was brief as far as the record is concerned. No pelvic examination was done, even though it is apparent that the physician was careful to obtain an acceptable menstrual history. One wonders if the doctor put his hand on this young woman's abdomen or listened to the bowel sounds after the initial examination. As rapidly as this patient's condition was deteriorating, it is reasonable to speculate that had careful monitoring been done, the bowel sounds would have been found hyperactive, and the abdomen itself would have been more generally tender with some distension, suggesting the need for an abdominal x-ray.

We had no diagnosis when a narcotic was given to relieve the symptoms, which, if carefully observed, would have led to the suspicion of a rapidly progressing process demanding early exploration of the abdomen.

It was the weekend, the ED was busy, and the tendency was, as it frequently is, to bet on the "odds" and not think about the "long shot." Almost every time, when confronted by a patient with an acute problem, a physician needs to prepare for the worst while hoping or the best.

12.   NEEDED—DOCUMENTATION IN QUOTATION MARKS

Allegation—Failure to transfer to appropriate facility in timely manner
Physician Issue—Failure of telephone communication physician-to-physician
Patient Issue—Severe and permanent brain damage
Outcome—Small settlement; clinical issues large

CASE STUDY

In our best efforts to do what is clinically appropriate, we can, and do, rely too much on our recall of the sense of a conversation with a patient, a nurse, or even a colleague rather than on verbatim documentation. Such verbatim documentation is not always easy to come by because of the particulars of a situation in which we may find ourselves. We may be in the room with a very sick patient or on the telephone giving instructions to a patient or a parent about a sick child or in the emergency room on a busy shift. Wherever we are, unless there is verbatim documentation, sometimes the conversation with a person or the instructions given, when reconstructed later, can distort the picture of what really happened.

A mentally retarded man was brought to the ER after midnight. The history obtained from friends was that the patient had been involved in a fight and had been struck over the head several times by his adversary with a stick. The patient appeared intoxicated and in fact had a blood alcohol level over twice that considered to be legal evidence of intoxication.

The patient was almost impossible to control. He got up off the stretcher several times, walked about in the ER, and had to be escorted back to his place by the nursing staff. On physical evaluation, the man's vital signs were unimpressive except for an initial blood pressure of 146/110 mm Hg. This changed in about 20 minutes to 132/94 mm Hg. The initial reading was attributed to the patient's restlessness and agitation. Neurologically, the patient seemed in command of his faculties to the extent expected of an intoxicated and injured emergency patient. He responded appropriately to questions and followed simple commands. He appeared to be oriented as to time, place, and person. He claimed no memory of the altercation and the injury that brought him into the ER. It was noted that while his pupils reacted normally and were of equal size, there was some constant external deviation of the left eye, which both the patient and those who accompanied him said had been present all of his life.

There were contusions over the occipital region, along with a small laceration in this area. Some blood in the right ear canal obscured the tympanic membrane, raising the question of a basilar skull fracture. The nature of the injuries and the possibility of the fracture were of sufficient concern for the ER physician to think that neurologic evaluation and observation in a Level I trauma center were indicated.

On contacting the medical center, the ER physician had a conversation with the neurosurgical resident about his patient and the possible need for more skilled care than was available at the community hospital some distance away. The consultant in the center told the attending ER physician that the center was extremely busy and that the CT was "backed up." He urged that, if possible, the scan be done locally and that the results of that examination be made known to him. At that point, the case would be discussed in the light of the CT examination and transfer decided on at that time.

While the physician was on the phone with the trauma center, the patient became much more agitated, aggressive, and somewhat belligerent. On re-evaluation, the patient's left pupil was beginning to widen, and his level of consciousness began to decrease. Twenty minutes after the first phone call the same neurosurgical consultant was contacted and told of the change in status of the patient.

Authorization was given for immediate air transport. The patient was intubated for transport, and about 90 minutes elapsed between the time the decision to transfer was made and the patient's arrival at the center, two and a half hours after his admission to the community hospital ER.

On arrival at the center, the patient was on full respirator support and deeply comatose. A CT examination revealed a large right-sided epidural hematoma requiring emergency surgery and decompression. Postoperative support included a tracheostomy and a jejunal feeding tube. He continues to function at the brain-stem level.

A lawsuit was filed alleging a failure to transfer to an appropriate facility in a timely fashion, causing severe and permanent brain injury.

LOSS PREVENTION COMMENTS

Although only a relatively small settlement was required in this case, the issues raised are very pertinent to many different areas of our professional lives. The allegations of a failure to do something in a "timely fashion," resulting in some injury that would not have occurred had the action been taken in a more "timely manner," are increasing in frequency and severity. These charges can and do involve us no matter what our field of practice might be.

The essence of this issue was that the attending ER physician believed that in recommending the CT be done locally because the machine in the Level I trauma center was "backed up," the receiving physician was refusing to accept the patient at that time. He testified to this belief in pretrial discovery deposition. The neurosurgeon, on the other hand, testified that he never refused transfer at any time. On the record it became apparent that the two physicians involved in the transfer decision were at odds as far as their memory of events was concerned.

Documentation on both ends of the transfer was brief and could support either view. On the transferring end of the conversation, there was not any recorded evidence that would support the testimony of the doctor in the community hospital ER. There was not a statement that "neurosurgical consultant denies transfer until after CT done." On the receiving end, the same is true. It would have been helpful if the neurosurgical consultant had documented, "Since our CT is backed up at the moment, collective decision made to expedite the CT at local facility if time and condition of the patient allow." The lack of this kind of descriptive documentation on both ends of this conversation allowed the plaintiff to contend that the community hospital's ER physician had delayed the action, allowing brain damage to occur.

The settlement was relatively small, but the issues in this case are very large indeed!

13.   CERVICAL SPINE INJURY—QUADRIPLEGIA

*Allegations—For emergency physician, failure to assess
            patient properly; for radiologist, failure to interpret
            x-rays correctly*
Physician Issue—Failure to diagnose injury in timely manner
Patient Issue—Quadriplegia
Outcome—Very large settlement

CASE STUDY

A 33-year-old intoxicated man became involved in a fight with another man. During this altercation, the patient was thrown down against the pavement, the most obvious injury being a long laceration of his forehead on the left. Almost immediately 911 was called, and within 18 minutes the injured man was in the emergency department of an urban hospital.

The initial ED note indicated vital signs that were normal,

described the laceration and stated, "States unable to move arms." An untimed note by the ED physician records the laceration, other abrasions, "neck supple?" and states, "Full range of motion in all extremities." Orders included Philadelphia collar, cross table lateral films of the C-spine, CT C-spine, and blood ETOH. Vital signs recorded at four and six hours after admission to the ED were again recorded as being in the normal range.

A second untimed note by the ED physician recorded the repair of the laceration of the forehead and stated that the x-rays had shown a compression fracture of C6 and that the patient was being held in the ED for observation because he was severely intoxicated. The blood alcohol level was reported at 256. Eight hours after admission to the ED, the CT was reported as showing a fracture of C5-6, with bone fragments in the spinal canal and physical findings consistent with cord damage at that level. A neurosurgical consultation was requested at this time by the admitting ED physician. Here time becomes confusing. A shift change occurred in the ED, and both ED physicians are on record during the first hour of that shift, which began at 7:00 AM, seven hours after the patient was first admitted to the department. The second ED physician records normal C-spine films 15 minutes before the note by the first ED doctor that ordered the neurologic consultation. Within five minutes of the "normal C-spine" report, the CT report indicated the fracture noted by the first ED physician.

About 10 hours after admission, the spinal cord injury protocol with large doses of steroids was begun, with the caveat that the hospital pharmacy had only half enough of the drug and the rest was being obtained from another pharmacy. It was two hours after the injury that the remaining steroid was obtained and given.

Eleven hours after the patient was admitted to the ED, the radiologist who reported a "normal C-spine" corrected that report by an addendum stating that in retrospect the fracture was possibly discernable on the plain oblique film.

As the patient's intoxication began to clear, the complaints of pain became more prominent. The neurosurgeon's evaluation of the patient concluded with the decision to immobilize the patient's neck using Gardner-Wells tongs. The course of the planned surgical treatment required transfer of the patient to another facility.

After the immobilization and the subsequent surgery, there remained a long course of rehabilitation. Four months after injury the patient was stable enough to be discharged home to continue rehabilitation treatment. At this time the patient was regaining more function in his left arm and hand.

A lawsuit was filed charging that the first ED physician and the radiologist were negligent. The contention was that the ED physician did not properly assess the patient's injury in a timely fashion and did not stabilize the patient in a timely manner. The radiologist did not properly interpret the x-rays, leading to a failure to diagnose and treat the patient's injury in a timely fashion. A large settlement was necessary.

Loss Prevention Comments

The events in this case leading to the lawsuit, and the subsequent loss either by settlement or jury award, are repeated, with variations, with frightening frequency. The common features are an intoxicated patient, an injury, a failure to appreciate early indications of the severity of the situation, and a less than adequate x-ray examination or interpretation. The points of emphasis are obvious in retrospect, but frequently are obscure at the time of the initial encounter.

It is difficult to evaluate a patient who is markedly intoxicated. In spite of the severity of the injury, the patient is frequently somnolent whether or not there is any evidence of head injury. They do not respond appropriately to history taking, initial examination, or pain. Sometimes they are combative and abusive, requiring the patience and persistence of a saint to adequately assess the situation. We are less likely to be sympathetic and caring toward such a patient and are more likely to become angry at being disturbed by such an obnoxious individual!

However, such a patient will frequently give very important information or show significant physical findings during the patient evaluation. It is of utmost importance to listen to what is said. In this case, the first note on the record was, "States unable to move arms." One has to wonder if this complaint was communicated to the physician verbally at the time, or if the recorded statement was the only way the doctor knew about it; if the latter was the case, how soon was the note read? At any rate, this vital piece of information was not acted on promptly.

The recorded statement by the ED doctor, "Full range of motion all extremities," is confusing. Was this a full range of passive motion he was talking about? Did the statement confuse the issue for subsequent examiners?

This patient was brought in with a cervical collar in place. Is it appropriate to do the necessary examination to record "neck supple?" Could further neurologic injury have been done by that maneuver?

How often is a cross table lateral x-ray of the C-spine adequate?

How often does that view show all the cervical vertebrae? How often does the attending ED physician report in his note just how many of the vertebrae are seen and the course of action to be taken to secure more help from radiology? How frequently does the ED physician call the radiologist in the middle of the night to assist in the evaluation of this kind of patient or the adequacy of the films that have been taken? The confusion in the record of multiple physicians reporting on the x-rays of the spine, including the radiologist's initial report of a normal C-spine, although corrected quickly, suggests that there might have been some delay in appropriate action.

The delay in instituting the spinal cord injury protocol in a patient who comes into the ED with the statement, "I can't move my arms," is hard to overlook. Why was there a delay? Even in the face of an inadequate supply of the drug in the ED, why wasn't the steroid begun sooner? Immobilization of the neck and the subsequent stabilization occurred in a timely manner once the appropriate people were involved.

The many questions raised in the discussion of this case all have some clinical relevance. They are prompted by the record. In this case, as in any other, it is vital that the record correctly reflect the plans and actions of the treatment team. Here that includes the ED physicians and nurses, the radiologists, and the specialists called in consultation. The sum of these questions does not begin to approach the number of questions asked by the plaintiff's attorney after the suit is filed.

Here we have a young man left quadriplegic by an injury that was presented to us within 20 minutes of its occurrence. Did any of our actions cause the injury in the first place? No! Did any of our actions contribute to this devastating result? Probably not, but maybe so!

14.   WHAT'S WRONG WITH THIS PICTURE?

Allegation—Failure to diagnose heart disease or do proper work-up
Physician Issue—Ignored risk factors (family history)
Patient Issues—Acute myocardial infarction; death
Outcome—Six-figure settlement

CASE STUDY

A 40-year-old man came to the emergency department of a metropolitan hospital complaining of diarrhea, fever, cough, and chest tightness for three to four days. He had been treated for hypertension in the past but volunteered that he stopped taking the high blood pressure medication more than a year ago. Further history revealed that the man was a smoker. The tightness in the chest seemed to be aggravated by deep breathing. There had been no sweating.

The physical evaluation revealed temperature 97.8°F, pulse 62/min, respirations 18/min, and blood pressure 90/56 mm Hg. The patient appeared in no particular distress, the vital signs were stable, and the patient was well oriented. The respiratory system seemed normal. The breath sounds were described as distant and clear. The cardiovascular system was thought to be normal, with normal rate and rhythm. There were no infiltrates on the chest x-ray. WBC count was 13,000/cu mm. The diagnosis was "viral syndrome," and he was treated conservatively with fluids and an antihistamine and told to return in three to five days if the symptoms were no better. The blood pressure was rechecked prior to his leaving the ED and found to be 99/56 mm Hg after an IV fluid challenge.

At about 3:00 AM the following day the patient was found unresponsive by his wife and returned to the ED with CPR in progress. There was no response, and the patient was pronounced dead at the scene.

A lawsuit was filed charging the ED physician with failure to diagnose heart disease and failure to do proper work-up in the face of symptoms suggesting heart trouble. There was trouble finding expert testimony, and when a physician was found who would testify for the defendant doctor it was thought that his testimony was weak. A six-figure settlement was reached on the courthouse steps.

Loss Prevention Comments

What were the symptoms suggesting heart trouble? Diarrhea, cough, low-grade fever, and chest tightness!? There was the history of smoking and hypertension and that he stopped taking his blood pressure medicine about a year before this episode. His physical examination was not suggestive. The chest x-ray was normal, and the WBC count was 13,000/cu mm. He was virtually free of pain when seen in the ED.

On the suggestive side for heart pathology was the history of smoking and hypertension. Still, so far, I don't believe the symptoms were suggestive enough to charge our doctor with medical malpractice.

What was the compelling reason that a cardiac work-up should have been done? The history of smoking and high blood pressure are certainly risk factors, but were they enough for the expense of EKG, enzymes, etc.? The most tell-tale sign that should have been taken seriously was the fact that this hypertensive patient who had not had treatment for a year was no longer hypertensive. This patient had an admitting blood pressure of 90/56 mm Hg, and even after a fluid challenge, his blood pressure was 99/56 mm Hg on discharge from the ED. This hypotension, with an only slightly suggestive evaluation, should have prompted the full cardiac work-up before the patient was discharged from the ED.

15.   A YOUNG WOMAN FAINTED

> *Allegation—Failure to diagnose*
> *Physician Issues—Fainting; unexplained numbness in legs;*
> *   "notify attending in AM"*
> *Patient Issues—Waiting in ER; not seen by attending promptly*
> *Outcome—Seven-figure settlement*

CASE STUDY

A previously healthy 19-year-old college student, a smoker, fainted and in ten days she was dead! On attempting to stand, the patient fainted, became incontinent, and was brought to the hospital by ambulance. The history indicated that as she began to revive, she complained of numbness in her legs but appeared to be disoriented. Her blood pressure was recorded at 160/96 mm Hg and pulse 96/min. The complete physical examination as recorded revealed entirely negative findings, with the lower extremities said to be "negative." By the time she had been in the emergency department for about an hour and a half, she was alert and oriented.

Within 30 minutes of her admission, the appropriate laboratory work had been ordered, IV fluids were being administered, and blood gases were reported to be normal. Shortly thereafter the laboratory reported normal blood counts and electrolytes and a blood alcohol had been reported as negative. About 45 minutes into her ED admission, her pulse was recorded at 36 to 40/min and the blood pressure 105/38 mm Hg. As the bradycardia continued, she was found to respond inappropriately to verbal stimuli, responding on one occasion, "It hurts."

The record indicated that the first "admission note" was written about one hour after admission and contained a more complete history of the event as given by the patient. Just when this communication with the patient took place is not recorded. She stated that she suddenly experienced severe pain in both sides of her neck and numbness in both legs. Then she lost consciousness. The physical examination at that time revealed her pulse at 56/min and blood pressure 130/100 mm Hg. Her skin below the knees was said to have been "icy cold," and sensation to pinprick was absent. She obeyed oral commands and appeared anxious and frightened. She is recorded to have said, "I'm very tired."

At this point (4:00 AM), the ED physician wrote admission orders (signed by the nurse) including seizure precautions, renal laboratory work, bed rest, and a regular diet. The IV was to be kept open. The attending physician was to be notified "in the AM." The working impression was that the patient had experienced a seizure. One hour after admission to the hospital, the nurse assisted the patient with the bed pan and recorded a "cranberry-colored, foul-smelling stool." She had three such stools in the first hour of her hospital stay. The attending physician was called and ordered a CBC STAT, stool culture, hemoglobin, and hematocrit at 10:00 AM.

The CBC revealed a WBC count of 24,500/cu mm after the ED WBC count had been 12,000/cu mm. Again the patient complained of no sensation in her legs. She continued to have the bloody stools. Four hours after admission, 7:00 AM, she again denied having any sensation below the knees, and the toes on the right foot were said to be cyanotic. The nursing notes record that the patient was sleeping at 10:00 AM.

The attending physician gave orders (signed by an LPN) in the morning at 10:10 AM for strict intake and output, IV fluid challenge, Foley catheter, urinalysis, amylase, and blood culture. At 10:30 AM the nurse's notes indicate that the attending physician "visits." At this time the attending physician recorded that the patient had been eating a sandwich when she felt the sharp pain in the neck, attempted to stand, felt dizzy, vomited, and lost feeling in the lower extremities below the knees. On examination the blood pressure was 110/70 mm Hg and pulse 80/min; there were decreased bowel sounds, with some distension and vague tenderness in the lower abdomen. There were no palpable pulses in the lower extremities and no sensation below the knees to pinprick. The attending physician's impressions were recorded as (1) loss of consciousness-simple faint with possibility of seizure, (2) abdominal cramping and pain on pressure over the lower abdomen, and (3) absent pulses—? saddle embolus.

A surgeon was consulted, who believed that the possibility of a saddle embolus existed and ordered a sonogram of the abdomen. This revealed a widening of the aortic root, with the suggestion of aortic dissection. An aortogram confirmed this impression, and preparations were made to fly the patient to a tertiary care center.

About 13 hours after onset of this illness, the patient arrived at the center and was taken immediately to the operating room for aortic exploration and grafting. This was done requiring the use of a prosthetic valve. Postoperatively, she developed renal failure and full-blown DIC with necrosis of her extremities distally. She died about a week later.

A lawsuit was filed charging the ED physician with negligence in failing to diagnose the patient's condition. The attending physician was not made a part of the lawsuit.

LOSS PREVENTION COMMENTS

Where would the possibility of aortic dissection have been on your list in the differential diagnosis of this case? In a young woman, previously healthy, with the only risk factor recorded being that of smoking, most of us would not have had this very high on our list of possibilities.

Two physicians were involved in this young woman's care from the beginning: the ED physician and the doctor to whom she was admitted on orders of the ED physician. Strangely enough, the attending physician was not a party to this lawsuit. Usually everybody in sight is listed by the plaintiff attorney, and one wonders why this was the case. Could it have been that had this lawsuit gone to trial, the attending physician was counted upon by the plaintiff attorney to point fingers?

The ED physician saw this patient about two hours after her arrival in the ED. This is the way the record reads. All notes prior to that time were generated by the nursing staff in the ED. But when she was seen for the first examination by the ED physician, the skin of the legs was said to be "icy cold," and there was no sensation to pinprick bilaterally below the knees. Additional history was elicited that revealed that at onset she experienced severe pain in the neck and numbness below the knees. The patient was hypertensive when she arrived in the ED, but became hypotensive and bradycardic in the first hour of her stay. This condition continued for an hour before the recorded examination by the ED physician. She was alternately confused and lucid during this time, and she was considered to be in the post-ictal stage of a seizure, although she gave no history of previous seizures.

There was no mention in the ED record that the ED physician conferred with the attending physician prior to admission, which led us to believe that the ED physician had authority to admit patients under the care of the "on-call" physician without prior consultation. The orders were those of the ED physician but were signed by the nurse. The order by the ED physician that the attending physician was to be called "in the AM" is evidence that he was assuming the responsibility for the patient postadmission until the attending physician came to see the patient the next morning. One presumes that under these circumstances the ED physician had privileges to work in the hospital as well as in the ED. We were left to believe that the ED physician was assuming the role of the attending physician beyond that already his by being the ED physician for that shift.

The "cranberry-colored stools" were repeatedly mentioned in the nurse's notes after admission, and because of it the nurses called the attending physician and received orders for cultures and sensitivity, renal studies, and follow-up on the blood counts. At least seven bloody stools were noted, along with abdominal pain from the time of her arrival in the ED. She was confused, somnolent at times, had pain in her abdomen, with bloody diarrhea, and the loss of sensation and motor function in her legs.

It is apparent that nobody on the treatment team was too excited about this patient. The attending physician was first called and notified of her admission two hours after the fact and four hours after the onset of her symptoms. He did not come into the house to examine his patient, and when he was notified about the continuation of the bloody diarrhea the second time he gave some orders that were signed by the LPN. Shortly thereafter, "Dr. (attending) visits."

The practice of allowing the direct admission of a patient from the ED by the ED physician for another attending physician is to be condemned. Almost always, the presence of a condition worthy of the patient's admission to the hospital suggests that the attending physician needs to begin assuming his rightful responsibility in the ED. Otherwise, the ED physician is assuming far too much responsibility, clinically, ethically, and legally. Both the attending physician and the ED physician should demand that practices like this be stopped by the medical executive committee.

In this case, this young woman needed all the clinical expertise and support she could get and needed it that night. She did not get it, nor the diagnosis, which, though rare, could have and should have been made hours earlier. That in the presence of an aortic root dissection the prognosis was grave at best is little consolation when the system fails as it did here. The large amount of money required to settle this claim is only a sobering reminder of our unmet responsibilities.

We can and should do better!

16.   "PARAMETERS" IN THE EMERGENCY ROOM

Allegation—Wrongful death
Physician Issue—Accident details not taken into account
Patient Issues—Blunt trauma abdomen; inadequate
*   examination; failure to transfer to trauma unit*
Outcome—High six-figure settlement

CASE STUDY

At 11:20 PM on September 7, a 54-year-old man was brought to the emergency room by ambulance following an automobile accident. The ER physician smelled alcohol on the patient's breath. There was a small laceration on the left side of his face, and he had lost three teeth, but had not lost consciousness. There were some abrasions and contusions on the chest, and it was apparent that the patient's face and chest had struck the steering wheel.

Further examination as recorded revealed: BP 108/70 and P 94. Heart: Rate and rhythm normal, no murmurs were heard. Chest: No tenderness to percussion. Abdomen: No muscle guarding or rebound. No organomegaly. Treatment: Suture of the laceration face; head and wound sheet given; return five days. The patient died at home about 36 hours later.

Autopsy revealed blunt trauma to the chest and abdomen, multiple fractures of the ribs on the left, and transection of the duodenum with marked pneumoperitoneum and free gastric contents (800 cc), with fulminant peritonitis. Cause of death was listed as septic shock due to fulminant peritonitis.

On the day of the patient's death the physician's office record showed, "While in hospital ER, I asked the driver what caused the accident. He said he didn't know. The driver was treated and released the AM of 9/8" (the day before death).

The details of the accident were recorded in the patrolman's report, which indicated that the car skidded 42 feet and was airborne for about 100 feet before coming to rest on a hillside. It was not clear from the record whether the physician was aware of the details of the accident or not.

A lawsuit was filed demanding $2 million and charging wrongful death. Settlement was reached for a large amount.

LOSS PREVENTION COMMENTS

Whatever the reason, the physician who saw the patient in the ER did not take into account the details of the accident itself. He mentioned in his office record his questioning of the patient about the cause and apparently left the subject with the patient's answer that he did not know. This clearly points to at least two possible conclusions: although the patient gave no history of unconsciousness, there might well have been some amnesia for the events of the accident itself, or that the physician did not inquire of anyone who knew the details.

When confronted with the victim of a motor vehicle accident (MVA) in the ER, the physician must take into account details about the wreck that are known or suspected by those who observed the scene, i.e., the emergency medical services (EMS) technicians, the law enforcement officers, witnesses, etc. Skid marks, seat belt restraints, air bags, roll overs, being airborne and the like are all vital to the assessment of possible injuries to the victim. The odor of alcohol on the breath is another important consideration. How much alcohol? The usual "couple 'a beers" or a liter of whiskey? Again, witnesses or those accompanying the victim may have vital information.

The autopsy findings indicating the extent of blunt trauma to the upper abdomen certainly suggest that the patient's ER assessment and treatment might have been below an acceptable standard. Transection of the duodenum is not uncommon in victims of MVAs who have undergone sudden deceleration, causing the driver to be thrown against the steering column with such force that the portion of the duodenum fixed against the spine is divided. What was recorded about the accident suggested that the damage to the face and the contusions and laceration of the chest wall had been produced by contact with the steering wheel. "Multiple rib fractures, left chest," when viewed against the physical examination in the ER, "Chest—No tenderness to percussion," suggest inadequate evaluation or a patient unable to respond appropriately because of alcohol anesthesia, concussion, or something else related to the accident.

In recent years there has been an evolution in the management of trauma throughout the country. Tennessee is no exception. The trauma center development, which has seen the hospital emergency rooms designated and licensed as Level I, II, or III trauma centers, has established, if you will, a "standard of care" for the evaluation and management of patients who are victims of trauma. The EMS technicians all across the state are under guidelines as to where to transport these patients based on the on-site evaluation of the extent of injury. The most seriously injured are transported initially to the Level I centers unless they require stabilization in another facility before transport is deemed to be in the patient's best interest. This would certainly imply that such a clinical judgment could be made by a physician in an ER with a designation other than Level I, or no designation as a trauma center.

This trauma center movement was developed from the experience of trauma surgeons through the impetus of the American College of Surgeons. It could be called one of the earliest developments of "parameters" of appropriate care, about which we will be hearing more and more as various specialty societies, the AMA, and even the physician-owned medical liability insurance carriers become involved. Whether we like it or not, this is the reality with which we as practicing physicians are faced.

In this case, is it proper to infer that this patient, probably a victim of his own excesses, would not have died if he had been initially transported to a Level I trauma center? Certainly not! But, judged against the current standards (parameters), which are in great measure the result of the trauma center development, the inference of a deviation from an acceptable standard of care was so strong that this case had to be settled out of court.

17.   BIG PROBLEM—SMALL HOSPITAL ER

Allegation—Inadequate assessment; history and physical;
            failure to diagnose; failure to consult
Physician Issues—Documentation inadequate; inappropriate
            use of narcotics in absence of diagnosis
Patient Issues—Unrelenting headache; two visits to ER; death
Outcome—High six-figure settlement

CASE STUDY

A 19-year-old female with a two-year history of recurrent headaches came to the emergency department in a small rural hospital at 7:00 PM complaining of headache of two hours' duration. The headache was aggravated by movement of the head and accompanied by photophobia. She was alert and oriented appropriately. The blood pressure was recorded as 126/78 mm Hg, the pulse was 76/min, and the temperature 98.4°F. Respiration was said to be "deep, quiet, and regular." The rate was not recorded. The neurological examination was recorded as "grossly intact." Nail beds were pink and refill was normal. The heart, lungs, and abdomen were described as "benign." The patient was said to be anxious, crying, and hysterical, but cooperative with the examination. She had been nauseated and had vomited on two occasions during the two hours since onset of the headache.

Further elaboration on the physical examination reveals that she appeared to be in pain. The range of motion in the extremities was normal, the neck supple, and the fundi described as benign. The diagnosis was "headaches," and she was treated with Phenergan, Toradol, Fiorinal #3 and told to see her regular physician in the AM if the pain did not subside. At this point, it is fair to say that the emergency room physician's documentation of the history and physical was unorganized and fragmented and parts of the record were illegible.

The patient returned to the emergency department about four hours after her initial visit with the same complaints. The physical was repeated and was said to be unchanged. The blood pressure was not recorded at this visit. This time she was given Demerol and Phenergan by injection and discharged from the department to see her regular physician in the AM. Within an hour, the patient returned to the emergency department in respiratory arrest. Resuscitation was unsuccessful. An autopsy was done and the findings were internal hydrocephalus due to obstruction of the ventricles.

A lawsuit was filed charging the physician with "inadequate history and physical, inadequate testing, failure to consult, and negligent failure to make a diagnosis in a timely manner." The lawsuit asked for $2 million damages.

Loss Prevention Comments

We do not know how careful the physician was in his history and physical on this unfortunate young woman. We do know that the documentation of that part of the encounter was woefully inadequate. We do not know about her history of headaches except that in the investigation of this claim, the emergency department personnel remembered that there was a two-year history of this problem. We do not know whether there was anything unusual about this particular headache. The answer to the question as to whether this headache differed in type or severity to previous headaches is extremely important. We know that the pain was accompanied by nausea and vomiting and that movement of the head made the pain worse. The record mentions that photophobia was a part of the picture. We do not know whether these complaints were a part of previous headaches nor do we have a description of the onset of the pain. Was it unilateral at the start? Did the photophobia begin before the pain started? How was relief obtained with the previous episodes? How long did the headaches usually last? The physical examination seemed to be less than acceptable in this setting. There was mention of normal range of motion and the absence of "visual difficulties or diplopia." We do not know about any lateralizing neurological signs, i.e., unequal reflexes, Babinski's up or down on each foot, or whether sensation was impaired. Upper and lower extremity reflexes were not recorded.

On her second visit to the emergency department the record of the findings was almost identical to the first visit. The record indicates that she was "calm/sleepy/cooperative." She was treated with Demerol and Phenergan and an ice cap was applied to the base of her neck. We do not know how long she stayed in the department but she could not have stayed more than a few minutes. She came in at 11:06 and when she came back in moribund it was still the same date, which indicates that she died before midnight. On the first visit, the statement was made that she was, among other things, "hysterical." It almost appears that the physician never got beyond this initial impression.

In a small community hospital where there may be lacking the necessary specialist backing in a case like this and where specialized testing, when available, usually requires that personnel be called out, the doctor is obliged to err on the side of caution and secure all the help available. Certainly on the second visit the physician in charge should have got a CT, should probably have called a neurologist for a phone consult if one was not resident locally, and should have carefully monitored and documented vital signs in addition to keeping a patient like this under observation until this assistance was obtained.

Would this approach have made any difference in the outcome? In view of the autopsy findings, it is doubtful. However this lesion is treatable, and every opportunity must be taken to provide the patient with all the support possible in this setting. From the available record it did not appear that this was done in this case. A settlement of near seven figures was required since defense was thought to be nearly impossible.

18.   FACTS AND FINDINGS IGNORED

Allegation—Failure to diagnose pulmonary embolism
Physician Issues—Morbid obesity; inadequate evaluation
Patient Issue—Death
Outcome—Six-figure settlement

CASE STUDY

A morbidly obese 25-year-old female telecommunications operator weighing over 500 lb came to the emergency department with a history of pain in both sides of her back for a week. She said that she had been getting more short of breath since onset and had developed a cough. A nurse's note reads, "SOB. Says she feels like she has gas in her chest." The history does not contain other facts about the back pain, shortness of breath, cough, or discomfort in her chest.

The physical examination is largely confined to the vital signs, the pulse oximetry findings, and the chest x-ray. The pulse was recorded as 132/min, respirations 32/min, and blood pressure 177/111 mm Hg. The record indicated that the blood pressure had to be determined by using a thigh cuff on the forearm and palpating the radial pulse. The thigh cuff would not go around her arm. The pulse oximetry showed 85 percent. The remainder of the documentation is very brief and is largely unreadable. "CXR V pneumonia R" is legible.

She was in the ED for about 30 minutes, discharged home on oral antibiotics, and advised to call her regular doctor in two days. The following day she was found dead in her apartment. No autopsy was done. The death certificate listed cardiopulmonary failure as the primary cause of death with obesity as secondary cause.

Barely within the year a lawsuit was filed charging, "Negligent failure to diagnose pulmonary embolism." Despite the massive obesity, very able defense experts were not able to support the management of this case. They pointed out that without an autopsy no one could positively diagnose a pulmonary embolism, but they further pointed out that with the presenting symptoms and the findings available to the ED physician, the patient should have been evaluated further in the hospital. A six-figure settlement closed the file on this case.

LOSS PREVENTION COMMENTS

The difficulties in the examination of a morbidly obese patient are well recognized. One venerable chief of medicine at the medical school where I graduated would not accept a patient of this kind in his practice, or so it was told when I was under his tutelage. To some of us, and I include myself, this level of obesity is so offensive that we may not be as attentive to detail and as conscientious about our evaluation as we customarily are. Could this have happened here?

The patient said she had had back pain for a week. No attempt was made by the physician to document the precise location of the discomfort or to describe its distinguishing characteristics. She further said that she had been increasingly short of breath since onset and that she felt that she had "gas in her chest." The location, character, and degree of this symptom were not documented. A cough was a part of the history, but there was no note as to its type or frequency, or whether or not it was productive.

She had tachypnea (respirations 32/min), tachycardia (pulse 132/min), and hypertension (blood pressure 177/111 mm Hg), and the pulse oximeter revealed a very distressing finding of only 85 percent O_2 saturation. No blood count or blood gas determination was done that might have helped to evaluate the chest findings. The chest x-ray was reported by the ED physician as, "CXR V pneumonia R." The radiologist reported a perihilar infiltrate on the right consistent with pneumonia. The "V" following the "CXR" appeared to be either a check mark indicating that the x-ray was ordered, or a "V" indicating viral pneumonia. Such was the difficulty of deciphering this record. Had the record contained some comment about the findings and a little more effort to sort out the problem facing this young woman, the outcome could have been different. Absent all this needed information, the patient was given antibiotics and sent home, to see her doctor in two days.

In the environment of litigation against a physician, the medical record is all that anyone has to either defend or indict the physician and his management of the case. One can almost unfailingly predict that illegible, scant documentation by the physician that does not comment on the history or the available abnormal vital signs will prove an insurmountable obstacle to the defense. It was so in this case. Defense expert witnesses, familiar with the situation and about the very real difficulties encountered in the clinical evaluation and management of a patient so obese, could not support the handling of this case. They pointed to the tachypnea, tachycardia, hypertension, and low O_2 saturation with the suggestion of pneumonia on the x-ray as findings demanding further evaluation in the hospital.

Would that have prevented this patient's death? Probably not, but this incomplete and largely illegible medical record was of no help to the physician involved here, or to his defense.

III

Gynecological Surgery

As in all surgical subspecialties, a good presurgical record is required. This record must contain the clinical conditions that justify the surgical intervention and a thorough record of informed consent. This is particularly true because of the hazard to adjacent structures in the pelvis that are vulnerable to injury during the procedure. The urinary tract is the area where most of these injuries occur. These are truly considered hazards of the procedure but if not disclosed in the informed consent they can become the reason for a charge of negligence. It goes without saying that the standard of care must be followed with respect to protecting these structures, i.e., the identification of the ureters by surgical dissection, the bowel particularly when cautery or laser is used for dissection or hemostasis, and the vascular structures that can be injured by trocar in laparoscopic surgery.

Surgery occasioned by complications of pregnancy or delivery is usually not complicated. Because it is not, the danger can be increased by treating the event as routine and overlooking something fundamental to a good outcome. Previous facts with regard to the pregnancy or the past history regarding complicating medical problems must be taken into consideration by the surgeon. Bleeding problems that may have become apparent during the labor and delivery, hypertension or proteinuria that may have been reported during pregnancy impact the surgeon's responsibility and must be considered.

It is important the these potential complications be given careful attention in the medical record so it will be apparent that efforts have been made to protect the patient during and following surgery. Some of the cases presented here illustrate some of the more common problems for the gynecologist.

19.   LEGAL TRAPS IN BREAST DISEASE

Allegation—Failure to diagnose breast cancer in timely manner
Physician Issue—Office system failure (reports)
Patient Issue—Delay in appropriate diagnosis and treatment
Outcome—Six-figure settlement

CASE STUDY

During routine breast self-examination, 26-year-old Mrs. Gray (divorced with two small children) noticed a lump. After some procrastination, she made an appointment to see her Ob/Gyn, Dr. Black. During this examination on January 10, 1983, a 2-cm. nodule was found at the three-o'clock position. He also noticed some "cystic mastitis" areas around the nodule. Mrs. Gray was sent for a mammogram, which was performed the next morning. When the written report returned indicating fibrocystic disease of the breast, Dr. Black phoned her informing her that the mammogram was negative for cancer but that she had a diffuse disease in the breast which might be caused by prolonged breast-feeding and to return after her next period for a recheck of the breast mass (the phone call was documented, but the instructions to return were not included; Mrs. Gray later denied having received the instructions to return for recheck). Mrs. Gray did not return.

During the next several months, Mrs. Gray noticed that the mass continued to increase in size, but she did not immediately return to the doctor due to her poor financial situation. Her family finally convinced her to seek a second opinion. She scheduled an appointment with another gynecologist, Dr. White, who saw her within two weeks. By this time it had been six months since the first examination. Dr. White saw her July 14, 1983 with complaints of a breast mass present for six months and that had been steadily increasing in size. His examination showed a solitary mass now 4 cm x 2 cm at three-o'clock position. On palpation, the mass was believed to be cystic, tender, mobile, and unattached to surrounding tissue. There were several 0.5-cm nodules also noted in the same area. Dr. White obtained a phone report of the January mammogram, and based on his examination and the report he diagnosed fibrocystic disease and recommended she decrease her caffeine intake by excluding coffee, tea, chocolate, and colas to see if the size of the mass decreased. If the mass did not decrease, she would need a breast biopsy.

One month later, August 16, 1983, Mrs. Gray returned to Dr. White with complaints of heavy and painful periods. No breast examination was conducted on this visit. Dr. White did ask if she had decreased her caffeine intake, which she indicated she had been unable to do. She was then instructed to return after her next period for recheck of the breast. This instruction was documented in the record, and Mrs. Gray later denied the instruction.

Two weeks later, Mrs. Gray became alarmed at the steady increase in size of the mass and decided to see a surgeon for biopsy. The biopsy proved the lesion to be an infiltrating intraductal carcinoma. A radical mastectomy was performed and all 18 lymph nodes were positive for metastasis. The cancer spread to her spine despite aggressive chemotherapy, and she ultimately died of the disease.

Loss Prevention Comments

Dr. Black's phone call to Mrs. Gray following the mammogram showing "cystic mastitis" should have been documented in his record along with his instructions to return for follow-up examination after her next menstrual period. Had specific instructions to return been documented, in all probability Dr. Black could not have been successfully charged with negligence.

Some six months later, Dr. White saw Mrs. Gray and was given a history of a mass in the breast said to be increasing in size. Dr. White obtained a report of the January mammogram and elected to advise the patient on a dietary management for fibrocystic disease. With an enlarging mass in the breast of six months' duration, Dr. White's appropriate management would have been to refer the patient to the surgeon for his opinion and his surgical intervention if the surgeon felt that appropriate. This assumes, of course, that Dr. White does not do breast surgery. Although the exclusion of caffeine from the diet for a period of one month might possibly be defended even in the case of an enlarging breast mass, again there was no documentation in the record proving that the patient was definitely instructed to return in one month for re-evaluation.

When a physician who does not do breast surgery finds a mass in the breast of a patient and elects to order a mammogram, he should probably also elect to involve in the care of the patient a surgeon who could be responsible for definitive surgical treatment if that became necessary.

The mammogram is an excellent test, but it does have definite limitations. These limitations should be communicated to the patient, who should not be told she definitely does not have cancer, based solely on a mammogram. The scenario above is all too frequent. Even when the mammogram does not show any evidence of malignant disease, an enlarging mass in the breast deserves biopsy.

20.   GOOD MEDICINE—LETHAL SIDE EFFECTS

Allegations—Inappropriate use of medication (Pitocin)
Physician Issue—Error in medication orders (physician to
  nurse)
Patient Issues—Water intoxication; brain damage
Outcome—Six-figure settlement

CASE STUDY

A 28-year-old woman with a history of menometrorrhagia since menarche at age 14 had had three previous pregnancies, two ending in spontaneous early abortions. She was two weeks postpartum, having delivered a healthy female infant after an uneventful pregnancy.

About ten days postpartum she began to have some vaginal bleeding. She experienced significant cramping and had passed large clots for four days when she was admitted to the hospital.

Vital signs on admission revealed a blood pressure of 126/70 mm Hg and temperature of 99.6°F. Her chest and heart were within normal limits. Her uterus was enlarged to the umbilicus and moderately tender. She was pale, but blood studies showed only a slight leukocytosis of 12,300/cu mm and a PCV of 30 percent with a hemoglobin of 10.6 gm/dl. An ultrasound examination of her abdomen showed some translucency of the uterine cavity and fluid in the cul-de-sac. A D&C was scheduled, and the following orders were given preoperatively: (1) NPO, (2) 1,000 cc Ringer lactate with 10 U Pitocin at 50 cc/hr IV, (3) Kefzol Gm 1 in IV q 8 hrs.

The D&C yielded a small amount of tissue, and the uterus was packed. Orders were given that the packing be removed in 48 hours. Considerable "ooze" was noted during the entire procedure. The following day a progress note indicated "moderate bleeding continues," and orders were made to give 250 cc D5RL with "Amp II Pit."

The next day the bleeding appeared to have slowed, but still continued, and orders were written for "Alternate D5W and D5RL 500 cc with Amp II Pit in each at 150 cc/hr IV. Methergine .2 mgm q 4 hrs IM until bleeding controlled."

The third day after surgery the patient was allowed to go to the bathroom. Orders were to "keep IV going until AM." The nurse's notes revealed that the patient complained of severe headache and vomited a "large amount" at 4:30 PM. At 8:30 PM there was "scant uterine bleeding." At 9:30 PM the patient was found in the bathroom unresponsive with dyspnea. Convulsive movements of extremities were observed. A code was called.

The lab work revealed chloride of 77 mEq/L and sodium 107 mEq/L. Severe brain damage resulted. A lawsuit was successful.

LOSS PREVENTION COMMENTS

Severe hyponatremia (water intoxication) is a known side effect of Pitocin. Because Pitocin produces water reabsorption through the renal tubules, hemodilution occurs, resulting in water intoxication, severe hyponatremia, cerebral edema, and even death.

The initial order for 10 U Pitocin in an IV was appropriate. Subsequent orders were for "Amp I" or "Amp II" Pitocin without specifying 5 or 10 U. In this case the nurses continued to fill the order with 10-U ampules in the IVs. During the 54 hours following the D&C the patient received in excess of 100 U Pitocin per 24 hours.

The *PDR*, in describing the recommended use of Pitocin, says, "The total dose should not exceed 30 U in a 12-hour period due to the risk of water intoxication."

Like so many medications, Pitocin can be indispensable in the management of specific situations, but its use demands careful attention to the possibility of adverse side effects. This kind of attention necessary to its use was lacking, producing severe injury to the patient. Had the order for Pitocin specified 5-U ampules, the total dose received by the patient would have been well within recommended guidelines. Did the physician intend to give the Pitocin in 5-U ampules? Probably. Did the physician allow too much discretion on the part of the nurses? Absolutely!

21.   I THOUGHT I SAW THAT REPORT

Allegation—Failure to diagnose in timely manner
Physician Issue—Office system failure (reports)
Patient Issue—Delay in treatment
Outcome—Six-figure settlement

CASE STUDY

At age 45, our patient began to experience severe hot flushes associated with sweats, sensation of rapid heartbeat, fluttering in the chest, and so on. The patient stated that these episodes were much more common and much more severe following or during exercise and/or eating.

It was in 1983 that these symptoms began. A routine physical examination was nonrevealing, and laboratory work, including a packed cell volume, white blood cell count, and urinalysis was likewise negative. A Pap smear showed no significant abnormality. The diagnosis of menopausal syndrome was made, and the patient was treated with supplemental estrogens.

The patient continued to complain of excessive "menopausal" symptoms, and in 1986 her physician ordered a follicle-stimulating hormone (FSH) assay and a luteinizing hormone (LH) assay; both were found to be within normal limits. Throughout 1986 her symptoms continued, and she also complained of some irregular bleeding. Physical examination again was within normal limits, and the pelvic examination showed no significant abnormality of the uterus or adnexa.

Because of the irregular bleeding, which began some three years after onset of the severe menopausal symptoms, a dilatation and curettage (D&C) was done with negative findings, and following the D&C, a CT of the abdomen and pelvis was also done. The report was never seen by the attending physician. We presume that it had been lost in the mail or in his office.

The patient's symptoms continued, and sometimes in the two years following the CT the patient felt a "knot" in her stomach. At this point, the CT examination of two years before was reviewed. At that time a mass had been present in the liver, and a repeat CT at this time showed a significant growth of the mass.

With respect to the evaluation that followed the D&C, the patient had been informed repeatedly by the physician that "everything was all right." The patient had not specifically inquired as to what the CT showed, but thought that since her physician had said that "everything was all right" that the CT examination must have shown normal findings. She was not told that the report had been lost.

The patient was admitted to the hospital for elective surgery to biopsy and/or remove the mass in the liver. At surgery, the mass was located without difficulty. It was of tennis-ball-size and was removed without significant difficulty. It had the clinical appearance of a carcinoid tumor, and indeed pathology confirmed that clinical impression.

In the course of the work-up that showed that the CT examination two years before had not been taken into account, the patient became angry and filed a lawsuit. In the discovery process, it was apparent that the tumor had grown on CT examination comparing the one two years prior to surgery and the one immediately before surgery.

Although expert testimony was available to discount the

importance of the two-year delay as far as definitive surgery was concerned, experts on the other side were willing to say that the patient's prognosis was not as good because of the two-year delay. It proved to be impossible to defend the attending physician, and a large settlement was required.

LOSS PREVENTION COMMENTS

Some way we must develop systems in our practice that prevent "lost reports." This is a common occurrence regardless of practice discipline. It would seem relatively simple to develop an office system where if a report was not returned within a certain period of time, inquiry could be made of the laboratory and/or radiologist as to what the report said. However, the frequency of claims of this type indicates that this must be an exceedingly difficult thing to do.

There are many systems in offices across Tennessee that are designed to prevent this kind of occurrence. In none of the offices where such a system is in place am I aware of a suit like this having occurred. The most frequent system, I believe, is to maintain a separate file for the medical record of a patient for whom tests have been ordered or surgery done. This file is not reentered into the routine filing system until all of the reports ordered by the physician are present in the file and have been initialed by him. In other words, if, when our patient had the D&C two years before the definitive surgery and the first CT was done, the patient's file in the physician's office would have remained in the "waiting for report" file until that CT report had been returned. It does complicate the system to some degree when diagnostic tests are done while the patient is in the hospital and the physician is not aware of the report while his patient is hospitalized. However, in almost all of the areas of the state with which I am familiar, an additional copy of the x-ray or laboratory report is sent to the physician's office when a hospital test is done. Since this is true, such a system would protect the physician from an incident of this type.

An additional safeguard is to routinely put all test reports that come to the physician's office on his desk to be read and initialed by him before they are made a part of the file. In our case, there was no report in the office file because, our physician alleged, none had been sent. However, in the development of the case, records were available in the radiologist's office that showed that the report had been dictated and mailed.

From previous experience the defense knew that if this case went to court, the attitude of the jury could be negative as far as our doctor was concerned because of the repeatedly stated position that the physician who orders a test is responsible for making sure that the test is done and reported properly. In other words, a layman would ask, "If the test is important enough to order in the first place, doctor, you should make sure that you have the results in hand at an appropriate time!"

The other inescapable finding in this case that made settlement absolutely necessary was that the diagnosis here had been delayed at least two years, thus definitive treatment was delayed by that same period of time. It's very difficult to convince a lay jury that the two years did not make any difference, when one would have to say that had the report been acknowledged two years previously, the surgery would have been done at that time rather than waiting the two years.

Again, look at the systems in your office that could protect you from this kind of lawsuit. Make sure that all reports ordered by you, whether outpatient or in the hospital, become a part of your patient's office record. Assign a responsible employee to the specific task of ensuring that this is done, and, if necessary, develop written protocols as to how this task should be carried out.

All would agree that this should never happen, and yet it very frequently does.

22.   HELP NEEDED—NOT CALLED FOR

Allegation—Lack of informed consent; injury to adjacent
       structure
Physician Issue—No documentation of attempt to identify
       ureter
Patient Issues—Multiple operations; prolonged hospitalization
Outcome—Six-figure settlement

CASE STUDY

In 1983, our patient was 36 years old and already had had a long history of pelvic pain. When the patient was age 28, an operation disclosed endometriosis. Prior to the second surgical procedure, the patient again complained of progressively severe pelvic pain, particularly during the menses, and the examiner noted irregular enlargement of the uterus consistent with fibroids. The right adnexa had been found to be thickened, tender, and at times to contain what appeared to be a large and tender follicle cyst.

The patient underwent a total abdominal hysterectomy with a

right salpingo-oophorectomy. Extremely dense pelvic adhesions were commented upon in the operative note, but the operation went well and convalescence was uneventful.

In 1988, at age 41, our patient developed increasing pain in the pelvis, particularly on the left, and on examination was found to have a left ovarian cyst, confirmed by ultrasound; the patient was admitted to the hospital for a left salpingo-oophorectomy.

Except for the pelvic examination, which showed the enlarged left adnexa, which was tender and relatively fixed, the preoperative laboratory work and physical examination were within normal limits. The operative note referred repeatedly to "dense adhesions." There was no operative note that indicated that an attempt was made to skeletonize the left ureter, but in discussion with the surgeon after the fact, he stated that attempt was made but proved to be impossible due to the severe dense, generalized adhesions.

The surgeon proceeded with the operation, and almost immediately after surgery the patient began to complain of inordinate pain in the left lower abdomen and in the left flank.

The diagnosis of a transected and ligated ureter on the left was made within five days of the operation. One attempt was made to surgically repair the lesion, but this proved to be unsuccessful. On the second attempt a successful repair of the ureter was accomplished.

The patient had been in the hospital for a number of weeks, she had had three operations, and she had lost her job. In a subsequent lawsuit, defense proved next to impossible, and a six-figure settlement was necessary.

LOSS PREVENTION COMMENTS

A thorough review of the record and examination of both the doctor and the patient indicated that there was no problem with the informed consent process. There had been an adequate description of the surgery and its risks and benefits, and specific reference had been made to the rather significant danger of injury to adjacent structures. In fact, a videotape had been shown in the doctor's office that spoke directly of injuries to the urinary tract, including the ligation of a ureter that this patient experienced.

Although the consent proved to be adequate within an acceptable standard, there were other severe deficiencies in this patient's management. Experts who reviewed the record were critical because once the surgeon found that he was not able to skeletonize the ureter because of adhesions, there was no mention of the possibility of calling in a urologist to catheterize the ureters from below so they could be easily identified in the pelvis.

Experts were also critical of there being no attempt by the gynecologist to call in a more experienced colleague and ask for assistance at the table. This occurred in a medical center of such size that this kind of consultation would have been both possible and desirable. Again, the very important point must be made that even when informed consent is adequate and appropriate, quality considerations in the delivery of care are paramount in the assessment of potential liability on the part of the physician.

23.   A "CUT" IN THE DARK

Allegations—Lack of informed consent; severed ureter
Physician Issue—No documentation of attempts to identify
    ureter
Patient Issues—Delayed recovery; additional surgery
Outcome—Low six-figure settlement

CASE STUDY

A 45-year-old woman had a total abdominal hysterectomy and a right salpingo-oophorectomy ten years ago because of uterine fibroids with excessive bleeding and a right tubo-ovarian mass that proved to be an old tubo-ovarian abscess. The operative note describing that surgery emphasized that marked adhesions required extensive blunt and sharp dissection in order to remove the diseased structures. The note described the identification of the ureters on both sides from the pelvic brim inferiorly.

The patient came to her Ob/Gyn primary physician complaining of pain in the left lower abdomen radiating into the back. The physical examination revealed a tender mass in the left adnexal region, and ultrasonography was reported to show a cystic mass in the region of the left ovary. The patient was given a broad spectrum antibiotic for one week and told to return to see her physician. The findings on pelvic examination were essentially unchanged except that the tenderness was somewhat decreased. Surgery was recommended.

After a thorough discussion of the planned operation, including the possibility of injury to structures adjacent to the tubo-ovarian mass, surgery was scheduled. At operation, adhesions encountered were much worse than expected. There were no identifiable cleavage planes, and by slow tedious blunt and sharp dissection the left adnexal area was exposed. The expected 7-cm cystic mass was found thoroughly stuck to the posterior peritoneum. With difficulty the mass was freed up and a clamp was placed, allowing the excision of the cyst. The operative note did not describe the left ureter or attempts to identify it.

Postoperatively the patient had more than the expected amount of pain posteriorly on the left side. A low-grade fever up to 100°F orally continued for about four days after surgery but returned to normal on antibiotics. The postoperative urine was within normal limits.

The patient was discharged on the sixth postoperative day but continued to require oral analgesics because of pain in the left lower abdomen and back. She was seen two weeks after surgery, and because of continued pain an x-ray (KUB) was done, which showed an enlarged kidney shadow on the left. Further investigation by cystoscopy and left ureteral catheterization showed the left ureter to be completely blocked. Corrective surgery followed initial operation by about 16 days, and although the left ureter was successfully implanted into the bladder, a vesicovaginal fistula developed and two successive operations were required to correct the problem.

After about six months, with the patient recovered, a lawsuit was filed alleging a lack of informed consent and negligent surgery in that the left ureter was severed, requiring the additional operations, hospitalization, and loss of time. The patient complained that although her discussion with her surgeon did mention the possibility of injury to adjacent structures, she was not thoroughly apprised of the seriousness of such a complication. Since the operative note following the total abdominal hysterectomy and right salpingo-oophorectomy some ten years earlier had emphasized the severe adhesions, she contended that her doctor should have anticipated that problem and taken the appropriate precautions relative to protecting the left ureter.

Since there was no description in the operative note of the attempt the surgeon said that he made to identify the left ureter, it could not be substantiated that an acceptable standard of care was followed. On this basis a settlement was recommended.

LOSS PREVENTION COMMENTS

In our surgeon's preoperative conversation with his patient he talked about the possibility of injuring adjacent structures including the urinary bladder and the ureter. He said he made a judgment at the table that attempting to skeletonize the left ureter was more of a risk to his patient than proceeding to carefully dissect the cyst and remove it.

The question must be asked, "What could he have done to prevent injury to the left ureter?" In this particular case, given the massive adhesions and the inability to palpate the ureter, a urologist could have been consulted to attempt to catheterize the ureter so that its course could be definitely determined. The experts who reviewed this case believed that the surgeon did not perform up to an acceptable standard in that the operative note did not describe any attempt to identify the left ureter, and faced with a failure to identify the ureter the operator did not call for help in the operating room to protect it.

The informed consent in this case was adequate. A defense could have been made if there had been good documentation. It is a principle worth remembering that the determining factor in all malpractice action is whether or not the care received by the patient meets the acceptable standard as established by our own colleagues.

24.   CARDIOVASCULAR WARNING SIGNS IGNORED

> *Allegations—Negligence on part of gynecologist, anesthesiologist, and CRNA; failure to take into consideration the past history of hypertension; failure to perform appropriate preoperative testing; failure to consult medical specialist for preoperative clearance*
>
> *Physician Issues—Preoperative examination normal; severe tachycardia early in anesthesia; anesthesiologist gave OK to continue*
>
> *Patient Issues—Preoperative severe anxiety; severe tachycardia early in anesthesia; tachy/bradycardia with coma requiring ventilator support; persistent vegetative state; death six years later*
>
> *Outcome—High seven-figure settlement*

CASE STUDY

A 33-year-old, divorced, gravida 2, para 2, the mother of two children, came to the obstetrician/gynecologist (Ob/Gyn), who had been her physician for a number of years, requesting a tubal ligation. She had had a cesarean section (C-section) with her second delivery and did not want to have other children. The operation was scheduled, and the patient was told when to report to the ambulatory surgery unit of the hospital.

The admission history and physical documented "no other

major problems." The previous C-section was noted. A part of the past history was illegible, but was thought to record "hypertension—pre-term—mild," without medication (apparently for hypertension) for over two months. The blood pressure was recorded at 136/78 mm Hg, temperature 98°F, pulse 88/min, and respirations 16/min. The examination of the heart revealed regular sinus rhythm without murmurs, and the pulse was said to be of a "good force." Examination revealed symmetrical breasts, clear lung fields, no bruits over the major vessels, and no palpable masses or tenderness. The surgical scar was noted.

In the preanesthesia note, the certified registered nurse anesthetist recorded a clear history of hypertension for which the patient took medication. Presumably this is the medication referred to in the physician's admission note—"no medication in over two months." The CRNA recorded, under "Cardiac," that the patient was treated for over a year for high blood pressure but had not taken any medication "this past year." The date of the admission was early in February. Under "Pulmonary," "emphysema" was noted. She was classified as ASA 1 for general anesthesia.

She was given Demerol, Phenergan, and Atropine preopera-tively and taken to the operating room. The CRNA recorded that the patient was "extremely apprehensive." Fentanyl, O_2, N_2O, and Ethrane were administered. Tachycardia of "over 150" was noted in the physician's operative note. In the postanesthesia note, the pulse rate was recorded at 180/min, continuing to rise to 212/min in a matter of seconds. The patient had been given 0.2 mg of Inderal IV at the onset of the tachycardia, and when the pulse rate continued to rise another 0.3 mg of Inderal was given IV. In minutes the pulse rate had fallen to 120/min, with the blood pressure remaining about 130/90 mm Hg. According to the physician's operative report, "the anesthetist" gave permission to continue the case, whereas according to the post-operative anesthesia note, a "decision was made to continue case."

With the patient under general endotracheal anesthesia with supplemental Pentothal, Anectine, and Metubine, after the skin incision was made the pulse rate again rose to 200/min, only to quickly fall to levels in the thirties. Atropine was given without response and was repeated, again with no response. The bradycardia persisted, and the blood pressure was unobtainable. Isuprel was given, and a cardiologist was called. External cardiac massage was initiated, $NaHCO_3$ was given IV, and a Dopamine drip was begun. (The timing of these events is not in the record, but the entire sequence of events had to have occurred within minutes after the induction of anesthesia.) The blood pressure was recorded at 80 mm Hg, and the next recorded pulse rate was 142/min with the blood pressure

LET THE RECORD SHOW

110/80 mm Hg. Narcan was given IV, and the patient was taken to the ICU breathing spontaneously, with small reactive pupils and responding to tracheal suction via the endotracheal tube. The anesthesia note recorded, "Earlier the left pupil was dilated and did not respond to light."

The patient remained in a deep coma and after three months in the hospital was transferred to a nursing home, where she remained in a vegetative state, dying over six years later. A lawsuit was filed charging negligence on the part of the Ob/Gyn, the anesthesiologist, and the CRNA in the failure to perform proper preoperative diagnostic procedures, failure to obtain clearance from the appropriate specialists before surgery, a lack of proper preoperative sedation in this extremely apprehensive patient, and for not canceling the surgery after the initial episode of tachycardia (cardiovascular instability). A seven-figure confidential settlement was reached, closing this very tragic case.

LOSS PREVENTION COMMENTS

Millions of successful general anesthetics are accomplished in this country each year, many of them in patients who are far more compromised than this patient appeared to be. She was to have a short, simple procedure requiring minimal anesthesia, and in fact the plan was to do it without endotracheal intubation. Only after the initial episode of tachycardia, with the decision to proceed with the surgery, was intubation carried out. The plan was probably appropriate. The patient was not!

There are several clues in the record, most of them documented immediately after the fact, that in retrospect alert us to the danger to this patient. The history of hypertension significant enough to require treatment for a year was barely mentioned by the surgeon. A slightly more detailed account of the disease and its treatment appears in the preoperative evaluation done by the CRNA after admission to the ambulatory surgery suite and immediately before the preoperative medication was given. The facts were known to the Ob/Gyn, who had mentioned the hypertension, its treatment, and the fact that treatment had been discontinued only two months before surgery. Was the medication stopped on advice of the treating physician, or did the patient stop it without physician direction? Did the Ob/Gyn know which had occurred?

The CRNA stated that the patient was "extremely apprehensive." We can surmise that the CRNA had seen many patients preoperatively so that her characterization of this patient would indicate that the observation was certainly significant. Did the CRNA alert the surgeon about this? The preoperative sedation seemed to be routine. Should there have been more or different preparation? Was the outcome related to the hypertension or to the "extreme apprehension"?

Almost immediately after the anesthesia was started the tachycardia developed, with rates recorded variously at "over 150/min," 200/min, and 212/min. Because the response to Inderal IV was prompt and encouraging, the decision was made to proceed under different anesthetic precautions. An endotracheal tube was put in place, and the anesthetic agents were changed. Attention was given to assure sufficient oxygenation, but the patient again exhibited cardiac instability with severe tachycardia, followed by bradycardia and subsequent "cardiopulmonary arrest." Though cardiopulmonary resuscitation was begun promptly, the outcome was a patient in a vegetative state for almost seven years before she died at the age of 40.

It is easy to attribute the tragic events in this case to a number of facts that singly or together could have triggered this horrible cascade: the history of hypertension and emphysema, extreme apprehension, tachycardia, the beta blocker, bradycardia, hypotension, asystole, and hypoxic brain damage. Though we cannot know for sure the effects of these on the outcome, this case was reviewed in detail on at least two occasions by experts in the fields of obstetrics and anesthesiology, and no one could be found who could support its management.

The lessons provided by this case seem clear. We ignore the history of any disease at the peril of the patient. We must be on unassailable grounds to continue an elective procedure in the face of events that cause us to abort the first attempt.

IV

Orthopedic Surgery

The orthopedic surgeon is frequently the target of litigation. Why is that? Perhaps it has something to do with the fact that although most orthopedic injuries can be visualized pre-operatively by x-ray or other imaging techniques, the approach to those injuries requires a great deal of ingenuity and variation from case to case. The "routine" hip fracture is almost never "routine"! The same is true of most bone injuries. The x-ray may not tell the whole story and the magnitude of the repair procedure can only depend on what is discovered during the surgery. Because of this the surgeon must be careful with the informed consent process so as not to give the impression that all will be well but must make the patient aware of the potential risks of what cannot be definitively determined before the surgery.

The follow-up is in many cases long and tiresome for the patient and likely to give rise to dissatisfaction and concern. A good physician/patient relationship is the best protection in these instances. Because the healing is usually a protracted process, the surgeon doing the procedure frequently must leave to an associate or colleague some of the follow-up. In this familiar setting, the communication between the operator and the colleague must be thorough and documented in the medical record.

Because orthopedic surgeons are skilled in interpreting their own x-rays, it sometimes happens that the overread of the film by the radiologist does not conform to that of the orthopedist. There must be a system in place in the physician's office to identify these rare occurrences and take appropriate action.

In the teaching setting, where there will be a resident with a responsibility for rounds and assessment of the patient, the attending must take into consideration the level of training and experience of the resident and communicate with him or her in the progress notes in a manner that instructs the junior member of the team thoroughly.

At all times it must be made clear that any question in the mind of the resident should be the occasion for a call to the attending.

The orthopedic surgeon so frequently approaches the patient and is expected to treat him or her with only the clinical knowledge of the referring physician in his possession. In these instances, the surgeon must be especially careful that all the clinical bases are covered with documentation by the referring doctor including all the back-up lab and x-ray studies available. There can be no substitute for confidence in the medical condition of the patient the surgeon is expected to treat.

A word must be said about worker's compensation and some of its hazards. The patient is usually not satisfied with the fact that the injury occurred at work and is not a "happy camper" when first seen by the orthopedist. The controversies that can occur between the physician and the patient over the degree of disability following treatment can be another reason for the patient to be dissatisfied. We have seen medical malpractice lawsuits against the surgeons in this setting. Because of this potentiality, the medical record must be good enough to defend the doctor if necessary.

The cases presented here are demonstrative of some of the more common problems faced by the orthopedist and offer some suggestions relative to avoiding litigation.

25.   COMMUNICATION THROUGH THE RECORD

Allegation—Failure to diagnose compartment syndrome
Physician Issue—Documentation failure (physician to
        physician)
Patient Issues—Deformity of leg and shortening
Outcome—Large settlement

CASE STUDY

A 10-year-old boy was admitted to the hospital with a spiral fracture of the femur sustained during a football game. The day after admission he was placed in balanced traction, holding the fracture in good position. His admitting orthopedic surgeon, Dr. Green, suggested to the patient's mother the possibility of placing her son in a "cast-brace" in order to decrease his hospitalization time. The mother agreed, and the "cast-brace," which extended from the groin to the ankle, was applied on July 17, 1982, two weeks after the initial injury.

On the evening of the cast application, the patient complained of pain in the leg, which was treated with narcotics. Following an examination, the resident noted "neurovascular status intact." The following morning, July 18, Dr. Green examined the patient and noted, "Refuses to move toes for fear of pain. Neurovascular status intact. Cast bivalved to the skin from groin to knee."

Dr. Range, an associate of Dr. Green, examined the patient on July 19, as this was Dr. Green's day off. The patient was continuing to complain of pain below the knee requiring periodic narcotic medication. Dr. Range's note stated, "Cast spread over thigh—circulation okay—no motor function." Opposite this progress note was an order to "spread cast over thigh." At 4:00 PM on the same day, some six hours after Dr. Range had seen the patient, the nurse noted that the cast seemed to be too tight around the ankle and that there was a "blister" at the upper margin of the cast on the anterior aspect of the thigh near the groin. Two hours later, 6:00 PM, Dr. Smith, an orthopedic resident, was called to check the patient relative to his complaints of pain below the knee. He observed Dr. Range's note, "No motor function," and was unsure about what was meant, but he decided not to call Dr. Range. On examination, he found some pain with toe motion but noted that the capillary refill was good. He did not write a progress note, nor did he describe the pulses verbally at that time. Dr. Smith marked the cast to be trimmed in the area where the "blister" had been noted. Two and a half hours later, the nurse reported that the patient complained of pain over the lateral aspect of the upper calf and she called the resident, Dr. Smith, to see the patient again. No progress note was made by the resident, but he ordered the cast to be trimmed further. The nurse again noted a "blister" in the area where the cast had been trimmed. The patient apparently got some relief and slept for about six hours.

At eight o'clock the following morning the nurse noted that the cast appeared tighter around its lower margin and the patient complained of pain in his calf on movement of his toes. About 10:00 AM Dr. Green saw the patient, found the increased pain over the tibia, some decreased sensation, and considerable pain on passive motion of the foot, both on dorsiflexion and plantar flexion. He diagnosed tri-compartment syndrome and immediately took the patient to surgery for a decompression fasciotomy. In surgery, after the cast was removed, no dorsalis pedis or posterior tibial pulses were palpable, and there was decreased sensation over the course of the common peroneal nerve. At surgery, approximately one third of the calf muscle was devitalized and had to be removed. Following the fasciotomy, pulses returned, and the patient began to move his toes slightly. Gradually the patient regained the full range of motion in his hips and knees and was left with only a 5° equinus contracture. He had a smaller calf and 1 cm shortening of the leg on the affected side.

Suit was brought charging the attending orthopedic surgeon, his partner, and the resident with deviating from a reasonable standard of care due to their failure to diagnose the compartment syndrome earlier. The plaintiff had no trouble finding expert testimony stating that the care of this patient fell below an acceptable standard in many areas: (1) With the patient complaining of pain in his leg, the notes stating "neurovascular status intact" were inadequate, since there was no description of pulses, temperature of leg, motion, sensation, etc. Capillary refill, which was described, was said to be unreliable in determining vascular status. (2) With continued pain below the knee, the bivalving of the cast only over the thigh was inadequate treatment. (3) The meaning of Dr. Range's note "no motor function" was never quite clear, and indeed if there were no motor function, the cast should have been removed immediately, and circulation should have been more carefully observed. (4) Dr. Smith did not call Dr. Range to determine what was meant by "no motor function." His own examinations at that time and at a subsequent visit were not documented. (5) The testimony of the resident physician, Dr. Smith, was confusing and inconsistent because he relied solely on his memory. Experts stated that his care was below the standard, both in his approach to the complaints and in his failure to document his findings.

LOSS PREVENTION COMMENTS

Three physicians were intimately involved in the care of this young patient. In this situation, progress notes were not detailed enough to adequately describe the condition found and the treatment given, and therefore no one involved in the patient's care was properly informed. Both the resident and the attending's associate were below the standard in this regard.

Compartment syndrome is such a devastating complication that it should be very aggressively managed. Any reasonable suspicion of this complication should certainly call for the removal of the cast and meticulous observation of the involved extremity.

Communication between the physicians was extremely poor, thus the opportunity to intervene early in this serious complication was missed, and patient injury occurred. There was negligence on the part of all those doctors, and a sizable payment resulted.

26.   A MISSED OPPORTUNITY?

Allegation—Surgery on wrong side

Physician Issue—Failure to localize approach
Patient Issues—Protracted pain and disability; additional
*   surgery*
Outcome—Six-figure settlement

CASE STUDY

A 29-year-old truck driver sustained a lifting injury to his back while unloading freight in December of 1984. Five days after the injury, he reported to his primary care physician with pain in his low back, with some radiation into the right leg.

Physical examination revealed only a 3+ straight-leg raising test on the right and significant limitation of motion in the low back. The patient was treated with bed rest, heat, and analgesics, and after no improvement in 10 days was referred to an orthopedic surgeon for evaluation and treatment.

Two more weeks of conservative therapy followed, including some effort at mobilization with passive exercises, heat, analgesics, and rest on a hard bed. Again, there was no response.

In March, some three months after the initial injury, the physical examination again revealed limitation of motion in the back, positive straight-leg raising on the right, but there were no objective findings of motor or sensory deficit. The DTR were recorded as being "okay." Routine x-rays of the back showed no significant abnormality. A CT scan and myelogram showed an extradural defect on the right involving the L4-5 space.

Chemonucleolysis followed, and after what appeared to be some initial improvement, the patient continued to complain of pain, required analgesics, and was unable to return to work.

In September of the same year, a repeat CT scan and myelogram again revealed the right extradural defect at the level of L4-5. The record indicated that conservative therapy had failed, and a lumbar diskectomy was scheduled.

The surgery was done on the left side due to some confusion that developed in the preoperative preparation and draping. The operative note indicated that disk material was located centrally and on the right and was removed. Following the surgery, the patient was fully informed as to the operative approach from the left side instead of the right.

Again there was little or no relief. Pain persisted all the while, and analgesics were required. Attempts at physiotherapy failed, and a repeat CT scan again revealed the central bulge at the L4-5 interspace.

The patient failed to keep a scheduled appointment with his orthopedic surgeon and in December of the same year was reoperated upon by another surgeon. Shortly after that operation was done, a lawsuit was filed. Expert witnesses for the defendant doctor and the patient were both deposed. The initial operating surgeon and experts for the defense all testified that although it was a deviation from an acceptable standard of care to approach a right extradural defect from the left, it can be done, and sometimes herniated disk material can be satisfactorily removed. The operating surgeon believed that all of the significant disk material had been removed at the initial operation, and his experts testified that this was certainly possible. Expert witnesses for the patient contended that it was indeed a departure from an acceptable standard to approach a lumbar diskectomy from the wrong side and that, therefore, results could be expected to be less than optimum.

There was substantial question that the preoperative CT scan was significantly different from the postoperative CT scan. Recovery was slow, and a significant disability resulted.

The extent of psychosomatic overlay was difficult if not impossible to assess. A substantial settlement was necessary to avoid a jury trial.

LOSS PREVENTION COMMENTS

Worker's compensation back injuries are known to be very difficult cases. Both the employer and the employee have a vested interest in prompt and aggressive management of the complaint. The worker needs to get back to work, and the employer needs an able worker. With this kind of pressure on the physician to "fix it," it is almost impossible to remain totally objective in the evaluation and approach to treatment.

In this case, while there was no evidence of mismanagement in the initial approach to treatment (chemonucleolysis), one wonders about the three months' delay between the initial injury and definitive treatment without any record of vigorous physical and occupational therapy. Additionally, there was no record of an objective neurologic evaluation. There was, however, in more than one location in the record, the note that reflexes were "equal and 2+" and that there was "no evidence of motor or sensory deficit."

There is no record of any involvement of the employer in a "early return to work attempt." In fact, after the chemonucleolysis, there was little in the way of systematic physical therapy. This may have been the time when a thoughtful application of what we know about physical/occupational therapy could have prevented further surgery. Apart from heat, a hard bed, and analgesics, little was done to encourage rehabilitation. Even though approaching a right L4-5 extradural defect from the left was considered negligence and a significant settlement resulted, one must wonder how differently this case would have turned out if, from the very beginning, aggressive use of modern physical/occupational therapy had been employed. This kind of approach involves the best efforts of employers, physicians, physical therapists, and patients.

Confusion between left and right is very frequent in the practice of medicine. Usually the confusion is clarified before an invasive procedure is done, but when the confusion leads to surgery on the wrong side, as it did here, we pay! In the checklist completed preoperatively, the surgeon should be asked to confirm the correct side of the abnormality.

Neurosurgeons and orthopedic surgeons, who generally manage these cases, definitively pay very high malpractice insurance premiums. The worker's compensation back injury is a fairly frequent cause of malpractice litigation, and the losses in this area are considerable. Perhaps the early and aggressive approach to rehabilitation employing all modalities at our command could result in a reduction in the risk to all concerned.

27.   THE SCHEDULE vs. THE PATIENT

Allegation—Failure to take into account preoperative studies
Physician Issues—Surgery done before reports of preoperative
studies; tight schedule
Patient Issue—Intraoperative myocardial infarction
Outcome—Six-figure settlement

CASE STUDY

A 38-year-old man sustained a knee injury in a fall on the job at a construction site. He had a long history of alcohol abuse and peptic ulcer disease, for which he had been seen regularly by his family physician. There was a strong family history of coronary artery disease in that the patient's father and an older brother had both had coronary artery bypass surgery. Two weeks after his initial injury, the patient was admitted to the ambulatory surgery service at 7:00 AM scheduled for arthroscopy of the left knee at 10:30 AM. The physical examination done by the attending orthopedist five days prior to admission documented no positive findings except for those related to the left knee. The preoperative orders included a complete blood cell count, urinalysis, partial thromboplastin time (PTT), chest x-ray, and electrocardiogram. All the initial orders were carried out on the patient and, at the time, the anesthesiologist made his preoperative rounds. All results were reported on the chart and were within normal limits. During this visit, the patient told the anesthesiologist that he had some epigastric discomfort. The patient attributed this to his fasting state. The anesthesiologist ordered STAT cardiac enzymes at 9:30 AM. The blood was drawn for these tests at 9:40 AM. At 10:00 AM the nurse administered the preoperative medication as ordered.

The operating surgeon arrived in the operating room about 10:40 AM and discussed with the anesthesiologist the cardiac enzymes that were not as yet reported. The patient denied any discomfort; the vital signs were stable, and both the anesthesiologist and the orthopedist thought that there was no good reason to delay the surgery. Within minutes after general anesthesia had begun, the patient suffered cardiac arrest, and attempts at resuscitation were unsuccessful. By this time the cardiac enzymes were reported and were strongly suggestive of an acute myocardial infarction.

A lawsuit was filed against both the orthopedic surgeon and the anesthesiologist.

LOSS PREVENTION COMMENTS

This young man had been followed and treated regularly by his primary care physician for complaints attributed to alcohol abuse and peptic ulcer disease. This was known to the orthopedic surgeon, but the surgeon made no effort to involve the patient's primary care physician in his plans for surgical treatment. The plaintiff position, supported by expert testimony, was that the orthopedic surgeon was negligent in not making contact with the patient's primary care physician regarding the past history and his plans for surgery.

The anesthesiologist promptly reviewed the patient's history during his preanesthesia visit and, because of the epigastric discomfort, ordered the cardiac enzymes STAT, assuming that the results would be reported before the scheduled surgery. He failed, however, to delay the preoperative medication until after the enzymes had been reported, and further, he agreed to begin anesthesia before the tests were reported. The plaintiff contended, again with the support of good expert testimony, that the anesthesiologist was negligent on both counts.

The orthopedic surgeon was accused of negligence for proceeding with the surgery before he had all the clinical evidence in hand with respect to the preoperative condition of his patient. No expert testimony could be obtained that the defendant physician had acted within the acceptable standard of care.

Other allegations complicating the defense pertained to the decision to operate in the ambulatory surgery area in view of the positive family history and in view of the continuing complaints related to peptic ulcer disease. The implication was that more attention was paid to cost containment, the surgical schedule, and the convenience of the physicians than to the welfare of the patient.

No good legal defense could be mounted; consequently, a large settlement was necessary.

28.   DAMN THE TORPEDOES—FULL SPEED AHEAD!

Allegation—Wrongful death due to errors in surgical technique
Physician Issues—Wrong drill used; informed consent documented but denied by family
Patient Issue—Death due to surgical errors
Outcome—Low six-figure settlement

CASE STUDY

During the past few years, a 72-year-old woman, who all of her life had been actively involved in civic affairs, church work, raising her family, and caring for her grandchildren, became progressively disabled because of severe degenerative arthritis in the right hip. The disability became severe enough to greatly limit her ability to enjoy life and take care of basic necessities around her home, i.e., cleaning, light cooking. She found increasing difficulty in getting about, even when she used a cane.

During this period of time, she had been observed by her internist, who had carefully followed and treated her. At the point when her pain and disability became intolerable, her primary care physician referred her to a well-trained, board certified orthopedic surgeon.

The preoperative laboratory work was within normal limits except for generalized osteoarthritis with extreme arthritic change in the right hip including a marked reduction in the joint space, severe hyperostoses about the acetabulum, and significant pain even on passive motion through a limited range.

The possibility of a hip replacement had been discussed with the patient by her internist over the past two or three years. Both had elected to defer the operation until pain and disability demanded some attention. The patient entered the hospital well prepared emotionally for the event. The standard hospital consent form, as well as a more elaborate typewritten form, was signed by the patient. The form discussed the operation in some detail, described the benefits in rather glowing terms, and dealt with the risks adequately but without emphasizing many of the potential hazards. The patient readily signed the informed consent document and proceeded to surgery the morning after admission. There was no physician's progress note regarding informed consent.

During the surgical procedure, the surgeon was given a drill that had no guard in place, but he was heard to say he would use a shorter drill and proceed with the operation. Indeed, the surgeon did proceed in what appeared to be an uneventful fashion, but, prior to leaving the table, the patient was noted to have a fall in blood pressure and an increase in pulse and was noticeably pale.

Blood loss was suspected, and a general surgeon was called who explored the pelvis, finding a significant tear/perforation in the right iliac artery.

An attempt was made to repair the artery, but mobilization and ligation of the artery proximal to the tear proved technically very difficult, and during the attempt to control bleeding the patient died despite the intervention of a general surgeon called by the attending physician to assist and the vigorous use of blood, blood products, and fluids.

LOSS PREVENTION COMMENTS

When an otherwise healthy patient enters the hospital for some elective, definitive surgical procedure, it is without doubt a severe shock when death is the outcome. The patient was greatly loved by her family and admired by her friends and was somewhat of an institution in her community. In a careful retrospective study of this case, the following points were found to be significant:

While the informed consent document was considered to be adequate and probably met an acceptable standard of care for informed consent in total hip replacement, there was no notation by the surgeon on the form or in the chart stating that he personally had dealt with the patient relative to the risks involved in this surgical procedure. A member of the patient's family was present when the physician made his rounds on the evening prior to surgery and did not recall any mention of any risks to the surgery, even though at this point the doctor did discuss the postoperative management, including early exercise and physical therapy. The picture painted to both the family and the patient was one that anticipated a very satisfactory outcome, but it did not deal candidly with the potential danger of anesthesia or the surgical procedure itself.

Without any question there was a technical error in this operation. The decision by the surgeon to proceed with a "shorter drill" without a guard proved to be fatal to his patient. Why was it inappropriate to delay the procedure until a proper guard could have been secured to place on the drill? Why could not another orthopedic surgeon have been summoned to the operating room to assist in making the decision as to whether or not to proceed with the surgery? It appeared that during the procedure, in spite of the obvious danger involved in not using a guard, the surgeon took the "damn-the-torpedoes" attitude and proceeded with what he intended to do in the first place.

These difficulties in the management of this case made it impossible to secure expert witnesses who would confirm the decisions and the technique used by the operating surgeon. Settlement of this claim was almost mandatory in light of these circumstances.

The settlement in this case was large, but it would have been much larger without the prompt reporting of the incident following the patient's demise. This prompt reporting allowed an approach to the family of the deceased that promoted settlement and avoided trial. Because of the prompt promoting and the aggressive activity on the part of the claims attorneys, the family of the deceased did not employ counsel, and settlement was made promptly.

29.   TAKE A LEFT—OR WAS IT A RIGHT?

Allegations—Surgery on wrong side
Physician Issues—Failure to identify and mark side of
*   problem preoperatively; defense impossible*
Patient Issue—Complications directly resulting from failure to
*   identify correct side*
Outcome—Usually large settlements (depends of magnitude of
*   loss)*

We have all had the experience of examining a patient, looking at an x-ray, making a diagnosis, and prescribing treatment, only to find that when we began to dictate the record we could not remember which foot was injured. "Do not let the left hand know what the right hand is doing," is a biblical admonition that has to do with the secrecy with which we should give to the needy. Physicians have a tendency to take this advice much too far when it comes to procedures to be done on only one organ of which there are two, one on each side. One of the earliest cases we had was of this type and involved the removal of the wrong kidney. But it seems that in recent years we might have trained a lot of young doctors who grew up looking for the wart on the hand before being sure whether that hand was the left or right. That, of course, is an exaggeration! But, in reality, SVMIC has paid many more claims in the past few years that grew out of this confusion than in its early years. Maybe it just seems that way, and maybe it is true only because more doctors and more procedures are involved. At any rate, instead of one case, I thought it might be well to look briefly at several with that as the common denominator.

CASE STUDIES

• On one occasion a very prominent surgeon was to operate on a patient suspected of having a malignancy in the right upper lobe of lung. The x-ray was on the view box, and the patient had been turned with the appropriate side up by the operating room crew when our illustrious surgeon entered the operating room with his usual flourish. He immediately looked at the view box where the film was displayed and went over to the table and assisted the crew in turning the patient on his other side despite the objections of the rather mild-mannered anesthesiologist. With the wrong side up, the chest was opened and, to no one's surprise but the surgeon's, the left lung did not have the lesion. At this point, our surgeon ordered the assistant to close and went to see the distraught family. It is rumored that he said, "Well, we are now absolutely sure that the left lung is free of cancer. After he recuperates for a while, we'll go after it in the right lung." Of course the surgeon did not say such a thing, but it makes a good story. SVMIC paid a healthy settlement for this confusion of right and left.

• The orthopedic surgeon had scheduled an arthroscopic procedure on the left knee of his patient, whom he suspected of having a cartilage tear. He entered the room where the left knee had been shaved and draped for the surgery. Because the operating camera had not been positioned in the usual way, the surgeon became confused, shaved and prepped the right knee, and proceeded to push the scope into the wrong knee joint. He became aware of his mistake immediately, backed out of the good knee, and did the appropriate surgery on the left knee that did have the injury. As soon as the patient recovered from the anesthesia, his doctor did what he should have done. He informed the patient of the error and assured him that the two-stitch incision on the right knee would not cause any trouble. Despite the "good" relationship that existed between the surgeon and his patient, a small settlement had to be made. It came as no surprise that the patient developed some rather troublesome pain and disability in the knee without disease, which was much in evidence until the settlement was made.

• An 82-year-old woman sustained a fracture of the left hip, and the procedure planned for her was a prosthesis. She was appropriately worked up, examined by an internist and the anesthesiologist, and scheduled for surgery about eight hours after admission. The patient went to the operating room at the scheduled time, and it was learned only then that the proper instruments were not available. The staff started frantically scurrying about looking for appropriate substitute instruments. After they were found, the patient was anesthetized. There was great confusion, and the surgeon left the room to scrub. When he returned to the operating room, the crew had prepped and draped the wrong hip. The operator did not recognize this until, on making the proper incision , he failed to find the expected hematoma. A closer examination of the patient and the films resulted in the incisions being closed, the patient being properly positioned on the table, and the surgery being carried out on the broken hip. There was an uneventful recovery with good healing of both incisions. A settlement was negotiated with the participating hospital that covered the added expense of an extended length of stay, more pain than was anticipated, transportation of family to and from the hospital, and other incidentals.

• Another patient, a 31-year-old man, had pain in both ankles after exercise. X-rays showed osteophytes on both, but the symptoms were worse on the left. Surgery was planned and scheduled for the most symptomatic ankle. For no apparent reason both the operating crew and the surgeon became confused as to which ankle was the one to be operated upon. The surgery was done on the right ankle by mistake. Again, the surgeon (not the same one that scoped the good knee) fully disclosed to his patient the error that was made. After a few months the operation was to be done on the correct ankle. There could be no arguments; a small settlement was required to avoid a lawsuit.

• A 37-year-old woman had back and leg pain. A good examination and appropriate testing revealed a herniated disk at the L5-S1 level. Conservative treatment failed, and surgery was done. The operation was uneventful, and she seemed to improve. Later, pain recurred in the back and leg, and a work-up by a different neuro-surgeon showed that the first operation had been done at the L4-L5 level instead of where the disease had been located: L5-S1. The additional operation, expenses, and significant pain and disability resulted in a lawsuit for $3 million. A six-figure amount was required to settle this case.

• The symptoms resulting from a ruptured disk in the thoracic spine can be confusing. In this case of a 41-year-old man complaining of numbness in the right leg and penis and weak dorsiflexion of the

foot, necessitating the use of crutches to assist ambulation, the correct
diagnosis was made fairly quickly by use of the MRI. The radiologist
reported that the lesion was located at the level of T9-10. A right
hemilaminectomy disclosed a large mass of calcified disk material in
an anterior position, which required an anterior approach. Six days
after the initial surgery a thoracotomy was done by a general surgeon,
with an anterior laminectomy at the T9-10 level by the neurosurgeon.
The patient showed improvement but again developed weakness
about a month after discharge from the hospital. It was at this point,
on careful re-examination of the original studies, that the lesion was
found actually to be at the T8-9 level rather than at T9-10. A reoperation
at the correct level had to be done, again requiring an anterior
approach. Recovery was slow, but after six months the prognosis
looked good for a normal return to work. This case was settled before
a lawsuit was filed. Due to the extensive surgery on three occasions,
months of disability, and rather enormous hospital bills, a six-figure
sum was negotiated.

• A 25-year-old man injured his back while lifting a roll of
carpet at his workplace. He was referred to an orthopedic surgeon
who, with the help of the CT scanner (this was before the routine use
of the MRI), made a diagnosis of a ruptured IV disk at the L5-S1 level.
Surgery was done, but the patient continued to have pain. After three
months of physical therapy, he was not improved. On re-examination
and repeat studies, it was found that the surgery had been done at the
L3-4 level by mistake. In this case, a lawsuit was filed, and the case was
tried resulting in a jury verdict of just under $200,000.

LOSS PREVENTION COMMENTS

There is very little room for argument when a procedure is
done on the wrong side! Most of these accidents are settled before or
as soon after the suit is filed as possible. Many are disposed of without
the necessity for litigation. Some go to trial because a reasonable
settlement cannot be negotiated. All of them cost us all premium
dollars!

There is almost never a reason that absolves the surgeon of
liability in these cases, and usually that liability is thought to be the
primary factor. I have heard and read of many routines adopted by
surgeons in an attempt to prevent these mistakes. Indeed, it does
appear that there should be some foolproof scheme we could all
adopt. Marking the extremity with an arrow or the words "NOT HERE"
has been advocated. Rechecking the level of the disk by imaging
studies on the operating table is done frequently. Surgeons who have
avoided taking out the wrong kidney, working on the wrong disk,

scoping the wrong knee, and the like may be just plain lucky. I doubt it! I believe these physicians more often than not take some time immediately before the knife is put to use to orient themselves to the patient and the complaint. Use any trick that will work, but bear in mind that confusing left and right, up and down, and even patients with the same name does occur.

I believe Davy Crockett was quoted as saying, "Be sure you are right; then go ahead." That motto put into practice consistently would eliminate these common errors and save lots of premium dollars.

30.   MISS THAT IN RESIDENCY?

Allegation—Failure to diagnose Lisfranc fracture; failure to note the radiologist's report
Physician Issue—Conservative treatment in face of injury
Patient Issue—Increased disability due to delay in treatment
Outcome—Modest settlement

CASE STUDY

A 21-year-old man was brought into the emergency room of a community hospital following a motor vehicle accident (MVA) in which he had sustained multiple injuries. The initial history indicated that the patient had been restrained by a seat belt when his Jeep flipped over, and he had to be extracted from the wreckage. The injured man admitted to having consumed a "six-pack" prior to his accident. There was no history of loss of consciousness.

The evaluation by the ER physician revealed "no acute distress, vital signs stable—Awake and oriented. Alcohol on breath. HEENT: About 1.5-in semicircular laceration on left cheek with moderate ecchymosis. Tympanic membranes visible and without abnormalities. Neck: Nontender. Rectal not done. Genitourinary: No rectal blood or scrotal hematoma. Extremities: Moderate ecchymosis bilateral ankles; dorsales pedis and PT pulses intact. About a 2-in laceration left lateral ankle."

X-rays of the "chest, C-spine, facial with zygomatic, bilateral ankle/foot" were ordered and the laboratory was asked to do hemoglobin and hematocrit. Fluids were given through large-bore needles, and a Foley catheter was placed. The lacerations were sutured after Betadine prep and irrigation.

The patient went to the radiology department at 4:20 AM, about one hour after arrival in the ER; the radiologist read and reported the films the same day. The significant findings reported were a slightly displaced fracture of the right fibula and a nondisplaced fracture of the base of the fifth metatarsal of the right foot. The following is the radiologist's report: "Left foot: Lateral displacement of the second through the fifth metatarsal. Appears to be minimal lateral dislocation of the first metatarsal. Although not well seen, appears a fracture of base of third metatarsal. Findings represent a homolateral Lisfranc fracture dislocation. There is a disruption of articulation between navicular and medial cuneiform and dorsal dislocation of medial cuneiform. Disruption and widening of articulation between middle and lateral cuneiform."

The ER physician wrote admission orders about six hours after the patient arrived in the ER. He ordered ice to contusions, bed rest with bathroom privileges, elevate foot on pillows, and further orders from the attending physician. The patient was received on the floor with both feet in splints with elastic bandage wraps. It was noted that the toes on both feet were warm.

The attending orthopedic surgeon saw the patient for the first time at 5:00 PM, about 14 hours after admission to the hospital. He apparently reviewed the films made the night before and concluded that "None of the fractures will require ORIF (open reduction with internal fixation); however, will not be able to weight bear for 10 to 14 days until pain and swelling subsides. Will weight bear first on the right."

The history and physical as dictated reflected the above impression in that the attending physician described the fractures of the right as "a nondisplaced fracture of the lateral malleolus and a nondisplaced fracture of the base of the fifth metatarsal." In his "plan," the attending physician again stated that none of the fractures would require ORIF. On the day after admission, the attending physician saw his patient about mid-afternoon and made arrangements for physical therapy to teach the patient the transfer technique from chair to bed, etc. On the second hospital day, the patient was discharged home with his feet in well-padded compression splints and dressings.

The discharge summary refers to "some medial deformity of left arch." The attending physician again speculated that in 10 to 14 days a walking cast would be applied on the left side with gradual weight bearing. Note the AP's shift to "left" for initial weight bearing, without diagnosing the Lisfranc fracture on the left.

One week after discharge, the patient was seen in the office of his orthopedic surgeon and both feet and ankles were again x-rayed. His records state, "Feet show fractures have maintained alignment throughout. Still has some slight angular deformity of left first metatarsal. . . . Placed in SLWC on left with cast boot; will be allowed progressive weight bearing on the left." Although a cast was applied to the right, no weight bearing was allowed.

The young man was seen again five weeks after the injury, and again x-rays were made. Again "all fractures maintained alignment with early callus formation and bone healing." Two weeks later he was seen by his attending physician. "Can allow progressive weight bearing bilaterally."

It is interesting to note that three days before the above visit, the patient showed up in the office of another area orthopedic surgeon requesting an opinion. Five days later he went to yet another orthopedic surgeon asking for an opinion. From both of these physicians, the patient received the news that he would require an operation to attempt to reduce the fracture dislocation of the left foot. Each of the consultants confirmed the diagnosis that had been made initially by the radiologist on the initial films made on order of the ER physician within an hour of the patient's arrival at the community hospital. Both surgeons explained that the surgery would be very difficult and, in all probability, would necessitate a fusion of his left forefoot.

On the day that the patient was scheduled to return to his attending orthopedic surgeon, he was admitted to another hospital under the care of the first consultant for his surgery. From the description of the surgery, it is clear that the intervening eight weeks had seen the development of sufficient callus that reduction of the dislocation was impossible and, indeed, a fusion was indicated.

On this same day, there appeared in the outpatient record of the original physician such self-serving language as, "consistently argued with and exhibited lack of compliance regarding restrictions recommended to him. At the time of the five-week visit, we had feedback from multiple sources that he had been weight bearing on both extremities contrary to instructions." Also in that office note, the original physician entered into the record, "Also refused surgery early on regarding right first metatarsal bone." A week later another similar note appeared in the outpatient record. "Did not keep appointment again. In view of the irresponsible circumstances of his injury, along with his unwillingness to cooperate with treatment, recommendations, advice, or follow-up, we can't feel responsible for either the cause or the outcome of his injury. I cannot help someone who refuses care."

Because of the delay in diagnosis and the consequent delay in appropriate treatment confirmed by the two consultants the patient had sought out, either on his own or on the advice of friends, and because their records had been secured by the plaintiff attorney, defense of this lawsuit was impossible and a settlement was made on behalf of the original orthopedic surgeon.

LOSS PREVENTION COMMENTS

I am told that a Lisfranc fracture dislocation can be difficult to see on x-ray. That offered little comfort in this case because the radiologist had "hit the diagnosis on the head." Did the attending orthopedist ever look at the radiologist's report? He must have looked at the films, but it is doubtful that he ever carefully read the report. I am aware that the orthopedist is an expert on x-ray interpretation of bones and joints. I wonder how many times the interpretation of a radiologist is so completely ignored. This discrepancy was very damaging to our defendant doctor.

It is interesting to note, and probably of significance in the area of physician/patient relationship, that the attending orthopedist did not see his patient during the first 15 hours of his hospital stay. One cannot help but conclude that this physician got off to a very poor start with his patient.

The attending physician does state in his discharge summary that there is "some medial deformity of left arch." He apparently missed the significance of that finding because he states later on his plans for the patient to begin ambulating and weight bearing first on the left, which he attempted to do as early as four weeks after the injury. The very self-serving notations in the orthopedist's office records make it likely that one or both of the consulting surgeons had somehow warned their colleague of impending trouble. Even if not prompted by the news of possible trouble, it was unwise to include in the record information that had not been recorded contemporaneously. It would have been just as easy to recall this later in the course of the impending litigation, and it would not have appeared so "phony."

It appears that this patient was setting his doctor up for litigation. I don't know of any way to be aware of this kind of patient behavior. In this case, if indeed the patient had exhibited the anger, resentment, and noncompliance that his doctor refers to after the "fat is in the fire," his physician could have confronted his patient with how he, the physician, feels about this kind of behavior and even suggested a consultation with one of his colleagues rather than let the patient move in that direction on his own.

Most of the time the game of "CYA" is lost by the one who plays it.

31.   FALSE SENSE OF SECURITY

Allegation—Failure to monitor postreduction
Physician Issue—Failure to act on observations by resident
*   and nurses*

Patient Issues—Contracture at elbow; claw-hand deformity
Outcome—Six-figure settlement

CASE STUDY

Following a fall from the "monkey bars" on the school playground, a 7-year-old boy was brought to the emergency room of a children's hospital. After examination by the ER physician, the orthopedic surgeon on call was notified by phone. The office staff of the surgeon asked that the orthopedic resident be called to see the child.

The notes by the ER physician documented the fall at school. The examination noted that the patient was awake and alert, that there was swelling and deformity of the left elbow, and that no radial pulse could be felt. A pulse was identified by Doppler.

The resident recorded that the child was alert and in pain. The swelling/deformity was again commented on, and the region of the elbow was tender. Examination of the affected arm further revealed, "No radial pulse on left but a weak pulse on Doppler." Good sensation was recorded, and there was full range of motion of all fingers.

The orthopedist's note stated, "100 percent displaced left supracondylar fracture." In less than 15 minutes after admission to the ER the child had been premedicated. A procedure note, written as an addendum to the admission history and physical, stated that the elbow was prepped in the usual manner, a hematoma block was given with good analgesia, and fracture was "reduced without difficulty." The elbow was taped in flexion and supination of the forearm. A posterior splint was applied, and the postreduction x-rays showed "some residual displacement, but well within the acceptable range with excellent position." Added in conclusion was, "Neurovascular status remained intact throughout."

The patient was admitted to the hospital for overnight observation, and a follow-up x-ray was interpreted as being satisfactory, although some posterior displacement persisted. Neurovascular checks were ordered at one-hour intervals. Shortly after reduction, about one and a half hours after admission to the ER, the resident recorded that the pulse was absent in the ER but was present on Doppler examination. At two and a half hours after admission, the resident recorded "good capillary refill."

On the patient's admission to the hospital, the nurse recorded "fingers slightly cyanotic and cool." Four hours later, the nurse stated, "Fairly warm fingers and color improved—pink now, cool and blanche well." About 12 hours after admission a resident's note states, "Decreased sensation all fingers especially over the median distribution ulnar?

Otherwise difficult to assess." Nurses' notes continued to record warm and pink fingers.

On the morning after admission, about 18 hours after the injury, a progress note states that there is decreased sensitivity over the median distribution but that this seems to be improving. Good capillary refill is mentioned. After an x-ray showed no change in the fracture, the child was discharged by the resident to see the attending surgeon in three days. The resident's discharge summary correctly relates the history of the injury and the reduction of the fracture. Some decrease in sensation over the median nerve distribution is still recorded and the fingers remained "dusky."

On the initial visit to the orthopedic surgeon, the same impaired sensation of the involved arm was reported. The speculation was that the nerve had been contused and would require a little more time to "wake up." At this time the surgeon reviewed the situation with the parents and spoke of possible damage or swelling involving the nerves in the arm. Subsequent visits continued to show a very disabled arm but a flawless position of the reduced supracondylar fracture.

This child had a severe contracture of the involved arm and hand that required multiple operations. There was complete palsy of the median and ulnar nerves. Permanent disability to that extremity is virtually total, with contracture at the elbow and a "claw-hand" deformity. A lawsuit was filed charging the attending physician and resident with negligence in the care of this little boy.

LOSS PREVENTION COMMENTS

One of the first principles taught about supracondylar fractures is to pay primary attention to the neurovascular status of the extremity. This is especially true if there is any significant degree of posterior displacement of the fracture. The critical marker is the radial pulse. The radial artery crosses the elbow in close proximity to the distal humerus, and thus with any posterior displacement of the distal fragment, the artery is subject to marked kinking and, in the process of reduction, is in danger of being pinched or severed at the fracture site.

In this case, the only mention of the radial pulse by a physician is that it is absent. Doppler examination is said to indicate some flow through the radial artery. How much? In retrospect, it can be said that the flow indicated by Doppler was too little! The nurses did the neurovascular checks at one-hour intervals, but this was limited to color and capillary refill. Color was referred to as "dusky" on more than one occasion.

The arm was "taped in flexion" after reduction of the fracture. With the swelling at the fracture site that was described at the initial examination, one could anticipate problems with adequate circulation, and this was aggravated by the fixation in flexion. Even with the early appearance of loss of sensation along the median distribution, there was no attempt to relieve the problem by reducing the amount of flexion at the elbow. True, the reduction might suffer, but the viability of the arm is the real concern.

What happened in this case? Did the attending physician depend too much on the observations of the residents? Did the residents depend too much on the "neurovascular checks" done by the nurses? Did they all put more faith in the Doppler findings than in the time-honored palpation of the radial pulse? Whatever the answer to those questions, the facts are that a 7-year-old little boy has a lifelong deformity of his arm that might have been prevented.

There is little doubt that the treatment team erred in not more adequately assessing the circulation of the arm when the radial pulse was found to be absent. There is likewise little doubt that the attending physician failed in his responsibility to monitor the care of his patient by those residents and nurses, who could not be expected to have his degree of judgment.

This child did not get acceptable care when measured by a standard considered to be reasonable. The negligence here was such that defense of the attending physician and the resident was not possible. A six-figure settlement was required.

32.   HOW TO SHOOT YOURSELF IN THE FOOT

Allegation—Negligent application of cast
Physician Issues—Failure to monitor extremity; completion of
    chart after the fact
Patient Issues—Prolonged physical therapy; recovery without
    residual
Outcome—Moderate settlement

CASE STUDY

The patient is a 20-month-old boy who was playing at home with his parents at about 9:30 PM on October 8. He fell while playing, causing pain in his right leg. It seemed to the parents that he fell on a small plastic toy, a GI Joe. The child cried a lot after the fall, and the parents held him until his crying subsided and then put him directly to bed. The little boy cried out several times during the night, and the following morning whenever his parents attempted to pick him up, he screamed, obviously in pain.

The parents took the child to the emergency room of their community hospital at about 6:00 AM on October 9. It was apparent in the ER that this little boy was complaining with any movement of his right leg. An x-ray of the leg revealed a spiral fracture of the right femur at the junction of its lower and middle thirds; it was in very good position. The right leg was splinted, and the patient was admitted to the hospital for casting under general anesthesia.

The orthopedic surgeon first saw the little boy at 10:00 AM in the operating room after talking to the parents. A hip spica cast was applied on the right, and the postcasting films showed the fracture to be in good position.

In the recovery room, the baby cried a lot, although seeming to react normally. No neurologic or vascular checks were recorded in the recovery room. The surgeon visited the patient on two occasions while the patient was still in the outpatient surgery area, and neurologic and vascular checks were recorded by the physician to be normal on both visits. After discharge from the recovery room, again neurologic and vascular checks were done by the physician and recorded as normal. The baby was crying perhaps more than the nurses expected. They had called the physician on two occasions and secured orders for sedation. X-rays of the femur were reported as showing indentation of the soft tissues of the thigh, but the fracture remained in excellent position. The patient was discharged a little before 7:00 PM on October 10, and the parents were told to return him to see the orthopedic surgeon in a week. By 7:15 PM the patient was back in the ER crying with pain. The ER note said "circ OK." The father reported that his son seemed to have lost "feeling" in his toes. At 10:00 PM the child was still crying constantly. The cast was bivalved. The note by the surgeon recorded "sensory and motor loss below the knee."

The orthopedic surgeon consulted a colleague in a nearby medical center who confirmed the motor and sensory loss and suggested the possibility of a peroneal nerve injury. It was further suggested that after healing of the fracture occurred the child be given physical therapy in the rehabilitation department of the children's hospital.

The fracture healed without further incident, and when the cast was removed some four months after injury, physical therapy was begun and continued for three years. After that time there was no evidence of residual neurologic damage.

A lawsuit was filed charging the orthopedic surgeon with negligent treatment. The contention was that the casting had been done improperly, causing "indentation of the soft tissues of the thigh" producing the nerve injury, and because of this negligence, the little boy had suffered needlessly for many hours and had required months of expensive therapy.

LOSS PREVENTION COMMENTS

A thorough investigation of this case revealed several facts that essentially allowed the surgeon no defense. It was noted that there was no careful documentation of the patient's neurologic status preoperatively, thus ruling out the logical contention that the nerve injury might well have been the result of the injury sustained at home.

The child's chart had been completed some three weeks after he was discharged from the hospital and the nerve injury was apparent. This called into question all of the doctor's observations that neurologic and vascular checks were normal. No such checks had been made by the nurses in the recovery room.

The nurses had thought that the child cried more than would ordinarily be expected. They had received phone orders from the surgeon on two occasions for pain medication. After the father had observed the child's inability to move his toes and had brought him back to the ER, it was three hours before the surgeon arrived to evaluate the situation.

The physical therapy had required much travel, with loss of work time by the parents, and it had been very uncomfortable for the little boy. He had recovered without residual, but had lost three years of his childhood.

In summary, this innocent child was caused to suffer needlessly. The medical record had been completed late, and this caused some doubt as to its accuracy. In addition, the documentation was poor, and the patient had been three years in recovery. A sizable settlement was reached.

33.   OUTCOMES CAN BE VERY UNEXPECTED

Allegations—Negligence in doing surgery initially; failure to adequately stabilize fracture in first operation

Physician Issues—ORIF indicated on first operation; fracture appeared stable at close of first operation; jousting (?); second surgeon possibly could have prevented the lawsuit

Patient Issues—Multiple operations; pain; disability; medical expense

Outcome—Low settlement in relation to expenses

CASE STUDY

A 55-year-old woman who fell in her home 48 hours earlier entered the emergency department of a rural community hospital because her arm had been very sore since the fall but had begun to be very painful in the past few hours. Her husband convinced her that she needed to have some attention. The ED physician found that her forearm had some minimal dorsal angulation in the mid-shaft. She gave a history of hypertension for which she had been on treatment for about five years. She thought that her blood pressure had been under control for the most part. Review of systems was otherwise unremarkable.

An x-ray of the forearm showed what the ED physician believed to be a segmental fracture of the mid-shaft of the radius with some comminution and a simple fracture of the ulna in mid-shaft. The radiologist identified in addition a small butterfly fragment involving the distal end of the proximal fragment of the radius. After an appropriate work-up, the patient was scheduled for surgery. Prior to surgery her blood pressure was recorded as 160/90 mm Hg.

At surgery and under adequate anesthesia the fracture was reduced with great difficulty. The surgeon's judgment at the time was that internal fixation was indicated. Through a 4-in incision two butter-fly fragments were identified. A single K-wire was used to fix the butterfly fragment to the distal fragment and a five-hole compression plate was employed to stabilize the fracture line. Some difficulty was encountered during the fixation of the plate, and two nuts had to be fixed to the screws on the opposite side of the bone to secure the plate. A pressure dressing was applied and a sugar-tong cast used for immobilization.

About a month later, because angulation had occurred and the screws were no longer in place, it was elected to reoperate. On this occasion a longer, tube-shaped plate was used to maintain the reduction. The K-wire previously placed across the fracture was left in place. Postoperatively, the arm was suspended on an IV pole, and x-rays done after the procedure showed the bone in good alignment. Because of some swelling, the cast was split and rewrapped. The following day the cast had to be removed and reapplied. Four days after the second operation, the patient was discharged from the hospital.

For five months, it appeared that the fracture maintained good position but no healing was seen on x-ray. With a diagnosis of non-union of the fracture of the radius, the third operation was planned. At surgery, a break was found in the semi-tubular plate used in the previous surgery. All the hardware was removed, including the K-wire, and a Nicoll graft was performed using the right iliac crest as the donor site. Again a plate and screws were used to maintain stability of the fracture site. The operative wound was closed and a site dressing applied. Again, a sugar-tong cast was used for immobilization. X-ray revealed the metallic plate and screws holding the fracture in good position. The arm was suspended from an IV pole, and she seemed to be doing "very well" at the time of discharge on the third postoperative day.

Six months after this third operation an x-ray showed some resorption of the broken ends of the radius and the Nicoll graft seemed to have "melted away." A fourth operation was planned, in which the surgeon planned to use a full thickness cortical and cancellus graft from the right tibia. The procedure seemed to proceed without incident. The tibial graft was held in place with four screws on each side of the fracture site. She tolerated the procedure and was discharged home on the seventh postoperative day with a cast on her right arm and a boot-walking cast on her right leg.

About two weeks after this fourth operation, an outpatient x-ray showed that two screws had pulled out of the distal end of the radius, but the remaining screws were intact and the position remained good. An x-ray done a month later showed good position of both bones of the forearm. The long-leg cast was removed from the right leg and an x-ray was normal except for the bony defect created by the donor site. There was some wound drainage that stopped spontaneously. X-rays four months after the last procedure showed the donor site almost completely filled in, and there seemed to be some evidence of healing of the radius fracture. About seven months after the last operation there was obvious non-union of the radius fracture. Further surgery was discussed with the patient but was not recommended. The surgeon believed that the patient should accept the non-union and wear a splint.

The patient did not accept this recommendation, went to another orthopedic surgeon, and had another operation. Three and a half years after the initial surgery the patient had not healed the radial fracture, and still other surgery was recommended. A lawsuit was filed charging the first orthopedic surgeon with negligence for operating on the patient initially and negligence in the first operation because of defective fixation of the fracture in that the screws pulled out of the bone and the surgeon had to put nuts on the screws to hold them in place. At the time the lawsuit was filed, the fracture had not healed and yet a sixth operation was being considered.

LOSS PREVENTION COMMENTS

In a situation like this, one feels for both the patient and the surgeon. It reminds me of the story of Tar Baby and Brer Rabbit. You remember that in the altercation between the two, Brer Rabbit's right fist stuck, then the left fist, then the right foot, and finally the left foot. In this case, the surgeon seemed not to be able to turn loose of this patient because nothing seemed to go according to expectations. Should he have attempted a closed reduction first? With this kind of comminuted fracture in the mid-shaft of the radius on the dominant side, experts agree that an ORIF is indicated. Could the surgeon have been more careful in preparing the broken fragments to accept the plate and screw? Did the fact that the screws pulled out of the bone suggest that he did the application carelessly? Experts took both views on these questions. Of course, we can be sure that, in retrospect, the surgeon wished he had tried the conservative approach first. It appears that his decisions were made with care and that healing just did not occur!

Was the litigation precipitated by the second orthopedic surgeon? Did he cast some doubt that the correct course had been followed by the first doctor? In all probability, the fact that another surgeon felt called upon to operate on this patient made it appear that more could be done than already had been done. Since there appeared to be no animosity between the patient and her first surgeon, would it not have been better for the second surgeon to have made some attempt to explain just how these things can happen in the best of hands? He could even have tried to associate the first surgeon in the further care of this difficult problem. One cannot help feeling that the second surgeon could have prevented the lawsuit against his colleague in some way! Wouldn't it be interesting if the second surgeon were sued later because he did not do an adequate informed consent discussion as to the poor chances of success of his own efforts?

Although the settlement was probably not enough to cover the patient's expenses, the first surgeon was put in a position of defending himself for having followed the standard of care and, in spite of that, having gotten a poor result through no fault of his own.

34.   GO THOU AND DO LIKEWISE

Allegations—Negligence in that patient continued to have
pain and disability
Physician Issues—Treatment met standard of care; excellent
medical record

Patient Issues—Continued pain and disability
Outcome—Defense verdict

CASE STUDY

A 59-year-old female patient was seen for the first time by a board certified orthopedic surgeon in the emergency room following a fall. The patient had been visiting her son and had slipped on ice leaving the hospital. She immediately complained of pain in her right wrist. She was brought to the emergency room where an examination revealed obvious deformity. X-rays showed a displaced fracture of the right distal radius, a Colle's fracture. Treatment was discussed with the patient and a closed reduction under local anesthesia was done. After reduction, a sugar-tong splint was applied and postreduction x-rays were obtained which revealed satisfactory positioning of the fracture fragments. The patient was then admitted to the hospital that evening and remained for two days.

The patient was seen in the office two weeks after complaining of marked swelling in her fingers, thought to have resulted from dependency and lack of exercise for the fingers. The patient was reinstructed on exercises and elevation, and the sugar-tong splint was changed to a short arm cast. The patient was unable to tolerate the cast and returned one week later. The cast was removed and a fiber-and-Velcro splint was used for immobilization of the wrist.

The patient continued to complain of swelling of her fingers, along with severe and unusual pain in her arm, mostly associated with supination and pronation, and numbness in her thumb. She was then readmitted, and further evaluation was done. The electromyogram (EMG) suggested a diagnosis of sympathetic dystrophy, for which active range of motion exercises and analgesics were prescribed. She appeared moderately improved on discharge ten days after admission.

Three weeks later the patient called stating that her right wrist was worse and that she felt something shift inside her wrist. The patient did not come into the office as instructed on that day but did return one month later. Despite vigorous physical therapy, the patient continued to complain of pain and swelling of her wrist and fingers. Resection of the distal ulna was considered, but more conservative treatment, a stellate ganglion block, was used. Following this, the patient continued on physical therapy, but continued to experience pain despite a normal EMG.

The patient then filed suit alleging that after treatment for her injury she continued to experience severe pain, swelling, and deformity, in addition to the loss of use of her right forearm and hand.

Loss Prevention Comments

This very unfortunate outcome of treatment has a happy medicolegal ending. Sympathetic dystrophy is a known and fairly common complication of this type of injury. Our orthopedic surgeon had an excellent medical record, documenting his discussion with the patient of the possibility of this complication under the best of circumstances. He stayed close to his patient, and he responded appropriately at every stage of the postreduction course. The patient was made aware of what was being done for her and why. This case illustrates dealing with a bad result before, during, and after the fact.

Had it not been for a real "hired gun," who was discredited before he had a chance to give testimony, this lawsuit would not have been filed in the first place. It was dismissed on summary judgment on behalf of our orthopedic colleague.

"Go thou and do likewise!"

IV

General and Vascular Surgery

This field of medical specialization is broad indeed, but the claims against these practitioners have shown a relative decrease in the past decade. In the beginning of the physician owned medical malpractice insurance movement the predominance of claims in this area amounted to near 80 percent coming out of surgery or some invasive procedure. Now we find that claims against the so-called "cognitive" specialties, i.e., Internal Medicine, Pediatrics, and Family Practice, are approaching half the total number. Again, this is a relative decrease apparently due to the increase in the number of claims that fall into the nonsurgical or procedural category.

The hallmarks of claims seem to come out of unrealistic expectations on the part of the patient or family coupled with an outcome that is surprisingly worse than expected. Indeed, since bad results will occur despite all of our efforts, the management of the unexpected or bad result is the best way that claims can be reduced.

The first step in the management of this phase of the problem that the surgeon faces is the process of informed consent. It is in this area that care should be taken to make the patient and family as fully aware as possible of the risks as well as the benefits of the planned procedure. This process is generally more than a single conversation. It is rather the entire spectrum of examination, testing, planning, and dialogue that takes place between the patient and the surgeon. The important thing is for the dialogue to take place even if the patient comes to the surgeon with all the preliminaries done. The patient should know about the procedure, the benefits expected, the risks possible, and the alternatives to the procedure. And the patient should be invited to ask any questions that are important to him or her. There is NO substitute for the documentation in the medical record of this process between the patient and the physician. Added to the documentation should be the physician's impression that the patient and/or family has understood what has gone on.

The rule about a bad or unexpected result is, "Run toward it, not away from it!" Engage the patient or family in a conversation as early as possible when aware of the fact. Explain the outcome, what led to the outcome, and what can be done about it. In my experience, a claim is most frequently brought to find out what really happened. The surgeon should express appropriate concern or grief depending on the severity of the situation being confronted. One can express a sincere apology for things that may have gone wrong without admitting fault. If the truth demands that one admit to an error of judgment or technique that has produced the bad result, it is less of a risk to openly deal with that than to attempt to conceal the fact. In this circumstance, the physician should be very careful about blaming himself without consultation with peers and legal counsel in order to get an objective view of the facts of the case. It can, and has, happened that the surgeon is so overcome with guilt because of the result that a statement is made that is later used against him.

The innovations in medical technology occur with surprising regularity: laparoscopic surgery, laser use in surgery, the expanding use of CT and MRI in diagnosis, the improving sophistication in ultrasound imagery for diagnosis or the guiding of invasive procedures to mention only a few.

It is vital that the surgeon/proceduralist be appropriately trained and credentialed before using such devices in the treatment of patients. Soon after the emergence of a new device or use of an old device for which there has not been formal residency training, the specialty and subspecialty organizations usually issue guidelines for the training of surgeons in their use. It is important that physicians who would use the technology comply with the policy statements of their individual boards or societies relative to its use.

It is also important for the hospital in which the new device is to be used to develop credentialing requirements for members of the medical staff. Many surgeons who have not been residency trained in these advances will find themselves needing to put them to use in the practice. It is here that training, experience, and credentialing will be challenged most often in the legal environment. Plaintiff counsel will insist that the jury take into account all the complexities of the new technology, the training, or lack of it, that the defendant physician has had, and the learning curve usually required before the surgeon/ proceduralist is able to safely employ the device or method without the guidance of a peer expert in its use.

The cases presented here deal with many of the above issues. Regardless of technical expertise, if a bad result occurs, the physician/patient relationship usually determines whether or not a medical malpractice lawsuit is filed charging the doctor with negligence and failing to follow an acceptable standard of care.

35.   DOCUMENTATION AND POSTOPERATIVE MANAGEMENT

Allegation—Negligent postoperative management
Physician Issues—Judgment call not to resect; failure to
        aggressively manage postoperative complications
Patient Issue—Death
Outcome—Lower six-figure settlement

CASE STUDY

A 55-year-old white man was seen in the hospital emergency room with cramping abdominal pain he had for 12 hours. For the past six hours, he had also had intractable nausea and vomiting. He had an appendectomy at age 8, and had had mild hypertension for the past five years, which was adequately controlled on furosemide (Lasix) 20 mg daily. Physical examination revealed a temperature of 100°F, pulse 110/min, blood pressure 130/90 mm Hg. Examination of head, neck, chest, and heart were within normal limits. The abdomen showed slight distension, generalized tenderness, and hyperactive bowel sounds. An abdominal x-ray showed evidence of small bowel obstruction. His white blood count was 27,000/cu mm, with 92 percent segmented neutrophils. Serum sodium was 139, potassium 3.9, chloride 98, and CO_2 28 mEq/liter. He was admitted to the hospital with a diagnosis of probable small bowel obstruction.

Shortly after admission he was taken to surgery, where he was prepared for an exploratory laparotomy. An IV was started and a large dose of antibiotics given. When his abdomen was opened, a closed loop small bowel obstruction was found, caused by an adhesive band from his previous appendectomy. The loop of the small bowel was cyanotic but intact. On release of the obstructing band, the physician carefully explored the remainder of the abdomen and noted no additional pathology. By that time the bowel had greatly improved in color. Though the area where the adhesive band had crossed the small intestine was still described as somewhat "bruised," the surgeon believed it was viable and decided not to resect it.

The postoperative orders were of a routine nature, calling for 5 percent dextrose in Ringer's lactate solution IV at 125 cc/hr, nasogastric tube to suction, turn cough, and deep breath every two hours, routine vital signs, measure intake and output, and sit on the side of the bed to dangle in the morning. The patient was kept in the recovery room for about an hour and then was returned to his room at about midnight. During the night his blood pressure was in the range of 100/70 mm Hg and his pulse was 100-110/min. His eight-hour output was less than 100 cc. The nurse notified the physician at 8:00 AM that the patient's temperature had increased to 102°F, and a Tylenol suppository was ordered. At 10:00 AM the surgeon found his patient very lethargic, with temperature 103°F, blood pressure 88/50 mm Hg, pulse 122/min, and respirations 26/min. Stat blood cultures, electrolytes, and CBC were drawn and he was prepared for immediate re-exploration, where a perforation was found at the site where the adhesive band had crossed the small bowel. The area was resected and an end-to-end anastomosis was performed.

Postoperatively the patient was sent to ICU, where aggressive antibiotics, IV Dopamine, etc., were employed in his treatment. His course was downhill, and six hours after surgery he went into cardiac arrest. Resuscitation efforts were unsuccessful. The laboratory later reported that the blood cultures grew a Gram-negative organism.

About one month after this patient's death, the surgeon was called by the record room at the hospital and told that an attorney had inquired about the records. At this point the surgeon dictated his operative note, but he dated it on the date of surgery. Further developments in this case revealed that the plaintiff attorney had secured conflicting statements from hospital personnel regarding the patient's treatment, contradicting the surgeon's operative note on the initial surgery.

The significant question in this case was whether or not the surgeon followed an appropriate standard of care by deciding not to resect this "somewhat bruised" area of small bowel at the initial surgery. Proof developed prior to litigation revealed that operating room personnel's description of this area of small bowel was diametrically opposed to the surgeon's description.

In spite of these difficulties, an expert witness testified that the surgeon's decision not to remove the bowel was a judgment call that could not be second guessed. On the other hand, the surgeon was deemed to have fallen below an acceptable standard of care due to his lack of aggressive postoperative management. Postoperative orders were not detailed as to how often vital signs were to be monitored or under what circumstances the surgeon was to be notified; postoperative blood studies were not ordered, aggressive antibiotic therapy was not continued postoperatively, and the surgeon had not seen this severely ill patient for approximately ten hours after surgery.

Although documentation of the aggressive efforts to treat this man was somewhat sparse, dictation of the operative note a month after the event, with erroneous dating, cast such a shadow over the entire case that the surgeon was at an extreme disadvantage, and a sizable loss resulted.

LOSS PREVENTION COMMENTS

(1) Operative notes should be dictated as soon after surgery as is physically possible.

(2) Orders for postoperative management should be detailed, reflecting the surgeon's concern for close and adequate observation. In this case, the surgeon should have been specific about the circumstances in which he was to be called, i.e., falling blood pressure, inadequate urine output, etc. Although preoperative electrolytes were normal, postoperative electrolytes should have been ordered, since intestinal obstruction, nasogastric suction, and previous treatment with furosemide all tend to disturb electrolyte balance. The compromised bowel should have signaled the possibility of perforation and Gram-negative sepsis, and the surgeon should have been personally involved much earlier in the patient's postoperative management.

(3) Postoperative management should be as aggressive as the operative treatment and tailored to avoid or observe the most frequent and severe postoperative complications of any given procedure.

(4) This patient was maintained in the recovery room for only an hour. Upon his return to the floor, he was observed by nursing personnel who are generally less accustomed than recovery room nurses to the management of patients in the immediate postoperative period.

36.   VICARIOUS LIABILITY AND THE PHYSICIAN'S ASSISTANT

Allegation—Failure to appropriately treat diabetes
Physician Issue—Surgeon's PA failed to follow diabetes
Patient Issue—Marked visual loss secondary to DKA
Outcome—Six-figure settlement

CASE STUDY

A 60-year-old woman with adult-onset diabetes was admitted to the hospital for work-up of possible gallbladder disease. Control of the diabetes had been satisfactorily maintained for the past ten years with 25 units NPH insulin every morning. A thorough outpatient work-up revealed no significant findings except for her controlled diabetes and cholelithiasis.

Preoperative laboratory work was essentially within normal limits except for a fasting blood sugar of 190. Urinalysis was negative for sugar and acetone. Prior to surgery, the physician's assistant (PA) visited the patient, introduced himself, and explained that he would be assisting her physician during her care in the hospital. The following morning the patient was taken to the operating room where an uneventful cholecystectomy was done. Intraoperatively the patient received 5 percent dextrose in Ringer's lactate solution at a rate sufficient to keep urine output at 30 cc/hr. Intraoperative urine tests revealed a trace of sugar but no acetone.

Postoperative orders written by the surgeon included IV of 5 percent dextrose in 1/4 normal saline to keep the vein open, discontinue IV when American Diabetic Association (ADA) clear liquid diet is tolerated, a blood sugar at 4:00 PM, and a sliding scale insulin coverage as indicated by urine sugars every four hours. The 4:00 PM blood sugar was drawn as ordered and was reported at 210 mg/dl.

The patient progressed most satisfactorily in the immediately after surgery. The ADA clear liquid diet was begun on the third postoperative day as ordered. Urine testing before meals and at bedtime following the administration of the clear liquid diet revealed 1+ to 3+ blood sugars. No report as to acetone was done. Subcutaneous insulin was given before meals and at bedtime per sliding scale as ordered.

On the fourth postoperative day, the patient complained of anorexia and generalized abdominal discomfort and shortly developed rather marked nausea and vomiting and later hypotension. The surgeon's PA was notified, saw the patient promptly, and, anticipating possible dehydration, ordered IV fluids to be administered at 125 cc/hr. Nasal gastric suction was also instituted to empty the stomach and alleviate the nausea and vomiting. The PA did not order any laboratory work, and the operating surgeon was not consulted.

In reviewing the orders, the nurse noted that the type of IV solution was not specified. The nurse called the PA, who ordered 5 percent dextrose in water, which was begun at 125 cc/hr. The patient was also given 50 mg of hydroxyzine (Vistaril) IM for her nausea and vomiting. Following this she became very drowsy, the vomiting diminished, and she slept soundly for eight hours or more.

When she was seen on morning rounds by the surgeon and the PA, the patient was found still to be very lethargic. Stat laboratory work revealed a blood sugar of 1,200 mg/dl and pH of 7.1. She was immediately treated appropriately with bicarbonate, fluids, and insulin, and her ketoacidosis was reversed over the next 24 hours, but her vision markedly deteriorated. Her regular ophthalmologist had examined her just two weeks earlier and believed that this was due to severe microvascular changes in the retina directly related to her severe ketoacidosis in the hospital.

The patient sued the physician, the PA, and the hospital alleging that she was improperly treated postoperatively, leading to severe ketoacidosis, which resulted in her marked visual damage.

LOSS PREVENTION COMMENTS

The law allows the use of a variety of personnel to assist us in our practice of medicine. In the case of unlicensed physician's assistants, the law sets out fairly detailed parameters for their use. Among other things, the law requires that "before a physician's trained assistant may render therapy or treatment to a new patient of the supervising physician, or to a regular patient of the supervising physician expressing a new or previously untreated condition, that patient's problem shall be personally evaluated by the supervising physician."

It is clear that both the physician and the PA were acting outside the law in this particular situation. Even if the physician had a detailed protocol under which the PA was allowed to participate in the postoperative management of patients, this particular patient had certainly experienced a change in her condition and thus the law would require the personal evaluation of the attending physician.

Under a doctrine known as "vicarious liability," it is unlikely that the physician would escape liability if the PA departed from a strictly written protocol. In this situation, the hospital also could find itself liable, since it is assumed that the hospital has some responsibility for the activities of persons participating in patient care.

The case written is clearly one where the PA acted far beyond his level of competence. This case could conceivably be a situation where punitive damages would be called for by the plaintiff counsel, alleging that there was flagrant disregard of statutory requirements in the relationship between the physician and his assistant.

We need help in practicing medicine. We need competent paramedicals in many areas of our practice and can hardly do without them. We must constantly keep in mind, however, that the privilege of using paraprofessionals in our practice assumes that we take the responsibility for their supervision.

37.   LEGAL SUICIDE: WEAPON—THE MEDICAL RECORD

Allegations—Negligence in performing umbilical hernia; no documented informed consent; inappropriate remark in medical record—"turkey"

Physician Issues—Informed consent lacking; sloppy documentation
Patient Issue—Further surgery required
Outcome—Modest settlement

CASE STUDY

A 50-year-old white man was admitted to the hospital from the office because of pain in the epigastrium which had been previously described as an "epigastric hernia" or lipoma by another doctor. The patient was extremely obese, and the epigastric hernia/lipoma was palpable only with the patient in the upright position. He also had pain in the left wrist, which was a result of repeated injuries. The patient came in asking for surgical relief of these conditions.

EKG indicated a first-degree AV block. Laboratory work was within normal limits, as was the chest x-ray. X-ray of the left wrist showed an old un-united fracture of the navicular bone, which affected the joint surface of the radius, and early arthritic changes.

The patient was taken to surgery, and under general anesthesia the epigastric hernia was repaired and two large fragments of bone were removed from the wrist. The patient made an uneventful recovery and was discharged, to be followed in the clinic.

Six weeks following surgery the patient presented to the office complaining that the "lump" that was to have been removed at the time of surgery had not been removed and in fact still existed just above the scar. The lump was believed to be either the epigastric hernia or lipoma that was to have been removed at the time of repair of lower hernia, or diastasis of the rectus muscle. The surgeon documented his office records accordingly, stating "the little lump was missed in the fatty supine abdomen." In addition, the surgeon documented that he offered to remove the lump on an outpatient basis free of charge.

The patient indicated that he desired to think it over and further indicated that he might ask the surgeon's partner to remove the mass since the partner had operated on another family member.

Following this discussion the surgeon communicated to his colleague by documenting in the record the following: "Partner, please do the necessary, but handle this turkey with kid gloves in order to avoid a lawsuit."

LOSS PREVENTION COMMENTS

This was obviously a difficult obese patient with extensive diastasis of the rectus muscle. The "epigastric hernia/lipoma" may or may not have been a true hernia through the midline fascia in the epigastrium.

The eventual sizable loss in this case was apparently due entirely to inadequate and faulty medical records. There was no documentation of informed consent dealing with the possibility of complications in this fairly simple problem enormously complicated by obesity. The risks of recurrence or failure of adequate repair should certainly have been dealt with.

The record contained a virtual admission of negligence in the statement "the little lump was missed in this fatty sizable abdomen" without explanations of how easily this could have occurred or pointing out that with the patient in the supine position there was no evidence of the abnormality. The reference in the note to his partner referring to the patient as "a turkey" was highly inappropriate and would have never been understood by a jury. Settlement was essential.

This loss was produced not only by an omission of any acceptable process of informed consent, but also by an inappropriate admission of negligence and a slang reference to this patient totally out of place in a medical record. This physician committed legal suicide using the medical record as his weapon.

38.   AND GOD SAID, "THAT'S THE IDEA"

Allegations—Negligent surgery; failure to remove all of
*   localizing needle*
Physician Issue—Jousting by second surgeon
Patient Issue—Further surgery required
Outcome—Small settlement

> *God said, "Cain, where's Abel?"*
> *Cain said, "I have enough trouble looking*
> *   after myself. Am I supposed to look*
> *   after that character, too?"*
> *And God said, "That's the idea."*

CASE STUDY

A 29-year-old woman, having found a knot in her right breast while taking a shower, was sent by her primary care physician to see Dr. White, a general surgeon. After examination, Dr. White ordered a mammogram, which was reported as showing a small mass but "no obvious sign of malignancy." Dr. White admitted the patient for an outpatient excisional biopsy. The mass was small, and the radiologist assisted in localizing the mass by using a needle wire guide.

Under brief general anesthesia, the mass was removed, and the postoperative note by the surgeon stated, "Lesion totally removed with the wire guide remaining in place." The pathology report confirmed that the lesion was totally removed but made no mention of the wire guide.

Patient returned for the routine postoperative visits. Her incision healed nicely, and at a three-month postoperative visit all was well and no further follow-up appointments were made.

Thirteen months later the patient went to see Dr. Green, a surgeon in the same city on the same large hospital staff. Her complaint was pain in the right breast "ever since my breast was operated on last year." She indicated that the pain was much worse in the past two weeks. A mammogram ordered by Dr. Green showed a small metallic object that appeared to be "a fragment of needle or wire." Dr. Green proceeded to remove the small fibroma that had developed, along with the 5-mm piece of the previously used needle guide wire.

The patient did well postoperatively, but filed a lawsuit against the first surgeon. After the usual long length of time taking the necessary statements, depositions, filing motions, etc., a small settlement was required.

LOSS PREVENTION COMMENTS

This case is not very important from the standpoint of monetary loss, but it is extremely important to Dr. White, the accused surgeon. He justly feels the victim of a system that was not inclined to treat him like the good and caring physician he believes himself to be. Several aspects troubled him: (1) The patient never complained to him of pain postoperatively. His notes make no mention of pain and he knows that he would have paid attention to such a complaint. (2) He looked at the needle guide and noted in his postoperative note that it had been removed. (3) He didn't pay any attention to the lack of any mention of the wire in the pathology note. It is the policy of that hospital to send everything removed at an operation to pathology. He assumes that they did and that the pathologist failed to mention the guide because it was so incidental to the main lesion. (4) He didn't even know until the suit was filed that a colleague had seen his patient and removed the small piece of wire.

It is true that Dr. White is a good and caring physician. He has good rapport with his patients and generally enjoys his contact with them. He is active on his hospital staff and has never had any question raised about the quality of the care he gives to his patients. No one doubts that Dr. White looked at the removed needle guide and truly believed it to be completely intact.

Be that as it may, the intraoperative notes made by the operating room (OR) nurse failed to mention a guide wire, but on deposition she stated that she knows she put the wire in the container with the tissue specimen if it was given to her, because, "That is our routine and I always do." As a matter of fact, the OR nurse admitted that she had no real recollection of the events that day in the outpatient OR almost three years before. She had to rely totally on the notes she made at the time.

The pathologist's testimony was very similar in that he had no real recollection of the event; he was even stronger in insisting, however, that had the needle guide been included in the bag with the specimen, it would certainly have been a part of the report.

There is no indication that Dr. Green openly criticized Dr. White's care. He was not guilty of jousting in the sense that he really "knocked Dr. White off his horse." But neither could we assume that Dr. Green's conscious purpose was to scrupulously avoid conduct that could be interpreted as critical to Dr. White's care. We don't know what Dr. Green said to the patient, but he didn't call his colleague and inform him of the visit of the patient and the presence of the small foreign body. We have no reason to believe that he said to the patient, "Look—Dr. White is a good surgeon. Things happen like this frequently. At the worst, it's an honest mistake and we really don't even know who made it. Why don't you let me call Dr. White and discuss it with him? I'm sure he'll remove it and not even charge you a fee." Had that been the spirit of the approach used by Dr. Green, there is a better-than-even chance that the patient's anger would have been softened and a satisfactory resolution could have been reached without involving lawyers. Our relationship to our patients and to each other is almost never adversarial until or unless attorneys are brought into it. So it makes good sense to keep them OUT, whether they are after us or our colleagues.

Because of this litigious environment in which we are forced to practice, we are, or should be, our colleague's keeper!

39.   "MINOR" SURGERY

Allegation—No informed consent in record; injury to common duct
Physician Issues—Reference to procedure as "minor"; no discussion of procedure in record
Patient Issue—Additional surgery
Outcome—Six-figure settlement

CASE STUDY

A 56-year-old man was admitted for an elective cholecystectomy with a history of "indigestion" for a number of years. A careful history revealed several bouts of epigastric pain associated with nausea and vomiting, requiring narcotics for relief. The bouts ordinarily occurred within two to three hours after a heavy meal and were not influenced by antacids. He had had no jaundice.

On two occasions, studies of the upper GI tract by x-ray failed to reveal evidence of peptic ulcer disease. Oral cholecystogram showed "no function," and sonography demonstrated stones. This seemed to be a clear-cut case of symptomatic cholelithiasis requiring surgical treatment.

In this day, when most major surgery is more dramatic and newsworthy than the removal of a diseased gallbladder, both the surgeon and the patient approached the task as "routine." In fact, the patient remembers the surgeon characterizing the planned operation as "routine" and "minor."

At operation, a diseased gallbladder was found containing palpable "small" stones and, although no jaundice had been reported in the history, x-rays were made during the surgery and showed "prompt emptying of dye into the duodenum without evidence of common duct obstruction." Surgery proceeded with the removal of the gallbladder, immediately after which the surgeon noted significant spillage of bile into the operative site. Examination disclosed that the common duct had been severed; this required a Roux-en-Y procedure to re-establish biliary tract continuity with the small bowel.

The immediate postoperative course was marked by prolonged and significant biliary drainage from the operative site, but eventually, in about four weeks, drainage ceased and healing occurred. About eight weeks postoperatively, however, the patient developed chills, fever, and jaundice, and subsequent studies revealed "intrahepatic" obstruction of biliary ducts. Reoperation was done in an out-of-state medical enter to which the patient was referred by his attending surgeon.

Six months after the second surgical intervention, a lawsuit was filed charging the original surgeon with, among other things, "failure to secure informed consent from the plaintiff patient" and "negligence in the performance of surgery in that the common duct was carelessly severed."

The medical report contained a rather long and detailed "consent form," which had been signed by the patient and witnessed by a hospital nurse. In the text of the "consent form" the patient agreed to allow the hospital and "members of its professional staff" to treat him in the "manner appropriate to my medical condition," understanding that there was no "guarantee of successful outcome stated or implied." In sworn testimony by the plaintiff, the descriptive terms of "routine" and "minor" were attributed to the surgeon in reference to the original surgery. There was no indication in the record that the surgeon had personally discussed the surgery in detail with his patient. The surgeon said that he had. The patient said that he had not.

Expert testimony by a qualified surgeon was highly critical of what appeared to be a failure on the surgeon's part to carefully investigate the possibility of anatomic anomalies of his patient's biliary tract which, according to the expert, were present in a significant percentage of all people. He pointed to the intraoperative x-rays as evidence that the surgeon himself was suspicious of the possibility of some common duct problem or he would not have ordered them. On the other hand, expert testimony was plentiful that the surgeon had acted in accordance with an acceptable standard of care and that although the surgical result was in fact terrible, it was a sometimes unavoidable hazard of the procedure.

LOSS PREVENTION COMMENTS

It is always wise to approach any operative intervention or invasive diagnostic procedure as if it were to be performed on a beloved member of one's own family. Gallbladder surgery is in fact "routine" and "minor" most of the time, as are bronchoscopy, arteriography, and a host of other "tests." But what occurred in this case can and does happen, and our patients have the legal right to be informed as to the potential for the "nonroutine" as well as the "major" possibilities in their own cases.

A large settlement was necessary in this case, not because our colleague was "negligent" in his surgical care of this patient, but because he had been negligent in his obligation to openly and honestly discuss possible complications of gallbladder surgery with the patient and to record that discussion in his medical record.

40.   IT'S NOT MY FAULT—IT'S HIS

Allegations—Negligent failure to expose operative field
Physician Issues—Behavior; angry in OR; jousting; blaming
*   assistant*
Patient Issues—Subsequent surgery; pain and disability
Outcome—Six-figure settlement

CASE STUDY

The patient is a 29-year-old woman with a history of abdominal pain for three months. The pain was usually postprandial, described as cramping, and associated with nausea consistently, and frequently with vomiting. There was no real food dyscrasia, but the patient reported that almost any type of food could precipitate an attack, particularly if the meal was a large one.

The physical examination revealed essentially normal findings except for some tenderness in the right upper quadrant. No masses were detectable. The routine laboratory findings all were within normal limits, but the liver function studies were abnormal. The SGOT was reported to be 157 IU/L, SGPT 246 IU/L, and the serum bilirubin 2.4 mg/dl.

Two days after examination the patient was scheduled for outpatient endoscopic retrograde cholangiopancreatography (ERCP); it was accomplished under intravenous sedation and showed multiple small gallstones. The architecture of the pancreatic duct system was unremarkable, but the biliary ducts were not well visualized, presumably due to some technical difficulty encountered during the examination. Surgery was scheduled for the next day.

During the surgery there was some difficulty in securing adequate exposure, and the operating surgeon became very angry. Exploration of the abdomen did not show any abnormality except for the gallstones, which were easily palpable within the gallbladder. None could be felt in the common duct area.

The gallbladder was removed, and the abdomen was closed in the usual manner. There was excessive bile drainage from the biliary bed, and on the third postoperative day the patient was obviously jaundiced. Reoperation was necessary, and the patient was transferred to another hospital where she was explored the day after her arrival. Two subsequent operations were required to re-establish the continuity of the biliary tract.

A lawsuit was filed, charging the surgeon with negligence in the performance of the cholecystectomy. The summary of the operation by the first operator accused the assistant of failing to provide adequate exposure during the operation. Perhaps by pointing fingers at others, the defendant surgeon called more attention to himself. That attention led to the further development of the case against him, which made defense of the case extremely difficult, if not impossible.

The surgical specimen revealed that the common duct was smaller than usual and had been severed some 3 cm proximal to the duodenum. The cystic duct was found to come off the common duct high near the bifurcation of the left and right hepatic ducts. Expert testimony by the pathologist and the second surgeon indicated that the dissection was not carried proximal enough to reveal the takeoff of the cystic duct; thus the small common duct was mistaken for the cystic duct and was severed and largely removed.

LOSS PREVENTION COMMENTS

This surgeon revealed his confusion early in the operation by becoming angry and upset. Perhaps if he had stepped back from the table for a brief time to collect himself, patient injury could have been avoided. His complaints that the assistant did not give him proper exposure were patently hollow. If indeed exposure had been recognized as a real problem, the surgeon was obliged to address that problem before proceeding. He did not, and blaming someone else was seen as a self-serving act without real foundation.

Abnormal anatomy in the biliary tract is not unusual, and the surgeon who does this type of surgery needs to be thoroughly familiar with the various anomalous situations that he could face. To begin the resection before the dissection is complete courts disaster. Injury can occur in this region despite the greatest skill, but when it does occur, the evidence of that skill must be apparent. In this case it was not!

41.   THE SYMPATHY FACTOR

Allegation—Negligent deviation; using uncross-matched blood; failure to operate in a timely manner; failure to control bleeding

Physician Issues—Postoperative bleeding; type-specific blood given on emergency basis; no deviation from acceptable standard

Patient Issue—Death

Outcome—Jury award: modest six-figure given

CASE STUDY

It was a typical early-season high school football game. The game had just begun when a defending back was hit by a legal block and taken out of the play. The block came from the left side, and almost immediately a spectator on the sidelines noted that the young player who had been blocked appeared unconscious for a very short time, during which there were seizure-like movements. The player appeared to regain consciousness and was immediately taken from the field and transported to the local hospital by ambulance. According to the observers, the injury occurred about 7:00 PM, and the patient arrived at the local hospital about 15 to 20 minutes later.

The initial examination in the emergency room revealed a conscious 14-year-old with some contusions and abrasions on the left side at about the lower edge of the rib cage. Although the young man complained of pain at the site of the injury, there was very little tenderness in the area. The blood pressure was low at about 70/50 mm Hg, the pulse was 110/min, and respirations were shallow, and there appeared to be splinting of the left chest on inspiration.

The usual blood work was ordered and was in the process of being done. While IV line was being started the ER physician noted that the pulse was becoming faster, the abdomen more distended, and blood pressure falling. Blood was ordered, and two units were given as soon as it became available. Although the pressure came back to the 70s and the pulse was stronger, more blood was given without the usual cross-matching. It was apparent that there was continuing intra-abdominal bleeding and the patient's condition was deteriorating, so it was elected to give him the type-specific blood as rapidly as possible. A Foley catheter was placed, and no urine was found in the bladder. Within 20 minutes of the patient's arrival in the ER, a board certified general surgeon was on hand.

The patient was intubated, a nasogastric tube inserted, and he was taken to the operating room with the diagnosis of a ruptured spleen secondary to the injury during the football game. The surgeon ordered two more units of blood to be given during the operation and opened the abdomen about one hour after the injury. As expected, the abdomen was filled with blood and the spleen was shattered into four separate fragments, which were removed along with a small accessory spleen. The splenic hilus had been controlled from the beginning of the splenectomy, and no significant abdominal bleeding was noted. On exploration of the abdomen under these controlled conditions, a perinephric hematoma was found and seemed to be stable. A large Penrose drain was placed deep into the operative site and the abdomen was closed in the usual manner. Blood loss was estimated to be about 4,000 cc.

Postoperatively the patient continued to be profoundly hypotensive, significant quantities of blood came from around the drain, and some bleeding was noted around the IV sites. A PTT was reported at 91.6, seconds and arterial blood gas analysis revealed a marked acidosis. Bicarbonate was given, and it was elected to send the patient to the teaching center primarily because the surgeon believed that a coagulation problem might be beginning and the university hospital could better manage the blood and blood products that were going to be needed.

The patient was transported by helicopter and arrived at the university hospital about five hours after the injury. On the basis of the information obtained from the surgeon in the local hospital, he was taken directly to the operating room and explored. Bleeding continued during the operation and the PTT was reported at >100 seconds. Despite the heroic efforts of the operating team and many, many units of blood and blood products, the patient died about 18 hours after arriving at the university hospital.

A lawsuit was filed, charging the surgeon with negligent deviation from the standard of care by using uncross-matched blood, by not operating on the patient in a timely manner, and by not using appropriate means to control the bleeding.

LOSS PREVENTION COMMENTS

This tragic death of a 14-year-old high school freshman was mourned by his classmates, his teammates, and the entire community. As could be expected, his parents were devastated and angry that their son had died as the result of an injury sustained in his first appearance in a high school football game. As time went on, the anger became focused on the person who could not save their son. One can only surmise that they took their anger to a plaintiff attorney who saw an opportunity to file a lawsuit that, before a hometown jury, could be made to seem like an event that could have been prevented by more appropriate action on the part of the local surgeon. He knew that he could win a judgment if he could make the 12 laymen on the jury feel like they had to do something to demonstrate their sympathy for the parents.

There are "experts" available who will be purists at the drop of a hat and find all kinds of excuses for saying that a colleague should have taken a different course of action and that it was negligent not to do so. It was from the "experts" that the charges came. Giving the type-specific blood without taking the time to cross match it with the patient's serum was a decision made in the thick of battle to save this young man's life. Who can honestly contend that it was negligent to do so? It is easy to say in retrospect that the surgeon should have taken the patient to the operating room before he allowed the two units of blood to run in. Was it negligent to reason that the delay was justified in an attempt to better prepare the injured young man for the surgery that had to follow? After the operation, during which the doctor believed that the bleeding had been controlled, the bleeding continued. With the PTT at a level that caused the surgeon to correctly believe that a coagulopathy was beginning, was it wrong to conclude that his patient's best chances lay with the transfer to the university hospital where there would be more blood and blood products available?

Negligence is not in making the wrong decision! Negligence is failing to take all the evidence available and bringing it to bear on the decision in a reasonable manner. Who can say that the surgeon did not do just that!?!

There was plenty of expert testimony to refute all the contentions made in the complaint and the "expert" opinions that supported them. There simply was no negligence involved in this case. The surgeon made careful and well thought-out decisions in his management of this tragic injury. Why then did the jury find negligence on the part of the surgeon and award money to the parents? We are left with the conclusion that in their deep feeling of sympathy for the parents who had lost a fine son, the jury made an effort to assuage their grief with a lot of money. That effort had to be a failure!

This case and the many like it that are lost because of the jury's sympathy for the grief of a family over such a terrible loss and the many such cases that are settled before trial because of the fear of a result like this must make a strong case for tort reform and some kind of an alternative dispute resolution system.

42.   OUT OF HIS LEAGUE

*Allegations—Negligence in not transferring patient to
        vascular surgeon; improper attempts to re-establish
        blood flow to damaged leg*
*Physician Issues—Not trained in vascular surgery; supporting
        staff inexperienced; physician did not attend postop;
        small rural hospital; inadequate documentation*
Patient Issues—Prolonged convalescence; loss of leg
Outcome—Seven-figure settlement

CASE STUDY

A 37-year-old farmer arrived at the emergency room of a small-town hospital about 6:00 AM, having been shot in the left leg while deer hunting. There was a previous history of a fracture of both bones of the leg in childhood which had healed uneventfully. On examination of the extremity there was some deformity, instability, and crepitation of the leg about 3 inches below the knee consistent with a fracture. There was a small round wound on the anterior surface of the leg at about the junction of the upper and middle thirds, which appeared to be a wound of entrance. A large gaping exit wound was present on the posterior surface of the calf opposite the small entrance wound and about 2 to 3 inches below the popliteal fossa.

The patient was complaining of severe pain in the leg, and there was active bleeding welling up in the large wound. The blood pressure was 50/0 mm Hg and the pulse was 126/min. While pressure dressings were being applied to the leg, large bore IV lines were established in both arms. The pressure began to improve, and on the way to the operating room (OR), x-rays of the leg revealed comminuted fractures of both the tibia and fibula corresponding in position to the bullet wounds.

In the OR the extremity was prepped and draped after endotracheal anesthesia had been started. With the patient on his right side, the wound was explored. There was no recorded examination of the leg prior to anesthesia.

Under anesthesia, both the popliteal artery and vein were found to be severed by the injury. Debridement was accomplished, and the artery ends were brought together in a primary anastomosis. The vein was found to be so badly damaged that it was ligated. These vessels were injured about 5 cm below the popliteal fossa. The wound was irrigated with a large amount of sterile saline, and fasciotomies were done in an effort to prevent damage from the postoperative edema. A posterior plaster splint was applied to the extremity to stabilize the fracture after loose closure of the wound.

The patient left the OR about seven hours after arrival in the ER. A nursing note revealed that pulses were heard with a Doppler before moving the patient to the bed, but none afterward. In the next several hours there was some confusion as to whether or not there were pulses in the extremity. At times the Doppler study was said to reveal a pulse, and at other times the findings were questionable. Intravenous heparin was begun. At about 3:00 AM, 20 hours after arrival in the ER, the patient was complaining of more pain, and the Doppler study did not reveal a pulse. Neurologic checks during the night revealed decreased sensation in the leg and foot.

Despite these equivocal findings, the surgeon was not called during the night. He was contacted about 8:30 AM and told of the reported blood work and the decreased pulses and sensation in the involved foot. "Doctor will come to see patient," was documented. He did not come to see the patient until about four hours after this communication. He examined the patient and ordered a left leg venogram. With the report that "deep veins of the calf and thigh cannot be identified," the patient was returned to the OR at 1:30 PM where, again under general anesthesia, clots were removed from the arterial repair and a segment of saphenous vein was used to repair it. Again an unsuccessful attempt was made to repair the popliteal vein.

The only progress note made by the surgeon during this

admission was recorded after this procedure. The note was labeled as a "Brief Op Note." He recorded that the preoperative diagnosis was "clotted popliteal artery" and that this was repaired with interposition of a saphenous vein graft. He estimated the blood loss at 1,500 ml and stated that the patient was returned to the ICU in stable condition. There was no note recording the time the patient was returned to the ICU, but at 7:30 PM the nurse's notes recorded that pulses were not found by Doppler and that the doctor was aware. The foot was cool and pale. Throughout the night the patient's condition did not change, and at 3:30 AM the surgeon returned to the hospital and ordered the transfer of his patient to a medical center about an hour's journey away. The transfer occurred almost 48 hours after admission. During this admission the patient received adequate supportive care in the form of blood, fluids, and antibiotics.

At the receiving hospital, under the care of a vascular surgeon and an orthopedist, the popliteal vessels were repaired and the fracture stabilized. A prolonged hospitalization followed, during which it first appeared that an acceptable extremity might be salvaged. Fasciotomies were done, wound care was instituted, skin was grafted to cover the granulations, and the patient was able to return home for a brief time. However, about three months after the initial injury, because of a deep chronic draining wound, amputation above the knee became necessary.

A lawsuit was filed alleging negligence in not making a timely transfer to a vascular surgeon, in ligating instead of repairing the popliteal vein, in using the right saphenous vein to repair the right popliteal artery when the right popliteal vein was compromised, in not identifying and dealing with one segment of damaged popliteal artery, and in failure to do adequate fasciotomies.

LOSS PREVENTION COMMENTS

In the "retrospective world" of a medical malpractice lawsuit, perception very frequently becomes reality. Of course it is unfair without a thorough examination of the facts to suggest, as the title of this case does, that the surgeon in this case was "out of his league." How does the world do that? By examining the medical record. What does that record suggest to the examiner? Unfortunately, the medical record becomes the legal record in a medical malpractice lawsuit. Any facts that are brought forward by anybody that are not corroborated by the medical record are suspect.

Here we have a man with an extremely serious gunshot wound involving the leg just below the knee. There was no recorded circulatory examination of the extremity made before the patient was under anesthesia. It was recorded that the hypotension present on admission had been corrected by the intravenous fluids started in the ER. The wound, just on superficial inspection, would have raised the strong suspicion of significant damage to the circulation below the knee. There was some indication of heavy bleeding on admission to the ER, and after pressure dressings were applied, the OR examination revealed that there was some continued bleeding, but the dressings were not described as "soaked." Again, retrospectively, certainly some consideration should have been given to transferring this young man to a facility where a vascular surgeon was available.

This was a 40-bed rural facility where one might perceive that there probably was some lack of the latest technology and that there might well be a shortage of personnel with experience and training in handling such a serious injury. Retrospectively, one would have to raise the question as to whether this was the appropriate place to try to definitively manage this type of injury.

The surgeon was not board certified in surgery. He might have had a world of experience in the management of vascular injuries of this magnitude, but that would have to be questioned. Should he have deferred to a more experienced surgeon in a better equipped facility? The development of this case from a proof standpoint certainly suggested that he should.

The record in this case raised more questions than it answered. Why was there no recorded assessment of the circulation in the leg before the patient was taken to the OR? Why did the surgeon attempt to repair the popliteal artery primarily when this is almost impossible to do even when the vessel is cleanly divided? Why did he attempt the repair on the second operation with the saphenous vein from the same leg when the deep circulation was so severely compromised by the destruction of the popliteal vein? Why did he delay in seeing the patient for almost 12 hours after operation when the nurses were reporting both circulatory and neurologic deficits? Why was it that the only progress note in this patient's chart appeared after the second operation and still contained no substantive information? After the second operation, why did the surgeon delay another ten hours to transfer his patient to a tertiary care facility when the circulation had not been improved and that facility was only one hour away? There proved to be no satisfactory answers to these questions. Expert witnesses were all critical of the care this patient received.

With all of these unanswered questions, we are left with the conclusion that this physician underestimated the injuries to his patient and overestimated his ability to cope with them. We are left to conclude retrospectively that this surgeon was trying to pitch in the majors with a class-A arm. It appears that he was truly "out of his league"!

43.   IN-OFFICE SURGERY? SAME STANDARDS PREVAIL!

Allegations—Negligent in performing surgery without
tourniquet; surgical injury to digital nerve and artery;
inadequate informed consent
Physician Issues—Office surgery to save patient money;
visibility and control of surgical field compromised
Patient Issues—Inadequate explanation of risks of surgery;
prolonged convalescence; missed work; deformed
finger
Outcome—Modest six-figure settlement

CASE STUDY

The patient was a 38-year-old female cashier who complained of a painful enlargement on the palmar side of her long right finger partially in the retinaculum at the base of the digit on the radial side near the index finger. The examination by a board certified general surgeon revealed a firm, small, smooth mass about 5 mm in diameter, which he felt sure was a ganglion cyst. Since this lesion was more painful when the patient used the hand during the course of her work, both she and her surgeon thought that it should be removed. The procedure was described to the patient, and she requested that it be done in the doctor's office since she had no health insurance and desired to hold down the expense of the operation as much as possible.

Although there was no documentation of the informed consent discussion, the surgeon said he informed his patient that the procedure could be done in his office and he would do it under a "regional block." He further warned his patient that there was a possibility that the nerve on that side of the finger could be damaged but indicated that the chances of that were remote. The surgery was scheduled for the next week.

The office note stated that the surgery was done under "local anesthesia—some bleeding encountered—vessels clamped on the radial side—question of nerve injury." The patient was informed of this possible complication and advised that if she experienced any complication, i.e., bleeding, numbness, or pain, she should report to the emergency department of the local hospital.

About four hours after the operation, the patient came to the emergency department as directed and complained of numbness, pain, and a bluish discoloration over the entire finger. Her doctor was notified, and he requested a consultation by a hand surgeon who came, evaluated the condition, and under general anesthesia did a repair of a "small laceration of the digital artery and a reapproximation of the completely severed digital nerve."

In the operative report, the operating surgeon stated that the "digital artery on the ulnar side seemed to be pulsating normally, but it does not appear to be carrying enough blood to adequately perfuse the entire finger."

Three days after the repair she returned to the hand surgeon's office for dressing of the operative site. The patient said that in dressing she had stretched the finger, causing some pain, but the physician did not think that she had injured the repair. The patient complained of some altered sensation in the finger, and the surgeon's note speculated that "she might experience some ischemic numbness, which should clear in time." He redressed the hand and advised the patient's primary surgeon that the finger should be kept in flexion for five to six weeks, but he did not feel that his follow-up would be needed. That patient was referred back to her original surgeon for continued care.

The patient was seen several times in the office of her primary surgeon, and at each dressing the wound was reported in his office record as "looking good." After six weeks in flexion, the patient was begun on active exercises under the direction of a physical medicine specialist in an orthopedic rehab center. She made some progress over the next four months and was advised to continue home exercise and to return for follow-up in about six months.

She returned to the rehab office in about four months, complaining of continuing pain and a failure to gain a full range of motion in the finger. The original surgery was nine months old, and she continued to have pain that kept her up at night and, because of the pain and limitation of motion, she could not do her previous job. She was advised by the therapist that the problem was a complex one and that there were no simple solutions. The therapist thought that with continued massage and exercise she would "eventually" improve. She was referred back to her original surgeon for continued follow-up. She did not return. She was left with a diagnosis of a flexion contracture of the right long finger and reflex dystrophy involving the radial side of the hand.

A lawsuit was filed, charging "negligent injury of the artery and nerve of the right long finger," failure to use a tourniquet in the performance of the operation, all of which had necessitated the second operation, caused continued pain, and some degree of permanent injury and disability. The charge also included fraudulent concealment of the nature of the risks of the surgery as well as the nature of the resulting pain and disability.

LOSS PREVENTION COMMENTS

There was little merit in the charge of fraudulent conceal-ment, and it was eventually dropped. Expert testimony would not agree that it was acceptable to do this kind of operation without a tourniquet. The question of the exact kind of anesthesia was also a problem. The office record had mentioned a "regional block" on the first visit, but in the description of the procedure, the language "local anesthesia" was used. The expert thought that if the "local" was indeed a regional digital block the standard of care was met, but only if a tourniquet had been used.

In the performance of the procedure, the injury to the digital artery occurred, obscuring the operative site with blood. The digital nerve appeared to have been "severed," which probably occurred with the same move that injured the artery, or in the effort to control bleeding, a clamp had divided the nerve.

The complications of reflex dystrophy and flexion contracture were almost certainly due to the nerve injury and the prolonged immobilization in flexion that was necessary. It is a fact that injury to the digital nerve and artery is a hazard of this procedure even under ideal circumstances. The problems here seem to be that the primary surgeon did not create "ideal circumstances." He failed to document that he had informed the patient of these risks of the procedure. The patient denied that he did. He did not use a tourniquet, which was mandatory in this kind of surgery. In his effort to accommodate the wishes of the patient to "hold down expenses," he did not do the procedure as he would have done in a patient who was insured. The effect was that he had no defenses against the charges of negligence. The patient did have significant disability and expenses, and after almost three years of investigation, discovery, and negotiations a settlement was agreed to in the six-figure range.

44.   LOSS OF CHANCE

Allegations—Negligent care postoperatively; failure to refer to reconstructive surgeon

Physician Issues—Poor oversight postoperatively in hospital and after discharge;de-gloving injury (dominant hand); prognosis poor at best

Patient Issue—Loss of hand

Outcome—Large, six-figure settlement

CASE STUDY

A 20-year-old patient with a severe industrial injury to his dominant hand came to the emergency department of a small hospital after catching his hand in a roller device. The hand was virtually degloved from the wrist distally, but the skin remained attached to the dorsum of the hand distally from the mid-metacarpal level. There was a compound fracture of the third finger, extensive soft tissue damage to the third, fourth, and fifth fingers, and dislocation of the fourth finger at the distal interphalangeal joint.

Initial evaluation revealed some extension of the third, fourth, and fifth fingers but almost no ability to flex them. Although there was a suspected wrist drop, the record stated, "No sign of severe nerve damage." The tips of all fingers were very dark on initial examination. The surgeon who was on call was the physician who did most of the occupational medicine at this institution. He was not a board certified surgeon.

In the operating room the fractures were stabilized and the flexor tendons identified and repaired. Vascular injury was suspected. The deep skin lacerations were repaired by approximating the degloved skin in such a way that the wound was covered. The ends of the fingers remained very dark. The hand was stabilized in a plaster splint with the wrist in the functional position and was elevated by suspending the hand from an IV pole with the elbow flexed at 90 degrees. The nurse's notes refer to a "cast" and to the fact that the hand remained cool to touch. Massive antibiotic therapy was prescribed.

On the first day after injury, about 18 hours after the surgery, the hand was "cool" and "all fingers move." There were few progress notes indicating the progress of this difficult case. On the third day after injury the fingers were "black." The following day the patient was discharged from the hospital. He was seen in the physician's office three days after discharge with the "fingers still black." Additional antibiotics were given. Eight days after discharge from the hospital, with no documented change, the patient was referred to a plastic surgeon for "possible skin grafts." This consultant believed the condition of the patient's hand too severe for him to treat, so he transferred him to a teaching center on the same day. The entire hand was "black," and with a diagnosis of gangrene of the hand, a disarticulation at this young man's wrist was necessary.

A lawsuit was filed charging the surgeon with negligence on three counts: (1) negligence in failing to provide adequate care while the patient was in the hospital; (2) negligence in failing to provide adequate care after discharge from the hospital; and (3) negligence in failing to refer the patient to an appropriate specialist in a timely manner.

Although there was good expert testimony that the hand was not salvageable to begin with and that the treating surgeon was not responsible for the amputation, other factors in the case and other expert testimony made a large settlement necessary.

LOSS PREVENTION COMMENTS

What were the "other" factors in this case? The most damaging of these was the fact that the medical record did not support the physician's close attention to this patient. Progress notes were sparse and not substantive in general. The physician's descriptions of the hand were cursory and incomplete. There was not repeated assessment of the neurovascular status of the extremity. One could detect that the hand was getting darker day by day. Following hospitalization, this patient with a very threatening injury was seen only twice in an eight-day period, after which he was referred to a plastic and reconstructive surgeon for "possible skin grafting." That quote in and of itself could be, and was, interpreted to indicate that the treating surgeon did not have a good grasp of the severity of the injury he was treating.

The point was made that this surgeon was not board certified, and it was substantiated that he had not treated a similar injury in the past. The adequacy of the hospital and its personnel to care for an injury of this type was questioned, and indeed there was no proof that the skill level of the nurses included the observation of and care for such an injury. Probably the most damaging testimony of all was the contention that if there had been a chance to preserve this hand, it was to be found in a center where major trauma was treated and the services of a hand surgeon trained in the microtechniques of vascular and nerve repair were available. It was pointed out that such a center with the necessary staff was present less than an hour away from the site of the injury.

It is probably true that the end result would have been the same no matter where, how, or by whom this patient was treated. However, the courts place great weight on "loss of chance," which was the principal reason this case had to be settled.

45.   WHEN IN DOUBT—OPEN!

Allegations—Negligence in performing laparoscopic cholecystectomy retained remnant of gallbladder
Physician Issues—Operative note ("difficulty visualizing gallbladder"); questionable indications for surgery; failure to convert to open operation

Patient Issues—Prolonged convalescence; additional surgery
Outcome—Modest six-figure settlement

CASE STUDY

A 20-year-old poorly controlled type-I diabetic patient was referred by her family practitioner to a general surgeon because of persistent complaints of right upper quadrant (RUQ) pain. In the course of months of observation of this patient for her diabetes mellitus, her complaints of RUQ pain had become worse. She had vomited on rare occasions but had been nauseated frequently with the pain. There was no typical radiation of the pain, and a clear connection with diet was not apparent. The pain did occur most often after meals, but at times was independent of food intake. An ultrasound examination of the abdomen had been obtained and no gallstones were revealed.

The surgeon examined the patient, recorded some RUQ tenderness, and ordered an oral cholecystogram, which showed no visualization of the gallbladder. A repeat attempt was likewise unsuccessful. A laparoscopic cholecystectomy was recommended and scheduled as an outpatient procedure. It was finally done about four weeks after the patient was referred to the surgeon. The operative note describes "difficulty visualizing the gallbladder," so that it was elected not to do an intraoperative cholecystogram. Due to persistent and severe postoperative site pain, the patient was admitted to the hospital.

The pain continued, a low-grade fever developed, and the WBC count and liver enzymes were slightly elevated. IV antibiotic coverage was begun on the first postoperative day, but the patient continued to have pain and fever. Despite vigorous attempts to control the diabetes, on postoperative day 5 the patient developed severe diabetic keto-acidosis (DKA) which was controlled after 24 hours of intensive care intervention. CT of the abdomen revealed significant amounts of free fluid, which both physicians involved believed to be bile. The patient was referred to a nearby medical center for treatment, and a laparotomy on the following day revealed an open remnant of the gallbladder on a long segment of the cystic duct, which was draining into the peritoneal cavity. The patient recovered uneventfully from this second surgical procedure but continued to have bouts of abdominal pain requiring further evaluation.

The surgeon was sued alleging negligence in the performance of the surgery leading to peritonitis, DKA, and re-exploration. Expert review of this case revealed that defense would be difficult because of substantial questions of the appropriateness of care.

LOSS PREVENTION COMMENTS

Several questions can be explored in retrospect about this case. First, one might ask about the indication for cholecystectomy in the first place. Acalculous cholecystitis requiring surgical intervention is not common. Perhaps in this case the question of the origin of the RUQ pain could have been observed and explored medically over a longer period. Upper gastrointestinal complaints are common in poorly controlled diabetics. In the absence of stones, perhaps the last option considered should be surgical removal of the gallbladder for this kind of complaint.

Second, the surgeon must have wished a thousand times that he had converted this operation to an open cholecystectomy. Complications are known to occur more frequently following laparoscopic surgery than with the open procedure. Though the complication rate has some relationship to the "learning curve" in this technique, even in the most experienced hands it still seems to be higher. Surely, when there is "difficulty visualizing the gallbladder," opening the patient cannot be the wrong decision.

Third, there seems to have been an inordinately long period of observation postoperatively before the decision was made that this patient must be explored. Of course, the presence of the DKA required its control, but with the persistent pain and fever, perhaps reoperation could have been done earlier. One can appreciate the hesitancy to subject a diabetic patient to further intervention, but the question is one to raise.

This patient, after two major operations, recovered and returned to her preoperative state still complaining of abdominal pain- a bad result where there are questions about the standard of care. Settlement of this case was necessary.

46.   I KNOW A LITTLE BIT ABOUT A LOT OF THINGS

Allegations—Negligent surgery for hiatal hernia; negligent postop care; attending left town for few days postop
Physician Issues—Complicated history; x-ray findings inconsistent; true diagnosis in doubt; "sick in the head" in record; delay in treatment of operative complication
Patient Issues—Prolonged postop pain/suffering; death
Outcome—Moderate six-figure settlement

CASE STUDY

At age 46, an obese woman, married and the mother of two teenage children, went to the attending physician, a general surgeon, with a five-year history of "esophagitis." Eight years earlier she had been told that a GI series showed an antral ulcer, for which she was treated with diet, antacids, and antispasmodics, with some relief but not ever the complete cessation of symptoms.

The patient made numerous visits with the symptoms she attributed to "esophagitis." Several x-ray studies of the upper GI tract had failed to reveal pathology. The gallbladder had been studied several times, and no pathology had been reported. She had had a hemorrhoidectomy about five years before and had been treated off and on for "depression" with various antidepressants and other psychotropic agents. During these years she had treatment for "cystitis" and had been told that she had "mastitis." Throughout this time she continued to complain of epigastric burning, attributed to "esophagitis."

About four years after the above encounter, the patient was admitted to the hospital for further testing. Another upper GI series failed to reveal fluoroscopic evidence of GE reflux. The attending surgeon did an endoscopic (EGD) esophagogastroduodenal examination, reporting "free regurgitation into the distal esophagus. Linear streaking in the distal one third of the esophagus typical of esophageal inflammation." Aggressive treatment of the condition consisted of H_2 blockers, antacids, elevation of the head of the bed, and antispasmodics, and because the patient appeared "depressed," tricyclic antidepressants were again prescribed. Another year followed, with only intermittent relief of symptoms. Again, she made numerous visits with a multitude of complaints.

About a year later the attending surgeon consulted a gastro-enterologist in a nearby medical center. The consultant repeated the EGD examination, and though he noted some reflux, there was no visible esophageal pathology. There did appear to be some inflammation in the stomach and duodenum. A biopsy of the stomach revealed some "chronic inflammation."

The complaints continued despite more treatment with all the drugs previously used, with little or no relief. Again, the visits were frequent and the complaints were multiple.

One year later the patient was admitted to the hospital in her home town complaining of a "burning substernal pain." A thorough cardiac work-up was negative. Another EGD was done, and this time a "gastric ulcer" was found; a biopsy was negative for malignancy. Propranolol was added to the regimen because of the chest pain, and a month later, because of continued complaints, antidepressants were again prescribed.

One month after this visit the patient was seen by her attending surgeon. The office record revealed that "patient decided to have a repair of her hiatal hernia." The attending surgeon's note followed— "patient sick in the head." Although "hiatal hernia" was found in one of the earlier studies, it had not been a prominent finding. It must be assumed that the attending surgeon had attributed the symptoms of reflux to the hernia, or, perhaps, to her being "sick in the head."

The patient was admitted to the hospital, and a type of fundal plication was done. The operative record described "hiatus admits 4 fingers," stated that the routine abdominal exploration was negative, and described the procedure. During the dissection of the gastro-hepatic ligament, serious bleeding was encountered requiring six units of blood; deep sutures were required to control the bleeding. The spleen was lacerated during the procedure and was repaired. The patient appeared to be doing well when she was taken to the recovery room about six hours after the case began. She reacted from the anesthesia appropriately and went to the SIU.

The first postoperative day the patient had fever to 101°F, tachycardia, and an elevated WBC count. She was examined and found to have significant lower abdominal tenderness. She continued to have fever which was treated empirically. Within three days following the surgery, with continuing fever, she became edematous and dyspneic and evidence of renal failure developed. She was then transferred to the medical center in a nearby city.

On the same day of transfer, the patient was taken to the operating room, where at exploration the anastomosis line was found to have disrupted, and there was a fulminant peritonitis with copious gastric secretions present. The dyspnea progressed and ARDS was apparent. Renal function continued to deteriorate, requiring dialysis. Long and heroic efforts were made to save this patient, but she died some eight weeks after the first surgery.

The medical center record contains for the first time the history of an extremely unhappy life. There had been a bad marriage for years, the teenagers had given their mother much trouble, and the family income had depended on the factory job held by the patient until about two months before her death.

LOSS PREVENTION COMMENTS

The study of this very long and complicated record revealed a general level of care that seemed to be below the standard. Adequate consideration of this patient's social and psychiatric history had never been part of the picture. In retrospect, one could conclude that the frequent visits and multiple complaints literally cried out for someone to look at the whole picture.

The patient "decided to have repair of her hiatal hernia." Multiple studies produced inconsistent findings. The effects of prolonged stress on the GI tract are well known but were never adequately considered in this case, and, except for the demeaning remark "sick in the head," we have little indication that the attending surgeon ever seriously considered this very important part of this patient's picture.

The surgical procedure at the community hospital was difficult to defend in at least two areas. The stomach was transected very close to the esophagogastric junction, without leaving the customary cuff of stomach by which to secure a better anastomosis. The decision to repair the spleen rather than remove it in the face of this very long and bloody operation was the subject of criticism by expert witnesses on the plaintiff's side and a fact that defense witnesses were not anxious to defend. Postoperative care was also marginal. With evidence of some intra-abdominal complication, as evidenced by the fever, the lower abdominal tenderness, the tachycardia, and her generally deteriorating condition, most of the reviewers considered the delay of four days very likely to have been a contributing factor to this patient's death. Another area of criticism by expert reviewers was that the attending surgeon had not done a pyloroplasty and vagotomy to aid the stomach in emptying.

And, if that were not enough, the attending surgeon left town the day after surgery without informing either the patient or her family. His coverage was a generalist who had seen the patient on a few occasions during her long history of complaints.

This patient presented great difficulties to the attending surgeon; she was truly difficult and demanding. It appeared that his reasoning went something like this: "I think I know what's wrong with her, but the evidence is inconsistent. I don't know how to treat her ... I've tried everything I can think of ... so ... let's operate." The poorest of all choices! Get expert help with the "depression"? Yes! Refer her to the medical center for management help and not for "rule out or rule in"! A teacher of mine used to tell us, "Any dimwit doctor can treat the straightforward case, but it takes a real doctor to diagnose and manage the patient with this kind of psychosomatic overlay."

Taking all the above into consideration, the only factor that made this case impossible to defend under any circumstances was the remark, "Sick in the head." This remark would have provided the jury with ample room to conclude that the attending surgeon didn't know what was wrong with his patient; he really thought she was a mental case but operated on her anyway! A six-figure settlement closed the books on this tragic story. I doubt, though, that the books will ever be really closed on this case in the mind and heart of the attending surgeon.

47.   PRICE OF THE LEARNING CURVE

Allegations—Trocar injury to left iliac artery and vena cava; lack of informed consent
Physician Issues—Failure to address vascular injury by converting to open procedure; competence in laparoscopic surgery
Patient Issues—Postop shock; coagulopathy; death
Outcome—Large six-figure settlement

CASE STUDY

A 22-year-old obese college student was seen by her primary care physician complaining of pain in the right upper quadrant (RUQ) with radiation to the back for three days. The symptoms began following a meal. The examination revealed some tenderness in the RUQ, and the physician thought that a presumptive diagnosis of cholelithiasis was justified. She was referred to a surgeon for further evaluation.

Before the patient saw the surgeon, he ordered an ultrasound examination of the abdomen that showed a "sizable echo focus" in the gallbladder. It was a week before the patient saw the surgeon, who stated in his record, "She has no insurance and is a student. She is checking with the health department for coverage."

When the patient expressed to the health department physician some reluctance about having the operation, she was instructed to go on a low-fat diet, given a mild sedative/antispasmodic, and told to return if she did not improve. Four days later she returned to the health department with continuing pain and indigestion and more tenderness in the RUQ than she had had on the previous examination. The WBC count was found to be 13,000/cu mm with a left shift. She was advised to return to the surgeon, and arrangements were made for her to be admitted for emergency surgery.

The patient was admitted to the hospital that day, and a laparoscopic cholecystectomy was scheduled for the following morning. The work-up done in the ED on the afternoon of admission revealed an obese 22-year-old with some tenderness in the RUQ. She weighed 224 lb and was 5 ft 2 in tall. Her temperature was 99°F, pulse 96/min, and blood pressure 118/80 mm Hg. She was not jaundiced, and her heart and lungs were thought to be normal.

She had "large pendulous breasts, not examined," and pelvic and rectal examination were "deferred." The abdomen was obese with "mild tenderness in the RUQ." (When the breasts, pelvis, and rectum are recorded only to comment that no examination of these areas was done, one wonders whether the patient was carefully examined before her surgery or not.)

The operative note describes an uneventful operation except to say, "She had some hypotension during the procedure." The anesthesia record does indeed record a fall in blood pressure about 30 minutes into the operation with a corresponding increase in the pulse rate. The hypotension responded to a position change and more IV fluids. The pulse rate remained 30/min higher than baseline throughout the operation.

About five hours after the operation, this note was made in the record: "Postop pt. pale, lethargic, usual abdominal tenderness. BP 108 systolic. Pulse 120, Hct 27. Will repeat. If Hct. continues to fall, may need exploration." The hematocrit did indeed continue to fall, and re-exploration was done as an emergency procedure by another surgeon with the attending surgeon as assistant. The operative procedure was styled, "Exploratory laparotomy with ligation of mesenteric bleeders, ligation of the left iliac vein, and 8-mm Gore-Tex interposition graft right iliac artery." The postoperative diagnosis was documented, "Hemorrhagic shock secondary to operative through-and-through laceration of right iliac artery, laceration of left iliac vein, and multiple lacerations secondary to trocar injury." In a postoperative progress note, the operating surgeon stated, "Replacement: 1900 cell saver, 10 units bank blood." The anesthesia note reported that the patient had experienced a "respiratory arrest" when she arrived in the operating room.

Despite all efforts on the part of the team, this patient's condition continued to deteriorate, and about six hours after the emergency procedure, the surgeon's note documented the decline in his patient, stating, "Pupils now dilated to 8-10 mm. Non-reactive." A consultation was secured from a hematologist, who believed that the patient had developed a "coagulation dysfunction." Her condition continued to deteriorate, and she developed what appeared on a CT examination of the head to be a brain stem hemorrhage. All heroic efforts were discontinued about 20 hours after the re-exploration.

A lawsuit was filed charging the attending surgeon with "negligently inserting the trocar, lacerating the left iliac artery and vena cava, and lack of informed consent." Settlement of this case required the payment of a large amount of money in the high six-figure range.

LOSS PREVENTION COMMENTS

This case confronts us with some very interesting problems, almost none of which can be answered from the clinical record. First, while the trocar injury is a known hazard of the procedure, it is difficult to escape the conclusion that undue pressure was exerted on introduction of the instrument. It is also reasonable to expect that vascular injury could result from this kind of entry and that a careful search for injury would ensue and well might require the surgeon to convert this to an open procedure. The record does suggest that the surgeon may have delayed his appointment with the patient while she checked "with the health department for coverage."

It is now known that the laparoscopic cholecystectomy is associated with a serious complication rate several times that of the conventional open cholecystectomy. Should this be included as a part of the preoperative discussion with the patient, balancing the shorter hospital stay, the reduced morbidity, and the much quicker recovery and return to normal activities against this known fact about the complication rate? It is also known that the learning curve for this procedure is longer than originally thought. Should the surgeon be proctored by an experienced laparoscopist for more cases than the usual requirements in the typical medical staff credentialing policies? What kind of training had the attending surgeon had, and how many of his cases had been proctored by a surgeon experienced in this kind of procedure? At the time of this operation, was the surgeon still in the "learning curve"? Also, what is the learning curve anyway? As the patient's advocate in the doctor/patient relationship, should we all be giving more attention to these questions? The obvious answer to all of these questions is a resounding YES.

There is no question as to the valuable place of laparoscopic surgery in the armamentarium of the surgeon. In our enthusiasm to embrace new technology, however, we must balance its use with very strong issues of patient safety.

48.   TOO GOOD TO BE TRUE!

Allegations—Delay in diagnosis and treatment; death
Physician Issues—Confusing case; logical decisions;
defensible case made indefensible by changing record

Patient Issues—Catastrophic illness; chance of recovery very
doubtful
Outcome—Six-figure settlement

CASE STUDY

A 67-year-old woman was admitted to a community hospital
from her physician's office with a history of generalized abdominal
pain for 24 hours and nausea with vomiting for 12-hour duration; the
patient denied any prior trauma or unusual dietary intake, though she
did give a history of two previous episodes of transient upper
abdominal pain during the past month, occurring within 30 minutes
after a meal and accompanied by some belching and a sensation of
fullness. The pain was nonradiating and subsided spontaneously after
30 to 45 minutes.

The present illness began 15 to 20 minutes after a normal
meal and persisted, becoming gradually more intense. There had been
some colicky symptoms following onset and four loose, watery stools
during the first eight hours of the present attack. The patient stated,
"My stomach feels like it will burst."

Past history was unremarkable; she reported no previous
surgery. The patient's attending physician was a board eligible general
surgeon, who had seen her in his office with the second of her
transient attacks, but at that time the pain was subsiding and the
examination revealed no reason to further evaluate the patient.

The physical examination done at the visit prior to
hospitalization revealed a temperature of 99°F, blood pressure 100/70
mm Hg, pulse 88/min, respiratory rate 14/min. The positive findings
were limited to the abdomen, which was generally tender with
minimal splinting but no rebound tenderness or localization. Bowel
sounds were present and questionably hypoactive and, though there
was possibly some distension, the patient was moderately obese and
this was difficult to evaluate.

After admission the WBC count was 9,000/cu mm with normal
differential. Blood chemistries were within normal limits including
glucose, creatinine, and electrolytes. KUB showed some large and
small bowel gas but no definite distension, and the radiologist who
reported on the film the morning after admission gave "ileus" as his
impression. The patient was ordered NPO and intravenous fluids (D 5-
NS) at 125 cc/hr were begun.

The morning after admission, Saturday, the surgeon made
rounds and found the patient about the same, having passed scant
flatus but no stools. Her abdomen was essentially unchanged but did
appear more distended. An NG tube was passed, and about 250 cc of

bile-stained, guaiac-negative material was obtained. IV fluids were continued, and a repeat KUB, CBC, urinalysis, and electrolytes were ordered for the morning. The patient was not seen by her attending physician the rest of that day, during which her pain gradually became worse, some vomiting occurred around the NG tube, and the temperature rose to 101°F.

The attending physician found his patient on Sunday morning feeling worse, having more pain and definitely more distended. The KUB was read by the attending physician as "essentially unchanged" from the admission file; the radiologist was not called. The WBC count was 11,000/cu mm with 20 percent bands forms. The serum sodium was 130 mEq/L, but the potassium was 2.8 mEq/L. The abdomen was more tender, and there was some rebound tenderness and guarding in the right lower quadrant; bowel sounds were not heard.

The patient was taken to surgery with the suspicion of a ruptured appendix. On entering the abdomen the surgeon found a large amount of serosanguineous fluid with a foul odor, and exploration revealed a massive infarction of the small bowel with multiple perforations. Resection and anastomosis was accomplished, but despite massive antibiotic therapy and aggressive support, the patient died on the third postoperative day.

A lawsuit was filed charging negligent delay of diagnosis as the cause of death.

LOSS PREVENTION COMMENTS

As the case developed, the defendant physician had several problems. He saw his patient only once during the first 36 hours of her hospital stay. On careful re-evaluation of the x-rays, some calcification could be seen in the upper abdominal aorta, which might have alerted him to the possibility of ischemic bowel disease. But despite the seriousness of the situation, expert testimony was available to demonstrate that the physician performed within an acceptable standard of care and that even with the most aggressive efforts of diagnosis and treatment chances of recovery were almost nonexistent.

The defendant did well with this deposition despite a vigorous and lengthy examination by the plaintiff attorney, and the case looked extremely good for him. The plaintiff attorney became suspicious that things might not be as they appeared, however, and thought that the office records were "too good to be true." Under oath, the defendant's nurse testified that about ten days after the lawsuit was filed, she was asked to bring the patient's office records into the physician's office, and together they altered the records by rewriting each entry; they then destroyed the original medical record. Although the defendant testified that the alterations were made to more clearly indicate what really happened, his credibility was lost, a large settlement was paid and the surgeon's professional liability was not renewed.

Moral: *Don't alter files after a lawsuit has been filed, even to correct an obvious error! It is much easier to defend mistakes than to try to restore credibility.*

49.   POSTOPERATIVE DELAY

Allegations—Delay in treating complications of surgery
Physician Issues—Tried conservative approach; finally
    referred for definitive surgery
Patient Issue—Prolonged postoperative morbidity
Outcome—Outside standard of care in the delay to refer for
    definitive surgery

CASE STUDY

A 53-year old woman was discovered incidentally to have gallstones about 10 years before her referral to a general surgeon. She had equivocal episodes of upper gastrointestinal symptoms on rare occasions for the entire period. During the year before her referral, the symptoms of "indigestion, bloating, heartburn, and upper abdominal pain" had become more troublesome and frequent. The pains were said to occur mostly at night, keeping her awake, and were sometimes relieved by antacids. Although the pains had become more trouble-some in the past year, she had not required narcotics for relief. She gave no history of other GI symptoms and had not had fever, weight loss, or change in bowel habits. The pain had been attributed to a known hiatal hernia with gastroesophageal reflux. Antispasmodics had been used along with the antacids. She had hypertension and adult-onset diabetes that had been under good control by diet alone.

The physical examination revealed a moderately obese woman with no abdominal tenderness or masses. The stools were free of blood. A recent ultrasound examination revealed two 1.5-cm gallstones.

Because of the long history of abdominal symptoms, the presence of gallstones, and the failure to respond to conservative treatment, including a low-fat diet, the patient was scheduled for a laparoscopic cholecystectomy to be done as an outpatient. In the physician's office there was a thorough discussion of the risks and benefits of the planned procedure, which included a book giving a good description of the operation and possible complications. The surgery was totally uneventful. The findings were compatible with chronic inflammation of the gallbladder, and she was able to be discharged on the day of surgery to go home.

She was seen as an outpatient in the physician's office frankly jaundiced, two days after she had become very nauseated and vomited several times. This seemed to respond to antiemetic suppositories, and at the time the patient seemed to be improving and the jaundice was thought to be clearing some. Laboratory tests on this visit revealed elevated liver enzymes and total bilirubin of 9.5 mg/dl. The WBC count was normal. One week later the patient was again seen in the office and was thought to be "about the same." She was still "very jaundiced." She was admitted to the hospital under the care of a gastroenterologist. Ultrasound examination revealed "slight dilatation of the biliary tree."

The patient was examined endoscopically and the common duct was found to be "markedly narrowed," with some dilatation of the structure above the point of narrowing. "Multiple surgical clips" were present in the area of the narrowing, but the stricture was said to be "smooth" suggesting a "benign" process. A stent was placed across the stricture, with "almost complete" emptying of the contrast media from the intrahepatic duct system. Three days after the placement of the stent the patient returned to the hospital with pain, chills, fever, and subscapular pain. The patient was again examined endoscopically, at which time the stent was removed and replaced with a larger stent. A sphincterotomy was done and the stricture was dilated. The bilirubin on admission was 5.5 mg/dl, and on discharge it was 1.5 mg/dl. It was now a month since the initial surgery. Two weeks later there was a negative quantitative nuclear medicine scan.

With no evidence of bile duct obstruction and feeling well, the patient was advised that a trip out of the country with her husband was all right. Two days after her arrival, however, she was ill with fever and the stent was thought to have become obstructed. She returned to her home in the states, where studies ordered by her gastro-enterologist revealed "worsening of hepatic function consistent with hepatic parenchymal disease. . . . Between the removal and replace-ment of stents a repeat cholangiogram was done and again showed a high-grade stricture." At this time "definitive" surgery was recom-mended by the physician.

Because the patient had moved to another city, her care was transferred to a biliary reconstructive surgeon there. It was agreed that "she did need permanent internal drainage of the stenotic common hepatic duct." She had a hepaticojejunostomy and excision of the scarred portion of the common hepatic duct. Postoperatively, the patient did well and was tolerating a normal diet two weeks after surgery.

LOSS PREVENTION COMMENTS

Common duct injury is a known complication of chole-cystectomy—whether it is done as an open procedure or is done laparoscopically. This patient had unmistakable signs of common duct injury with obstruction within a few days of operation. Thorough evaluation of the complication was done by the attending surgeon and consultants, who thought that she had sustained a thermal injury to the common duct and that the initial approach to therapy ought to be placement of a stent across the area of injury. This began about two and a half weeks after the operation, but the team seemed reluctant to move more aggressively toward permanent treatment. Most of the experts who reviewed this case believed that the delay in ordering the first ERCP was unacceptable and that repeated stenting and dilatation of the duct should have led to surgical correction much sooner.

When a video made during the operation was viewed by experts, it was their opinion that it could be interpreted as showing some hesitance and awkwardness by the operating surgeon. Surgeons who make a practice of giving their patients copies of the videotape made at surgery might consider that from a medicolegal standpoint, the tape, if it is used in litigation, can only be used to aid the plaintiff and not the defendant surgeon.

This case was settled primarily because no expert could be found to fully support the management of this case in which the common duct was injured as a complication of laparoscopic chole-cystectomy.

50.   DEADLY DELAY

Allegations—Delay in diagnosis and treatment
Physician Issues—Delay of FP in seeing patient after
        admission; delay by surgeon in performing operation
        after diagnosis; physicians pointing fingers at each other
Patient Issue—Death
Outcome—Surgeon, family physician, and anesthesiologist all
        participated in large six-figure settlement; most
        apportioned to surgeon, next to family physician, and
        lesser amount to anesthesiologist

CASE STUDY

For the previous eight years, this 69-year-old man had been seen by his family physician for hypertension, gout, glaucoma, degenerative joint disease, and a variety of routine complaints. He was a moderately heavy smoker, was overweight, and had a history of hematuria for which he had been referred to a urologist, but no definite diagnosis was made as to the etiology of the complaint.

Treatment of the hypertension consisted of a mild diuretic and a low-salt diet. The documentation of his blood pressure readings during this time ranged between 180/90 mm Hg (under treatment) and 220/110 mm Hg when treatment was interrupted. Documentation of the encounters between the patient and his doctor was poor, with visits usually being documented with the impression only and no other indication of blood pressure, treatment, advice, or instructions as to return visits. He had been hospitalized once during this interval for acute gout, Bell's palsy (right), and hypertension. The treating physician in the hospital had been the consulting internist. Following the patient's discharge from the hospital, the internist wrote to the referring physician: "Thanks for the referral of (patient's name) during his recent admission. The discharge diagnosis: (1) Bell's palsy, (2) hypertension, and (3) gouty arthritis. He will be returning to see me in follow-up care."

This man was seen by the internist twice following this hospital stay. On these two visits, PA, lateral, and oblique views of the chest were documented, with a final interpretation of some pleural thickening that was not thought to be of significance, and cardiomegaly presumably due to the man's longstanding hypertension. There was no documentation of treatment or change. The patient was seen only twice by his FP between this hospital stay and his final admission.

About two years after this patient's last visit to his internist, he had right flank pain with radiation to the right groin. By 8:30 in the evening the pain became so intense that relief was absolutely necessary, and he reported to the emergency room of the hospital where both his FP and internist were on the medical staff. History revealed some "tarry" stools, but he denied any urinary tract symptoms.

The ER physician's examination revealed temperature 97.2°F, respirations 20/min, pulse 88/min, and blood pressure 180/110 mm Hg. Medications being taken were recorded as Timoptic, Naprosyn, Zyloprim, Corgard, Lasix, and Micro-K. About 30 minutes after the patient arrived, the shift changed and another ER physician took over. Again, this doctor recorded the complaint of severe pain in the right flank radiating to the groin, with nausea but no vomiting. The patient told of three black stools the day of admission and hematuria two months earlier. He stated that his gout was in remission. Physical examination of the abdomen showed a mass in the right lower abdomen slightly below and lateral to the umbilicus. The bowel sounds were thought to be normal. Rectal examination revealed bright red blood at the os. Guaiac was 4+. The prostate was normal, and the impression was probable right ureteral calculus. About one hour after his arrival in the ER, the patient was given 1 mg Dilaudid. The blood pressure was recorded at 190/120 mm Hg. More narcotic was given, and an hour later the patient was asleep, with a blood pressure of 130/80 mm Hg. The laboratory reported WBC count 11,300/cu mm, RBC count 5,180,000/cu mm, hemoglobin 15.3 gm/dl, hematocrit 46.7 percent, platelets 308,000/cu mm. Urinalysis showed 2 to 5 RBC/HPF. KUB x-ray showed extensive degenerative changes in spine and right hip, and a normal gas pattern. No abnormal mass or calcification was seen.

The ER physician called the FP on call for the patient's doctor and discussed hospital admission. The patient was admitted about three hours after he came to the ER, with admission orders by the ER physician to "notify Dr. (patient's physician) at 7:00 AM of patient's admission and room number. Notify Dr. (covering physician) of any changes in condition tonight. IVP in AM as soon as possible after 4:00." Orders were written for the urine to be strained for stones and for narcotics to control pain. The nurse's admission note stated: "New admit, no acute distress. Denies any urinary difficulty. Family states he has passed some bright red blood per rectum tonight." He required narcotics once during the early morning hours, but two hours later he was "calling out" in pain, needing more medication. He complained of severe right groin pain radiating to the back. The IVP was done about 9:00 AM. The report indicated only an enlarged prostate. Otherwise the examination was normal.

When the patient returned from x-ray, he was said to be cool and clammy. He denied pain but complained of "feeling bad." The blood pressure was measured at 184/112 mm Hg. The charge nurse was notified of the elevated blood pressure. The diaphoresis reported as following the injection of the dye subsided in about 30 minutes, but within 15 minutes the blood pressure was recorded at 210/120 mm Hg. The charge nurse called the doctor's office. She learned at that time that the answering service had not notified the attending FP at 7:00 AM as instructed. At 11:00 AM, the nurses were still waiting for a call from the FP. The blood pressure remained high. The internist who had previously seen the patient was on the floor and, on request of the nurses, ordered 20 mg of Procardia sublingually. In a short time the blood pressure was recorded at 158/90 mm Hg, and the internist would have seen the man, but both the patient and his wife refused an examination by him. The family specifically requested another internist.

It was 3:00 PM when the attending FP came to the hospital to see his patient. His examination found the abdomen to be "very obese, bowel sounds normal, no tenderness or masses." At 5:00 PM the attending FP wrote an order for the requested internist to see the patient. Shortly afterward the requested internist examined the patient and ordered a STAT CT of the abdomen with the presumptive diagnosis of a ruptured and leaking abdominal aortic aneurysm (AAA). Prior to this examination, the nurse's notes recorded: "Diaphoretic. Moist and clammy. Placed in Trendelenburg." The blood pressure was not recorded this time, but one could assume that it was low. Volume expanders were ordered, and the patient was transferred to ICU.

At 5:15 PM the laboratory reported WBC count 17,200/cu mm, RBC count 4,740,000/cu mm, hemoglobin 14.3 gm/dl, and hematocrit 42.5 percent. The CT report indicated an aneurysm involving the lower abdominal aorta below the renal arteries measuring 5 cm in diameter and projecting toward the right. There appeared to be some "reaction" in the mesentery adjacent to the aneurysm. At about 6:00 PM, the internist examined the patient again and wrote as a progress note: "The BP is up to 110 systolic. There is a pulsating mass in the right lower abdomen. No bruits are heard and the abdomen is quiet." A vascular surgeon was consulted immediately.

At 8:00 PM blood work was reported as WBC count 10,000/cu mm, RBC count 2,780,000/cu mm, hemoglobin 8.4 gm/dl, hematocrit 25 percent, and platelets 212,000/cu mm. A note was written by the surgeon, timed by him as 9:00 PM to 4:00 AM, describing the surgery for the ruptured AAA. Times recorded in the operating room show that the patient arrived in the OR at 8:45 PM. The anesthesiologist arrived 30 minutes later, and the surgeon did not begin the operation until about two hours after the patient got to the OR. Cardiac and renal complications in the postoperative period caused the patient's death.

A lawsuit was filed against four physicians. The FP, the surgeon, and the internist were all charged with delay in the diagnosis and treatment of this patient. Punitive damages were demanded for "willful and wanton negligence." The anesthesiologist was charged with causing cardiac failure and respiratory difficulty by injudicious administration of fluids during the surgery.

In the development of this case, the physicians pointed fingers at each other, making settlement much more difficult and expensive. Finally the surgeon bore the chief responsibility because of his delay in treating this severe emergency. The FP was charged with a significant amount of the settlement for his delay in seeing the patient after his admission to the hospital. A lesser part of the settlement was charged against the anesthesiologist.

LOSS PREVENTION COMMENTS

The standard of care in our profession demands that we put our patients first. In the case of both the FP and the surgeon, there were reasons at the time that seemed to mitigate the actions of each. In the aftermath of the death of the patient, these reasons were seen as excuses only and could in no way justify the FP's delay in seeing his patient for at least four hours after he learned of the man's admission, but about 12 hours after the actual admission. Although the surgeon said he was involved with another emergency, there could be no reason why another surgeon was not called if the first one was not immediately available. The surgeon's progress note was seen as an effort to hide the true facts of his delay. This surgeon had a reputation of holding on to patients at all costs rather than asking for help from his colleagues. There were no physicians willing to testify that he was within the standard of care in this case. The anesthesiologist, in retrospect, could have been severely criticized for the amount of fluid given during and immediately after the surgery.

In view of the very real chance of a "shock" verdict by a jury sympathetic to the patient's widow and his children and a willingness to "punish" the doctors for what the jury might well have believed to be careless and uncaring behavior toward a patient in a very real medical emergency, settlement of this suit was considered necessary.

51.   CONSIDER FIRST THINGS FIRST

Allegations—Traumatic rupture of esophagus; delay in diagnosis and treatment
Physician Issue—Lack of physician-to-physician communication
Patient Issues—Sepsis and death
Outcome—Settlement

CASE STUDY

A 67-year-old woman, who had been previously diagnosed as having an esophageal hiatal hernia, was seen in the emergency room complaining of chest pain which began following her evening meal two days before. She was admitted by the emergency room physician with orders for a barium swallow and surgical consultation.

The barium swallow, done early the next morning, demonstrated a fairly high-grade esophageal obstruction by a 2.8-cm foreign body located above Schatzki's ring in the distal esophagus. The patient was then taken to the operating room where, under general anesthesia, the esophagoscope was passed without undue difficulty and a moderate amount of meat was removed in multiple sections with the foreign body forceps. Afterwards, the esophagoscope was passed to its entire length, apparently into the hiatus hernia. Following the procedure, the patient was returned to her room in an alert and responsive state.

Approximately 30 minutes later the patient complained of severe chest pain, for which she was treated with nitroglycerin sublingually without relief. She was immediately seen by a cardiologist, who, following a cursory examination, reached the diagnosis of possible pleurisy, and the patient was transferred to the intensive care unit for overnight observation; a portable chest x-ray revealed possible pneumonia but also demonstrated what appeared to be a foreign body in the distal esophagus.

On morning rounds the patient was found to be restless, dyspneic, and with diffuse chest pain. Repeat chest x-ray revealed subcutaneous emphysema in the neck and over the upper chest wall. There was also some left pleural effusion that appeared to be located posteriorly. Serial chest x-rays and arterial blood gases were done for the next three days, whereupon, with the patient being five days postesophagoscopy, the possibility of perforation was entertained. After a chest tube was placed in the left posterior chest, evacuating approximately 200 cc of purulent fluid, the patient's chest x-rays improved, but her arterial blood gases remained marginal.

The sepsis associated with the perforated esophagus failed to respond to antibiotic therapy, and the patient ultimately progressed to irreversible cardiopulmonary arrest. Autopsy revealed acute mediastinitis and pleuritis with bilateral pleural effusions due to a traumatic laceration of the distal esophagus.

Loss Prevention Comments

In reviewing the essential features of the case, one is prone to react with dismay that the possibility of perforation of the esophagus did not occur to the attending physicians much earlier. The factors that seem to have contributed to this delay in diagnosis were several, which again in retrospect seem hard to explain.

First, the chest pain 30 minutes following the endoscopic examination was clinically typical of myocardial infarction, with sweating, pallor, transient hypotension, and classical pain radiation. To further complicate the picture, there was an EKG that showed changes, which when compared to a previous tracing suggest this. Though the portable chest x-ray showed only "possible pneumonitis," a pulmonary embolus was seriously considered. Apparently no other possibilities were entertained.

Second, the chest x-ray done the second day showed subcutaneous emphysema, which was overlooked, presumably due to a delay in getting the radiologist's written report into the record. (The films were taken Friday morning; the written report was typed that day, but was not seen by the surgeon until Monday, the fifth day postendoscopy.)

Third, and probably the primary reason for a large financial settlement, was that the surgeon had had little previous experience in esophagoscopy and in deposition had to admit that he had never seen subcutaneous emphysema before. Recognizing the incomplete removal of the meat, he attributed the patient's symptoms to either the retained foreign bodies or some cardiopulmonary complication.

Finally, there was no documented evidence that there was any real communication between the physicians involved in the management of this unfortunate patient. Real coordination of medical effort in this case probably would have resulted in an earlier diagnosis and would possibly have prevented the tragic outcome. This apparent lack of coordination of physician efforts occurs with alarming frequency in medical practice. Don't let it happen to you!

VI

Surgical Subspecialties

Claims that arise against physicians from these areas of medical practice, exhibit the same risks as their General and Vascular colleagues with the possible exception that it may be even more necessary here to get timely and complete information from the referring physician. In the hospital setting, the consultant has the benefit of the chart and the information in it if indeed the medical record is complete enough. If not, a conversation with the referring doctor is mandatory. I believe it is always preferable to converse with the colleague about the patient and not be bound by only the written word on the chart. Very few of us are able to paint a word picture in the record as complete as we can in conversation with a colleague.

Reports from the laboratory or the x-ray department need to be scrutinized carefully. For example, when the report of a film of the cervical spine does not show ALL the vertebrae, any decision relative to a neurological complaint or suspected deficit must not finalized until the image is complete. This error is specifically mentioned only because it occurs repeatedly and comes back to haunt the physician who has missed the consequences of injury to the neck and cervical spine.

It seems that the more specialized a practitioner becomes the more he or she can become isolated from the total picture. In all of medicine there can be found examples of physicians who build walls of isolation around themselves in order to focus on their field of expertise. The negative side of this practice is that most diagnoses are not pure. Most patients come to us with more than one thing going on. We cannot afford to shield ourselves from the total patient. If we do, patient injury is almost bound to occur.

The subspecialist is perhaps under even more obligation to be very attentive to the informed consent process. Frequently brought into the management of a case after other physicians have been involved with the patient, one may easily forget the particularities of risk of a given procedure to the individual. One such case is presented in this chapter.

A word about the pathologist. Accustomed as we may become to proceeding with definitive treatment on the authority of the frozen section, this may never be a good idea. There is no literature that indicates that there is an unacceptable risk in waiting for permanent studies. Mistakes on reading the frozen section are much more likely to occur than when the doctor is dealing with a permanent section, and even with the pressures of managed care, the wait is justified to avoid the removal of a healthy organ or the failure to remove a diseased one.

NEUROLOGICAL SURGERY

52.   A GOOD DOCTOR—A BAD RESULT

Allegation—Negligence in replacing CSF
Physician Issues—Admission against interest; operating room
*   error in failing to identify CSF*
Patient Issue—Death
Outcome—Florida case, no known litigation

We will depart from presenting a "fictionalized" Tennessee case and use a case from Florida reported in the press. Perhaps you read it. The case was a tragic example of a relatively routine surgical event ending in catastrophe.

The patient was undergoing surgery for cancer that apparently had involved the eye. Since the dura was to be opened during the operation, some spinal fluid was removed preoperatively, and the syringe labeled "CSF" was set aside for reinjection at the end of the procedure. Sometime during the surgery, an ophthalmologist brought to the operating room an unlabeled vial of glutaraldehyde to be used to preserve the eye tissue removed at surgery. Somehow this vial of clear solution was also labeled "CSF," and at the close of the procedure both the real cerebral spinal fluid and the mislabeled glutaraldehyde were reinjected into the patient. The result was coma and death within a few days.

The surgeon, faced with the awful truth, responded in his own grief, "I accept full responsibility." This was the reaction of a good doctor motivated by all the very deep emotions that make for a good doctor/patient relationship, but he was responding in a way that could be legally devastating.

The surgeon reacted almost automatically out of his training and experience; he looked at this tragic result and asked himself the searching question, "What could I have done differently that might have prevented my patient's injury?" Every good physician goes through the same soul searching when confronted with a bad and unexpected result. All our clinical pathology conferences and morbidity and mortality conferences are pointed in this direction. There is probably no other way to become a good physician. We know that there is always something that we did or something that we did not do that might have made the difference. So we can hear ourselves saying, "I accept full responsibility."

Obviously this surgeon was not "fully responsible" in a legal sense. He may well have had no legal responsibility. There was the ophthalmologist, who dropped off the unlabeled toxic substance. There was the surgical team, who obviously handled and labeled the real CSF. It is unlikely that the surgeon himself personally supervised the adding of the toxic material to the real CSF for injection into the patient.

One thing is certain. When our treasured ethical concerns for the patients we serve are translated into the adversarial arena of the legal process, they simply do not fit. To remember this is to avoid the understandable but legally damaging way this surgeon reacted.

53.   CLOSE COUNTS ONLY IN HORSESHOES

Allegations—Failure to diagnose and treat in a timely manner
Physician Issues—Good and careful evaluation; wrong diagnosis
Patient Issue—Paraplegia
Outcome—A six-figure settlement

CASE STUDY

The patient, a 30-year-old nurse, came to her primary care physician complaining of numbness in her right knee and toes, which had developed fairly suddenly about three months before. She remembered the day the symptoms developed; there was no history of pain or trauma. The primary care physician referred her to a neurosurgeon.

A detailed neurologic examination was recorded in the outpatient medical record, including the history of a "lazy eye" on the left, with confirming physical findings, some motor spasticity in the lower extremities, worse on the right, temporal pallor of the optic disk, symmetrical hyperactive deep tendon reflexes upper and lower extremities, absent Babinski's signs bilaterally, and lack of superficial abdominal reflexes. The neurosurgeon's impression was "possible demyelinating disease." Mild sedation was prescribed and the patient was to return for re-evaluation in ten days.

At this second visit her legs were "improving," and the nurse thought that she could return to work in "ten days or so." She did return to work approximately three weeks after her initial evaluation but three days later again consulted the neurosurgeon, complaining of "dizziness." On this occasion she was admitted to the hospital, where further work-up, including evoked potentials, cerebrospinal fluid examination, and IgG and myelin-based protein studies were done. The results of these tests, along with continued physician evaluation and observation, were suggestive of a demyelinating disease, and the patient was discharged with the diagnosis of "probable MS."

Two months later the neurosurgeon noted that his patient was now "ambulatory with cane." Six months after the initial visit to the neurosurgeon and nine months after the development of symptoms, the patient reported to another physician, requesting a second opinion regarding the diagnosis of multiple sclerosis. Again, extremely thorough evaluation, medical history, physical examination, and results of tests done by the first neurosurgeon were found to support the diagnosis of multiple sclerosis, but he believed that even in the absence of any history of trauma, CT of the spine should be done. This examination revealed a lesion at T9 and T10, and thoracic and lumbar myelograms revealed a "partial block at T9 and T10 predominately extradural." Following the myelogram the patient showed some neurological deterioration, and an emergency thoracic laminectomy was done, revealing a herniated intervertebral disk at T9 and T10. The patient is now paraplegic.

LOSS PREVENTION COMMENTS

Every physician has had the experience of very carefully evaluating a patient by physical examination and history, arriving at an impression, and proceeding to order appropriate studies designed to confirm his initial impression. This might be likened to focusing so intently on a single tree that one loses sight of the forest. This appears to characterize the trap that this physician fell into in dealing with this particular patient. The initial very careful history and physical examination certainly pointed toward a demyelinating disease, and considering the sex and age group, the preliminary diagnosis of multiple sclerosis was extremely logical. As the laboratory and other clinical studies progressed, all seemed to confirm the initial impression.

A very important consideration in our management of patients is cost control. We are increasingly aware of the financial burden we place on our patients when advanced technologic procedures are employed that cost a lot of money. This may have influenced our physician in his failure to order other tests on his patient earlier in her course.

There are few areas in medicine where a wrong conclusion, no matter how logical, drawn from the information at hand, can be as devastating as it is in the specialties of neurology and neurosurgery. Even though this patient seemed to be following a very predictable course with the initial diagnosis of multiple sclerosis, in retrospect it would have been extremely valuable for our physician to have consulted a colleague in his own field. As medical litigation becomes increasingly important in our lives and as awards in medical malpractice continue to escalate, we need to become increasingly sensitive to our patients' dissatisfaction with the course of their illness. In this case, one wonders if the patient gave any indication to our attending physician that she was not satisfied with his management of her case. Had she done so, he could have called for a consultation, and in all probability, even if the results were unchanged, the litigation could have been avoided.

Perhaps we could also conclude from this case that when we are dealing with a situation where consequences of a wrong conclusion are so devastating, our patients would be better served and some bad results prevented if we cast aside all thoughts of cost containment and used all the technologic tools available to rule out other possible diagnoses.

54.   DECISION ABSENT GOOD DATA

Allegations—Failure to diagnose and treat in a timely manner
Physician Issue—X-ray of neck unsatisfactory as to C7
Patient Issues—Persistent difficulty swallowing; minimal activity
Outcome—Modest six-figure settlement

CASE STUDY

After an automobile accident, a 73-year-old man was brought to the emergency department of a very fine hospital. He complained chiefly of pain in the neck and had multiple bruises and abrasions over the extremities and a deep laceration of the scalp. He reported no loss of consciousness and appeared to be neurologically intact. There was full motion in the neck, but motion was somewhat painful.

The lacerations and abrasions were attended to, and an x-ray study of the cervical spine was requested.

The x-rays were reported to show some degenerative changes but no other abnormalities. Some disk space narrowing consistent with the patient's age was present at the C4 and C6 level. The report did not mention whether there was good visualization of C7. The skull films were reported as normal. Despite the negative findings, the patient was admitted to the hospital because of his age and the severity of the accident itself. In the hospital, the patient continued to complain of pain chiefly in the back of the neck, which was aggravated by motion. With the ED findings, the attending physician followed the patient closely, doing a neurologic examination every day with consistently negative findings. Medication for pain and a cervical collar were prescribed.

In addition to the neck pain, the patient also developed marked soreness in the chest. Findings indicated some late appearing ecchymoses over the sternum, where it was thought the chest had come into contact with the steering wheel. X-ray studies of the chest were negative. Again, the neurologic examination was not revealing. Rotation of the neck was very limited because of pain. Aggressive physical therapy was begun the second hospital day with electrical stimulation, cold, and heat.

On the third day of hospitalization, there were some vague complaints of roaring in the head and continued marked pain in the neck. There did appear to be some improvement and lessening of the pain on this day. The following day, hospital day 5, the attending physician ordered more imaging of the head and neck and a neurosurgical consultation. It was a day later before the neurosurgeon made his evaluation of the patient. His findings were no different from those of previous examiners, and his conclusion, based on the negative CT studies, was again severe cervical strain. The radiologist suggested that a myelogram be considered if the consultant believed that a herniated disk was a good possibility.

For the next two days the patient continued to complain bitterly of pain in the neck. He was more comfortable with the soft collar off and was reported by the nurses to "hold neck when moving." He was given Valium and Feldene and seemed to improve slightly; the pain was slightly less and, subjectively at least, the motion in his neck was a "little better."

On the fifth day of hospitalization, the patient complained of having more pain since he started the physical therapy. Examination showed more tenderness along the paravertebral muscles of the neck, but nothing further. CT scans of the head and neck were ordered, with particular attention to the possibility of a herniated nucleus pulposus

(HNP) in the areas of C5, C6, and C7. The report showed mild degenerative changes but no evidence of a ruptured disc. There was also the suggestion of an arteriovenous malformation (AVM) in the left temporal area. Conservative therapy was continued.

With consistent complaints of some dizziness and a "roaring" in the head, along with the stiff neck, a cerebral arteriogram was ordered to determine whether or not the AVM could be leaking, but no leakage was seen. An ulcerated plaque was found at the origin of the right carotid artery, but no surgery was thought to be indicated. He was discharged home taking Valium 10 mg three times a day and Feldene and ASA one tablet each daily.

Two weeks after discharge the patient was seen by the neurosurgeon who had been consulted while he was in the hospital. There was "no significant progress since leaving the hospital." Still, the neurologic examination was reported as normal. Readmission was advised for the restudy of the possibility of a fracture or a ruptured disk in the neck. After consulting with the original attending physician and a neurologist, the neurosurgeon ordered a bone scan, MRI, and x-rays of the cervical spine with the neck in flexion and extension. These x-rays showed marked subluxation of C2 and C3 with widening of the lamina "usually seen after fracture dislocation." The MRI confirmed the subluxation. Repeat x-ray studies of the neck revealed fracture lines in both laminae of C2 with anterior subluxation of "one-third the distance of the vertebral body."

An anterior open reduction was recommended, with a thorough discussion of the risks and benefits of the surgery. The patient was told that there was an 80 percent chance of a good result. Illustrations of the surgery were drawn and the possibility of paralysis and even death was discussed. The possible consequences of not having the surgery were also thoroughly discussed with the patient and his wife. The patient was resistant at first but consented to surgery to be done two days later. Films made in the operating room revealed the reduction to be good.

In the early morning hours of the night after the surgery, the patient developed acute shortness of breath. Chest x-ray revealed some cardiomegaly but no significant congestion. His neck collar was adjusted with some relief and the edema in his neck previously noted was thought to be less the afternoon of the first postoperative day. Signs of congestion continued with cough productive of "large amount of grayish sputum." During the second postoperative day the patient became more restless and demanded to smoke. The nurses' notes record that he was found smoking with the oxygen turned off on at least three occasions. He became more confused and restless and this became progressively worse until the fourth postoperative day, when he became combative, wanting to go home, and had to be restrained. Portable lateral x-rays of the neck showed that the superior-most screw seemed to have backed out and that the degree of anterior subluxation of C2 on C3 was at that time estimated to be 10 mm. He was transferred to the ICU, where the surgeon applied Gardner-Wells tongs with 15 lb of cervical traction. Shortly thereafter the patient developed bradycardia and a code was called. There was a prompt return to a normal sinus rhythm after he had been intubated and put on a ventilator. He was said to respond appropriately and his color had improved.

A consultation with a pulmonologist noted that the patient's dyspnea seemed to be related to the position of the neck and the swelling around the operative site. His PO_2 had been 50, with a normal CO_2 while he was breathing room air. With the patient improved, the neck collar was left off and the traction was reduced to 10 lb. Repeat cervical spine films showed a "few mm" of subluxation. In order to achieve better pulmonary control, a tracheostomy was done. The following day the patient developed a fever and a chest x-ray showed some infiltrate interpreted to be pneumonitis. All agreed that a nosocomial infection had occurred, and on appropriate antibiotics the fever came down. Repeat x-rays showed no significant change in the degree of subluxation.

Nevertheless, the patient was unable to swallow, thought to be due to the impingement of the anterior plate on the esophagus. Since stabilization of the neck was essential, a posterior fusion with removal of the anterior plate was done. Following this surgery there was stormy and slow improvement, mainly involving the persistent difficulty in swallowing. He was able to be discharged about six weeks after admission.

Four months after discharge the patient was still having difficulty swallowing, with frequent aspiration. His physicians told him at this time that nothing further could be done. He was minimally active and was encouraged to gradually increase his activities and be seen again in another four months.

LOSS PREVENTION COMMENTS

The lawsuit that followed charged that the failure to diagnose the fracture and subluxation in a timely manner was negligent and led to the bad result. In the course of the litigation, the general surgeon who admitted the patient and the orthopedic surgeon who participated in both attempts at fusion were nonsuited, leaving the neurosurgeon and the radiologist charged.

This was a very difficult case, and the result probably was not worse because of the delay in diagnosis. However, the patient did continue to complain of severe neck pain despite the reassuring x-ray studies, and he was discharged from the hospital only to be readmitted with the same complaints two weeks later. The finding of the AVM on CT of the head and confirmed on arteriography confused the picture. Until readmission, the x-ray studies had consistently been reported as normal, but also one has to be impressed with the wording of the reports, which could lead to the impression that since the initial films had failed to clearly show C7, the radiologist was concerned that C7 be shown clearly. In addition, the degenerative changes repeatedly reported at C4, C5, and C6 made the ruling out of a ruptured disk in that area more of a challenge. On readmission, however, the pathology present at C2-3 was demonstrated promptly on lateral views of the area, and, as is so often the case, on re-examination of the previous films could be said to have been there all the time. It is interesting to note that the MRI, which in 1987 had to be obtained in another institution, made no real contribution to the correct diagnosis.

There was a discrepancy in the record that could have been critical to the credibility of the neurosurgeon had the case gone to trial. His discharge summary stated that the patient was "immediately placed in Gardner-Wells tongs for stabilization," when no record of this appears in the record until the third postoperative day.

Delay in diagnosis of cervical spine injuries comes up frequently in malpractice lawsuits. The lesson to be learned here again is perhaps best stated in the two rules that follow: The first is to listen to the patient when there are complaints that cannot be fully diagnosed and understood on the basis of any of the studies. The second is to insist on clear visualization of the entire cervical spine.

Because of the acknowledged delay in diagnosis, the extreme expense of the management of the case, the permanent disability, and the presence of "experts" second-guessing our colleagues, prudence dictated the settlement of this case for a modest amount.

UROLOGICAL SURGERY

55.   THE LOSER FINALLY WINS

Allegations—Delay in appropriate intervention; negligence in choice of surgical intervention
Physician Issues—Noncompliant patient; alcohol abuse; failed to act on ureteral obstruction

Patient Issues—Prolonged pain and suffering; damaged kidney
Outcome—Modest six-figure settlement

CASE STUDY

The "loser," a 28-year-old man, was seen with a history of gross bleeding from the urethra with some burning on urination. In the past this young alcoholic had been treated for peptic ulcer disease and eight years previously had a purulent urethritis typical of gonorrhea. This had subsided with penicillin treatment, but a urethral stricture caused some difficulty urinating and bleeding. A meatotomy and dilatation had been repeatedly recommended. On this admission his general physical examination had been unremarkable, including the prostate.

An IVP showed "moderate obstructive uropathy on the right due to a 3-mm stone distally in the ureter about 3 cm above the uretero-vesicle junction." The patient was discharged with a 10-day supply of nitrofurantoin macrocrystals (Macrodantin) with instructions to return following the treatment. When he returned to his urologist, a meatotomy was done and the outpatient record showed that the "stream improved."

Some five months later he was seen in the emergency room with marked epigastric pain, nausea, and vomiting. On this occasion his alcohol abuse was noted, and he had a serum amylase of 571 U/L. Studies revealed cholelithiasis and some urethral obstruction. A diagnosis of acute pancreatitis was made, and he was discharged on a regimen of diet, H_2 blockers, and NO ALCOHOL!

Two months following this admission, this "loser" was seen by his urologist, whose office record stated that he "continues to complain of the same old problem: pain over the flanks and halfway down the penis." Treatment again was Macrodantin. One week later the "urine almost normal," and one week later another IVP showed an irregular calcification low in the right pelvis measuring some 6 to 7 mm. "Mild obstructive uropathy present on the right." Again the patient was placed on Macrodantin.

Three months later another IVP showed no function on the right for one hour, then marked hydronephrosis above a stone in the lower right ureter measuring about 1 cm in diameter. A traumatic extraction was followed by the placement of a stent in the lower right ureter. Because the pain was much more severe than usual, the stent was removed sooner than planned, and he was discharged on trimethoprim and sulfamethoxazole (Bactrim) and meperidine and promethazine (Mepergan) for pain.

Later the patient had to be admitted with severe abdominal pain.

A pancreative pseudocyst was diagnosed and surgically treated, and a follow-up IVP showed "mild to moderate hydronephrosis on the right."

Shortly after discharge, a suit was filed against the urologist charging unnecessary surgery, pain and suffering, and significant financial loss. A settlement in six figures was necessary; no adequate defense could be developed.

LOSS PREVENTION COMMENTS

The cold medical record in this case made settlement absolutely necessary! An obstructing stone in the lower right ureter was ignored for a year before definitive treatment was instituted. What factors in this case could have contributed to a good doctor overlooking the obvious in this way? Some possibilities come to mind.

First, this was a very undesirable patient! He was a drunk, who had first been encountered with gonorrhea, which had caused a urethral stricture.

Second, he was a known alcoholic with physical complaints directly produced by his habit, and he made no known effort to change his lifestyle.

Third, he had multi-system complaints, all seemingly related to alcohol, and he was continually complaining of symptoms that he could have controlled or greatly moderated, but he would not.

Fourth, the urologist in this case did the easiest thing in the world to do. He continued to attribute all of this patient's symptoms to his known problem of urethral stricture, ignoring the more serious problem. In all probability the urologist, who routinely read his own x-rays, did not take note of the radiologist's reading of a stone a year before its extraction.

Fifth, after the repeat study showed the stone to have enlarged and the obstruction to have become more marked, it was three more months before intervention. This delay had to be due to some over-sight, or "falling through the cracks."

Perhaps the most evident trap in this case is the trap of the extremely undesirable, obnoxious patient. Maybe this man deserved his fate, but not at the expense of his doctor. Yes, this loser really did win!

56.   TO SPEAK IS NOT NECESSARILY TO BE UNDERSTOOD

Allegations—Fraudulent concealment; path report
Physician Issue—Claimed that he informed patient by phone,
    not documented

Patient Issue—Unwanted pregnancy
Outcome—Modest settlement

CASE STUDY

A 30-year-old man presented himself to a urologist requesting elective sterilization. The patient stated that he and his wife had a healthy 9-year-old daughter and he desired a vasectomy, in part because his wife had been taking the pill for eight or nine years and desired to quit. They had also decided to have no additional children. Past history revealed that the patient had had nasal surgery and was allergic to codeine. The physical examination was within normal limits except for the presence of sebaceous cysts. The urologist proposed admitting the patient to the hospital to do the vasectomy as well as to excise the sebaceous cysts. The patient agreed and a general surgeon was contacted regarding the excision of the sebaceous cysts.

The vasectomy was explained to the patient and wife while they were in the office, and the doctor maintained that all possible complications were discussed and postoperative instructions were given. In addition, a consent form was signed by the patient and his wife. There was no documentation of the discussion.

Two days later the patient was admitted to the hospital, where under general anesthesia he underwent a bilateral vasectomy and excision of the sebaceous cysts. The operative note describes identical procedures on the left and right scrotum, with approximately 1 cm of vas sent to pathology for identification. The patient was discharged the next day. The chart documents both verbal and written instructions having been given to the patient regarding postoperative care. The patient was to return in six weeks for a sperm count. Following that, he was to return in six months for a repeat count.

Four days following the patient's discharge, the pathology department generated its report identifying sections of both the right and left vas, but the microscopic diagnosis stated that one specimen was only "suggestive but not diagnostic" of a transected ductus deferens. The other portion was identified as a completely transected segment of an essentially normal ductus deferens.

When the patient returned in six weeks his sperm count was zero. He was to return in six months, but did not. Approximately three years later, the patient called the urologist stating that his wife was pregnant. A sperm count in the urologist's office revealed 1.5 million sperm per milliliter. Although no comment is made as to motility or morphology, the count itself would be far below the accepted range indicating fertility.

LOSS PREVENTION COMMENTS

This case illustrates the fairly frequent example of good care, preceded by adequate written and verbal information as to the nature of the procedure and its risks and complications, complicated by a known hazard of the procedure. Although the documentation of the preoperative consent discussion is virtually nonexistent, fairly complete written information was given to the patient, who simply did not comply with instructions to return six months after the vas ligation for a second sperm count.

Defense of this case was made virtually impossible by the alleged failure of the urologist to inform the patient of the pathology report. This led to a charge of "fraudulent concealment" by the plaintiff patient, and this charge voided the statute of limitations.

Why the failure to inform the patient? The system failed! The "system" called for direct communication between physician and patient. The physician said he informed the patient by phone of the pathology report. The patient said that he received no such information. There was no documentation of the call.

Our physician in this case was foreign born and had difficulty in communicating in the English language. His patient came from a rural area and had had no experience with an accent such as that of the doctor. It is possible that the physician did call, but because of the language difficulty he was not understood by his patient.

The importance of documenting important phone calls in the patient's record cannot be overemphasized. Had this been present in the patient's record, the lawsuit might not have been filed. Once filed, defense of the doctor would have the advantage. Our foreign-born physicians especially need to be aware of possible language problems and be doubly careful to make their verbal communications understood. Documentation in such a situation becomes even more important.

PATHOLOGY

57.   TAKE YOUR TIME—BE SURE

Allegations—Oral report premature; diagnosis not within reasonable standard
Physician Issues—Noncompliant patient; verbal report on frozen section; peer review challenge of report

Patient Issue—Unnecessary radical surgery
Outcome—Modest six-figure settlement

CASE STUDY

A 52-year-old patient reported to a surgeon who was considered to be a "breast specialist," with a history of tenderness in the right breast. The patient first noticed the tenderness about one month before her visit to the physician, and because she was knowledgeable about breast disease she delayed her appointment to be sure that the tenderness was not related to her menses. The doctor examined her breasts and located the area of tenderness without difficulty. The surgeon was not sure about the presence of a mass, but she informed the patient that she suspected that there was a small "lump" in the region of the point of maximum tenderness.

A mammogram was ordered, and the report was somewhat surprising in that the radiologist recorded "a focus of microcalcification in the central portion of the right breast." The patient was obese with very large breasts, and the tenderness did not seem to be in the area of the calcifications. The surgeon recommended to her patient that a biopsy be done under general anesthesia followed by a modified radical mastectomy if the frozen section was positive for malignancy.

Six days after the patient first visited the surgeon the biopsy was done, and the report was suspicious for cancer but not diagnostic. The day after the biopsy the excised specimen was x-rayed, and "no microcalcifications" were present. The report suggested that a repeat mammogram be done after healing had occurred. The patient did not return as suggested in the pathology report. There was no documentation in the attending physician's office chart as to whether or not the patient was advised of the recommendation of the pathologist.

About one year later, on a routine follow-up visit, the patient's attending physician reported to her that the "final diagnosis was normal." A repeat mammogram was recommended in three months.

Subsequent office visits documented healing of the surgical scar. The patient lost weight following her surgery, which was attributed to her own efforts at dieting. Three months later, which was 15 months after the initial biopsy, the mammogram showed "increase in mass density—the presence of microcalcifications—recommend excisional biopsy."

The excisional biopsy was performed as indicated, and the frozen section was reported orally to the operating room as "infiltrating ductal carcinoma." A modified radical mastectomy was done. The day following the surgery the report from the pathologist was "unequivocal diagnosis of carcinoma cannot be made on this specimen." Following exhaustive review of the specimen by several pathologists, the final diagnosis was "sclerosing adenosis."

A lawsuit was filed charging the pathologist with negligence. The contention was that the oral report of "infiltrating ductal carcinoma" should not have been made until after the permanent sections had been examined. The pathologists called as expert witnesses could not agree that the diagnosis of "infiltrating ductal carcinoma" was within a reasonable standard. A settlement was necessary in the case.

LOSS PREVENTION COMMENTS

Most all of us would agree that radical surgery should never be done until after a final diagnosis has been made. We are not infallible, however, and this was a confusing case. There had been a previous biopsy, and in retrospect we could say that the area in the initial mammogram that was suspicious was not a part of the excised specimen. The specimen did not contain the microcalcifications that were most suggestive of malignant disease.

When the pathologist suggested a repeat mammogram after "healing" had occurred, he surely did not contemplate that the surgeon would delay the examination for a year. In light of subsequent events, it seems that the pathologist so strongly suspected malignancy that when he saw the second biopsy specimen his diagnosis was tilted toward his strong assumptions. Consequently, he gave the oral report of carcinoma.

The surgeon was not sued, but there is certainly room to question her management of her patient. She did not insist on the repeat mammogram and follow-up, as suggested by the pathologist. Although the surgeon said that she verbally instructed her patient to return for the recommended mammogram, the patient denied it and there was no supporting documentation. In this confusing set of circumstances, the surgeon accepted without question the verbal report of the pathologist and performed a deforming surgical procedure on her patient.

There is not universal agreement that, even in the presence of confirmed carcinoma of the breast, the "one-stage" biopsy followed by immediate definitive/radical surgery offers a better prognosis than waiting a sufficient time to get the "final diagnosis."

In these days the pressure is on to expedite the diagnosis and treatment of our patients. Outpatient surgery for the biopsy and an inpatient admission for a radical procedure is cumbersome, to say the least. One could argue that in this case, the perceived need to rush through its management contributed to the outcome, which was certainly not satisfactory to either the patient or the physicians involved.

Perhaps we should daily remind ourselves that our patients deserve careful and considered management regardless of the bureaucratic hassle, which seems to be getting worse by the day.

58.   FROZEN SECTION ERROR?—RARE BUT DISASTROUS

*Allegation—Pathologist negligent; issuing wrong report;
        surgeon negligent; later dropped
Physician Issues—Confusing facts; peer review diagnosis;
        nonmalignant
Patient Issues—Loss of breast; premature and wrong
        diagnosis
Outcome—Moderate six-figure settlement*

CASE STUDY

A 50-year-old obese woman reported to her primary care physician complaining of soreness and some pain in her right breast. Examination showed a small, tender area of question in the upper outer quadrant of the right breast, and the examiner thought that there was indeed a small mass present. She was referred for a mammogram, and the radiologist reported an area of microcalcifications deep in the central portion of the breast.

The physician of record referred the patient to a surgeon, who, on the basis of the mammogram report, recommended a biopsy. In explaining the situation to his patient, the surgeon told her that the suspicious area in the breast was not in the location where the tender lump was found and should be further examined with a biopsy. He further explained to his patient that the suspicious area found by the mammogram was in a location that would require general anesthesia. She wished to think about this recommendation and discuss it with her husband but felt sure enough that she wanted the biopsy to allow the surgeon to schedule her for three days later. She reported at the scheduled time.

The biopsy was done under general anesthesia. The frozen section was very suspicious of cancer but not diagnostic. Mastectomy, which had been planned pending a malignant lesion, was not done. Permanent sections did not show the radiologically identified calcifications, and the pathologist recommended that a repeat mammogram be done after healing of the operative site had occurred.

The surgeon followed his patient after biopsy and did schedule a repeat mammogram in three months. The report of this examination showed that the lesion described on the initial study had not changed. A repeat study was recommended in three months. This examination was done as recommended and the report again showed no change. On recommendation of the radiologist, her surgeon planned another mammogram for six months later.

At the six-month checkup, the surgeon believed that there had been no change in his patient's physical examination. She had been on a diet and had lost weight, and the breasts were smaller and easier to examine. Study of the mammogram done at this time indicated that the findings represented "an increase in a mass density associated with microcalcifications. An excisional biopsy is recommended to determine the true nature of this condition."

At this point, the surgeon again explained the situation to his patient. He again went over the possibility of a radical procedure if the mass proved to be malignant. The excisional biopsy was scheduled for a few days later. Needle localization was used to precisely identify the area and a wide excisional biopsy was done. Frozen section was done on the specimen and the report was "infiltrating ductal carcinoma." While the patient was under anesthesia, a modified radical mastectomy was done. There were no problems associated with the operation. In the early postoperative period the surgeon learned that there was some confusion and disagreement in the pathology group about the exact nature of the lesion, but the prevailing opinion was that it was benign. The specimen was sent to a consulting pathologist in Tennessee, as well as to one at Sloan-Kettering Institute, for their opinions.

Within three or four days of the surgery, while the patient was still in the hospital, all the pathologists agreed that the lesion was, indeed, benign. However, one consulting pathologist stated that this was a lesion about which experienced pathologists might disagree.

The attending surgeon stayed very close to his patient, repeatedly assuring her that regardless of the true diagnosis, she was indeed cured of her disease. He made available to his patient all the many pathology reports. He continued to stress to his patient that the lesion was a hard one to be specific about; therefore, he could not criticize the pathologist who read the frozen section.

Some months went by before the pathologist and his group were sued, charging negligence in issuing a definitive opinion on a lesion about which there was some doubt. The surgeon was initially charged with negligence in failing to reassure his patient that the lesion was not malignant, thus contributing to her mental anguish. This charge was dismissed during the course of discovery and further investigation.

This woman had lost her breast and suffered through weeks of confusion about whether or not she had cancer. The plaintiff was very aggressive and the expert testimony was all on the side of the plaintiff. No expert could be found who would say that a diagnosis of "infiltrating ductal carcinoma" was within an acceptable standard of care, largely because in the presence of such an equivocal situation, permanent sections should have been done before committing this patient to such a disfiguring and emotionally shattering experience. It was argued that had the patient been aware of the differences of opinion regarding the definitive diagnosis, she and her surgeon would have waited and given even more time for further evaluation. A large settlement was necessary in this case.

Loss Prevention Comments

In medicine, when things go well in a given procedure or situation so consistently, it is easy to forget that in the same situation one can and does encounter unexpected complications. This is certainly the case with frozen sections. Almost always the surgeon can rely on the report of the pathologist to be correct. Almost always the surgeon can plan his approach at the table with confidence that the pathology report is accurate. "Almost always!" Then there comes a situation like this when surgeons and pathologists realize that occasionally (even if very rarely) there comes a time when the definitive procedure should be deferred until the permanent sections have been processed and a final report is issued.

OPHTHALMOLOGY/SURGERY

59.   PREVENTING/MINIMIZING PATIENT INJURY

Allegation—Negligence of all parties involved
Physician Issues—Lack of postop supervision of patient by
   attending; self-serving agreements with anesthesiologist
   and resident
Patient Issue—Quadriplegia
Outcome—Six-figure settlement

Case Study

An ophthalmologist treated a 30-year-old man who had been an insulin-dependent juvenile diabetic since age 5. The ophthalmologist had an unwritten agreement with the hospital he used that he took care of only diseases of the eye and that other conditions his patients might have or develop would be the responsibility of the hospital. During the time in question the anesthesiologist was supposed to take care of "the other medical problems," and a moonlighting orthopedic resident was employed by the hospital to "cover" at night. The anesthesiologist had an internist who had agreed to help in the management of this patient if necessary.

The ophthalmologist did a trans pars plana vitrectomy and scleral buckling with encircling band because of proliferative diabetic retinopathy. The operation was done under general anesthetic; the surgery went well and the patient went to the recovery room at 10:20 AM. In the recovery room, the patient was "lethargic but responsive to commands." About one hour and forty minutes after admission to the recovery room, the patient was asleep but could be awakened easily. Blood pressure was 136/76, blood sugar by Dextrostix was acceptable at 200, and the patient was discharged to his private room at 12:10 PM. Neither the operating surgeon nor the anesthesiologist saw the patient in the recovery room, but transfer to his room was made according to hospital protocol. The surgeon did not see his patient the rest of the day.

Postoperative orders specified that the patient by kept in the "seated face-down position," accomplished by having the patient sitting up in bed with his arms folded across a Mayo stand and his head resting on his arms. The ophthalmologist was to be consulted only regarding eye problems; the anesthesiologist and/or the resident were to be called about any other problem. The resident was not informed of this agreement.

At 3:30 PM the patient was "alert and responsive to verbal stimuli," and the position was maintained. At 7:30 PM, however, the nurses noted that the patient was "unresponsive to verbal stimuli," the blood pressure was 80/50 mm Hg, and a Dextrostix was found to be 80 mg/dl. Stat blood sugar was ordered and reported at 76 mg/dl. At 8:00 PM the resident was called. He came and administered 50 cc of 50 percent dextrose in water by IV push, noting that the patient was unresponsive but complained of pain in his eye and both arms.

At 1:35 AM when the nurse attempted to sit the patient on the bedside to void, the patient was found to have no sensation in his legs and could not move either of them. The resident was immediately notified and arrived at 1:40 AM. After examining the patient, the resident called the surgeon and reported his findings, but there was no documentation of this call by either of them. The resident insisted that he was told that the complaints were probably due to positioning and to put the patient in the prone position. The resident also insisted that the ophthalmologist said that if the patient did not improve with the change of position that he (the ophthalmologist) would call in a neurologist. The surgeon, however, said that the resident only called requesting a position change because of the patient's complaints of numbness.

The resident ordered the patient placed in the prone position but did not re-examine him before leaving the hospital at 6:00 AM. Nurses notes were made during the night, but the patient was not checked by the nursing staff between 2:00 AM and 6:00 AM, and the surgeon made no inquiry during the night as to whether his patient's condition had improved or not.

At 6:00 AM it was found that the patient still could not move his legs, but only after the patient complained at 8:20 AM of no feeling or movement in his arms or legs was action taken. The anesthesiologist was called, and at 9:00 AM the surgeon checked the patient and said he was consulting a neurosurgeon. At 11:00 AM the patient was actually examined by the anesthesiologist; a neurosurgeon examined him at 11:30 AM and arrived at a diagnosis of (1) possible C6 cord lesion, (2) with a vascular lesion, traumatic injury, or Guillain Barré syndrome to be ruled out. In the university center, after further diagnostic studies, a cervical laminectomy was done at C3-4-5 to decompress the cord, culture the area, and perform a biopsy.

Postoperative diagnosis was probable infarction of the cord, but cultures grew out alpha *Streptococcus*, not group D. The neuro-surgeon then changed his opinion to "transverse myelopathy, probably due to abscess." When quardriplegia persisted, the operating neurosurgeon still later changed his opinion favoring infarction of the cord.

Defense theory, supported by expert testimony: The vascular lesion and/or infectious process was the result of this patient's long-standing diabetes, and postoperative management did not contribute to the result.

The plaintiff's theory, supported by expert testimony: The postoperative positioning produced pressure on the cervicle vessels causing infarction, producing the result.

LOSS PREVENTION COMMENTS

All parties were clearly below an acceptable standard of care in the postoperative management of this case. The ophthalmologist did not examine his patient postoperatively the day of the surgery, even when he knew there were some questions about his condition. His "unwritten agreement" with the hospital, attempting to avoid responsibility for the overall management of his patient, was not only below the standard of care but ethically offensive.

The resident's failure to pursue the investigation of his findings of some neurological deficit by subsequent examinations and calling again for help was below any acceptable standard for a resident.

The anesthesiologist's failure to adequately ascertain the patient's preoperative status, failure to meticulously follow the patient postoperatively, and failure to act immediately on the knowledge of a neurological problem the morning after surgery were held by experts to be below an acceptable standard of care.

The hospital nurses' failure to follow this patient closely after they found that he was "unable to move his legs" was certainly below the standard. (They failed to examine the patient between the hours of 2:00 AM and 6:00 AM.)

These are only the most glaring problems in the case. Defense was rendered virtually impossible by substandard care in the face of this most serious postoperative complication. The patient's injury might well have been unavoidable, but his postoperative care was not pointed in the direction of preventing injury, or if it could not be prevented, of minimizing its effect.

PLASTIC/RECONSTRUCTIVE SURGERY

60.   EXCELLENT CARE—UNEXPECTED RESULT

Allegations—No informed consent; negligence in performing reduction of fracture of orbit
Physician Issues—Critical injury spine and face; excellent neurosurgical and reconstructive surgeons
Patient Issue—Loss of vision
Outcome—Negligence charge dismissed; six-figure jury award solely on lack of informed consent

CASE STUDY

In a single car, high-speed accident a 16-year-old boy sustained multiple contusions and fractures, including a fracture of the dorsal spine with significant displacement, which required emergency surgery to relieve and/or prevent pressure on the spinal cord. A laminectomy was done at T10 within the first 12 hours of admission, and the patient stabilized uneventfully. Within the first 48 hours after his surgery, some loss of upward gaze on the left was noted, but the patient denied diplopia and visual acuity seemed unaffected; on examination, however, there was some inability of the left eye to move upward with the right eye. The neurosurgeon who had attended the patient initially called in for consultation an excellent plastic surgeon with extensive maxillofacial experience.

Additional x-rays of his face revealed a fracture of the floor of the orbit on the left (a blow-out fracture), and surgery was planned to relieve what was felt to be some entrapment of the external ocular muscles. Surgery was carried out uneventfully with the reduction of the fracture of the floor of the left orbit and no apparent difficulties were noted during the operation, but upon reacting the patient complained of loss of vision on the left; it never returned.

A lawsuit was filed charging the plastic and reconstructive surgeon with negligence in the performance of the operation, as well as lack of informed consent. As usual, depositions followed with expert witnesses being summoned by both sides. Though absolutely no justification was found for the charge of negligence related to the surgical procedure, numerous expert witnesses were available to testify that failure to inform the patient and/or the parents of this 16-year-old boy of the possibility of the loss of vision as a complication of the surgery was a deviation from an acceptable standard. A trial followed, and there was a large jury award based solely on the lack of informed consent.

Loss Prevention Comments

More and more lawsuits are being brought, and more and more money is being paid out because, after a bad result, the plaintiff patient believes that he was poorly informed as to the possible consequences of a surgical procedure. In this case, this young man had excellent care from both his neurosurgeon and his plastic and reconstructive surgeon. The complication that occurred, causing him to lose the vision in his left eye, is extremely serious and extremely regrettable, but it nevertheless can and does occur in this kind of surgery, even when done by experts in the field.

The question normally is raised, "How much documentation is necessary to avoid this kind of lawsuit?" Our claims attorneys at SVMIC say that cases of this type where settlements are required or awards are given are those cases where there is no evidence in the record of any encounter between the patient and the operating surgeon during which an attempt is made to apprise the patient and/or family of the potential risks and benefits of the planned surgery. As was true in this case, the record is simply silent on the entire subject. The surgeon could not specifically remember warning of the possibility of blindness, however unlikely, as a complication of the surgery, and of course the parents stated that there was no mention of such a complication.

It is worth emphasizing that SVMIC has yet to lose or settle a case because of lack of informed consent where there is a note by the attending physician that he talked with the patient and discussed the risks and the patient seemed to understand the essence of the discussion. Any discussion should include any extremely serious complication that can occur, i.e., death, blindness, paralysis, loss of limb, so as to provide the patient with all of the knowledge that he needs to make an informed decision relative to consenting to allow surgery.

Patients have been conditioned to expect unrealistically good results from our efforts, and because of this, when an unexpected or bad result occurs, patients will always believe that they should have known about its possibility before the fact and, on occasion, this dissatisfaction will result in the filing of a lawsuit.

61.   WHAT HAPPENED TO THAT OWNER'S MANUAL?

Allegations—Failure to prescribe postoperative antibiotics; failure to maintain sterile precautions
Physician Issues—Not responsible for clinic's sterilization procedures; did not routinely prescribe postoperative antibiotics
Patient Issues—Care below standard for both physician and clinic; significant facial scarring
Outcome—Modest six-figure settlement

CASE STUDY

After suffering a facial laceration while doing some remodeling work, a 39-year-old carpenter sought treatment in a nearby free-standing emergency clinic. The laceration was approximately 2 inches long and fairly deep and had been sustained as the carpenter accidentally walked into a piece of scaffolding with a nail in the end of it. Bleeding profusely, the patient entered the clinic, where he received a tetanus shot. The wound was cleansed, the laceration was closed with 4-0 silk sutures, and the patient was sent home with instructions to apply ice and take acetaminophen for pain.

The patient experienced significant pain and swelling during the night and the following morning returned to the clinic, where a huge hematoma was noted at the laceration sight. He was immediately referred to a plastic surgeon, whose offices were located nearby.

The skin sutures were immediately removed and the hematoma drained. In addition, the wound was explored and a small artery was identified as the source of the bleeding leading to the hematoma. With the help of his office nurse, the plastic surgeon ligated the artery. Thereafter, the wound was re-evaluated and found to be free of any additional bleeding sites. The wound was then irrigated with an antibiotic solution and was closed in two layers.

Some three days later the patient began to experience some generalized aching, mild swelling, and beginning redness in the area of the facial laceration. The plastic surgeon was called and without seeing the patient prescribed an oral broad spectrum antibiotic, cephalexin (Keflex), 1 gm every six hours. The patient was advised to come to the surgeon's office in 24 hours if he had not improved.

The patient felt no worse the next day, so he did not return to see his surgeon, but the following day the facial swelling, redness, and tenderness were much worse. He called and related his symptoms to the surgeon's office nurse. After a 12-hour delay, the patient was able to see his doctor, who immediately admitted him to the hospital, where an emergency I&D was done, followed by five days of culture-specific intravenous antibiotics. The patient's symptoms resolved slowly, and complete healing resulted, but with significant facial scarring; the result of subsequent attempts by the plastic surgeon to revise the scar were cosmetically unsatisfactory to the patient.

A lawsuit was filed against both the freestanding clinic and the plastic surgeon alleging failure to properly close the wound, failure to maintain sterile precautions, and failure to prescribe antibiotics to prevent infection.

In the course of developing the lawsuit, the plaintiff attorney learned that while the plastic surgeon used only disposable equipment in the wound care, the freestanding clinic had its own autoclave and sterilized its own drapes, scalpel handles, hemostats, etc. No proof was presented by the defendant clinic that a protocol existed for the routine inspection of the autoclave as recommended by the manufacturer. Test runs of the autoclave assuring proper pressure and temperature requirements had not been done during the 12 months the clinic had owned it.

Expert witnesses were available in abundance to testify that the plastic surgeon should have prescribed systemic antibiotics following his management of the hematoma, which necessitated the exploration, the establishing of hemostasis, and secondary closure of the wound.

A sizable settlement was required, to which each defendant contributed.

LOSS PREVENTION COMMENTS

Do you have an autoclave? Do you follow the manufacturer's specifications as to periodic maintenance, with test runs for the reliability of that machine?

The use of antibiotics in an effort to prevent infection in a secondary closure of a facial wound is deemed indicated. In this case the plastic surgeon admitted in his deposition that his failure to prescribe antibiotics had been an oversight.

VI

Radiology

As this speciality becomes more subspecialized, it becomes more invasive and more subject to all the issues that bring it into the legal arena. In the last generation we have seen the practitioner evolve from one who interprets the still films that come out of the diagnostic operation to one who may use extremely sophisticated radiation therapy machines, needles, and catheters to do studies of organs and blood vessels, CTs, MRIs, PETs, three-dimensional ultrasound, and an array of other technologies that assist in the diagnosis of disease states.

With all of this comes the obligation to engage the patient in the process of informed consent with an understandable discussion of the risks and benefits of what the radiologist intend to do. The problems begin to escalate for radiologists when these aspects of risk management are left to the doctor who has asked for the diagnostic or therapeutic procedures.

There is now, perhaps more than ever, the necessity for the constant training and monitoring of employees. They may play critical roles in the calibration of machines and shielding of patients to protect from injury.

Reporting of results of studies take on an ever-increasing urgency. Support of the emergency department of the institution is a must. Overreads of x-rays done in satellite areas like the emergency department must be done in a timely manner and a fail-safe system of dealing with differences in interpretation of studies must be in place. The critical piece of this system is the identification of the person, or persons, who is responsible for communicating with the patient in whom interpretations may differ between the satellite area and the radiology department. Where this is not spelled out in policy, confusion develops and patient injury can and does occur.

The communication between the technologist doing or participating in the diagnostic study and the radiologist is crucial. Then there comes the clear-cut responsibility for the radiologist to notify the attending physician of findings that may have critical implications for the patient no matter when, or under what conditions, the studies are done. This is particularly dangerous for the patient when the institution is likely to be short staffed, i.e., on Sundays and holidays.

As the radiologist becomes more and more a consultant in the true sense of that word, more claims occur involving the radiologist and systems must be developed with the primary intent of preventing patient injury.

62.   A MONUMENT TO FAILURE

Allegations—Negligence on all physicians and hospital
Physician Issues—Radiologist failure to notify attending of
    emergency condition; surgeon failure to acquire
    radiology report; technician failure to notify
    radiologist of severe pain on barium enema
Patient Issues—Wrongful death; pain and suffering
Outcome—Large six-figure settlement

CASE STUDY

A 60-year-old man who six years earlier had had a diagnosis made of diverticulitis had been asymptomatic for five years and had been active and healthy until the present illness began three days earlier. On admission, he complained of increasingly severe cramping abdominal pain. On two occasions during the past few months he had noticed a small amount of bright blood following bowel movements. He attributed the blood to "hemorrhoids" and did not consult his physician. Since the cramping abdominal pain began, he had not had a bowel movement.

On physical examination the patient was found to have some generalized abdominal tenderness. The bowel sounds were "normal to hyperactive." A plain film of the abdomen revealed slight gaseous distension of the colon. A barium enema was ordered, with preparation by soap suds enema. After multiple attempts, the colon was thought to be clean enough for a satisfactory barium study.

It was about 4:00 PM Thursday when the barium enema was begun. While a technician was administering the barium, the patient complained of a brief episode of severe abdominal pain, but the enema and fluoroscopy continued and multiple films were made. On expelling the enema, some bright bleeding occurred, which was reported to the technician.

The radiologist dictated the findings late in the day. The following day the report, which showed a "constricting lesion in the mid-sigmoid," was transcribed. The report added that "a small amount of barium is seen outside the lumen of the bowel." Neither the pain during the enema nor the bleeding that followed were made a part of the report, which was delivered to the patient's chart at 3:00 PM on Friday.

The surgeon went to the x-ray department after finishing in the operating room and before he made rounds on Friday evening. He looked at his patient's films and agreed with the diagnosis of a lesion in the sigmoid colon. He either did not see or did not recognize the extravasation of barium.

The patient developed some fever early on Saturday morning, with leukocytosis, increasing abdominal distension, and pain with generalized tenderness. A ruptured bowel was suspected, and full antibiotic coverage was ordered at that time. No bowel sounds could be heard, and by midday on Saturday the patient had fever of 103°F. He had been receiving nothing by mouth (NPO) and had had nasal gastric suction since admission. All findings suggested peritonitis secondary to perforation of the bowel. Monday morning CT of the abdomen revealed fluid accumulation in the peritoneal cavity and despite the compromised condition of the patient, surgery was done consisting of a left colectomy and colostomy. The surgeon considered that "due to the peritonitis" time should not be taken to reestablish continuity of the bowel, as there was extreme peritoneal contamination with purulent material in the pelvic area. Multiple drains were used in an attempt to provide drainage and prevent further abscess formation.

The patient's condition rapidly deteriorated. Fever continued and two additional attempts were made to drain the peritoneal abscesses. Sepsis was present and even with culture-specific antibiotics, the patient died on the fifth postoperative day.

Six months later the surgeon, the radiologist, the x-ray technician, and the hospital were sued. Ultimately, a large settlement was required, with all the defendants contributing equally.

Loss Prevention Comments

The x-ray technician who knew of the severe pain during the administration of the barium enema and the bleeding that followed made no written report.

The radiologist who saw the extravasation of barium made no special effort to inform the surgeon, even though this is a true medical and surgical emergency. The surgeon read the films himself, but did not see the extravasation, which ultimately killed the patient.

Although the surgeon had done a good job of securing and documenting informed consent, he was not attentive to the spouse, who after the initial grief of her husband's death became very angry at all concerned. When she learned of the perforation of the colon, the delayed x-ray report, etc., she filed her lawsuit.

The hospital was charged with negligence in the delay of getting the report of the radiologist transcribed and on the chart. Every error made in the care of this patient was critical to his treatment. All the errors converged on our patient and his death became a monument to our failure.

63.   DON'T TAKE OFF WITH YOUR TANKS HALF FULL

Allegations—Failure to complete x-ray examination; delay in diagnosis of cord compression secondary to fracture T12
Physician Issues—Multiple injuries; failure to assess T12 fracture with additional studies; delay in diagnosis
Patient Issues—Cord compression; neurological damage leg
Outcome—Modest six-figure settlement

CASE STUDY

A 42-year-old man was seen in the emergency room after being injured by a heavy falling object. He was fully conscious upon admission, complaining of injury to his left ankle with pain and swelling. He additionally complained of back and left lateral chest pain. He had no respiratory difficulties. Examination revealed a badly displaced left ankle, which x-rays showed to be due to a badly displaced bimalleolor fracture. X-rays of the spine showed a compression fracture of the 12th dorsal vertebra, and x-rays of the chest showed a fracture of the sixth left rib, undisplaced.

The patient was transferred to the intensive care unit overnight for observation and stabilization of his condition. The following morning, with his vital signs stable and his condition good, he was taken to surgery where an open reduction of the left ankle was done. His postoperative course was uneventful. Bed rest was ordered until his back pain subsided. He was then placed in a back brace, and ambulation was permitted with the aid of a walker. He did well and was discharged on the seventh postoperative day.

Eleven days later he was seen in the office. X-rays of the ankle showed good reduction, and x-rays of the lumbar spine showed compression fracture at D-12 unchanged. The patient complained of lack of improvement in his back discomfort. Neurological consultation was immediately obtained, but the patient failed to keep that appointment and returned to the attending physician's office one month later. The ankle was healed. He was advised to continue to wear the brace, and physical therapy was begun.

He was seen for two additional office visits at one-month intervals. He continued to complain of back pain, and an increase in exercise was recommended. The next office visit six weeks later indicated continued back pain with the development of numbness in the left leg. Referral to a neurosurgeon was obtained and the patient kept this appointment. The neurosurgeon recommended hospitalization for further evaluation. A CT scan and myelogram revealed a 50 percent compression fracture with impingement on the spinal cord. An anterior decompression of the spinal fracture was done. Suit was filed alleging that insufficient x-rays and examinations were made to properly diagnose and treat his initial spinal injury.

LOSS PREVENTION COMMENTS

Diagnostic studies done under emergency conditions frequently are lacking in completeness and/or quality to the extent that precise determination of the degree of the injury is not possible. With this in mind, both the radiologist and the attending physician should develop systems to alert each other and themselves of further studies needed prior to a final diagnosis and treatment plan.

In this case, there was no record of any spinal x-ray films except the anterior/posterior exposure. Without at least a lateral view of the spine no good estimate of the possibility or probability of the cord compression on weight bearing could be made. Apparently the radiologist, on seeing the D-12 fracture on the anterior/posterior view, did not indicate that a lateral view would be necessary for correct assessment of the injury, nor did the attending physician indicate that a lateral film should be obtained when the patient's condition stabilized. The emergency room record and the admitting progress note should contain mention of further studies indicated. With such a system in place, significant patient injury could probably have been avoided, as well as the resulting malpractice suit against the attending physician.

The system failure illustrated in this case is analogous to the airline pilot who takes off with half enough fuel to take the plane to its destination. Doctor, look at the "gauges" to determine whether or not your studies are complete enough to get your patient to the "destination" of "reasonable" diagnostic and therapeutic efforts on your part.

64.   ONGOING SUPERVISION OF STAFF—A NECESSITY

Allegations—Failure of calibration of radiation therapy
          machine
Physician Issue—Quadriplegia secondary to transverse
          myelitis
Patient Issue—Paralysis lower extremities
Outcome—Large six-figure settlement

CASE STUDY

A 58-year-old woman had a modified radical right mastectomy
eight years before because of breast cancer. She had been treated
according to the standard protocol and following the surgery had
chemotherapy and radiation. The patient had done so well
postoperatively that after the five years of careful follow-up, her
physician elected to see her annually.

At the eight-year annual checkup, the patient complained of a
rather severe pain in the upper back and chest, which had begun only
two or three weeks before. A physical examination did not reveal any
significant abnormality. The mastectomy scar was examined
thoroughly, and a chest x-ray showed no evidence of lung pathology.
Some symptomatic treatment was prescribed and the patient was
asked to return within a month if the pain continued.

The patient's pain became worse and she did not wait a
month to return but returned to her primary care physician within
two weeks. At that point the patient was sent to the operating
surgeon for further evaluation.

Again, the physical examination showed no significant
findings. The examination included a very thorough evaluation of the
chest wall and axilla. Again, a routine chest x-ray was unremarkable.
Because the patient's pain had gotten worse in the two weeks that
intervened between her visit to her primary care physician and the
appointment with her surgeon, a CT scan and a bone scan were
ordered. Both showed evidence of metastatic disease in the upper
thoracic spine and the right clavicle.

The patient was having no neurologic symptoms except for
the local pain. It was elected to treat her with chemotherapy initially,
to be followed by radiation. She had a course of chemotherapy, to
which she responded clinically with a marked reduction in pain, and
the radiation therapy was to follow at an appropriate time after the
completion of chemotherapy.

The lesions were evaluated, and the radiation protocol was
established. The patient was to return at stated intervals until she had

completed the radiation protocol. She completed the treatments in the scheduled amount of time.

Three weeks after completing the therapy she began to complain of some numbness and weakness in her lower extremities. This rapidly progressed to involve the upper extremities, and she soon became a quadriplegic with only minimal function of the upper extremities; a diagnosis of transverse myelitis secondary to radiation was made.

LOSS PREVENTION COMMENTS

In reviewing the entire protocol for treatment, it was found that shielding had been inappropriate in the actual delivery of radiation to the prescribed sites on this patient's body. The inappropriate shielding had been used with every treatment and was believed by all involved in the case, including the attending physician, to be the cause of the patient's disease. A six-figure settlement was negotiated.

Catastrophes of this type do not occur often, but they do occur, and when they do they most often are due to a tragic mistake. There have been cases where the programming of the therapy unit has been at fault and even though the appropriate dosage had been entered into the machine, due to the programming error inherent in the computer of the unit the patient received much more radiation than had been intended. This did not appear to be the problem in this case.

There have been cases where the supervision of the technical people involved with actually delivering the treatment has been at fault. Instructions that were less than precise and the failure to monitor what the technician was doing with each treatment have been faulty. This was probably the error in this case.

Calibration of the machine has been a problem in some previous cases, but in this case that was not suspected. Here we have a situation where everybody involved admitted that inappropriate shielding had been used. The reason was not that there was a lack of awareness of the type of shielding that was appropriate, but simply that those responsible for setting up for the treatments did not attend to their responsibilities adequately.

You may say that this kind of tragic error will occur despite all our efforts to prevent them. Perhaps that is true. However, if this happens to one of your patients, the pain of high malpractice insurance premiums will be the least pain you will endure. The much greater pain will be the memory of the damaged patient.

Had this case gone to the jury, it was feared that the degree of negligence perceived by them, which was a part of the charges, might have led to the awarding of punitive damages.

To repeat, when one is involved in delivering this type of therapy, there simply must be a precise calibration of the machine to be used, the appropriate programming of the prescribed dosage and time into the unit, and the close supervision of technical people. The last of those appears to have produced this very tragic injury.

65. EXPECT THE BEST—PREPARE FOR THE WORST

Allegations—Negligence in treatment of contrast media reaction
Physician Issues—Radiologist not prepared to treat emergency; resident handed responsibility off to emergency physician; ER physician delay in giving IV medication
Patient Issue—Anaphylactic death
Outcome—Large six-figure settlement

CASE STUDY

A 20-year-old female college student reported to the emergency room with a history of pain in the left CV angle for 36 hours; she denied dysuria or hematuria. She was afebrile and normotensive, and a complete physical examination revealed no positive findings except for right CV angle tenderness to light percussion. There was no history of allergy.

Urinalysis revealed 10 to 20 WBCs, RBCs too numerous to count, with bacteria. No culture was done. A KUB film showed some calcification overlying the left kidney, which did not have the appearance of calculi.

The patient required narcotics to relieve her pain. She was given some analgesics and advised to see her private physician or the campus doctor in the morning. She was advised to return to the ER if her pain returned.

Five days after the above visit, the patient again came to the ER where the attending physician, a first-year surgical resident, obtained a history of pain in the left flank and left lower quadrant abdominal pain. There were no other symptoms and the patient was having a normal menstrual period. The physical examination, including a pelvic examination, was entirely within normal limits. An IVP was ordered.

The physician explained the procedure, including the possibility of a reaction to the contrast medium. The chart contains the note, "Allergic reactions explained, patient understands."

The following are "post-event notes":

- *12:40—CM (contrast media) IV—Reacted—Radiologist saw patient—Resident paged—Resident arrived—Couldn't make diagnosis—Called ER MD—Radiologist left room after resident arrived—ER MD directed patient be moved back to ER—Grand Mal seizure 1-2 minutes after CM injection. Patient immediately resuscitated.*
- *1:07—IV med—steroids—other IV meds given.*
- *1:58—Oral intubation—Pressors (Dopamine).*
- *2:10—BP 80/0 (palpation).*
- *3:30—Awake—Complaining of abd pain—Nodding appropriately to questions.*

In Critical Care Unit—
- *3:30—Progress Note (M4 student)—ER—1-5 min into CM IV—GM seizure lasting 3 min—Skin became mottled—Petechiae over lower extremities—Began to lose consciousness—Pink froth noted orally—Anesthesia succeeded in intubating the patient after several attempts—Larynx could not be visualized secondary to fluid—Initial ABG—pH 6.88—CO_2 58—O_2 55.3—Transferred to ICU BP 90/50—On ventilator.*

  DIC leading to death about 10 hours after receiving contrast medium.

Autopsy—Diagnosis: (1) Left ureterolithiasis; (2) Venous angioma— right parietal lobe of brain.

The autopsy report included a very scholarly report on contrast media reactions, pointing out: (1) 20 percent to 30 percent are anaphylactoid in type; (2) Fatal in 1/11,000 cases; (3) Anaphylactoid reactions=IgE mediated sensitivity (urticaria, angioedema, pruritus, bronchospasm, and shock); (4) Most seizures are during the injection of the contrast media or within 10 min; (5) Idiosyncratic reactions are not dose-related; (6) A disproportionate number of reactions occur in the 3rd and 4th decades; (7) Decrease in peripheral vascular resistance—Hypotension—Tachycardia— Dysrhythmias; (8) Respiratory distress is the initial symptom in about 20 percent of the cases.

This case ended with a very large settlement involving all parties. Contributions to the settlement were made by the radiologist, the ER physician, the resident, and the hospital.

Loss Prevention Comments

Many times in the development of a lawsuit against a physician it becomes apparent that even if all the grievous acts cited in the complaint were true, those acts had little or no effect on the outcome. In other words, the acts cited in the complaint were not the cause of the outcome. Lawyers would refer to this as not related to causation. In all probability, in this case nothing could have been done to change the result, but settlement was necessary because of the obvious fact that the activity that followed the seizure demonstrated that the treatment team was unprepared, disorganized, and confused. It appeared that there was no logical response from the physicians involved. The radiologist was not prepared to assume the primary responsibility even in the short time that it took to get help. The baton was passed again from the resident to the ER physician. The area was not prepared to deal with this occurrence even though it is here in the radiology department that these reactions occur. The patient had to be moved to the ER. The anesthesiologist called to intubate the patient had trouble doing so.

There was at least a 20-minute lapse in time before steroids were given. The adequacy of fluid replacement must be questioned as well as the ventilatory treatment on the basis of the ABG that was initially reported.

Although the prognosis for a patient who has a true anaphylactic reaction to contrast media is dismal, some of the victims survive. Survival certainly depends to a great extent, however, on preparation, recognition, and response. Expect the best, but prepare for the worst. That is the way we must approach our patient care.

66.   A DEFENSIBLE CASE MADE INDEFENSIBLE

Allegations—Negligence in failing to clear C-spine; radiologist
negligence in ailing to consult; attending negligence
in failing to admit for observation; attending
Physician Issue—Jousting (each blaming the other)
Patient Issues—Neurological deficit; quadriplegia
Outcome—Large six-figure settlement

CASE STUDY

A 17-year-old boy who had been autistic since birth and who had a lifelong history of seizures that proved very difficult to control had been followed all his life by the same physician, with frequent help from a neurologist who had also been involved with the patient for a long time. Even with maintenance anti-seizure medication using combination therapy, seizure activity occasionally required IV sedation to interrupt the attack.

During an unwitnessed seizure, the patient apparently fell and was in considerable pain. The emergency medical service was notified and on the initial evaluation before transport found reflexes in the extremities to be "positive," but the patient would grimace and moan when moved. He was therefore transported on a backboard with a cervical collar and a chin immobilizer. He was seen in the emergency department by his regular primary care physician who, after a difficult evaluation, concluded that there were no apparent focal neurologic deficits but that there was evidence of significant and unlocalized discomfort in the patient's neck.

X-rays of the spine were ordered, and both lumbar and cervical films were viewed by the radiologist and the attending physician. The radiologist reported that the films were negative. The mother was given extensive instructions on the care of her son and advised to return to the ED or to the physician's office for re-evaluation at any time. The attending physician did document in his office record that he received a phone call from the mother two hours after the patient's discharge from the ED informing him that the patient had had two seizures before leaving the ED and three more after arriving home. Again, the mother was advised to bring the patient in for re-evaluation, but she declined because she could see no change in her son's condition after the seizures. It is important to note that the mother had taken care of this patient for his entire life and consequently must have become accustomed to all kinds of unexpected behavior.

The following morning, on routine review of the films taken at night in the ED, the senior radiologist reported that the films were non-diagnostic because there was no visualization of C7 on any of the views. Before this report could be acted upon by the attending physician, the patient was brought to the ED about noon, unable to move his lower extremities, and having not urinated since the last seizure the night before. The presumptive diagnosis at this point was spinal cord injury, and the patient was transferred to the care of a neurosurgeon in the medical center.

On CT scanning of the neck no fracture was seen, but there was a "2-mm" forward subluxation of C7 on T1. An emergency exploration of this area with a posterior spinal fusion was done, and after a prolonged and complicated hospitalization the patient was transferred to a long-term care facility because continued care at home was not possible.

Because of the very serious injury and the devastating neurologic deficit, a multi-million dollar lawsuit was filed, charging both the attending physician and the radiologist with negligence in "carelessly" failing to clear the cervical spine and "carelessly" failing to get appropriate consultations. The attending physician was charged with "carelessly" failing to admit the patient to the hospital for observation and appropriate monitoring during the night.

LOSS PREVENTION COMMENTS

Failure to adequately evaluate the cervical spine after trauma of any kind is one of those claims almost automatically considered medical malpractice when a less-than-desirable outcome follows; in addition, spinal cord injuries that result in a significant neurologic deficit are among the most expensive. Lifelong care is necessitated by the deficit and usually must be carried out in a long-term facility of some kind, with the participation of various paramedical disciplines.

Although there were obvious problems in defending this suit, e.g., the failure to get x-ray views of the entire cervical spine, there were circumstances that should have mitigated the damages to some degree. The seizures, which were in all probability responsible to a certain degree for the neurologic damage, were not the fault of the physicians involved. The mother's failure to avail herself of the offered re-evaluation after the postdischarge seizures occurred was not the fault of the physicians. The attending physician had given the mother good detailed instructions in the care of the patient and had described in detail the signs to look for that would indicate the need for re-evaluation. There was the prompt review of the films in the radiology department, which had discovered the error. Much time and compassionate concern had been invested by the attending physician in the evaluation of his patient. Nobody is perfect! This is generally understood by a jury when this kind of prompt discovery of the error is in evidence.

One thing in this case, however, made the dangers of trial too great to consider. The physicians blamed each other for the outcome. This injury was serious, the evaluation of the injury was less than perfect, there was great sympathy for this unfortunate patient and his mother, and the monetary damages were calculated to be in seven figures. Nonetheless, not even all this made this case demand settlement. When physicians blame each other in such a situation, where each has some obvious responsibility, we lose everything we have going for us. The settlement required here was almost in the seven-figure range. The lessons? View all the vertebrae! Don't blame each other!

67.   TWICE THE DOCTORS—HALF THE CARE

Allegations—Negligence in failure to diagnose lesion of colon
Physician Issues—No clinical information on request for
        bariumenema; radiologist doing test not one
        reading/reporting on films
Patient Issue—Metastatic disease at time of study
Outcome—Jury awarded a large six-figure amount

CASE STUDY

A middle-aged woman was seen by her primary care physician with complaints of shortness of breath, weight loss of 10 lb in the past three months, and some vague pain in the right lower quadrant of her abdomen. Examination in her doctor's office revealed a rather profound anemia with a hemoglobin of 6.5 gm/dl and a PCV of 30 percent. She was referred to the radiology department of a hospital for outpatient upper GI series and a barium enema. Her physician planned an outpatient sigmoidoscopic examination after the x-ray studies.

The radiologist report indicated a 2-cm esophageal hiatal hernia on upper GI and "no constricting, inflammatory, or neoplastic changes evident" on the barium enema. The sigmoidoscopy was never done.

Two months later, after conservative treatment with diet, antacids, and antispasmodics, the anemia was not improved. Bone marrow showed "changes reflective of an acute to subacute reactive process." The patient's complaints continued two more months. An ultrasound study was done, revealing a 2-cm solid mass in the liver. Review of the barium enema revealed an overlooked lesion in the cecum, and two consecutive stool examinations showed occult blood.

Admission to the hospital was followed by a colonoscopic examination, which revealed a space occupying lesion in the cecum that proved on biopsy to be adenocarcinoma. Right colectomy was done and multiple liver nodules were found. The patient died about one month later.

Litigation in this case resulted in a sizable loss due to negligence on the part of the radiologist.

At first glance, this case shows a less than adequate work-up by the primary care physician. The history and the anemia would cry out for early stool studies for blood and the strong suspicion of large bowel pathology. But the primary care physician was not sued, so the case was processed in order to defend the radiologist and his corporation.

In the subsequent investigation two findings made defense almost impossible: First, the radiologist was given no clinical information on the request for x-ray studies, nor did he take any history prior to his studies. Second, the radiologist of record dictated the report of the barium enema, but the actual procedure had been done by a partner who had made notes on his findings.

Loss Prevention Comments

About 40 percent of paid claims on SVMIC radiologists result from misread x-rays. Would that figure be reduced by the requirement of pertinent clinical information on the request for studies? We believe it would. Would that figure be reduced by the radiologist who does the procedure taking a brief clinical history of his own? We believe it would. Should a radiologist dictate and sign the report of a procedure done by a partner? We believe he should not.

In this particular case, the primary care physician was spared because he was not sued. The team taking care of a patient must work together to prevent patient injury if medical malpractice losses are to be avoided in the present medicolegal environment.

VIII

General Medicine

The areas of medical practice encompassed by this broad name include Internal Medicine, Family Practice, and General Practice. The majority of patient encounters occur in the offices of physicians who are designated as one of the above. Consequently, the majority of chances for patient anger and dissatisfaction occur here. It has already been stated that the number of claims coming out of these practices was in the minority two decades ago. In the last decade, however, the number of claims in these areas has increased to the point that now the ratio between the proceduralist and the non-proceduralist claims is approaching one to one.

There are problems that stand out as the principal causes of claim and lawsuits against these so called "cognitive" physicians. Perhaps the most frequently encountered situation is patient injury that results from the failure of systems in the doctor's practice to assure that the ordering physician receives the report of studies done outside the office, initials these reports as having been read, and takes some action with regard to the patient. Patients believe that if the study is important enough to do it is important enough for them to be informed as to the results. At a minimum, the failure to do so produces anger directed at the practice and at worst, results in injury to the patient coming out of the delay in diagnosis and or treatment of a condition revealed by the report. Lost or misplaced mammography reports have been prominent in this setting. Defense of the doctor is almost impossible when this occurs.

Another "system failure" that figures prominently in the losses suffered by these physicians is the system to assure coverage of one's patients on days off, vacation, etc. The legal term applied to cases of this type is *abandonment*. Even in well run group practices, it does occur that an associate will not be available and there is confusion as to where the coverage responsibilities fall. "Who really is my doctor?" is the frequently asked or implied question.

A particular hazard occurs when more than one physician is involved in the diagnosis and treatment of a patient. Unless otherwise specified, the primary care internist, family physician, or general practitioner is considered the "quarterback" or coordinator of care rendered in this setting. It is essential that he or she take this responsibility seriously and play this role inpatient care. Often this involves regular encounters with the family who expect to be informed on a regular basis. This is a heavy responsibility and one associated with significant liability when not understood or acted upon.

Practitioners in these areas are doing more and more "procedures" that require the standard informed consent process. This kind of process may be needed with the use of drugs that have particular potential toxicity. Here the patient needs to know about the need to follow certain developments during the use of the drug, i.e., skin rashes, nausea, laboratory surveillance, etc. More and more drugs are in use that have the potential of doing significant harm and the patient must know how to assist the physician in avoiding damage from the medicine prescribed.

Communication skills are required in these practices perhaps more than in any others. Eye contact, listening, manifesting interest in the patient as a person, and, perhaps above all, the communication of the doctor's presence at critical times in the course of the disease process are expected and, if not apparent, can be the source of resentment and anger. Patients come to the physician with a need and consequently expect him to be committed to the meeting of that need. The best informed consent is the constant engagement of the patient during the process of the history taking, physical examination, laboratory testing, decision making as to diagnosis, treatment, and follow-up. Patients usually expect the physician to be a friend. Our obligation is to fill that expectation. In general, one does not sue a friend!

68.   SYSTEM FAILURE

Allegations—Failure to diagnose lung cancer
Physician Issues—Report in office not read—no follow-up;
    noncompliant patient
Patient Issues—Not notified of report; died of Ca lung with
    metastasis to brain
Outcome—Modest six-figure settlement

CASE STUDY

During Mr. Jones' first visit to a physician in approximately ten years, he gave a history of having been a two-pack-per-day smoker for "several" years and he did have a little "smoker's" cough. Three days prior to this visit he had noticed a small amount of blood in his sputum. Dr. Smith, a board certified family physician, told Mr. Jones he felt hospitalization was indicated for a thorough work-up of his complaints. Jones, very hesitant about hospitalization, agreed to a "short" stay in the hospital for, the tests.

During the course of the work-up, his chest x-ray showed some enlarged hilar lymph nodes and was suggestive of a "little pneumonia." When further radiological examination showed what was believed to be granulomatous disease, several sputum specimens were obtained for AFB and cytologic examinations. The patient was discharged from the hospital before all reports were returned to the chart, so he was told to return to Dr. Smith's office in two weeks for follow-up.

Shortly after the patient's discharge, copies of his x-ray and sputum cytology reports were delivered to Dr. Smith's office. One of the cytology reports indicated "clusters of cells suspicious for squamous-cell carcinoma." Dr. Smith briefly examined the report and made a "mental note" to follow up on this finding when the patient returned. The patient did not, however, keep his follow-up appointment.

Mr. Jones did return to Dr. Smith about six months later with fever, aching, and persistent cough. Influenza was diagnosed and appropriate treatment recommended. Dr. Smith did not notice the suspicious sputum cytology report. The patient never returned.

Dr. Smith later discovered that the patient had subsequently died of carcinoma of the lung after seeking treatment from another physician, who diagnosed lung carcinoma with metastasis to the brain.

LOSS PREVENTION COMMENTS

At least 40 percent of medical malpractice losses represent "system" failure. We set up some system to follow up on laboratory reports of this kind and the system fails; a critical report is lost in the shuffle and the treating physician finds himself in an almost indefensible legal position. This patient's care was excellent. His physician ordered appropriate tests and obviously was right on the mark as far as his work-up was concerned.

How can we avoid this type of system failure? First, there must be a procedure for handling all reports coming into the office from outside sources, i.e., hospitals, reference laboratories, pathologists, and consultants of all kinds. This system should recognize that the report of the laboratory work to the patient is a must. This can usually be handled by a phone call documented in the patient's records.

However, when phone contact cannot be made, a registered letter, return receipt requested, should be sent to the last address of the patient.

In this case, an appointment was given when the patient left the hospital, but the patient did not keep the appointment. Neither this appointment nor the missed office visit was documented in the patient's office record. No real proof of the appointment existed, so the discharge order to return to the office on a certain date was the only evidence that this appointment was made.

The consequences of a suspected positive cytology on the sputum specimen are so significant that courts have held that the treating physician must use all reasonable means to notify the patient. Check the system you have for handling incoming laboratory reports, documenting appointments given on discharge from hospital, and documenting missed appointments on the patient's record. In this case a lot of grief, time, and money could have been saved with attention to this kind of detail.

69.   IF ONLY I HAD SEEN HIM

Allegations—Failure to diagnose medication reaction
Physician Issue—Did not respond to repeated phone calls
Patient Issue—Severe toxic epidermal necrolysis secondary to
   medication
Outcome—Modest six-figure settlement

CASE STUDY

A 30-year-old father of two went to his board certified family practitioner complaining of tenderness in his right testicle along with some generalized nonspecific aching and soreness in the lower pelvis and rectum. He also stated he had noticed some blood in his urine for the last couple of days.

Examination by his physician revealed the testicle and epididymis to be normal in size and nontender. The prostate gland was found to be normal in size and neither hot nor swollen, but there was a "little tenderness" noted in the region of the right seminal vesicle. Based on this examination, a diagnosis of mild prostatitis with epididymitis was made and the patient was given carbenicillin (Geocillin), one capsule four times per day, pending results of a urine culture and sensitivity and urinalysis.

The urine culture reported later that day grew out a moderate amount of *Staphylococcus epidermidis* that was resistant to tetracycline and ampicillin. The urinalysis was apparently either not done or the doctor was not notified of the results.

When the patient returned following a 12-day course of carbenicillin therapy, examination in the office revealed the prostatitis to be "clearing fairly well," but there was still mild to moderate soreness in the region of the prostate and right seminal vesicle. In addition, the patient complained of excessive flatus and mild diarrhea. This was believed due to the carbenicillin, so the medication was changed to trimethoprim/sulfamethoxazole, one tablet twice a day for six weeks. The patient was instructed to call if he felt he was not improving.

Two weeks later the patient was seen complaining of vague abdominal pain in the right lower quadrant over the internal inguinal ring. Coughing or straining increased the pain, which would radiate into the right testicle. The patient also complained of low back pain and occasional urgency, but no dysuria. He further stated that he continued to have intermittent hematuria. The patient says he also complained of some itching and flaking of the skin on his calves although that complaint was not documented. Following these subjective complaints, a diagnosis of possible right inguinal hernia with continued prostatitis was made, and the patient was referred to a general surgeon for evaluation of his possible inguinal hernia.

Later that same day, the patient says he telephoned his physician several times with complaints of itchy watery eyes, nasal congestion, and blisters forming inside his mouth, but he was told that due to the heavy afternoon schedule the doctor could not see him until the next morning.

During the night the patient awoke coughing up blood and went to the emergency room of the local community hospital, where examination revealed a severe conjunctival infection with a yellowish discharge and confluent errosive lesions on the buccal and pharyngeal mucosa, some of which were hemorrhagic. There was a papular confluent rash over the internal surfaces of both upper thighs. The patient was immediately admitted to the hospital from the emergency room.

On the day after admission, the patient developed a generalized papular rash, and vesicles began to form over the papules. By the third hospital day, the rash was generalized and urologic consultation was obtained for a bulla that almost totally covered the patient's penis, obstructing the urethra. After this was debrided the patient was able to void. An ophthalmologic consultation was obtained because of continuous discharge from the eyes and marked photophobia; finally, a dermatologic consultation was obtained and the patient was diagnosed

as having toxic epidermal necrolysis, probably due to trimetho-
prim/sulfamethoxazole therapy.

When no improvement followed very aggressive therapy, the
patient was transferred to a university burn center for treatment of his
skin lesions, which were equivalent to second degree burns over 95
percent of his body surface. This hospitalization was of six weeks'
duration, and the medical expenses were massive.

The patient did recover, but he sustained extensive scarring,
leaving him permanently disfigured.

Loss Prevention Comments

This board certified family physician managed his patient as
many family physicians and/or urologists might have done, illustrating
again very clearly that when a bad result occurs, the entire management of a case is called into question. The initial urinalysis was
never reported, and the complaints of hematuria on more than one
occasion were never systematically investigated. It is difficult to
support the use of antibiotics in this case from the beginning. The
doctor did not document his telephone calls from the patient and
thus was unable to support his memory from his records regarding
this matter.

The extremely severe reaction to the trimethoprim/sulfa-
methoxazole combination emphasizes need for discussion between
the physician and the patient as to the possible complications from
medication.

The plaintiff's expert witness testified that the doctor was
below the standard of care in (1) failing to examine prostatic fluid, (2)
failing to diagnose the specific type of prostatitis, (3) failing to follow
up on the urinalysis, (4) negligently ordering trimethoprim/sulfa-
methoxazole after the culture grew what was probably a contaminant,
(5) failing to warn the patient of the risks of the chemotherapeutic
agent used, (6) failing to recognize the early symptoms of an allergic
reaction, and (7) failing to react to telephone calls indicating a
potentially serious problem.

There is little question that the physician's failure to see this
patient and personally involve himself in what the patient considered
a serious complication was the reason for this action having been
brought in the first place.

70.   RESPONSIBILITIES OF PRESCRIBING

Allegations—Contributing to addiction; failure to consult

Physician Issues—Refilling medication without examination;
  continuing psychotropic drugs without consultant
  support
Patient Issue—Noncompliant about return visits
Outcome—Modest six-figure settlement

CASE STUDY

A 28-year-old man was brought to the emergency room after fainting at home. In the emergency room, he was examined by a family physician, who found him alert, well oriented, and without obvious neurologic problems. A faint systolic murmur sounded like a click.

The patient was admitted to the hospital, where a cardiologist confirmed the suspected diagnosis of mitral valve prolapse. Associated with the characteristic heart sounds there was a disturbing sinus tachycardia with frequent supraventricular extrasystoles which completely cleared with small doses of propranolol.

Subsequent to the diagnosis of his heart condition and beginning of treatment, the patient developed a rather marked cardiac neurosis and stated that his fears had made him so nervous that he could not adequately perform his duties at work and that his job was threatened. His family physician believed he was dealing with a situational depression and described diazepam and amitriptyline.

When the patient returned for a follow-up visit in two weeks, he was found to be greatly improved. He was productive at work and appeared to be making a good recovery from the depression. His treatment was continued, and he was instructed to make an appointment to be seen in one month. The appointment was made, but not kept. The patient called his physician saying that he "never felt better" and requested a refill on his medication. The prescriptions were refilled by phone and the patient made an appointment for an examination in one month. Neither the phone call from the patient, the missed appointment, nor the prescription refill were recorded in the record.

This same pattern was repeated two more times, with the medication being refilled by phone request. Each time the physician would urge his patient to come in for an examination, and each time the patient promised that he would, but didn't. No notations were made in the record documenting these facts.

It had been over three months since the patient had been seen by his physician, when he called stating that his mother had died suddenly and requested temporary increase in his dosage of diazepam. The doctor complied but made the patient promise to come to see him as soon as he got back in town.

About five days later the patient was seen again in the emergency room, this time deeply comatose from an overdose of diazepam and amitriptyline. The overdose was successfully treated, but a lengthy hospitalization for drug dependency ensued and the patient filed a lawsuit charging his physician with contributing to his drug addiction.

LOSS PREVENTION COMMENTS

The plaintiff established by expert testimony that (1) the family physician was below the standard of care in continuing to treat a depressed patient without psychiatric consultation and that (2) the family physician was below the standard of care in continuing to prescribe the diazepam and amitriptyline without examining the patient.

The defendant physician had no documentation of the phone calls from his patient, the instructions to come in for examination, or the patient's repeated promises to do so. The patient denied that he was instructed to return for examination or that he promised he would. A sizable settlement of this claim was necessary.

Once again it was clear that when a swearing contest develops between a physician and his patient, unless there is documentation in the patient's record to support the contentions of the doctor, he cannot ordinarily be successfully defended.

71.   NOT HIM AGAIN!

Allegations—Delay in diagnosis of C-spine injury
Physician Issues—Undesirable patient (alcoholic); frequent
*   falls with minor injuries; lack of prompt x-ray services*
Patient Issue—Permanent neurological damage
Outcome—Large six-figure settlement

CASE STUDY

A 76-year-old man who had a history of alcohol abuse had been seen three times in the past six months following minor injuries from falling. On each occasion he had been treated by his family doctor in the emergency room and released to his family.

On June 7 the same patient was brought to the physician's office following an injury sustained when he fell down the steps in his home. His son gave the history that his father had "drunk too much whiskey." The injured man complained of pain in his anterior right chest, his low back, and his neck. The assessment in the office documented the pain and "a strong odor of ETOH on his breath." The blood pressure was 160/92 mm Hg, pulse 90/min, and respirations 14/min; on deep breathing he complained of the sharp pain in his anterior right chest, which limited the depth of respirations. The physician's note further recorded orders for x-rays of the chest, low back, and neck, for which the patient was sent in the company of his son to the hospital x-ray department.

In this community hospital, the radiologist was present only on Tuesdays and Thursdays, so that, since the injury occurred on Friday, the films were made and sent in their hospital x-ray jacket to the physician's office. The doctor looked at the films and saw no abnormality of the chest or back. He made no note on his office records about the films of the neck, however, and later stated he had no recollection of having seen them. He did not deny that the films were in the jacket but only that he had no recollection of having seen the x-rays of the cervical spine. There was no recorded examination, but the record contained notes of "no abnormality" regarding the chest and the x-rays of the back. Some Tylenol No. 3 was prescribed for pain and the patient was sent home with his son. There was no recorded instruction to return.

Two days later, June 9, the man was brought to the hospital emergency room still complaining of pain in his neck, and approximately two hours earlier he had begun to experience some difficulty moving the arms and legs. The emergency room nurse notes stated "unable to move arms or legs." The patient was referred to the medical center, where the paralysis was confirmed and skeletal traction was begun. He was admitted to the neurological ICU, where his condition worsened and he died from a cardiorespiratory arrest two days later. Ironically the patient died the same day the radiologist returned to the hospital, read the films, and dictated the report. He correctly reported a fracture of C6 with a subluxation of C5 on C6 that measured slightly over 5 mm.

The suit that was filed against the physician and the hospital charged negligence in the failure to make a timely diagnosis of the fracture and subluxation of C5 on C6 and to begin appropriate treatment. A large settlement was necessary by both the hospital and the physician.

LOSS PREVENTION COMMENTS

To be called upon repeatedly to attend to a patient for alcohol abuse is extremely frustrating, and it is very easy to become so resentful toward a patient of this kind that the fundamentals of good patient care are forgotten. The case presented could have developed because of these complex and powerful emotions. This was the fourth time in six months that the physician had been called upon to interrupt his care of other patients to take care of the consequences of behavior that might have been avoided. The three previous episodes resulted in very minor injuries. This one was the same kind of episode, and probably the attitude of the physician on this fourth occasion was such that he was less than completely objective and thorough in his approach to the patient.

The physician had ordered x-ray films of the chest and the cervical and lumbar spine, but he recorded seeing only the chest and lumbar spine films. Omitting or ignoring the film on the cervical spine was certainly outside an acceptable standard of care.

What is the position of the hospital that offers diagnostic services to outpatients but only to the extent as outlined in the hospital's contract with the provider? Should not the medical staff insist on some system that would provide the more prompt reading and reporting on diagnostic x-rays? Had the radiologist seen the film on the day of the injury, he would certainly have called the physician and reported such a significant finding. Perhaps in such situations as this, courier service could be used to transport films daily to the specialist with reports dictated over the telephone.

1. Every patient, even the very distasteful one, deserves a careful and logical evaluation of his complaints.

2. Today's standards would require prompt reporting of diagnostic tests.

The physician and the hospital both failed in this case and tragedy occurred.

72.   DOCUMENTED SELF-DESTRUCTION

Allegations—Delay in diagnosing cancer; alteration of record; jousting

Physician Issues—Delay in consulting (disputed); jousting by surgical consultant; alteration of record (credibility of defendant destroyed)

Patient Issue—Delay in definitive treatment

Outcome—-Modest six-figure settlement

CASE STUDY

An extremely obese 42-year-old man had been seen a few times by his family physician but was not regarded as a "regular" patient. Because of pain in the right lower abdomen and groin, this patient visited his physician. The occasional bouts of pain were described as dull and aching in character and were aggravated by standing and walking. Occasionally the pain increased on coughing. He further complained of constipation for the last several weeks.

The patient was morbidly obese, being at least 100 lb overweight. Blood pressure was 160/102 mm Hg and his temperature was 99.2°F. Examination of the chest and heart was unremarkable. The abdominal examination was very unsatisfactory because of the obesity, but there appeared to be no real peritoneal irritation. Some tenderness was present on deep palpation over the right groin area. Blood counts that were done were within normal limits.

The physician suggested the possibility of a right inguinal hernia, but in the absence of more definite physical findings, he was hesitant to commit himself to this diagnosis. The chart read, "Impression: Possible right inguinal hernia. Treatment (1) Lose weight. (2) Donnatal AC&HS."

About eight weeks after the initial visit, the patient again returned complaining of lower abdominal and right groin pain. He had had one brief episode of cramping abdominal discomfort associated with diarrhea and lasting approximately 24 hours. Examination was unchanged. Vital signs were essentially as they had been on the original visit and treatment was again symptomatic.

Six months after the initial visit the patient returned. He had not lost weight but complained of gradual worsening of his right abdominal pain. He stated that on two occasions he had had bright blood in the stool. The abdominal examination was unchanged. Rectal examination revealed no abnormal findings except that feces on the examining glove was guaiac positive.

The following morning a rigid sigmoidoscopic examination was done by the attending physician. There had been relatively poor preparation, and the scope could not be advanced beyond 20 cm, at which point the examiner could see an irregularity of the mucosal pattern but felt insecure about attempting a biopsy.

The attending physician telephoned a local surgeon and arranged for consultation, sending a copy of his medical record to the consultant. After routine colon preparation, the consultant conducted a flexible sigmoidoscopic examination, identifying the lesion and securing a biopsy. The pathologist reported an adenocarcinoma of the colon and shortly thereafter a left colectomy was done. There was some serosal involvement by the lesion and some mesentaric nodes were positive.

Within three months of the surgery, a lawsuit was filed against the original physician charging negligence because of the delay in diagnosing cancer. The plaintiff submitted a statement from the operating surgeon giving an opinion that the attending physician was outside an acceptable standard of care, which caused the delay in the diagnosis. Events later indicated that statements by the consulting surgeon critical of the attending physician may have been the reason the patient decided to file a lawsuit in the first place.

In the routine investigation of the lawsuit, the consulting surgeon submitted his own medical records. A part of his record was the copy of the attending physician's record sent to him when the consultation was requested. Copies of the attending physician's record were also secured by the claims attorney. Later when the defense counsel was employed for the defendant physician, another copy of the attending physician's medical record was requested.

In comparing these copies of the defendant physician's medical record, the following alterations had been made:

• After the attending physician had copied his record for the consultant and before the copy had been made for the claims attorney, an alteration of the record had occurred which added after the brief notes on the physical examination, "rectal exam—negative." This had been sandwiched in between the physical examination and the prescribed treatment. The ink was the same, and it appeared that the attending physician was attempting to conceal the fact that an alteration had been made.

• Defense counsel's copy of the record showed an additional alteration. Following the orders, "Treatment: (1) a 1,000-calorie diet; (2) Donnatal," and again sandwiched in between (2) and the next chart entry was "(3) Return one week if not better." Again the ink, pen, and handwriting were the same, giving the appearance that there was an attempt to conceal the record change. A large settlement was required.

LOSS PREVENTION COMMENTS

The patient in this case was a morbidly obese, noncompliant patient. The attending physician testified that a rectal examination was actually done and the patient was actually told to return one week after the second visit if he was not improved. The attending physician contended that the record alterations were made to make the record more accurate. He denied any attempt to hide the record alterations.

The management of this patient had indeed been within an acceptable standard according to most physicians who reviewed this case. Prompt action was taken with the finding of blood in the stools, and it could certainly be argued that given the difficulties with examination in a patient of this type, a definitive diagnosis was made in good time.

All the good defense that could have been developed was of absolutely no account in view of the record change. The attending physician's credibility was so badly damaged by this fact that no defense was possible.

The surgeon's criticism of the attending physician was without question the one event that created such doubt in the mind of the patient and his family that the lawsuit became a reality. That act of jousting was extremely damaging to the attending physician and will also damage its perpetrator in the long run. Jousting could be viewed as an act of aggression by one physician against another. It can never be justified! Ordinarily a good defense can be mounted against the results of jousting, but while jousting is aggression, changing the medical record is suicide!

73.   ANY OLD HIRED GUN WILL DO

Allegations—Delay in management of diabetic ketoacidosis; myocardial infarction secondary to above
Physician Issues—Consultant negligence in assessment of patient; poor documentation by attending
Patient Issue—Disability secondary to myocardial infarction
Outcome—Large six-figure settlement (attending, neurologist, hospital)

CASE STUDY

A 46-year-old male with insulin-dependent diabetes since age 17 entered the emergency room with a six-year history of severe headache, vomiting, and drowsiness. His attending physician was notified and came to the emergency room about 9:00 PM and conducted a physical examination.

The patient had a history of poorly controlled hypertension for the past three years. For several months he had shown some proteinuria, occasional red blood cells in the urine, and slightly elevated serum creatinine. He had also experienced some visual disturbances as a result of diabetic retinopathy. He presented the picture of multi-system disease based on the diabetes.

On examination, the patient was afebrile, his blood pressure was 190/110 mm Hg, pulse 94/min and regular, and respirations rapid and deep. The neurologic examination showed no localized deficit. Admission laboratory studies showed an elevated blood sugar at 536 mg/dl, normal hemogram, and a creatinine of 2.4 mg/dl. The urine was 2+ for protein and 4+ for sugar. An occasional red blood cell was present in the urine. The EKG showed ST-T abnormalities, which were considered to be nonspecific.

Because of the severe unrelenting headache, an impending stroke was feared and a STAT neurological consultation was requested. The neurologist consulted was not familiar with the details of this case, and the available progress notes and the admission note were of little help in this regard. He confirmed the nonspecific character of the presenting picture and ordered a four-vessel cerebral arteriogram. The test was carried out as an emergency procedure but no abnormalities were reported. The neurologist ordered a glucose tolerance test (GTT) in the morning.

The nurses questioned the order among themselves but did not notify the attending physician or the neurologist of their concerns. The attending physician had ordered a pre-meal urine test for glucose and a routine regular insulin sliding scale three times a day.

The next morning the attending physician cancelled the order for the GTT, not recognizing that the test had already been started and that the one-hour, post-meal blood sugar had already been drawn. By 2:00 PM that first day after admission, the patient was found to be more lethargic and flushed, with very deep and rapid respirations. The attending physician was called and immediately recognized diabetic ketoacidosis. The previously drawn blood sugar was reported at 1,264 mg/dl. During the successful management of the ketoacidosis, the patient complained of midsternal pain with some radiation into the neck. The EKG showed definite changes in the ST-T segments, prompting the cardiologist who was consulted to speculate that the patient had had a subendocardial myocardial infarction.

The remaining days of his hospitalization were uneventful and the patient was discharged with a diagnosis of diabetes mellitus, ketoacidosis, diabetic retinopathy, diabetic nephropathy, coronary artery disease, acute myocardial infarction, and hypertension.

Two weeks after discharge a lawsuit was filed charging the attending physician and the consulting neurologist with negligence. In the lawsuit, the plaintiff patient charged that as a result of the GTT, inappropriately ordered, he experienced an acute MI, rendering him totally and permanently disabled.

During the discovery stage of the litigation, a typical "hired gun" medical expert testified against everybody involved in the case except the cardiologist. He testified that within a reasonable degree of medical certainty, the GTT caused the ketoacidosis, which in turn produced severe hyperosmolarity which led to the MI.

Although several experts testified that the GTT probably had little or nothing to do with the outcome in this case, none would defend saying the ordering of the GTT was within any acceptable standard of care in this case, and none could defend the less than aggressive management of the severe ketoacidosis.

This case was settled before trial with a large contribution on the part of the attending physician and the neurologist. The hospital had previously settled.

LOSS PREVENTION COMMENTS

There are many questions of quality in the management of this case. The record would suggest that the attending physician did not appreciate the early signs of ketoacidosis that were present on admission and recorded in the emergency room record. Having admitted this brittle diabetic with evidence of both retinal and renal complications, the approach was at best sluggish. Instead of ordering frequent blood examinations for glucose, the physician ordered only that the urine be tested. Having asked for a consultation by the neurologist, the attending physician did not adequately inform him of the existing extent of this patient's disease. There was poor documentation in this regard.

The consulting neurologist did not adequately assess this patient either by history or physical examination, or he would at least have waited for the report of the admission blood sugar before ordering the GTT.

The hired gun was a poor one as hired guns go. But, when management is marginal and documentation is poor, any old hired gun will do!

74.   THE EMERGENCY ROOM ZOO

Allegations—Delay in management of drug overdose
Physician Issues—Negligence in management (resident);
*   failure to attend (attending physician); delay in*
*   reporting laboratory data*
Patient Issues—Delay management of drug overdose;
*   wrongful death*
Outcome—Modest six-figure settlement

CASE STUDY

About 6:00 PM one Saturday evening, a healthy appearing man was brought to the very busy emergency room. He was obese, extremely strong, extremely combative and difficult to control, and required multiple attendants to hold him on the stretcher and eventually required restraints. On admission to the ER his blood pressure was 120/50 mm Hg, pulse 120/min, temperature 99.4°F, and respiratory rate 36/min. Drug overdose was suspected and a drug screen was ordered. The patient was retained in the ER and monitored at irregular intervals. About seven and a half hours after admission to the ER, a drug screen was reported, and the salicylate level was reported as 100. The junior house physician, who was working in the ER that evening, did not recognize the significance of the high salicylate level and was therefore not as aggressive as he might have been in the management of his patient. But he did contact the attending physician on two occasions and was advised to order blood gases, which was done; in spite of his obvious confusion as to the problem with his patient, the attending physician did not come to the ER to assist in the management of this very difficult patient.

Again there was significant delay from the time the blood gases were ordered and the report was received in the ER. At about the time the report was made, the patient suddenly began to convulse and died.

A lawsuit was brought charging the resident, the attending physician, and the hospital with negligence in the care of this patient. A sizable settlement was negotiated on the part of all parties.

LOSS PREVENTION COMMENTS

It is difficult to exonerate the first-year resident, who admitted that he did not know the full significance of the salicylate level. Certainly by that time in his medical education he should have known that such a level was extremely dangerous. To his credit, he was very busy, running from room to room to attend to many more or less minor complaints. Of course, since the attending physician is responsible for the "supervision" of the house staff, it was his duty to personally involve himself in the management of the patient.

Complicating the problem was a laboratory that somehow sent the first report to the wrong area of the hospital, so that consequently it was seven and a half hours before the report arrived in the ER. In the ER, on a busy weekend night, it is easy to see how a patient might "get lost" in the rush; systems should be in place to track the laboratory work and to follow up if the report has not been received within the allotted time. The report of the blood gases ordered by the attending physician was also delayed.

This extremely unfortunate and tragic accident appeared to be the result of the confluence of activity of a junior house officer who knew less than he should have, an attending physician who felt that his resident knew more than he really did, and the lack of prompt and efficient systems to expedite the reporting of laboratory work, once accomplished.

75. RECERTIFICATION—A REAL HAZARD

*Allegations—Delay in diagnosis of aneurysm; failure to
    continue evaluation in face of denial by carrier*
*Physician Issues—Discharged patient on demand of carrier;
    failure to consider aneurysm*
*Patient Issues—Prolonged pain and suffering; death
    postoperative (ten months); pulmonary embolus*
Outcome—Modest six-figure settlement

CASE STUDY

The patient was an extremely obese man in his mid-sixties who came to the emergency room physician complaining of sudden, very severe pain in the left side of the abdomen. The patient characterized it as having a "pulling" or "stretching" quality. He gave no history of nausea, vomiting, or diaphoresis. He had been a heavy smoker (one to two packs/day) for 40 years; his alcohol consumption was only social and rare. He had been obese for his entire adult life but had gained some weight in the last six months. His father had a "heart attack" at age 55 but lived to the advanced age of 94. His mother had died in childbirth when he was small.

The physical examination revealed an obese man who gave his weight as over 250 lb. His blood pressure was elevated at 180/100 mm Hg. The examination of the abdomen was unremarkable except for hypoactive bowel sounds, some tenderness in the lower left side, and marked obesity. The abdomen was said to be markedly distended, but no masses could be palpated and there was no mention that auscultation had been done. Blood pressures were not taken in the legs and there was no mention of peripheral pulses. A rectal examination was normal.

Since the pain had been sudden and severe and due to the difficulties in evaluating this very obese man, he was admitted to the hospital for further study and observation. The admission laboratory tests were unremarkable. The urine was normal. The CBC showed a mild leukocytosis of 13,600/cu mm with a normal differential. The RBC count was reported at 4,700/cu mm with the PCV 41.4 percent and the hemoglobin 13.6 gm/dl. Chemistries, liver enzymes, and serum lipids were all within normal limits. The patient's routine medications,

Indocin for gouty arthritis and Lasix for mild hypertension, were
continued, and Demerol was ordered for pain.

The attending physician suspected large bowel disease and
ordered upper and lower bowel studies. He asked that stool be
checked for blood. The patient's pain was severe enough to require
narcotics for relief. Reports of these studies showed only a hiatal
hernia and some diverticula in the colon, without evidence of
diverticulitis.

The patient continued to have abdominal pain requiring
narcotics. Periodic blood pressures were systolic 150 to 180 mm Hg
and diastolic 100 to 110 mm Hg. An abdominal ultrasound revealed
possible gallstones but no other abdominal masses. The patient had no
stools, thus the occult blood studies were not reported.

On the third hospital day, the attending physician received a
call from the medical director representing the patient's insurance
carrier, stating that since he was not receiving any intravenous fluids,
etc., his insurance would not cover him beyond that day; thus the
patient needed to be discharged the following morning. The physician
had initially called the carrier and suggested to the nurse to whom he
spoke that his patient needed more time in the hospital. A discharge
order was written for that day. The physician's discharge note
reflected the conversations with the insurance company.

The patient was taken to his car, but before he could get in, he
collapsed. In the ER, he again complained of abdominal pain, but this
time on the right side in the upper quadrant. There was tenderness in
the RUQ but no rebound tenderness. Bowel sounds were said to be
present. Rectal examination was normal. The stool on the examining
glove was described as yellowish-brown and almost liquid. He was
again admitted with the diagnosis of abdominal pain.

The attending physician asked for an internist to evaluate his
patient at this time. The patient complained bitterly of inability to
void, which had not been a prominent part of his previous admission.
Catheterization yielded about 20 ml of urine, with some improvement
in the pain. The consultant wrote on the ER record, "plan to admit,
hydrate, and observe." The patient was transferred from the ER to the
floor. The nurse wrote, "In no acute distress. Skin warm, color OK.
Complaints of lower abdominal pain." About ten hours after admission,
at 5:00 AM, the patient complained that the Foley catheter did not feel
like it was working. At this time the urine was described as "amber."
Pedal pulses were felt bilaterally by the nurse but were said to be "weak."

On the morning rounds, the internist wrote that the admission
hematocrit was down to 29 percent, the pain was better, and that he
was awaiting the old chart in order to compare with the previous

hematocrit. He ordered an anemia study. The patient related his continuing abdominal pain to the inability of the Foley catheter to empty his bladder and the lack of a bowel movement.

These complaints continued throughout the day. The anemia study revealed only the low hematocrit and hemoglobin. An enema given about 10:00 PM the second night of this hospital admission yielded "golf ball-like" stool with "much relief."

The following morning the hemoglobin and hematocrit were continuing to fall. The hematocrit was 24 percent and the hemoglobin 8.0 gm/dl. The continuing complaints relative to emptying the bladder and the continued obscurity of the origin of the pain led the consultant and the attending physician to request an evaluation by a urologist. The history was reviewed, as was the admission examination. An IVP/cystogram was planned.

In the early evening hours the preparation for the IVP was begun. The patient had experienced pain during the night but had obtained some relief from a K-pad. He requested the bedpan, complained of severe abdominal pain, and collapsed. No blood pressure could be obtained. The code team was called.

The internist came to the hospital and called for the vascular surgeon who came, transferred the patient to the operating room, and, after intubation and induction, opened the abdomen to find a ruptured abdominal aneurysm. At least 4,000 ml of blood were present in the abdomen. The aorta was replaced from below the renal arteries to the iliac bifurcation, the blood was replaced, and the patient came off the table alive.

He suffered throughout the postoperative period from hypoxic encephalopathy, respiratory distress, and renal failure. He recuperated some, being able to be up in a wheelchair and about six weeks after surgery was transferred to a rehabilitation unit in the hospital. For another six weeks he seemed to be slowly improving.

About ten weeks after the initial admission, at 10:00 PM the patient asked for the bedpan. He suddenly stated that he "feels funny." The blood pressure began immediately to drop, the respirations increased, and the pulse rate became faster. He became progressively short of breath, requiring increasing oxygen. The blood pressure was barely audible at 60 mm Hg systolic. The patient was transferred from the rehabilitation unit to the ER for monitoring. Despite intravenous fluids, controlled respiration, vasopressor, and other supportive measures, the patient died about five hours after the sudden onset of dyspnea. The consultant believed a pulmonary embolus had caused his death.

LOSS PREVENTION COMMENTS

It is easy to second-guess the attending physician and the consultant in this case. This was an exceedingly tough case to figure out. The patient was markedly obese, and his abdominal findings were atypical despite his obesity. The ultrasound had not revealed any masses consistent with an AAA. The pedal pulses were said to be present but "weak." The symptoms referable to the urinary tract and the constipation were, to say the least, confusing. Between the first and the second admission, the abdominal pain changed from the lower left side to the upper right side. The consultant did not have the previous chart in order to see quickly that the hematocrit had fallen precipitously. Perhaps the physicians "chased rabbits" with bowel studies and urological procedures, but, again, that is easy to say from this perspective.

One must wonder what would have happened had the patient not been discharged. At the least the rupture and collapse would probably have occurred under more controlled conditions. More than likely, the attending physician and the consultant would have arrived at a vascular diagnosis with a little more time to study this very confusing patient. What can we learn? It must be obvious from this record that the attending physician did not agree that this patient was a candidate for discharge when he received the "word" from the medical director of the patient's insurance carrier that his patient would not be covered beyond that day. It must be a principle that we do what is clinically appropriate for the patient regardless of what the insurance company says. The source of payment for the hospital and ourselves must be secondary to our clinical judgment. We must not let anyone, including the patient, pressure us into doing otherwise!

76.   HEADACHE—AN IMPORTANT SYMPTOM

Allegations—Delay in evaluation and treatment of brain tumor; death

Physician Issues—Failure to assess intractable headache; poor intra-office communication; delay in consulting specialist

Patient Issues—Prolonged pain and suffering; death

Outcome—Large six-figure settlement

CASE STUDY

The patient was a 25-year-old man who would not have aroused the interest or concern of many physicians on the first visit.

He reported to the board certified family physician of the HMO to which he belonged with a five-day history of a pounding occipital headache. He gave no history of trauma but had a history of excessive beer drinking, the regular use of marijuana, and the occasional use of cocaine. He reported no previous headaches. Examination revealed no significant abnormalities. His blood pressure was recorded as 140/88 mm Hg. A cursory neurologic examination was within normal limits and there was no tenderness over the occipital region. He was treated symptomatically with a mild tranquilizer and aspirin and instructed to return to the clinic if he was unimproved in "several days."

One week after the first encounter he was seen again by the same physician, with the same symptoms. The headache was still described as "pounding" and located principally in the occipital region. Again the examination was considered normal. The patient stated that he was sleeping a little better. His blood pressure was unchanged. This time the diagnosis entered on the examination form was "headache of undetermined origin." A synthetic codeine preparation was prescribed. The record indicated that the physician planned a CT of the head and a neurologic consultation if the symptoms were not improved in a few days. Laboratory work, including a CBC and urinalysis, was reported as normal.

Five weeks after the initial visit, the patient was seen again with the same complaints of persistent, unrelenting headache. He reported only slight relief from the medication that had been prescribed. This time the examiner reported some worsening of the pain on movement of the head and thought there was "prominence" on palpation of the occipital area. X-rays of cervical spine were reported to show some "straightening," which was thought to be due to muscle spasm. An order was written to refer to a neurologist.

The patient was examined by the neurologist the following day. The specialist reported that there was no evidence of "root or cord disease"; he prescribed an NSAID and requested that the HMO arrange for physical therapy. The patient was examined by another HMO physician, a board certified internist who prescribed a muscle relaxant and ordered physical therapy. It was not until four days later that the physical therapy treatments began. The physical therapist reported to the HMO internist that the patient "loses his balance easily, complains of dizziness, and still has constant pain." Ten days later the patient reported to the emergency room but was told by the HMO's precertification nurse that he could not be certified as an emergency patient and was to see the original physician who first examined him at the HMO clinic. The ER physician did record "normal neuro" and felt that the difficulty was "musculoskeletal pain, anxiety, and depression," for which he prescribed a mild antidepressant. The following day the young man was examined by his original doctor, who reported, "Still having excruciating headache and doesn't want to go to work." A stronger narcotic was prescribed, along with an antihistamine decongestant, since the family physician's examination suggested some middle ear effusion. The record of this encounter ended with the statement, "Disability papers put on medical director's desk."

Three days after this visit, the patient went to the ER in a small town near the medical center where his examinations and treatment had started. He received some "pain medicine" for his severe headache on this first visit to the small town ER. He returned with the same symptoms twice and, on the same day and during the last visit, he experienced respiratory arrest. A CT was done showing "cerebral edema and a possible posterior fossa tumor." The patient was transported by helicopter to the medical center, where an EEG was compatible with brain death. An autopsy showed a medulloblastoma.

Loss Prevention Comments

This was an undesirable patient! He gave a history of regular alcohol and drug abuse. In all probability, the first examiner was convinced that the patient was continuing to abuse drugs and that his symptoms were, in some measure, due to that. The same physician saw his patient with some regularity for over a month. On the fourth visit, x-rays were done, which showed only some straightening of the cervical spine. At that time he properly consulted a well-qualified neurologist, whose examination supported the normal neurologic findings reported from the beginning of the patient's illness.

Perhaps the most tragic thing that occurred in this sad story was the HMO's refusal to allow admission to the hospital. They insisted that the patient was not sick enough to be hospitalized and referred him back to his primary care physician. At that time the patient was experiencing dizziness and difficulty maintaining his balance, in addition to his unrelenting head pain. Within a week the young man was dead!

Even though headache is one of the most common complaints that we deal with, it can be an extremely important symptom. This story chronicles a textbook picture of some organic etiology of the pain. It was unrelenting. As soon as the first dose of medicine wore off, the second was needed. More and stronger medication was required to control the pain and finally, about six weeks after onset, definite neurologic signs appeared.

Three physicians had a chance to make a timely diagnosis. The family physician, of course, had the longest exposure to the patient.

Should he have made a referral to the neurologist sooner? The internist, the senior member of the HMO clinic, who had approved the consultation, was informed by the physical therapist about the problems with dizziness and balance. This information may have been available to the HMO doctors as long as two weeks before the young man's death. As the senior physician of this group and a board certified internist, should he have initiated a return visit to the neurologist or directly ordered an outpatient CT? Then there is the neurologist. He is supposed to be an expert in these matters! Should he have ordered a CT examination as a part of his consultation? If he had, would the HMO have approved such an examination just on the basis of unrelenting and worsening head pain? During the investigation and development of this litigation, it became increasingly apparent that the jury's answers to all of these questions during trial would probably have been, "Yes!" The case was settled on behalf of all the physicians involved.

77.   WHO'S MY DOCTOR?

> *Allegation—Delay in diagnosing and treating cancer (FP; only physician sued)*
> *Physician Issues—Poor communication between treating physicians; failure to follow up on chest x-ray (all physicians); deviation on part of all physicians (FP, cardiologist, surgeon)*
> *Patient Issues—Loss of chance; palliative treatment; death*
> *Outcome—Large six-figure settlement*

CASE STUDY

Fourteen years after two visits to the primary care physician one week apart for an upper respiratory infection, the patient went to this physician with a history of having checked his blood pressure in the supermarket and getting a reading of 200/105 mm Hg; he made the appointment to have his blood pressure checked. Examination revealed a moderately overweight 54-year-old man with a blood pressure of 180/94 mm Hg. Otherwise the examination was not remarkable. A beta blocker and a mild diuretic were prescribed and he was told to return in three weeks. He returned at the appropriate time, feeling better, and with a 6-lb weight loss and a blood pressure of 160/88 mm Hg. No return visit was scheduled. One month later the patient was sent to the emergency room of a large hospital in a major city with a note from his physician. The ER physician saw the man, who was complaining of chest pain, some diaphoresis, and marked apprehension about his condition.

The examination in the ER consisted of the usual physical, which was essentially normal. The blood pressure was 145/90 mm Hg, pulse 110/min, and a chest normal to percussion and auscultation. An EKG revealed the characteristic findings of acute ischemia, and the chest x-ray was reported as showing an abnormality in the "right superior mediastinal contour, which may simply be related to ectasia of the vasculature. I could not entirely exclude adenopathy or mass in this area. Follow-up is recommended as felt to be clinically indicated. Impression: Right superior mediastinal abnormality. Ectatic vasculature vs. mediastinal mass or adenopathy. Follow-up or captured tomography is recommended."

The man was admitted with the diagnosis of myocardial ischemia and hypertension. On the next day the chest x-ray again was reported to show a "nodular appearing infiltrate projecting into the right upper lung area." An apical lordotic view was suggested to help to more precisely define the abnormality.

A cardiac catheterization showed severe coronary atherosclerosis and some dyskinesia involving the anterior wall of the left ventricle. The following day the patient had a CAB with six-vessel bypass grafting.

The man did well after surgery. There were almost daily chest x-rays, without specific reference to the previously described lesion. A letter to the referring physician on the fifth postoperative day described the excellent progress of the patient. Reports of all the x-rays taken in the hospital were sent to the primary care doctor. The discharge summary, which contained a reference to "pulmonary nodules," was sent to the cardiologist and the family physician. The patient was discharged with an appointment to see the cardiologist in two weeks. The patient was followed by the cardiologist with letters to the FP until about three months after surgery.

For the next year, the patient was followed by his FP. He was seen intermittently for medication refills, blood pressure checks, etc. On one occasion, the patient was seen by his FP for a "sinus infection." The history on that occasion indicated that he had "spit up some bright red blood." Antibiotics were given and the condition appeared to clear. The patient continued to do well until 14 months after the surgery when he called the FP's office complaining of right shoulder pain. Symptomatic treatment was prescribed over the phone, and he was instructed to come in if the pain persisted. Two months later he did come in with continued pain in the right shoulder. Every two weeks after that time the patient came in to see his doctor with continuing pain in the left chest and shoulder. He was treated symptomatically on each occasion.

The FP did a chest x-ray on one of the visits about 18 months after the initial report of a possible mass in the right upper chest. This film showed a well-defined lesion in the right chest, which was diagnosed as bronchogenic carcinoma and which proved to be inoperable. The patient was given palliative treatment, including x-ray therapy to the right chest.

LOSS PREVENTION COMMENTS

This case represents an example of the frequent failure to make a timely diagnosis and to initiate treatment. With too much regularity, these cases turn on a report or test that is overlooked or not received in the first place. In this instance, the FP felt that the consultants would follow up on a finding of such severity and, in a progress note a few days before discharge, the surgeon stated, "Will check the chest x-ray and get sputum cultures." The cultures were obtained, but the chest x-ray was not repeated. Even the discharge summary talks about the "pulmonary nodules" and states that the patient is "discharged with an appointment to see the cardiologist."

Where does the ultimate responsibility lie in a case such as this one? I am sure that those of us who regularly refer patients to a medical center for tertiary care would contend that the FP could reasonably conclude that the consulting surgeon and/or the cardiologist would follow up on this new finding first discovered on the admission chest film. In fact, a good case could be made for delaying this kind of surgery until some definitive diagnosis could be made with regard to the possible disease in the right chest. In reality, this man was subjected to a life-threatening operation when, depending on the circumstances, he might well have chosen to avoid such a surgical exercise had he known that he had a malignancy in his lung that was inoperable. On the other hand, the surgeon and the cardiologist would contend that they were justified in leaving the further investigation of the chest condition to the FP.

No matter on which side of this issue you find yourself, you must conclude that the practice of all three physicians involved was below the expected standard of care. The FP should have made note of the reports of the chest x-ray and repeated those studies when the patient returned to his care. It must be noted that the cardiologist saw this patient for two months following the operation and did not investigate the chest findings. The surgeon, who was the attending physician in the hospital, stated that the chest condition would be restudied before discharge. It was not!

To underline the vagaries of the legal environment in which we have to live, only the FP was sued and only the FP had to be

reported to the Data Bank! Under the current State Supreme Court
ruling establishing the doctrine of Comparative Negligence, all three
physicians could have been found negligent whether or not they had
been named in the plaintiff's action. The patient obviously believed
that his doctor was his family physician and held him responsible for
not following up on the abnormal chest x-ray.

78.   HAZARDS OF HEPARIN

*Allegations—Failure to diagnose and treat coagulopathy due
     to Heparin; wrongful death*
*Physician Issues—Failure to act on previous history of
     bleeding peptic ulcer;failure to act on falling Hct*
Patient Issue—Wrongful death
Outcome—Large six-figure settlement

In large hospitals where significant numbers of cardiovascular
surgical procedures are done and where cases of deep vein thrombosis
and pulmonary embolism are all too common, heparin medication
becomes so routine that its hazards come to be minimized in the
management of these problems. The following case is an ex-ample
of this danger.

CASE STUDY

A 71-year-old man with multiple health problems had in the
past been hospitalized for a bleeding gastric ulcer, acute urinary retention,
prostatic cancer with transurethral resection of the prostate (TURP),
COPD, and hematuria thought to be due to a post-TURP stricture of
the urethra. He was a known type-II diabetic and had been seen in the
hospital emergency room for blood pressures of 220-200/120-110 mm Hg.
     This present illness and hospitalization was brought about by
a history of sleep apnea, which had been investigated in the sleep
laboratory of another hospital. The patient was thought to have
"redundant pharyngeal tissue" that should be treated surgically. In the
preoperative work-up by a cautious otolaryngologist, a history of
exertional chest pain was discovered, causing the internist to admit
his patient to the hospital. His admission history did not record the
previous bleeding gastric ulcer, which had been treated in another
hospital, but did carefully document the exertional discomfort that
had been getting worse for the past few months and the other health
problems that were a part of the record at this hospital. The physical
examination was not remarkable and the laboratory work was within

normal limits, with a hematocrit of 44.2 percent. A cardiologist was consulted and cardiac catheterization was scheduled. A severe degree of stenosis was found in the left anterior descending coronary artery (LAD) with less obstruction in the right coronary artery. The circumflex artery was said to show some "irregularities without narrowing." Angioplasty done two days after the initial catheterization failed to open the LAD, and in fact some slowing of the flow was observed distal to the point of the dilatation site. An emergency coronary artery bypass graft (CABG) was done, with routine heparinization prior to the catheterization and surgery. Post-CABG the hematocrit was 40 percent. Bloody urine was noted per Foley catheter.

The day after surgery the hematocrit was recorded at 34.1 percent. Heparin was ordered at 100 mg every eight hours, and the following day the hematocrit was 28.6 percent. The patient began to complain of nausea, for which symptomatic treatment was given. When the hematocrit appeared to stabilize for a day or two, heparin was continued. By the third postoperative day, the patient had begun to have more abdominal discomfort, and while standing at the bedside he began to retch and vomit green emesis. The abdominal discomfort continued but was easily managed. Iron was given on the fourth postoperative day, with the hematocrit at 26 percent. Nausea continued and some abdominal distension was noted. Some serosanguineous fluid was noted oozing from the incision, and another cardiac surgeon was asked to follow the patient because he was thought to have had more experience with wound management and could offer the patient a better outlook. During this day the patient began to have some shortness of breath. Small, loose stool was reported but not described. Heparin was continued.

On the fifth postoperative day the hematocrit was 22.1 percent. Two units of packed red blood cells were given. A "good BM" was reported the following day but not described. An order was written to check all stools for blood. On the seventh postoperative day a black stool was reported and thereafter all stools were reported 4+ for blood. Heparin was continued and the hematocrit remained at 22 percent. On the night of the eighth postoperative day the patient became disoriented, and upon being turned on his side the following morning during his bath, respiratory arrest occurred. Resuscitation was not successful. An autopsy reported "exsanguination from a large gastric ulcer that had eroded into a medium-sized gastric artery." The 100 mg heparin flushes were continued during the last day of this man's life.

Both the internist and the surgeon were named in the lawsuit that was filed in this case, and a large settlement was negotiated.

LOSS PREVENTION COMMENTS

Perhaps the initial lesson to be learned from this case is that the past history must be complete and not limited to the patient's history in one institution or with one physician no matter how long and varied that history is. This patient's history of a bleeding ulcer at another institution was not part of his record of his last admission.

Of course, the tragic terminal event of massive GI bleeding could have occurred even had the heparin therapy been stopped days earlier. The PT/PTT determinations had not indicated that too much anticoagulant was being given. It would appear that the routine use of heparin in all CABGs had become so established that it escaped the daily evaluation of this patient's condition. Thus the abdominal symptoms and their possible implications were ignored.

It would be well to look carefully at your institution's "Adverse Drug Reactions" for heparin. If it is significant (and it probably is), consider developing a physician-led team to develop an institution-wide protocol for heparin use in all of its indications. That exercise could result in the prevention of patient injury and thus real medical malpractice loss prevention.

79.   PAST HISTORY REMAINS CRITICAL

Allegations—Delay in diagnosis of cancer; death
Physician Issues—Failure to act on inadequate x-ray
*   examination; failure to obtain past history from*
*   previous physicians*
Patient Issues—Severe pain and suffering; death
Outcome—Modest six-figure settlement

CASE STUDY

A 29-year-old woman had two episodes of bleeding at stool. The blood was bright red and on each occasion consisted of about a tablespoonful, or more. Her physician at the time promptly ordered a barium enema, which showed a 2-cm polyp in her transverse colon. A benign but "atypical" adenomatous polyp of the colon was surgically removed.

For the next thirteen years the patient was followed by her Ob/Gyn physician with the routine care for three uncomplicated pregnancies. Her physician did the routine gynecological follow-up with annual Pap smears and treated her for a variety of minor ailments. No studies of the colon were done and there was no record of stool guaiac exams having been done.

At age 50 she became a regular patient of a family physician, and the initial notes indicate that she was a "new (HMO) patient." She complained of recurrent headaches for thirty years. The history indicated that, in addition to the benign colon polyp, she had been studied thoroughly for her headaches, including a brain scan, which was at the time state of the art. During the ensuing three years, she was seen several times for the headaches and other routine complaints. The headaches were eventually controlled by Tofranil.

In April, the patient went to her FP for a routine examination and, with no significant abnormal findings, was instructed to continue the Tofranil for her headaches and return for follow-up in four months. It was six months before her next visit, and at that time she complained of increased constipation, straining at stool, and stated that the bowel problem had become very troublesome. Her weight was recorded at 13 lb less than it had been four to six months earlier. An unprepared sigmoidoscopic exam was attempted. The scope was advanced only to 10 cm. The mucosa was described as "irritated," and the stool was recorded as "faintly guaiac positive." She was given a bowel prep kit and scheduled for a barium enema a few days later.

The barium enema was done, and the report stated that, "A tremendous amount of bowel content, both formed and particulate, was present. The bowel content ruled out the detection of any mucosal lesions, but there is no gross constricting lesion seen." At the office, her physician recognized the colon study was compromised, ordered her to stop the Tofranil, prescribed a mild tranquilizer, and asked her to return in three to four weeks unless the condition worsened at which time another attempt at a barium enema would be scheduled. Interim stool studies for blood were negative.

Her weight loss continued and her constipation did not improve. A repeat barium enema showed an "apple core" lesion in the rectum. Surgery followed at which time advanced metastatic disease was found. A radical pelvic eviserectomy was done followed by radiation and chemotherapy. The patient died three years later. A lawsuit was filed charging her family physician with negligence in the delay of the diagnosis of cancer of the colon.

LOSS PREVENTION COMMENTS

By 1982 it was well known that patients who had adenomatous polyps of the colon were at risk for recurrence of this condition, with the additional risk of the polyps becoming malignant. While the epidemiology had not yet been completely developed, patients who had this disease and who had been treated surgically were advised to have screening examinations routinely.

There is no record of the surgeon's advice to the patient regarding follow-up, nor do we have a record of subsequent visits to the internist who referred her to the surgeon. We do know that she became a patient of the Ob/Gyn specialist about three years after the surgery, when the internist who referred her to the surgeon originally sent her to him because of a spontaneous abortion. His records revealed the history of the colon polyp. We also know that she continued under the care of this physician for about sixteen years.

The real problem with this case is the departure from an acceptable standard of care in that there was no known follow-up after the removal of the adenomatous colon polyp. Both the internist and the Ob/Gyn physicians may have strongly urged the follow-up, but there is no record of either having done so. In October the family physician was faced with a patient who had lost 13 lb and had complained of a definite change of bowel habits in the form of severe constipation. The barium enema was done promptly, but not repeated after the report indicated that the patient was so poorly prepared that he could not be sure about his findings. One wonders why the radiologist who performed the test did not urge that the test be repeated promptly. It may well be that this physician also did not follow the acceptable standard. It is true that under the care of this FP, three months went by before his patient was admitted to the hospital by another physician and the final surgery was done. During the three years that elapsed between this radical surgery and the patient's death, she had numerous complications from radiation and recurrent malignancy. She suffered greatly.

From a clinical perspective, perhaps as many as four physicians could have been charged with negligence. This patient should have had routine screening examinations during the years between her original surgery and her final surgical experience. That was the standard of care! However, from a legal perspective, the statute of limitations had run out on the internist and the Ob/Gyn. The radiologist probably was negligent, but his involvement in the case came so late that it probably made no difference in the outcome.

This leaves the family physician as the logical legal target. The question must be asked if the fact that this patient was a "new (HMO) patient" colored the FP's management. There was no recorded evidence that it did. The lack of giving the past history of surgery for a colon polyp the attention that the standard of care demanded could not be defended, and a six-figure settlement was negotiated. The past history is indeed critical to our management of most of our patients!

80.   FRAGMENTED EVALUATION

Allegations—Failure to diagnose aneurysm
Physician Issues—Communication by progress notes
*   inadequate; three physicians with different strategies;*
*   failure to appreciate severe and intractable pain*
Patient Issues—Severe pain and suffering; death from
*   ruptured aneurysm*
Outcome—Large seven-figure settlement

CASE STUDY

A 46-year-old farmer was seen in his local community hospital complaining of lower mid-chest and epigastric pain beginning about two hours after his evening meal. He had not eaten anything apart from his usual diet and denied having eaten an unusual amount of food. The pain began suddenly but was not severe at the outset. There was some nausea, and as the pain escalated in severity there was some sweating and one episode of vomiting. He was examined by the emergency room (ER) physician, who ordered a chest x-ray (CXR), an ECG, a CBC, and urinalysis; all were considered to be within normal limits. A narcotic was administered for pain, and at the patient's request he was transferred to the medical center where he had a long-standing relationship with an internist.

When he arrived at the center, he was seen in the ER. His regular physician was being covered by an associate, who responded promptly to his call and came to the ER where he reviewed the history, examination, and laboratory findings from the community hospital. The pain had subsided some with the narcotic administered at the other hospital, but the physician was impressed that with the pain there was some radiation to the upper back, and during the ambulance ride to the center the patient had told the EMT that the pain seemed to involve the left leg. The patient was under treatment for mild hypertension, which had been satisfactorily controlled on a small dose of propranolol for the past three or four years.

An ECG was repeated and again showed no abnormality. Enzymes were in the normal range and a repeat CXR was ordered for the next morning, with the specific note to do a CT of the chest if the plain film showed any abnormality. The patient was admitted to the hospital and spent a fairly comfortable night. The CXR was done the following morning and reported to be normal.

Having been admitted on Sunday evening, the following morning the patient was seen by his regular physician, with whom the patient reviewed his experience but stressed that his discomfort was more epigastric and that he seemed to be having some pain on swallowing that morning.

The patient had been treated some ten years previously for a peptic ulcer and at times since that would be careful about certain foods and take some antacid. The pain became worse by mid-morning with marked vomiting. More narcotic was given, and his physician asked his associate, a gastroenterologist, to examine the patient's upper GI tract.

By the time the endoscopic examination was done, the patient was having severe pain. The endoscopist commented that he could not advance the scope beyond the mid-esophagus, but that to that level the esophagus appeared normal. He speculated that his inability to advance the scope could be due to an extraluminal problem. Following this examination, the patient had extreme pain to which the nurses were not as responsive as the family thought they should be, and the family demanded that the nurses summon the attending physician. This was done, and a larger dose of narcotic was prescribed in a phone order. The nurses' notes commented on the pain being felt in the mid-chest, back, and lower extremities.

On the larger dose of narcotic the patient dozed some, but whenever he was conscious he was in severe pain. On that day after admission the patient was seen by both his regular internist and the gastroenterologist. The family made frequent complaints to the staff that the nurses were not attentive to the patient's pain. The usual battery of blood chemistries was normal and cardiac enzymes were not elevated.

The second night in the hospital the patient's pain was never satisfactorily controlled. The nurses again failed to attend to the complaints of the patient to the satisfaction of the family, who urged the charge nurse to call the attending physician about the severity of the pain.

CT of the chest was ordered for the next morning, but shortly after midnight, the patient cried out, sat up in bed, and collapsed; resuscitation efforts failed. An autopsy revealed a ruptured thoracic aortic aneurysm.

Loss Prevention Comments

It is extremely difficult in this type of case to ferret out the reasons that three extremely fine physicians would not make the diagnosis. The doctor who saw the patient on admission was obviously thinking along the lines of aneurysm. This was reflected in his admitting note that emphasized the back and leg pain and his order of a CT of the chest if the plain film of the chest was abnormal.

Since the x-ray of the chest the morning after admission was read as normal, no CT was done. The request for the x-ray did not suggest to the radiologist the suspicion of aneurysm.

When the regular physician saw his patient the morning after admission, the picture presented to him was one that directed his thinking to the GI tract. The gastroenterologist was directed by the previous history of peptic ulcer and failed to connect the difficulty encountered in the passing of the scope to the possibility of an aneurysm as the reason.

What can we conclude? The admitting physician probably attributed more importance to a negative CXR in assessing the probability of an aneurysm of the thoracic aorta than was warranted. Indeed, if the CXR were used as the only indicator, a majority of thoracic aneurysms would be missed. The attending physician accepted the assessment of his associate without independent scrutiny. The gastroenterologist, like the radiologist, had nothing in the request to examine the patient that would have pointed him in the right direction.

Extremely important in this tragic case was the failure of the physicians to appreciate the extreme nature of the pain. The family charged in the lawsuit that the nurses were negligent in not calling the attending physician on at least two occasions when the pain was not blunted by the narcotic. Perhaps the nurses were not aggressive enough in calling the attending physician.

The most compelling conclusion in this case that led to a very large settlement was that the record never indicated that the three involved physicians made contact with each other and put together the observations and thoughts that each was in a position to contribute. Progress notes were not absent but were brief. Nursing notes were not wonderful but were fairly expressive.

Do you remember the fable of the three blind men and their descriptions of the elephant? When more than one physician is involved in the management of a patient, it is essential that all the physicians put their observations and suspicions together or they can be characterized in the same way.

81.   STOP, LOOK, LISTEN

*Allegations—Failure to diagnose and treat tuberculosis in
        timely manner; severe brain damage*
*Physician Issues—Confusion as to responsibility by attending
        physicians; failure to act on laboratory reports; failure
        to follow up on initial x-ray evaluation*

Patient Issues—Young man (breadwinner); prolonged
hospitalization; severe neurological compromise
Outcome—Seven-figure settlement divided between all
physicians (FP, internist, pulmonologist) and hospital

CASE STUDY

A 45-year-old man reported to his family doctor with a
history of "feeling bad" for at least three weeks. The patient recounted
also that he had experienced chills and fever. On direct questioning,
he also told of night sweats. The physical examination was recorded
to show high-pitched expiratory wheezes and rales, a "red right
ear," and a fever of 102°F. A chest x-ray taken by the attending
physician prompted him to admit his patient to the hospital directly
from his office.

The hospital record revealed a differential diagnosis that
included both miliary TBC and collagen disease. The admission orders
included requests for STAT sputum, blood, and urine cultures, together
with routine comfort measures and theophylline for the respiratory
symptoms. These orders were carried out, and a direct examination of
the sputum was reported as negative for AFB.

On the second hospital day, the attending physician requested
a consultation from a specialist in internal medicine. The consultant
suggested possibilities that included tuberculosis and other granulomatous diseases and advised that a pulmonologist be requested to
bronchoscope the patient. The fever continued with spikes up to
104°F; a PPD was negative.

On the sixth hospital day the bronchoscopy was carried out.
The washings were negative on direct smear and a transbronchial
biopsy of the RUL was likewise reported as "negative." The febrile
course continued, with elevations of 102°F to 104°F. Repeat chest x-
rays continued to show the miliary changes, which were interpreted
by the consultant as "some kind of granulomatous disease."

During the third week of hospitalization, with the fever
continuing to reach levels of 104°F, a further report from the open-
lung biopsy revealed "multiple 1-mm nodules." During this time, the
cultures began to show "yeast." Antifungal therapy was started on the
21st hospital day.

During the fourth week of hospitalization, the patient began to
have severe respiratory difficulties with a fall in the PO_2 levels below
50 mm Hg and concomitant increases in the CO_2 levels. The patient
was transferred to the ICU, where he was given a bolus of steroids IV
(100 mg Medrol) and was intubated for a short time. He pulled the
tube out, and the anesthesiologist was unable to reintubate; they

elected to leave the tube out and support him with oxygen. The following day the patient had increasing respiratory difficulties, continued to have fever, and was reintubated and placed on a respirator. PO_2 and CO_2 levels were controlled within acceptable limits, but otherwise the patient's condition did not significantly change.

During the fifth week of hospitalization, the patient began to show neurologic symptoms including stupor, muscular rigidity, and some focal neurologic findings. The consulting neurologist suggested the strong possibility of TBC meningitis.

The patient continued to deteriorate both neurologically and from a pulmonary standpoint. Seizures began and continued over the next several days, being very difficult to control.

Cultures of both the urine and bronchial washings finally showed AFB; specific therapy was begun after a little more than a month in the hospital and three days after a nurse's note appeared in the chart, "Consultant aware that tests are positive for TBC." The patient left the hospital neurologically compromised some nine weeks after admission and was admitted to a convalescent center.

On careful review of the medical record, it was found that a follow-up report on the lung biopsy was positive for TBC and was reported in the record on the 21st hospital day.

A lawsuit was filed charging the hospital and all the physicians (except the neurologist and radiologist) with negligence in the management of this case. A seven-figure settlement was negotiated, with the hospital and all the physician parties to the suit contributing.

LOSS PREVENTION COMMENTS

In order to make sense out of a tragedy like this, we must look at each defendant and carefully fill in the blanks left by the record, which in no way excuse, but may explain to some degree, how this could happen.

Beginning with the family doctor and the attending physician, we have to ask how could he have missed the boat so badly? Reading between the lines, we have to conclude that his involvement was not as the physician ultimately responsible for the study of the patient in a systematic fashion. A logical approach to the problems of his patient was not reflected in his notes or in his orders. It appeared that he was waiting expectantly for somebody else to do something for his patient.

He started on the right track! How could he have been diverted in the course it appeared that he intended to follow? His initial suspicion from the chest x-ray made in his office was miliary tuberculosis (TBC). Again reading between the lines, it is possible that this generalist was deferring to the internist to make the critical decisions and begin appropriate management. In a patient this sick with the respiratory symptoms described, when the sputum is described as "negative," and with the radiologist agreeing that miliary TBC or some other granulomatous disease were the two most prominent possibilities, he seemed to lack the confidence to begin empiric therapy for TBC, which, in retrospect, probably would have effected a cure. He had all the definitive studies in process, and, even without a positive sputum or culture, treatment for this most serious and life-threatening condition was certainly indicated.

The internist, like the family doctor, began on the right road. On the second day of hospitalization he suggested miliary TBC as the first condition in his differential diagnosis. The request for his help in the first place was ambiguous. It did not request that he consult and continue to follow, nor did it suggest that he assume the primary responsibility for the care of this patient. His visits and progress notes were irregular, leading to the speculation at least that he did not feel like the attending physician intended for him to take an active role in the management of this desperately ill man. It is always necessary for the consultant to know what role the attending physician expects him to play in management. The consultation request should specify the expected involvement of the consulting physician. From the notes, however, we can conclude that even the consultant was focused on some kind of granulomatous disease, as indicated in his note on the sixth hospital day. It seems that both the attending physician and the consultant were thrown off the track by the absence of positive sputum, bronchial washings, transbronchial biopsy, and negative skin tests.

The pathologist involved found unmistakable evidence of TBC in the lung biopsy reported from permanent sections and special stains not available for the initial report. There is no record of a call to either the attending physician or the consultant regarding this all-important finding. The report was sent in the usual fashion to the floor and filed in the chart. It was not seen until sometime much later when a nurse wrote in her notes, "Consultant aware that tests are positive for TBC." This was after the patient had become severely neurologically compromised and even the appropriate treatment could not reverse the damage done. The possibility that a report will be lost in the hectic world of a busy hospital is such a good one that the pathologist or radiologist should by all means directly contact the physician with any report that could be of such a critical nature.

Of course, in retrospect, one could reason that the steroids given for the respiratory failure during the third week could have done great harm to this patient with fulminant TBC. He was a strong young man, the breadwinner of his family, and is now totally disabled and requires constant, skilled care, which could be required for many years in the future.

In spite of the evidence all around indicating failure to follow an acceptable level of care, in this case by the attending physician, the internist, the pathologist, and the hospital, one cannot help but believe that the basic negligence was a failure to communicate on the part of the physician team responsible for this man's care.

82.   EARLY CLUES MISSED?

> *Allegations—Delay in diagnosis and treatment of infectious disease (internist and pulmonologist); failure to attend postoperatively (surgeon)*
> *Physician Issue—Failure to aggressively treat infection; failure to consult infectious disease specialist)*
> *Patient Issues—Prolonged pain and suffering; death*
> *Outcome—Modest six-figure settlement*

CASE STUDY

This 39-year-old mother of two, who had a past history of URIs, sinusitis, and otitis media on many occasions, was seen by her primary care physician about three weeks before this Sunday visit to the emergency room with fever and vomiting. She was found to have bilateral otitis media and was given amoxicillin 500 mg four times a day. Today she came to the ER in a nearby large city after having developed severe retro-orbital pain associated with nausea and vomiting. She reported that she was no better after the three days of amoxicillin.

The ER work-up revealed a temperature of 101.6°F. The chest was reported as "clear." Laboratory tests revealed a WBC count of 6,100/cu mm with 86 percent segmented neutrophils, 6 percent band forms, and platelets at 61,000/cu mm. The "on-call" internist was called, who gave her Demerol for pain, 1,000 ml, D5RL IV, and Phenergan suppositories for nausea. "Follow up in my office in three days. Check the platelets at that time." The impression recorded by the ER physician was dehydration, upper respiratory syndrome, and thrombocytopenia.

The patient returned to the ER three days later, about four hours before the appointment that she had been given with the attending internist, again complaining of persistent nausea and vomiting. The retro-orbital headache had persisted and now she complained of bilateral earaches; her temperature was 101.8°F and again she was dehydrated. She was sent to the internist's office after this visit to the ER, where her past history was reviewed. On her first ER visit no antibiotics were given; on that occasion she was admitted to the hospital. The chest x-ray made on her first visit to the ER was reported to be WNL, but the attending physician thought that his patient had a "postviral pneumonia." Routine blood work was ordered in addition to cultures of sputum and blood. In the nurses' note the patient was said to have a temperature of 104°F and was quoted as saying ," He said I had pneumonia." The note further records pain on deep breathing and shortness of breath.

The laboratory reported a PO_2 of 68 mm Hg, with an O_2 saturation of 96.2 percent. Now the WBC count was 13,400/cu mm again with a marked left shift with 80 percent segmented neutrophils and 16 percent band forms reported. The platelets were reported at 54,000/cu mm. Treatment with Rocephin 1 gm every 24 hours was begun. The patient continued to complain of pain in the chest on deep breathing and shortness of breath, but the phrase, "respirations not labored," was repeatedly seen in the nurses' notes. The blood and sputum cultures were reported positive for *staphylococci* on the second hospital day. The chest x-ray continued to worsen with increasing opacity in the right lung.

A consulting pulmonologist reported that the chest x-ray was showing signs of necrotizing, which was consistent with *staphylococcal* pneumonia. Antibiotics were changed at this point, five days after admission, to nafcillin 2 gm every six hours.

The patient was repeatedly found by the physicians to be "lethargic." One of the consultants thought there were beginning signs of empyema after about a week in the hospital. Fever increased, leukocytosis was more prominent, and the right lung showed increasing opacity. With this degree of sepsis, the patient became anemic, requiring transfusions with packed RBCs.

After a week in the hospital, the patient developed diarrhea and was investigated for pseudomembranous colitis; a sigmoidoscopic examination was negative. Increasing signs of empyema demanded a consultation with a chest surgeon. Hypoproteinemia developed and worsened, with increasing peripheral edema. A paracentesis was done on suspicion of ascites, but none was found. A thoracentesis removed about 600 cc of the purulent fluid.

Dyspnea became steadily worse, and the surgeon thought that a thoracotomy with rib resection for adequate drainage of the empyema would be necessary for the patient to improve. During the second weekend of this patient's hospitalization, all of the physicians involved in her care, which included her internist, a consulting pulmonologist, another covering pulmonologist, and the surgeon, concurred in the decision to proceed to surgery.

After the surgery the patient went from the recovery room to the ICU, intubated and on controlled respiration. There was copious drainage from the right chest. The patient was very agitated and tried repeatedly to get to the ET tube. She was given morphine to relieve pain and control agitation. Marked tachycardia was present, with rates to 200 on the monitor. She was very restless, turning her head from side to side, and agitation was difficult to control. The PO_2 was recorded at 58 mm Hg and the O_2 saturation down to the low 90s. She became very acidotic and bicarbonate was ordered by the surgeon. About 14 hours after the operation, after diuretics had been given, the surgeon ordered a chest x-ray to be done STAT and asked that the ER physician compare the two films and call him about his observations. Lanoxin was given because of the tachycardia, steroids were used in large doses, and nafcillin was resumed in the preoperative dosage of 2 gm every six hours.

There were numerous changes in ventilator settings. Diuretics were given and more Lanoxin was given IV for persistent tachycardia. The patient continued to be extremely restless and difficult to control. Nothing seemed to work, and about 18 hours after the surgery she was found to have extubated herself. An attempt was made to oxygenate her with the AMBU and a face mask. Reintubation was accomplished by the attending physician but the #6 ET tube used would not stay in place. The code was ended about 80 minutes after it started. The autopsy revealed the expected extensive necrotizing pneumonia, with near complete consolidation of both lungs.

A lawsuit was filed charging the attending physician, the pulmonary consultant, and the surgeon with deviation from an acceptable standard of care. The attending physician and the pulmonary consultant were charged with failure to assess and evaluate the true condition of the patient in a timely manner and of not using an adequate dosage of the appropriate antibiotics.

The surgeon was charged with negligent postoperative management of the patient. Experts and peers concluded after many reviews that an effective defense would not be possible and a large settlement was made.

LOSS PREVENTION COMMENTS

On review, there seemed to be some clues in this case that were not considered by the attending physician and the first consultant, the pulmonologist. On initial encounter with the ER physician, the fever associated with upper respiratory complaints and the very unusual blood picture might have been considered to be a response to a severe and potentially life-threatening infection. The WBC count was only 6,100/cu mm, but the differential was very suspicious in that the segmented cells were 91 percent of the total and 6 percent were band cells. A very suspicious finding that might further indicate suppression of the bone marrow was that the platelet count was only 61,000/cu mm, and this thrombocytopenia persisted only to begin to improve slightly after antibiotic therapy and other supportive measures were begun.

After the chest x-ray showed pneumonia, the choice of antibiotic was a cephalosporin, which is not recommended as a first-line drug for gram-positive infections, which could have been suspected in this setting. As the patient got sicker, the dose of this initial antibiotic was increased, and it was only after culture diagnosis of *Staphylococcus* sepsis and pneumonia that an antibiotic that could have been effective was given. The reviewers were puzzled as well by the fact that, in the face of a worsening situation, a more effective antibiotic was not added to the treatment regimen. It would have also been extremely difficult to defend the lack of an infectious disease consultation at an early stage of this woman's illness.

The surgeon was probably asked for his opinion later than was ideal, but he cannot be blamed for that. Perhaps the right operation was done too late. The real fact that made this good surgeon difficult to defend was that he did not personally attend his patient during the last 18 hours of her life. He saw her about five hours after the surgery, but in the face of a progressively deteriorating clinical picture, he continued to give only one set of phone orders after another. Only after the extubation and the code was begun did he come to the hospital.

Without question, the nurses on duty during the post-operative 18 hours failed to apprise the physicians in charge of the patient's care of some critical information. Their assessment of the clinical condition was consistently misleading. While they reported the laboratory findings at appropriate times, they failed to stress the patient's severe discomfort and agitation. Had they been more clinically accurate, one could conceive that the extubation would not have occurred and that the patient just might have survived. Because of these nurses' failure to act according to acceptable nursing standards, the hospital joined in the large monetary settlement.

Would this case have had a good outcome if appropriate antibiotic treatment had been started in adequate dosage from the outset? Nobody can answer that question. That is not the question that we ever have to answer in the arena of medical malpractice litigation. When a bad result occurs and we find ourselves in the role of defendant physician, we have only to demonstrate by our medical record and the testimony of supporting colleagues that we have acted within an acceptable standard.

83.   WHO/WHERE IS MY DOCTOR?

Allegations—Failure to obtain physician coverage (no documentation); failure to diagnose cardiac complications
Physician Issues—No documentation as to coverage of patient (abandonment); hospital issues as to notification of physician
Patient Issues—Anger as to physician coverage; signed out against medical advice (AMA)
Outcome—Six-figure settlement

CASE STUDY

On the 16th of the month, a 64-year-old woman entered the emergency department of her community hospital with chest pain. She was a moderately obese, two-pack-per-day smoker, with a questionable history of diabetes and a strong family history of "heart trouble" and diabetes. She also had a long history of indigestion and heartburn, frequent headaches, and chronic back pain. She described her chest pain as aggravated by exertion, accompanied by some dyspnea, and having been present off and on for a week. She also described another type of chest discomfort that was increased by deep inspiration and relieved by holding her breath. She was seen and examined by the ED physician, who found her in no distress, with vital signs within normal limits, her blood pressure being 140/88 mm Hg. The chest was clear, heart sounds normal, and the abdomen soft, without tenderness or masses. The neurologic examination was negative. She was admitted to the hospital to the service of her personal physician, Dr. Green. Orders were written for serial EKGs and enzyme determinations every eight hours times three, an AP/lateral chest x-ray, Nitrol paste, Cardizem 30 mg daily, and Zantac 150 mg twice a day. He also scheduled an upper GI series (UGI).

The EKGs were interpreted by computer and said to show evidence of a possible subendocardial injury on admission. Over the next 12 hours the repeat tracings became less ominous but were still abnormal and compatible with some lateral wall ischemic changes of undetermined age. The enzymes, including the cardiac isoenzymes, the CPK, and MB band were within normal limits.

On the 17th, the day following admission, the patient was seen by Dr. White, covering for Dr. Green. He wrote a note documenting the reduction of chest pain since her admission and noted that UGI had been ordered because of her complaints of "indigestion." The nurses noted fever of 102.2°F, which was not commented on except that there was a telephone order by Dr. Green to give Tylenol for fever and to begin Ceftin 250 mg orally four times a day. The nursing notes did not document whether or not the patient was visited by Dr. Green. The second day of her hospital stay, the 18th, the patient was apparently seen by Dr. White, who ordered back x-rays because of the patient's complaints of back pain. Dr. White also noted a "decrease in chest pain," and that the patient was to have the UGI that day. The UGI was later reported as showing only some exaggerated esophageal contractions in the lower third. EKGs and enzyme studies done that day were essentially unchanged. The nursing notes revealed a good day with no changes in the patient's vital signs.

On the 19th, Dr. White wrote a progress note indicating that there was barium in the bowel, which made the back films unsatisfactory. The nurses noted no change in the patient's condition. She had no chest pain and had been resting quietly all day. On the fourth hospital day, the 20th, Dr. Green verbally ordered hydrocodone as needed for pain. A progress note that same day by Dr. Green recorded some chest pain and shortness of breath that AM. He also ordered a repeat EKG, which continued to show the nonspecific abnormalities without significant change. The pain is recorded on the nursing notes with the added description that it was worse on deep breathing. The shortness of breath was referred to in the nursing notes by the patient as "not unusual for me." She was given some of the pain medication for the chest pain and was said to have had no pain for the rest of the day.

On the fifth day of her hospitalization, Dr. White reported that the spine films showed "arteriosclerosis of the aorta and degenerative disk disease." On the same day the patient complained of nausea and attempted to induce vomiting by sticking her finger down her throat. A standing order for Phenergan was given by Dr. Green. Dr. White noted that the patient had experienced some "chest and left shoulder pain this AM." The heart and lungs were negative on auscultation. The EKG was reported again as abnormal but essentially unchanged except for occasional premature ectopic complexes. On the sixth day in the hospital, there was more chest pain and a nitroglycerin patch was applied. She complained of nausea, ate poorly, and was said to have a "nonproductive cough." The nurses noted an "audible wheeze" on auscultation of the chest. On this day the nurses reported that the husband had become very upset because Dr. Green, her regular physician, had seen her only one time since admission. The following morning, after one week in the hospital, the patient signed out against medical advice and went to another facility in a nearby large city.

On review of her chart from the community hospital, the admitting physician in the larger institution concluded that there was a likelihood of some myocardial injury on her admission there and that she might also have some pneumonia. Two days later there was a suggestion on the EKG of further myocardial injury, although this was equivocal. Echocardiography revealed some left ventricular hypertrophy and "severe mitral regurgitation." EKGs were reported as "consistent with inferior posterolateral infarction, but unchanged" from the time of her admission to the second hospital. There was also the suggestion that the patient was in some degree of congestive heart failure.

On the sixth day of her stay in the second hospital, the patient died from a sudden bout of ventricular tachycardia. All attempts to convert the arrhythmia failed. A lawsuit was filed against the community hospital and Dr. White.

LOSS PREVENTION COMMENTS

One could not say that this patient was benefited by her stay in the second hospital, but her care in the first hospital left much to be desired and could have contributed to the end result. It is obvious from the events that Dr. White was expected to see this patient while covering for Dr. Green. But we cannot be certain that Dr. White ever understood that and it was documented nowhere in the record! Dr. White was asked in a hallway conversation the day of her admission to cover for his colleague. He understood that this coverage was to continue for the next two days. The nursing notes do not help us to determine just who, if anybody, was seeing this patient regularly. Dr. White is noted in the nursing notes and the progress notes to have seen her on at least three days of her hospitalization, but with the "verbal and phone" orders and few progress notes by the physicians it is difficult to tell. One thing is certain about the record and that is that the discharge summary was dictated by Dr. Green about ten weeks after the fact of her hospitalization on his service in the community hospital and eight weeks after her death in the second hospital.

It is obvious that the anger that developed toward Dr. White because of the confusion over who was to see the patient led to the lawsuit against him. This is a case where the lack of a clear understanding between the two doctors, one that was supported by the record, was critical to the filing of the lawsuit and could have contributed to her death in the second hospital. A simple order on the chart and a progress note by Dr. Green, the patient's primary physician, that Dr. White was to cover for him for a specified number of days could have prevented the litigation. The misunderstanding and finger pointing between the physicians made it unwise to try this case, and it was settled for a significant amount of money.

84.   NEGLIGENCE IN A GOOD PRACTICE

Allegations—Failure to monitor anticoagulant (bleeding)
Physician Issue—Did not personally instruct patient on
*   discharge; failure to stop anticoagulant appropriately*
Patient Issue—Marked blood loss; retroperitoneal hematoma;
*   congestive heart failure*
Outcome—Modest settlement

CASE STUDY

Twenty years prior to this admission, a 70-year-old woman had a total arthroplasty of the right hip because of a non-union of a fracture of the femoral neck. She did well for approximately ten years, but because of severe pain and disability in the hip brought on by loosening of a component of the prosthesis, she required a revision of the procedure. She did well for about ten years before she again began to have disabling pain in the hip, once more requiring surgical attention.

Three years before this admission the patient had bouts of superficial thrombophlebitis, for which she had been maintained on Coumadin. She had hypertension, which was well controlled. In the past she had had pelvic surgery and had been receiving maintenance estrogen therapy for many years. She was admitted this time for a total revision of her hip prosthesis. She had stopped taking the anti-coagulant about a week earlier and had received clearance for the surgery by an internal medicine specialist.

The surgery was uneventful and the patient did well considering the magnitude of the operation. Postoperatively she received prophylactic heparin and Coumadin. Three and five days after surgery, the internist noted the prothrombin time (pro-time) was "sub-therapeutic," and the Coumadin was increased from 2.5 mg, which had been the daily dose during the heparin administration, to 5 mg daily. Six days after the operation, the patient was reported by the internist to be "stable," and the heparin was stopped. Two days later, the patient developed some calf tenderness and a venous sonogram was done; it was reported as normal. The patient was walking with minimal assistance and a walker at this time. She was discharged home two weeks after the operation. The internist noted three days before discharge that the control pro-time was 11.6 seconds and the patient 13.1 seconds, indicating that the anticoagulant was moving up toward the desired therapeutic level. On the day of discharge, the internist phoned in the take-home orders, which included continuing the Coumadin at 5 mg daily. She was given an appointment to see both her orthopedist and her internist four weeks after discharge.

She returned for these appointments and the internist found her to be making good progress with her home physical therapy. She did complain of easy bruising and the Coumadin was stopped. Laboratory data on this visit showed that the hematocrit was 34.4 percent and the control pro-time was 12.5 seconds and patient 35 seconds. She had 2+ blood in her urine (2 to 4 RBC/HPF uncentrifuged).

The following day the patient began to have pain in her neck and back and became extremely weak, diaphoretic, and dyspneic. She was admitted to her hometown hospital, where admission laboratory studies showed the hematocrit to be 18.2 percent with a hemoglobin of 6 mg/dl. The pro-time was calculated at 86.1 seconds for the patient and 12.5 seconds for the control. She was in heart failure. The CT of the abdomen and back showed extensive retroperitoneal hematoma. She had massive hematuria and bleeding from the GI tract on admission. She required six transfusions of packed RBCs and treatment for heart failure. She remained hospitalized for one week, most of that time being in the ICU, and was discharged home, weak but recovering.

The details regarding just why the patient filed a lawsuit are not known. One can safely assume that it was apparent to the patient and her family that the anticoagulant was not properly managed. To require readmission to a hospital within the first 24 hours after the first posthospital visit to her physician with massive blood loss would be reason enough to question the care she received. It is possible that the lawsuit was filed in order to find out the reasons why the patient was allowed to get so far out of control with the anticoagulant.

LOSS PREVENTION COMMENTS

The investigation of this case following the filing of the lawsuit revealed that at the time of discharge from the hospital following the hip surgery, the internist intended to instruct his patient to have her blood tested at weekly intervals. There was no documentation to this effect and the nurse who took the phone orders for discharge had carefully written the entire medical regimen, including all the medications and the correct dosage of each, and the instructions for physical therapy and exercise. One would have to conclude that if the internist had ordered the frequent blood tests, those instructions would have been included along with the others.

It was also found that the internist did not know that the capability of his laboratory was such that 35 seconds was the maximum time the pro-time machine would measure. That being the case, the surveillance of the pro-time was not only in error, but the determination of the pro-time on her return to the physician's office was wrong.

Although the patient recovered, the complications she suffered were life threatening and the pain and suffering occasioned by the retroperitoneal hemorrhage and the congestive heart failure were significant. The monetary loss of an additional week of hospitalization, including the days in the ICU, was also a factor.

Questions could be asked in the aftermath of a case like this. If the internist had returned to the hospital and personally discharged his patient, would he have recognized the need to be more explicit about the need for weekly blood tests until he saw her in his office? I believe that he would. He certainly could be expected to know the capabilities of his own office laboratory. Was he new to the practice in this office setting? Was he not properly oriented to the office systems so that this mistake could have been avoided? Was this a new machine with which he was not familiar? Nobody thinks that this physician's negligence was deliberate, but negligence it was, and it threatened the life of his patient. It also required a monetary settlement.

85.   LET THE RECORD SPEAK—PLEASE!

Allegations—No real indication for antipsychotic medication;
no informed consent in record
Physician Issue—Treatment by internist is within standard of
care in treating mild depression; claimed he gave
informed consent—just did not document it
Patient Issue—Very disabling complication; tardive dyskinesia
Outcome—Low six-figure settlement

CASE STUDY

In 1980, a 52-year-old woman began to feel fatigue and had increasing difficulty sleeping; she complained of a loss of interest in sex, had occasional hot flashes, and became unusually irritable with her family. She had had a vaginal hysterectomy in 1978 and was taking supplemental estrogens prescribed by her gynecologist. With these symptoms she consulted her personal physician, a general internist who had been her doctor since she was in her thirties. A complete physical examination was within normal limits and basic studies of blood and urine showed no abnormality. He treated her symptoms with amitriptyline hydrochloride (Elavil) 25 mg at bedtime, and she improved some as far as her insomnia was concerned but developed some nervousness that she thought was due to her medication.

After about six months, her doctor changed her medication to Triavil 2-25 to be taken morning and night, which she continued to take, as she found that it helped her a great deal. She was able to refill it regularly on telephone calls from her doctor to the pharmacist.

The patient continued to be significantly improved on her medication, and though she saw her doctor every three months during the first year of therapy, thereafter she saw him only about once a year. She had no trouble refilling her prescriptions for medication.

About four years after this treatment began, the patient complained to her internist that she frequently experienced brief periods of severe anxiety accompanied by a sensation of breathlessness. Again, a complete physical examination and routine laboratory studies were unremarkable, and she responded quickly to Mellaril 25 mg each morning. She was instructed to repeat the dose at noon if she thought she needed it.

Some six years after the beginning of treatment, the patient's family noticed some peculiar movements of her mouth and tongue. When the internist was consulted, he immediately referred her to a psychiatrist, who confirmed the suspicion of tardive dyskinesia. All the medication was stopped but the symptoms continued and gradually got worse. The only diagnosis appearing on this patient's record was "chronic depressive disorder."

A lawsuit was filed, charging negligence in prescribing antipsychotic medication over an extended period without appropriate indications, which was considered outside an acceptable standard of care. Also, there was no evidence of informed consent in the medical records, which were unbelievably illegible and sloppy. Many entries were incomplete and some were entirely missing. There were infrequent notes regarding prescription refills, but pharmacy records, which were introduced into evidence, revealed almost uninterrupted treatment with amitriptyline and phenothiazine derivatives since 1980.

While there was no record of informed consent, the physician testified that he remembered discussing complications with his patient but made no note about it. He further testified that he was aware of the remote possibility of tardive dyskinesia as a complication of the medication he had prescribed. Expert testimony was given that put the attending physician out of an acceptable standard by not discussing the possibility of severe complications with his patient.

Although the plaintiff asserted that the standard was not met in that she was not referred to a psychiatrist, the expert testified that it was well within an acceptable standard for an internist to treat nonpsychotic depression.

This case was ready for trial when the internist requested settlement within his policy limits, fearing a judgment in excess of his coverage, which was $200,000. Settlement was arranged.

LOSS PREVENTION COMMENTS

A depressive episode is one of the most common conditions encountered in the primary care practice of general internists and family physicians. It is so common and initial therapy as prescribed in this case is so frequently used that we do not keep potential complications in mind. In many cases, the results of treatment are good and the patient is inclined to comply poorly with instructions to return for evaluation. Complications of treatment are so rare that we do not use appropriate care in treatment and follow-up. It is easy to fall into the practice of refilling prescriptions by telephone and not putting it in the medical record. Here, a fine physician fell into all the traps present in a case like this. The public is very unforgiving in matters of informed consent. This serious complication of a certain class of medication is well known throughout the medical community. There was no compelling reason to use the medication. No psychosis was present. This lady could have exercised her right of informed consent if she had only been given the opportunity. The courts and our patients demand no less!

86. PATIENT CARE AND THE BUREAUCRACY

*Allegations—Failure to follow patient in nursing home
(abandonment); failure to control diabetes; failure of
nursing home to appropriately care for the patient*
*Physician Issue—Could document only one nursing home
visit in six months; fulfilled Medicaid policy for
evaluation every fifty days by phone; advanced disease*
*Patient Issues—Rapid progression of vascular disease; pain
and suffering as a result of neglect by physician and
nursing home*
*Outcome—Small settlement contributed to by both physician
and nursing home*

CASE STUDY

An 84-year-old white female stroke victim was admitted to a long-term care facility from a leading Tennessee hospital with the following orders signed by the medical director, who became the patient's attending physician:

(1) 1,800-calorie ADA diet
(2) AC urine for glucose, one time daily, sequentially before breakfast, lunch, and supper
(3) Up in chair ad lib
(4) Decubitus care per standing orders b.i.d.
(5) 15 units NPH insulin q a.m., AC

There was no note in the hospital chart at the time of discharge describing any decubitus lesions. The entry history and physical examination in the nursing home chart did not mention decubitus ulcers. Six weeks after admission a progress note on the record indicated no change in the patient's condition, but an order for "C&S on decubitus ulcers" was written.

During the following three and a half months, there were orders for different antibiotics on three separate occasions, the first of which was culture specific. The first antibiotic order was for Ampicillin, 250 mg, PO, q.i.d., for 10 days. No subsequent cultures were done for the changes in antibiotic therapy. On one occasion an order was written for a topical antibiotic to be applied "to the decubitus ulcers on the inner aspects of each leg." There were recertification forms for Medicaid signed at the required 60-day intervals, but no progress notes in the patient's medical record.

Six months after admission to the nursing home, the patient was readmitted to the general hospital where bilateral above-knee amputations were done. The patient died approximately 15 days after this hospital admission. A lawsuit was filed within a year of the patient's death charging both the nursing home and the medical director with negligence.

LOSS PREVENTION COMMENTS

A careful study of the patient's medical records in the nursing home and in the hospital revealed unmistakable evidence of advanced arteriosclerotic disease involving both the brain and the lower extremities. There were notations in the nursing home record indicating repeated telephone contacts with the attending physician, but only one physician visit could be documented. The tests for urine sugar were done with some regularity and ranged from 0 to 3+. No blood glucose levels were done. While the nurses' notes faithfully record "patient turned q two hours," there was no evidence that the "up in chair ad lib" order was ever adhered to.

This elderly diabetic patient obviously succumbed to the ravages of generalized arteriosclerotic disease. Even though in all probability the course of this disease could not have been significantly altered by more aggressive therapy, a sizable settlement was agreed to by both the nursing home and the attending physician.

According to experts who were involved in the review of the records in this case, the attending physician did not adequately supervise the patient's care while she was in the nursing home. Experts who reviewed the record agreed that decubitus care was substandard and that the diabetes was not monitored adequately. The "decubitus lesions" were never described or even precisely located anatomically in the record. Although the attending physician was "medical director" of the facility, the record did not show that the physician had been made aware of changes in the patient's condition in a timely manner.

The record did show that the system worked well enough to satisfy the bureaucratic requirements of recertification for Medicaid payment, but it did not reflect a comparable level of interest in the clinical management of the patient.

The number of patients who will be cared for in this type of setting can be expected to increase as our population gets older. The medical records must show the physician's direct supervision of patient care as clinically indicated. We must not allow any type of "regulation" to dictate the level of involvement in the care of our patients in long-term care facilities.

IX

Medical Subspecialties

These areas of medical practice require a degree of procedural or cognitive skills not required by the fields of general medicine. The same requirements of informed consent pertain here and do not differ as a process from those required in any other field of medical practice. However, as the area of involvement becomes narrower, the need for good communication with the referring physician becomes greater. When the consultant "hands off" the patient to another physician or to the "regular doctor," it must be clear as to the details of follow-up and who is to do what. As a rule, the referring physician expects to do the follow-up and it is of utmost importance that the consultant pass along to him the expectations as to follow-up care.

Jousting is a term used to identify the situation where one physician is critical of another. It is the opinion of those of us who deal extensively in medical malpractice issues that jousting occurs much more often than we can prove it. Usually it occurs when the critical doctor does not have in his possession all the facts. It is probable that the majority of lawsuits against physicians are brought about by the criticism, overt or implied, of another physician. We are truly "our brothers' keepers," and we must exercise the most extreme caution when expressing a differing opinion from that of another doctor. There are ways to do this without criticism or "one-up-man-ship."

The subspecialty consultant must become a part of the involved and caring physician team that is attempting to manage a sometimes difficult and critical presentation. This involvement must continue, whether formal or informal, throughout the treatment, follow-up, and convalescence of the patient.

The medical record should describe the situation that exists and the logical decision making efforts by the treating physician or physicians. If the record reflects a preoccupation with financial matters, life-style issues, or the like, it is easy to conclude that the attending was not primarily engaged and interested in the care of his patient.

The protection of the patient must be the primary focus of the physician. Sometimes, as in the case of mental/emotional problems, this means protecting the patient from himself. Though this is sometimes impossible, the medical record must reflect that a real effort was made by the attending to create an environment where his/her patient would be safe.

While the nuances of care may be different, our record must show our primary concern for the welfare of our patients.

CARDIOLOGY

87.   MYOPIC VISION (2 CASES)

Allegations—Failure to diagnose cancer in timely manner (1)
Failure to diagnose trauma aorta (2)
Physician Issues-Did not take into account radiologist's report
of chest x-ray (1-2)
Patient Issues—Inoperable lung cancer (1)Traumatized aorta
with rupture (2)
Outcome—Six-figure settlements (1-2)

CASE STUDY

A 55-year-old female was admitted to the hospital because of an acute bout of abdominal pain that required surgery. Her age and medical history of mild hypertension made a preop chest x-ray and potassium necessary as far as the consulting cardiologist was con-cerned. The EKG was normal and surgery proceeded uneventfully. Recovery was prompt. The radiologist reported what appeared to be a small nodule in the right apex of the lung and suggested further study. No further mention of this lesion appears in the patient's medical record until ten months later when she reported to her internist with some left upper chest pain and a troublesome nonproductive cough. Chest x-ray done at this time revealed a 10-cm mass in the right upper lung which seemed to involve the pleura. A review of the preop films showed the 1- to 2-cm nodule in the radiologist's report, which had been placed in the patient's chart two hours prior to surgery.

Following a one-car accident, a 34-year-old male was brought to the emergency room unconscious. He had not been wearing a seat belt.

X-ray examination in the emergency room revealed no obvious skull fracture. The CT scan of the head was normal. Physical examination showed some slight ecchymosis over the mid-sternal area. Chest x-ray was seen by the emergency room physician and the attending neurosurgeon at 2:00 AM. No notation of what they saw on the x-ray appeared in the medical record. The radiologist saw the film at 8:00 AM the next day and reported a suspicious widening of the superior mediastinum. The patient remained unconscious but showed definite signs of neurological improvement when he went into shock, arrested, and died. Autopsy showed a traumatized aorta, which had suddenly ruptured.

The details of these two cases are fictionalized, but similar situations occur with alarming frequency and involve all the physicians of record and their hospitals in litigation. It appears that we frequently become lost in the forest while looking intently for a single tree. Do surgeons only concern themselves with the systems involved in the presenting complaint? Do cardiologists only look at the EKG? Do emergency room physicians, faced with an unconscious patient, consider only the cranial contents in their differential diagnosis? Do neurosurgeons so focus on the neurological deficit that the possibility of multiple trauma is overlooked? The answer to that question should be NO! Yet that is precisely what happens many times.

What can we do? Radiologists, develop a system to follow up on abnormal readings when your advice for additional studies is ignored. Call the attending physician about any determination that suggests serious problems, even if your findings are subtle and inconclusive. Specialists, ask that x-rays or other reports not be filed in the chart until you have read them. It is a good idea to initial the report indicating that you have read it. Record the positive findings in the progress note you make. The clinically significant findings on all tests need to include what action is to be taken. Emergency room physicians, call the on-call radiologist for an opinion on the report when you need it.

Most importantly, attending physicians, you are morally, ethically, and legally bound to consider the whole patient and not just a single symptoms complex. Somebody on this team must be the quarterback and call the signals. That responsibility is yours unless you formally turn that patient over to another physician.

This system failure is a primary cause of lawsuits. We could eliminate this failure to coordinate and communicate by paying close attention to all our colleagues involved in the care of the patient.

88.   COME TO MY OFFICE IN THE MORNING

Allegations—Failure to diagnose recurrent myocardial
infarction/CHF; failure to attend the patient
Physician Issues—Attending relied on telephone information
only; did not come to emergency department to attend
the patient
Patient Issues—Progressive complaints one week; attending
did not examine patient
Outcome—Modest six-figure settlement

CASE STUDY

With very few exceptions, every physician who reads this will have made the title statement many times during the course of his practice. Most of the time such a statement is entirely justified and is extremely good advice, but once in a while an event occurs to make us realize that "come to my office in the morning" is a piece of advice that must be given with due regard to the circumstances.

A 58-year-old man had been treated in the hospital for an acute myocardial infarction complicated by severe, persistent pain and some congestive heart failure. His initial period of hospitalization was something slightly less than two weeks. He became pain-free after four or five days in the hospital, and although he developed significant pulmonary congestion, on proper diuretics and low-salt intake his lungs cleared; at the time of discharge he was pain-free and breathing easily.

On leaving the hospital he was given instructions about medications, which included nitroglycerin and a diuretic to be taken daily. A graduated program of exercise was prescribed and he was given an appointment to see his cardiologist two weeks from the time of discharge.

During the six days following discharge, there were four telephone calls from the patient, each time complaining of chest pain, and each time he talked with a resident who had seen him while he was in the hospital. He was advised to take his nitrogylcerin regularly, was reassured, and was reminded of his appointment with the cardiologist. Nine days after discharge, on a very busy night in the emergency room, he appeared at 3:00 AM with severe chest pain, marked diaphoresis, and extreme shortness of breath. The hospital was very crowded and there were no available beds in the coronary care unit (CCU). He was observed for about six hours in the ER and given morphine, IV diuretics, and oxygen support with marked improvement. His chest pain subsided and with oxygen he was no longer short of breath. After the period of' observation, he was allowed to go home and was told to "see his cardiologist in the morning." He returned to the ER two hours later in severe congestive heart failure, experienced cardiopulmonary arrest in the ER, and died two days later.

After a lawsuit was filed, the investigation revealed that this patient's four calls to his cardiologist had been handled by two different residents. Although they communicated with the cardiologist, there was no effort on their part or the part of the specialist to have the patient speak with the cardiologist himself. Investigation disclosed that on the night when the patient went to the ER with chest pain and shortness of breath, the cardiologist approved by telephone the resident's decision to allow the patient to go home after the six-hour observation period, during which he responded to treatment. Litigation resulted in a large settlement.

LOSS PREVENTION COMMENTS

The lawsuit charged the residents and the cardiologist with negligence in the care of the patient. One of the most damaging facts uncovered in the investigation, and one among others that led to the large settlement, was that the "crowded hospital" somehow influenced the decision by the resident and the cardiologist to allow this man to return to his home rather than keep him in the hospital.

Conditions other than those presented by the patient frequently influence our decisions relative to the patient's care; in this very tragic case, it was a "crowded hospital," "the unavailability of a bed in the CCU," and a genuine belief that the patient would be better off at home than he would have been in an unmonitored bed on a regular medical floor that led to his being allowed to return home. Sometimes, when there are no financial impediments to the care of a patient, we might do things differently than we would if the patient were going to be unable to pay his hospital bill. When we practice in an area remote from a tertiary care hospital, we might well "wait" for a patient to stabilize, but when given the same patient in a tertiary care setting our management would be more aggressive. Within limits, these variations in the management of patients under differing circumstances can be fully justified. However, when there is a bad result that can be linked to decisions we make because of circumstances other than those inherent in the condition of the patient, we put ourselves in a position that may be legally hard to defend if litigation results. In this case, it is entirely probable that this patient's outcome would have been the same even if he had been retained in the hospital, but it could also be argued the other way.

89.   AGGRESSIVE MISMANAGEMENT

Allegations—Failure to diagnose myocardial infarction;
ordering treadmill test
Physician Issues—Failure to interpret EKG; proceeded with
work-up in advance of diagnosis
Patient Issue—Death
Outcome—Large six-figure settlement

CASE STUDY

A 60-year-old man with known hypertension gave a history of occasional bouts of "pressure" in the chest and shortness of breath associated with mild to moderate exertion for the past two years. These episodes had been worse the past two months. The pain that brought the patient into the hospital was described as mid-sternal, radiating to the shoulders, and associated with some breathlessness and diaphoresis.

In the emergency room, the patient was found to have a blood pressure of 160/90 mm Hg. The chest and heart were normal to auscultation. The EKG showed small Q waves in leads III and AVF with "atypical but nonspecific appearing ST segments." The echocardiogram was reported out as "normal," as was the chest x-ray. Routine laboratory values, including electrolytes and serum glucose, were normal. The patient was admitted as a "rule out myocardial infarction." Admission blood pressure was 150/88 mm Hg. The patient was symptom-free. Both a thallium scan and an exercise tolerance test were ordered.

On the day of admission, while waiting for the treadmill test, the patient complained of chest pain radiating to both arms. The physician was called; he ordered a STAT EKG and nitroglycerin (NTG) sublingually. Before the NTG was given, the blood pressure was 190/112 mm Hg. With almost immediate relief of chest pain the blood pressure was recorded at 170/110 mm Hg.

The physician ordered that the treadmill test be done, and his MD associate was to remain with the patient until the test was completed. The EKG showed the Q waves persisting in leads III and AVF, and the T waves inverted in V4-5. As the exercise test proceeded, at 6 MET an atrial bigeminy was observed. The treadmill test was interrupted, and the thallium scan was begun. Cardiac arrest occurred with documented ventricular fibrillation. Prompt and aggressive CPR was ineffective, and the patient died.

A lawsuit was filed charging negligence in the failure to diagnose the infarction and in being out of an acceptable standard of care in ordering and proceeding with the treadmill test in the face of evidence strongly suggestive of acute myocardial infarction. No expert witness could be found to support the attending physician's conduct of this case. A six-figure settlement was negotiated.

LOSS PREVENTION COMMENTS

Our attending physician in this case was an experienced specialist in a fine urban medical facility. Could it be that he had become so accustomed to success in the aggressive management of acute myocardial infarction that he had lost the edge of urgency and guarded expectation necessary to make appropriate decisions in the assessment and treatment of this kind of patient?

In retrospect, I am sure that the physician could not believe he had ignored the many signs of instability in this patient! Was he too tired to make a good decision? Was he distracted by a too busy schedule? Was he impaired by chemical dependency? What was it that prevented this physician from the cautious management of his patient, which could have had a positive outcome? Whatever it really was will not appear on the chart. It was not to be found in the area of competence, experience, or training.

It is not easy to remain alert and properly focused constantly. It is, in fact, humanly impossible to do so. How can we prevent this type of behavior in ourselves? When we get tired, rest! When we become overly preoccupied, back away—go to a movie, take a walk, or do whatever helps us to refocus with clarity on the patient and his problem. Sometimes it can be a matter of life or death.

90.   SHARING RESPONSIBILITIES

*Allegations—Negligence in allowing air embolization during
    angioplasty attempt*
*Physician Issue—Apparent lack of communication between
    cardiologist and technician during infusion*
*Patient Issues—Some permanent neurologic impairment;
    lengthy hospitalization*
Outcome—Moderate six-figure settlement

CASE STUDY

A 60-year-old man was admitted to the hospital from the emergency room because of severe, intermittent pain in his chest brought on by mild to moderate exertion. A complete work-up revealed an abnormal EKG, and coronary angiography showed significant occlusive disease of his left coronary artery system. Both the anterior descending branch and the circumflex arteries showed marked narrowing. The treatment of choice for this patient was believed to be angioplasty. He was scheduled for this procedure on the fourth hospital day to be done by a board certified cardiologist with extensive experience in angioplasty.

On the day of the procedure, the patient was taken to the special procedure room and prepared in the usual manner. After a number of changes of guidewires through the dilatation catheter, the catheter was positioned in the left anterior descending artery and the lesion was dilated. The dilatation catheter was removed from the guiding catheter while the guidewire was left across the anterior descending arterial lesion. Six coronary cineangiograms were made, and the dilatation was considered successful. Just before the guidewire was removed, the technician was instructed to watch the pressure bag, as the fluid level was noted to be low. The guidewire was removed and the team prepared to catheterize and dilate the circumflex artery.

A different guidewire was inserted into the balloon catheter in order to attempt to dilate the circumflex artery. As this was done, it was noted that the pressure system was open to air and there was a retrograde flow of blood. The technician called this to the attention of the cardiologist who instructed him to close the system. Following closure, it was noted that the pressure system would not flush properly. After the technician made some adjustments to the pressure bags and the intravenous tubing, the system flushed correctly, and the guidewire was then inserted into the balloon catheter, but it was noted that the guidewire was bent. While the cardiologist was attempting to straighten the guidewire, the saline solution was flushing through the guide catheter in the aorta. It was at this time that bubbles were noted going through the pressure system attached to the guide catheter. This was called to the attention of the cardiologist, who attempted to "back-bleed" the system, thereby letting any air introduced out of the catheter. It was during this time that the patient had a seizure and became unresponsive.

Following the seizure, the emergency alarm was sounded and resuscitation procedures were immediately instituted. The patient was examined under fluoroscopy for any evidence of air in the cardio-vascular system, and none was seen. Following stabilization, the patient was transported by air to a hyperbaric chamber for further treatment.

The patient suffered injury and his hospitalization was extremely lengthy. He did recover, but he has permanent neurologic impairment and was unable to resume his $50,000-a-year job.

LOSS PREVENTION COMMENTS

The infusion of air into the arterial system is not unusual. In this case, both cardiologist and technician were experienced people. The procedure required the introduction of a main catheter into the arterial circulation, usually in the groin, from which point it is advanced into the coronary artery. Since the pressure in the arterial side is high, the catheter must be connected to an infusion system through which some solution must be forced under pressure at all times to prevent "back-bleeding" into the infusion apparatus. The catheter must also be capable of carrying the injection of contrast medium to precisely identify the position of the catheter in relation to the lesion to be dilated. A two-way stop clock is used to allow the infusion of fluid or contrast medium, each under pressure. If there is no fluid in the pressure system, air is pumped into the artery.

This is not an exceedingly complex procedure but it can be tedious and time-consuming, requiring changes in guidewires to allow for precise placement of the balloon-tipped catheter in order to dilate the lesion. Since the team is working under fluoroscopic guidance, the room light must be subdued.

In this type of procedure, where a physician must have the assistance of a technician, a protocol outlining the duties of each member of the team would help to prevent such unfortunate accidents. The physician member of the team must precisely define the duties of his assistants. When difficulties are encountered in the catheter placement, etc., perhaps another team member should be recruited. It goes without saying that one member of the team must be primarily responsible for maintaining the infusion system, ensuring that it is free of air at all times.

Our primary goal is the prevention of patient injury. Recognizing that injury will occasionally occur despite our very best efforts, we must continue to devise systems with that primary goal in mind.

NEUROLOGY

91.   NOT MY RESPONSIBILITY

Allegations—Negligence in performing MRI on patient with cardiac pacemaker; brain damage secondary to above
Physician Issues—No past history of pacemaker in record; failure to supply critical information to consultant

Patient Issues—MRI disabled pacemaker; arrest or prolonged
bradycardia; vegetative state post-MRI
Outcome—Five-figure settlement

CASE STUDY

A 72-year-old man went to his primary care physician with a history of generalized weakness. These "spells" were prolonged, lasting for days. There were no precipitating factors as far as the patient or the family could recount. The patient's wife had died some years before, and the family initially attributed the "weakness" to depression and loneliness. The family further told of memory failure and gradual developing loss of mental faculties manifested by such things as losing his way home from a neighborhood grocery and forgetting to eat or bathe.

Past history also included previous episodes of syncope, which had been found to be due to heart block, and had been treated by the implantation of a pacemaker. A physical examination including basic laboratory work revealed no explanation for the periods of "weakness."

The patient was referred by his primary care physician to a neurologist who in a telephone call to his specialist friend described the period of "weakness," the history of memory problem, and suggested the possible diagnosis of Alzheimer's disease. The neurologist examined the patient confirming no objective neurological findings that would explain the periods of weakness. He ordered magnetic resonance imaging (MRI). The magnetic field disabled the patient's pacemaker resulting in cardiac arrest and, after successful CPR, severe brain damage. He lived in a vegetative state for six months before his death.

Suit was filed charging negligence in the performance of an MRI on a patient dependent on a cardiac pacemaker. A settlement was negotiated before trial.

LOSS PREVENTION COMMENTS

The questions involved in this case are commonly encountered by the Claims Review Committee of SVMIC. Does the primary responsibility lie with the referring physician, who gave a good account of the present illness of his patient to the consultant neurologist but did not think to elaborate on the past history of heart block requiring the permanent pacemaker? Where does the consultant get general information about the patient? Does he rely solely on the referring physician's comments regarding the case, or does he repeat the history and physical already done by the primary care doctor?

These are good questions that frequently have physicians blaming each other in cases like this. Indeed, if this case had gone to trial, the legal defense of each physician could have been based on emphasizing the liability of the other. These cases seem always to cost more money than cases where the liability rests only on one MD.

If we are to prevent this kind of bad result, good communication must exist between the physicians involved. Except in case of emergency, the attending physician should supply his consultant with a written request for his services in the management of the case. This written request should be accompanied by a good history and physical examination, including all the diagnostic tests done and the interpretation of those tests.

The consultant is certainly responsible for taking a pertinent history and doing a physical assessment relative to the appropriate specialty. The consultant would also be required to know the negative aspects of any diagnostic test or procedure needed.

In all probability, both the primary care physician and the consultant knew that a patient dependent on a pacemaker would be in danger if subjected to an MRI. Each expected the other to protect the patient from this danger. Both had that responsibility, and both were negligent.

92.   GOOD SCIENCE—BAD LUCK?

Allegations—Failure to adequately treat seizures in a timely manner; unauthorized application of restraints; shoulder dislocations (hospital)

Physician Issues—Failure to attend patient on timely basis; failure to assist in disability insurance application

Patient Issues—Pain and suffering; surgical treatment dislocated shoulders; brain damage; anger (wife)

Outcome—Seven-figure jury award

CASE STUDY

A 41-year-old professional with extremely close connections to the medical community became ill with fever and generalized muscle aching three days before his wife took him to the hospital emergency room about 8:30 PM. On that day she had noticed some inappropriate speech in addition to the chills, fever, nausea, and vomiting he had been having for the preceding two or three days. He had taken Compazine 5 mg five times over the preceding 12 hours. He had seemed withdrawn and depressed. The evaluation done by the ER physician revealed generalized hyperactive reflexes and occasional myoclonic jerking of the extremities. Even though the patient had walked into the ER, he was found to be disoriented to time and place. He did know his wife. Based on his evaluation, the ER physician called the primary care internist who asked that a consulting neurologist be called in.

The neurologist performed a lumbar puncture, which was difficult and initially described as bloody but cleared as the fluid dripped. There was no noted increase in CSF pressure, and the specimen was sent to the laboratory for studies.

In his "Neuro Note," the consultant documented some total body stiffness with occasional myoclonic jerks. The reflexes were said to be 3+, with some mild clonus at the ankles. His impression was, "Depression; rule out encephalitis."

The patient's doctor, the internist, came to the ER and examined his patient. He wrote an admission note basically repeating previously documented information. He added the patient's history of asthma and the fact that steroids by inhalation and oral theophylline had been used regularly in his treatment. He added that while the patient followed appropriately with his eyes, the speech was guttural, monosyllabic, and not connected. He reported that the CSF glucose/protein was normal. Few cells were present but two lymphocytes were counted. His diagnosis was "cerebritis vs. psychosis."

When the patient arrived on the floor about four hours after getting to the ER, the nurse described a seizure lasting about two minutes, with the patient becoming stiff and purplish. The neurologist was notified about her observations and ordered Benadryl 25 mg IV. Because of the patient's severe myoclonic movements and seizures, the nursing supervisor applied restraints to the upper extremities. Throughout the night the nursing notes recorded, "neck and lower extremities more rigid," again, "restless with outbursts."

The neurologist re-evaluated the patient about 8:00 AM and reported an abnormal EEG with "high voltage slow/sharp." The CSF report was more complete but added little to the information The consultant believed that the best possibility was encephalitis due to herpes. A consultation with an infectious disease (ID) specialist was ordered. The seizure activity was confirmed, Dilantin was ordered, and the patient was moved to ICU.

The evaluation by the ID specialist agreed with the possibility of herpes encephalitis and started acyclovir empirically. Through the next 24 hours the seizures were largely controlled but with difficulty. The patient's inappropriate behavior continued, and the fever went to 103°F. The nurses' notes mentioned the patient grimacing with pain, still showing muscular stiffness, and talking in short, unintelligible phrases.

The following morning the patient looked better but was noted to have swelling about the shoulders, with severe pain on any movement of the arms. X-rays made late in that same day showed bilateral fracture dislocations of the shoulders that required reduction and pinning of the greater tuberosities. The orthopedic consultant called in to correct these injuries did so without significant difficulty.

Improvement continued with the patient becoming progressively more lucid and conversational. The patient was discharged one week after admission, requiring many weeks of physical therapy, and still has not regained normal motion in his upper extremities. While he has recovered a great deal of his mental capacity, there persists significant cognitive difficulty. Two months after entering the hospital the patient wrote to the neurologist, stating that his degree of physical impairment and his residual memory and other cognitive difficulties made him totally disabled under the terms of his disability insurance coverage. He enclosed a form for the physician to complete attesting to this fact. More than a month after the request, the neurologist wrote, regretting the delay but stating that the disability would depend on testing more sophisticated than could be done in a neurologist's office. He suggested that arrangements would be made for those tests by a psychologist.

A lawsuit was filed within the year of our patient's admission to the hospital, charging both the neurologist and the internist with failure to prescribe anti-seizure medications in a timely manner, failure to timely and aggressively treat the seizures that developed, and charging the hospital with applying restraints without a specific physician's order. In the very expensive lawsuit that followed, a jury rendered a verdict against both the hospital and the neurologist. A very large award was given.

LOSS PREVENTION COMMENTS

This was a very difficult case to evaluate. On two occasions the medical records were thoroughly reviewed, and the peer group involved failed to find significant deviation from an acceptable standard of care by the neurologist. The internist had been dismissed earlier in the litigation. Based on the testimony at trial, the jury felt strongly otherwise!

There was a 12-hour delay from the time of admission to the ER before anti-seizure medication was prescribed. Why was this? The question is valid in view of the fact that every physician who saw the patient described seizure activity. Is the resulting cognitive impairment a result of the disease alone, or did the patient sustain some cerebral hypoxia that might have been prevented had medication been prescribed earlier to control the seizures? Did the nurse make a faulty judgment about the use of restraints? Throughout the first night there were multiple entries in the record describing thrashing about, irrational behavior, and seizures. The policies of the hospital allow its supervisory nurses to apply restraints when there is the belief that injury to the patient or hospital personnel will be prevented. It was the contention that dislocations of the shoulders would probably not have happened if there had been no wrist restraints.

These are questions that involved expert testimony on both sides of the issue. There were legitimate differences of opinion voiced by equally qualified experts. The jury, as juries frequently do, decided in favor of the injured patient.

There are equally relevant questions that could be asked about the conduct of this case that have little or nothing to do with the pure clinical issues presented by this patient. The wife was very angry! She saw the suffering of her husband, and nurses appearing to be impotent to do anything to help him. She was aware of the nurses' calls to the physicians. On the terrible night of admission (her perspective), where was the primary care internist? How much time did either he or the neurologist spend reacting to her absolute terror? Imagine: your spouse, a very bright and rising professional, becoming sick with what both of you thought was a simple viral illness that had been going through the family and suddenly becoming irrational, out of contact with reality! You watch this suffering go on, first the seizures, then the problems with the shoulders, for what seems to be an eternity! Did either of her physicians share their own confusion with her and give her the assurance that they were walking this tragic trail by her side? After the ID specialist first examined the patient, there is a nursing note indicating that the physician spent a "long time talking with the wife." It is easy to conclude that this description is made against the backdrop of other physicians not spending significant time doing the same.

Should it have taken the neurologist over a month to reply to the patient's request for assistance with his application for disability? Did he know the details of the policy well enough to conclude that he, the neurologist, was not able, from his own knowledge, to attest to the disability of his patient? It is easy to come to the conclusion that, like many of us, there is a long delay with papers constantly piling up on our desks. In the circumstances that exist here, wouldn't it make sense to go out of one's way to accommodate this damaged man and his family?

We will never know how good or bad the "science" employed in this case was. We can only express an opinion. What we do know is that the jury, on hearing the evidence, like the wife became angry and expressed their opinion. The jury's opinion is what "goes to the bank"! Again, we must be impressed with how little we can do in some instances except express the concern, the warmth, the sincerity, the compassion that one human being owes another.

93.   THE RIGHT TO KNOW—THE DUTY TO COMMUNICATE

Allegations—Failure to advise of the lesion in the lung; failure to diagnose and treat lesion in the lung
Physician Issues—Each physician involved thought the other had informed the patient; failure of physicians to communicate with each other
Patient Issues—Progression of neoplasm of lung left untreated; loss of chance to improve under earlier treatment
Outcome—Moderate six-figure settlement

CASE STUDY

A 42-year-old waitress, who had been seen intermittently by her local physician for headache, was seen in the emergency room of her local hospital complaining of sudden acute onset of severe headache and neck rigidity. A lumbar puncture produced a bloody sample, and she was transferred to a larger facility where she was re-evaluated in the emergency room. With a provisional diagnosis of subdural hemorrhage, the patient was immediately taken for a CT scan, which showed a mild to moderate ventricular enlargement. Arteriograms showed a left internal carotid posterior communicating aneurysm. Treatment was begun with dexamethasone (Decadron), 8 mg IV every six hours, and the patient was placed in the intensive care unit for observation.

Shortly after admission to the intensive care unit, the patient developed a sinus arrhythmia with associated bradycardia. A cardiologist ordered a collagen disease work-up, including a chest x-ray, which the radiologist interpreted as showing a "fairly sizable nodular density in the right apical region which seems to be sharply demarcated."

Neurologically, the patient failed to improve. Following a craniotomy with clipping of the aneurysm, however, her condition stabilized; the cardiologist was satisfied with her condition, and signed off the case the day after surgery.

By the second postoperative day, however, the patient showed deterioration of her mental status, becoming lethargic and withdrawn, and complaining of a stiff neck; her husband stated that she was somewhat disoriented. Emergency CT scan was reported as essentially normal.

The next day PA, lateral, and apical lordotic views of her chest, ordered by the neurosurgeon, again showed "a coin lesion in the right upper lobe measuring 3x2.7 cm. It is irregularly defined on its inferior medial margin and is consistent with the presence of either a neoplasm or granuloma. Tomography is recommended for further evaluation."

The patient's neurological status slowly improved and she was discharged home in good condition to be seen in the office for regular postoperative follow-up visits.

On her three-month postoperative visit in the neurosurgeon's office, the patient complained of increasing pain in her back, hips, and ankles. She stated that she did try to return to work but was unable to, due to what was thought to be an inflammatory reaction related to preexisting arthritis. She was treated with nonsteroidal anti-inflammatory agents, but two months later she returned stating that the pain in her knees and ankles had increased. A bone scan revealed a relatively large area of abnormal activity extending from the clavical to the level of the second rib on the right, and CT of the thorax revealed a 9- to 10-cm mass in the apical plura of the right chest, believed to represent a primary malignancy.

The patient was evaluated by a thoracic surgeon who believed the lesion was inoperable. Following this, the patient filed suit against the operating surgeon, the cardiologist, the radiologist, and the hospital alleging multiple acts of negligence, including failure to advise her of the lesion in her lung. Careful study of this claim revealed numerous problems with defense, and a sizable settlement was necessary.

LOSS PREVENTION COMMENTS

One can easily argue that the delay in coming to terms with the lesion in the right apex had nothing to do with this patient's prognosis. Though this may be true, no one can justify failure to inform this patient about the lung problem, and certainly nothing could convince anybody that the prognosis for a 3x2.7-cm lesion aggressively managed is not generally better than the prognosis for a 9- to 10-cm lesion managed in any manner.

What could have prevented this tragic event? Communication! Neither of the physicians really communicated with the other two doctors involved, and nobody communicated with the patient. Each physician had a primary ethical duty to communicate with the patient. Each physician failed in his duty to his colleagues, but most of all, each physician failed in his responsibility to communicate with the patient.

The past generation has seen tremendous advances in the field of medicine. Have these lifesaving advances in the scientific and technological aspects of medical practice been achieved at the expense of your desire and ability to really communicate with your patients? If so, for most of them the price has been too high!

ONCOLOGY

94.   THE DEVIL IN THE LACK OF DETAILS

Allegations—Failure to adequately manage terminal state
Physician Issues—On-call oncologist admitted for regular physician; failure to react to laboratory reports; nurse failure to notify admitting physician of patient's condition
Patient Issues—Prolonged suffering in terminal state; anger on part of family
Outcome—Settled before suit (hospital and physician); five-figure amount contributed by both

CASE STUDY

The patient was a 50-year-old man with a known inoperable "non-small-cell" carcinoma of the right lung that had been diagnosed about one year earlier. It had been determined on exploration that the cancer involved the great vessels, making it inoperable. Radiation and chemotherapy had been given, with the patient having completed the initial course of radiation therapy about three months before this visit to the cancer clinic of the medical center hospital where his oncologist practiced.

Fever, cough, and some increased shortness of breath began on the day before he came to the clinic. His regular physician was not available on that day, so he was seen by an associate, whose examination revealed temperature of 101°F, blood pressure 130/86 mm Hg, pulse 108/min, and some shortness of breath. It was noted that he could walk independently, without much increase in his breathlessness. He had been taking ampicillin for about a week because other members of the family had various upper respiratory symptoms. The examination revealed diffuse rales and rhonchi bilaterally, and the chest x-ray showed bilateral infiltrates, thought to represent pneumonitis, in addition to some radiation reaction, and not diffuse malignant spread.

The physician admitted the patient to the service of his regular oncologist and ordered IV fluids, IV and IM antibiotics, and routine assessment of blood gases prior to beginning O_2 at 2L via nasal catheter. Cardiac drugs were continued on the same schedule taken at home. The patient was noted to walk to a wheelchair in the hall of the clinic without difficulty.

The patient was admitted about 5:00 PM. The routine nursing assessment was not completed. The admission laboratory tests were reported about 6:30 PM, but the critical finding of a PO_2, of 32 was not recognized as a value that needed to be reported to the admitting physician.

Three hours after admission, because of increasing complaints by the patient and his family, the nurse called the admitting physician and reported increasing shortness of breath and restlessness. At this time the PO_2, of 32 was reported. The attending physician thought that this value must be in error because it did not square with his clinical observation. He asked that the blood gases be repeated in the morning and ordered a diuretic IV. The patient's temperature was now 102°F, and Tylenol was ordered. Again, at 9:30 PM, there was a physician order for a slight change in the IV fluid rate. At 10:30 PM a phone order increased the nasal O_2 from 2L to 4L. Each of these orders had been given in response to laboratory reports called to the admitting physician.

At 7:45 AM the patient's regular oncologist was on the floor when the nurses reported that the patient was out of bed, sitting in a chair, with severe dyspnea. Additional diuretics were ordered and given, and the patient was transferred to a special care unit. On his arrival, he was unconscious and in respiratory arrest. A code was called, he was intubated, and while the code was in progress, the patient was sent to a critical care unit. On arrival at the CCU a normal cardiac rhythm and blood pressure had been re-established, but over the next 24 hours it became apparent that there was no improvement in the mental status, and a neurologist pronounced the patient brain dead. The family was advised, a corroborating second opinion was obtained, and the patient was removed from life support.

LOSS PREVENTION COMMENTS

The patient was surely in his last days with his disease process! Because of increasing difficulty at home, he was brought to the doctor for some relief from his distress. It was not that he died that made this experience intolerable for the family, but that he did not get any relief from his suffering in his dying.

The physician who is "on call" for an associate is at risk simply because he could not know the situation like the patient's doctor. In this case, the admitting physician trusted his clinical observation of the patient being able to walk from the examining room to a wheelchair in the hallway without a recognizable increase in shortness of breath more than he trusted the laboratory value of a PO_2 of 32. We do not know what the patient's resting PO_2 was at home much of the time. We cannot know what kind of tolerance for a low PO_2, the patient had developed during the past year of surgery, chemotherapy, and radiation treatments. The admitting physician should have reacted in a more definitive manner to this finding. He could have ordered an immediate repeat of the test if he believed that a laboratory error was a possibility. He could have come in to the hospital to assess the patient to make sure that his condition had not significantly deteriorated since seen about three hours earlier. He should have done both!

The nursing documentation was unacceptable. The initial assessment had not been completed. There was only the flow sheet which noted "abnormal respiratory status" at 6:30 PM, 10:30 PM, and 1:00 AM without any elaboration in the progress notes. There was no nursing documentation from 1:00 AM until the nursing note timed 7:45 AM (late entry), which described going into the room and finding the patient sitting in the chair experiencing real distress. Much of the negligence in this case has to be borne by the hospital, which, in fact, was the final determination.

The wife and daughter told of a nightmarish 14 hours. During that time their numerous complaints to the nursing staff appeared to be ignored. Numerous times the patient's increasing difficulty in breathing would be called to the attention of the nurse without any noticeable response. The wife stated that it was at her insistence that the physician had been called during the night. Finally, the 7:45 AM event brought the nurse only after the wife had begged for attention. At this time the attending physician was on the floor and immediate action was taken.

While it is easy to take the position that if there had been adequate and accurate nursing care, the physician would indeed have been in attendance, it was the physician's assumption that the PO_2 of 32 on admission must have been a laboratory error that began this cascade of events that perhaps led to an earlier and more painful death than was necessary. It is a certainty that the family felt abandoned by those whose job it was to attend to the needs of their husband and father. The settlement was participated in equally by the hospital and the admitting physician.

95.   DID SOCIOECONOMIC FACTORS INFLUENCE CLINICAL DECISIONS?

Allegations—Failure to treat with initial and more current
protocol; delay in surgical intervention after discovery
of mass in abdomen

Physician Issues—Change to less expensive protocol; repeated
discussion of the cost of his treatment with the
patient; requesting payment; failure to follow and
treat aggressively

Patient Issues—Pressure for payment when he had no funds;
life-style issues and financial status felt to contribute
to lack of aggressive treatment and follow-up

Outcome—Jury trial; large six-figure award

CASE STUDY

A man in his mid-twenties, who gave a history of living with a male companion, was diagnosed as having had an embryonal-cell testicular carcinoma, which had been removed in another city 10 months earlier. Following the operation, the patient received radiation and chemotherapy. A complete survey for metastases showed only some small periaortic nodes, which were unchanged from their preoperative appearance and size. He had been advised to follow up with a cancer specialist in the city to which he planned to move within six months but had delayed this visit by about four months.

He presented himself to his new physician with a history of hemoptysis. He was found to have extensive pulmonary metastases and a mass in the right upper quadrant of the abdomen displacing the ureter to the right. The patient's father promised to pay his son's bill but "carried on" about the young man's lifestyle. Six months of aggressive chemotherapy was planned and begun. There was gratifying response to the first course of chemotherapy. The markers were improved and the plan was to continue with the therapy.

After the second course of chemotherapy, there was a note in the patient's office record that "nobody has even made an attempt to pay some of the bills" and that the patient volunteered that the father "may have lied to me." Treatments continued as planned for two more courses, after which there was remarkable clearing of the chest lesions and the periaortic nodes had decreased by 50 percent in size.

Just before the fourth of six planned treatments, the record states, "Asked about his bill," and, "Please try." The family was found to be very dysfunctional due to alcohol abuse. The physician had written several letters to various agencies on behalf of his patient, but on this occasion, when asked to write more letters, the physician refused because "no effort has been made to reduce the rising balance." "The father's promises were never fulfilled. Cost of our laboratory work, labor, and drugs has thrown us into a negative flow." The chemotherapy was repeated for the fourth time. The physician wrote to a state agency, "Due to a dramatic response to chemotherapy, I have suspended treatments. Current prognosis—he has entered into what we believe to be a prolonged remission."

A month later the patient noticed a mass in his right abdomen, which was confirmed by his doctor. The record indicated that the patient "wants to watch it." The plan stated in the record was to "recheck the mass and consider radiation or chemotherapy." Two weeks later the mass was essentially "unchanged, possibly smaller" and two weeks after that the physician recorded, "I think this needs definitive treatment. Discussed therapy. The patient states that the parents are destitute financially and emotionally. He doesn't want chemo."

Three months later, because the mass was found to be causing some obstruction to the right kidney, surgical removal was carried out. At this time the tumor marker, AFP, was markedly elevated. Another course of more aggressive chemotherapy was begun and continued for four cycles, but the marker continued to rise and further pulmonary lesions appeared.

The patient was then seen at another center and thoroughly evaluated. The consultant commented that there was an "unfortunate delay" between his examination where he was initially treated and the institution of chemotherapy, which he described as "at lower doses and longer intervals than we would believe to be optimal." He referred the patient to yet another center for possible bone marrow transplant. This evaluation was underway when the patient filed a lawsuit against his physicians.

He was not considered to be a suitable candidate for the transplant, and died four months later, about two and a half years after his initial surgery. Almost five years of litigation continued with the discovery of many "experts" on both sides of the matter. A long trial followed, resulting in a large award.

LOSS PREVENTION COMMENTS

Experts differ on the details of a case like this. Many considered the treatment given by the involved physicians to have been adequate. Others, however, thought that the delay in follow-up from the time of the first surgery, the choice of treatment protocol, and the delay between the discovery of the abdominal mass and its removal were below an acceptable standard of care.

The comments in the record relative to lifestyle, while truthful, may have been unnecessary. The recorded discussions of payment of bills and family matters should never have appeared in the clinical record. In this situation, although unfounded, it is easy for the jury and the lay public to conclude that factors other than the disease process entered into the decisions regarding treatment. The jury award against the physician was very large, but the jury also found that the patient himself bore some of the responsibility for the delay in the initial follow-up after his move. Under the doctrine of comparative negligence, the award against the defendant physician was mitigated by the percent of negligence ascribed to the plaintiff patient.

GASTROENTEROLOGY

96.   SAME PROCEDURE—DIFFERENT STANDARDS

Allegation—Negligent performance of procedure
Physician Issues—Patient fell from table; subdural hematoma
Patient Issue—Head injury
Outcome—Modest six-figure settlement

CASE STUDY

A 55-year-old woman had been taking an anticoagulant for ten years following placement of a prosthetic mitral valve because of rheumatic fever in childhood. This patient had noted some inter- mittent bright bleeding at stool for at least six months. She had been examined by her primary care internist, who had found very dark fecal material on rectal examination strongly positive for blood by guaiac testing. Physical examination did not reveal anything suggesting the origin of this bleeding. The internist referred her patient to a local gastroenterologist for further investigation.

The specialist repeated the physical examination, again with negative findings, but the PCV and hemoglobin had fallen from 38 percent and 13.5 gm/dl respectively to 30 percent and 11 gm/dl respectively in the two weeks since the primary care internist had checked them. With the history suggesting that the bleeding had probably originated in the large bowel, a full colonoscopy was scheduled. The preprocedure PTT was reported as 23 seconds (normal 12). The endoscopy was to be done in the gastroenterologist's office at 8:00 AM.

Under intravenous sedation with a small dose of midazolam hydrochloride (Versed) and without an attendant, the specialist positioned the table for the examination by putting it in the head-down position. Before the procedure began, the patient slipped from the table, falling about three feet headfirst onto the floor and sustaining a 1.5-inch laceration of the scalp in the right occipital region. The patient was taken to the emergency room of a nearby hospital, where x-rays of the skull were negative; the laceration was repaired without incident. At this point, the gastroenterologist took his patient back to his office and finished the colonoscopy. No cause for the bleeding was found, and it was suspected that even though the PTT was within acceptable levels, the anticoagulant was the cause of the bleeding.

Following the procedure, the patient was admitted to the hospital for observation with the diagnosis of possible concussion. She remained stable through the next 24 hours and was discharged from the hospital to be followed as an outpatient. An H_2 blocker was prescribed, and the PTT was allowed to drift lower to a level of 1.5 times the control. No further bleeding occurred during follow-up period.

Three weeks after the injury the patient complained to her internist of increasing headaches, and a CT scan of the head revealed a subdural hematoma. She was referred to a neurosurgeon who performed a craniotomy, removing the blood clot. The patient's recovery was uneventful except for residual headaches, which gradually improved.

About six months after the event a lawsuit was filed charging negligent performance of the procedure. The contention was *res ipsa loquitur*, "the thing speaks for itself." A prompt settlement was negotiated.

LOSS PREVENTION COMMENTS

This case is presented to illustrate some very important facts regarding the world in which we care for our patients these days. This patient had her endoscopy done as an outpatient in order to save her some money. She was covered by insurance, but in her plan the out-of-pocket expense for the hospital, the operating room, etc., would have been considerable. The specialist's office was properly equipped, and the physician was certainly competent. But in the performance of this procedure some vital shortcuts were taken.

Although the intravenous sedation with midazolam hydrochloride did not appear to cause trouble, doing this without backup by help that can closely monitor the patient's vital signs is not acceptable practice. Even under the most ideal circumstances, the ability of this drug to cause serious respiratory depression is well known.

There were no restraints on the table to prevent this kind of accident. Head-down positioning is required for performing this procedure, and it is reasonable to expect that protection of some kind would be employed.

The physician's office medical records were not available for three weeks after the procedure. There was no documentation of a preprocedure evaluation, and no informed consent in the doctor's record. The absence of these fundamentals in the medical record indicated that preventing patient injury did not have a high priority in this physician's practice.

As more and more of the care we give is done in our offices or in an outpatient facility, it is absolutely essential that quality is not compromised. Our patients demand the same level of care as outpatients as they receive in the best of our hospitals. Keeping that in mind will be true loss prevention.

PSYCHIATRY

97.   WARNING SIGNS UNHEEDED

Allegations—Negligence in not ordering suicide precautions on admission; negligence in failing to notify county authorities as called for in policy

Physician Issues—Admitted by phone on suggestion of treating psychologist; not notified by hospital of patient's escape for two hours; agreed to violate policy and not notify authorities

Patient Issues—Suicide by hanging; found several hours after escape

Outcome—Modest six-figure settlement

CASE STUDY

A 25-year-old mother of a 3-month-old infant was referred to a psychiatrist by her obstetrician with a tentative diagnosis of post-partum depression. The problems that she related to the psychiatrist were extreme nervousness, periodic depression, and a "jittery feeling." She stated that her condition bothered her to the extent that she could not carry out her routine daily chores. She further complained that it was difficult for her to get organized and structure her day so that she could do her cooking and cleaning, and at the same time take care of her baby. Psychotherapy was recommended in lieu of drug therapy because she was still breast-feeding her child. The psychiatrist agreed with the diagnosis of postpartum depression.

After a trial of psychotherapy, the patient decided to stop breast-feeding her child so that she could take the medication prescribed by her psychiatrist as an adjunct to psychotherapy. Even with the medication, however, there was no improvement in her condition, and in fact it worsened. She expressed extreme hopelessness during counseling sessions, manifested by her remark that she was "never going to find her way out."

It was shortly after the institution of tricyclic drug therapy that the patient began to consider suicide as an alternative. Consequently she was hospitalized for three months, and although some improvement was seen, on the day after her discharge, the patient attempted to take her life and was immediately readmitted to the psychiatric institution for approximately four months. Treatment consisted of medication adjustment, along with counseling every other day. Toward the end of her hospital stay, the patient began to improve; her outlook was better, and she felt better about herself. She felt as though she was making a recovery.

The patient returned home to her family, but suffered a series of disappointments. After a long awaited family reunion was cancelled due to the sudden death of her uncle, in an effort to mitigate his wife's disappointment, her husband planned a long weekend away for the two of them but this had to be postponed because the baby became ill. Shortly thereafter, the patient began to exhibit signs of depression, and at the urging of her husband she began weekly visits to a clinical psychologist. After several sessions, the psychologist increased the sessions to three times a week, but the patient still failed to show any improvement. The psychologist recommended to the patient that she be readmitted to the psychiatric hospital, and made the arrangements with the patient's psychiatrist, but the patient requested that the admission be delayed a day or two so that arrangements could be made to have her child taken care of. The psychologist and psychiatrist both agreed. During this time the patient again attempted suicide, and she was again admitted to the psychiatric hospital.

The patient was admitted via telephone orders of the psychiatrist, which did not include suicide precautions, though she was placed on hourly observations. Shortly after midnight on the day of admission the patient was found missing from her room, but the attending psychiatrist was not notified for two hours. While the hospital protocol required that the county law enforcement agencies be notified in case of patient elopement, the psychiatrist determined that the patient's actions did not indicate suicidal intentions, so no notification was given. Several hours later the patient was found in the men's locker room of the hospital's gymnasium dead from suicide by hanging.

LOSS PREVENTION COMMENTS

There are at least three glaring errors in management, any one of which, had it been correctly handled, might have prevented this tragic event.Certainly suicidal precautions should have been ordered on admission, since this patient had been suicidal for many months, having made two suicide attempts.The physician simply overlooked the order for suicide precautions. Perhaps if her physician had attended her personally at the time of admission, rather than admitting her "via telephone orders," the outcome would have been different.

Although hourly observations were ordered, the patient was missing for two hours before her physician was notified.The hospital deviated from an acceptable standard of care in delaying notification of the physician. Case law determines that the hospital and physician were negligent in not notifying county law enforcement agencies, since hospital protocol requires it in a situation of this type.

These last two deviations from acceptable care are typical examples of "system failure."Though a "system" was in place to protect the patient, in one instance it was ignored by the hospital, and in the other, the hospital and doctor together agreed to override it. Successful defense was therefore deemed impossible, and a large settlement was made.

X

Pediatrics

The pediatrician has twice as many patients in fact as his patient roster indicates. Of course, this means that she is faced with the responsibility of treating both the child and usually the mother. This fact requires that communication with the mother of the sick child must be brought into the role of supporting the care given by the doctor. The successful pediatrician, while examining the child, is communicating in depth with the mother. All the risks and benefits of medication, the possible type of idiosyncratic reaction to medication, immunizations, etc., must be heard and understood by the adult. This is not difficult most of the time but can be impossible at others. Nevertheless, the best ally the doctor has is an interested and understanding adult caregiver.

One of the more frequent problems that arises in this practice is the failure of system to receive communication from this adult about the progress of the child that is being treated. It is here that an experienced office staff is essential. It is a mistake for the pediatrician to so shield herself from the caregiver of the child that input from that source is compromised. The office staff must err on the side of caution when taking a call from a distraught parent and allow contact with the doctor.

One of the most devastating conditions that pediatricians face is meningitis. In the case of a sick child, usually under treatment for an upper respiratory infection, whose fever continues, who is fretful out of proportion to the efforts to comfort him, or who may seem to resist being picked up communication with the physician is necessary. This takes judgment on the part of the person who attempts to triage the calls that come in to the office. Again, it is much better to err on the side of interrupting the physician than to miss the opportunity to examine the CSF early enough to begin appropriate treatment. The majority of claims in this specialty area are characterized by charges of failure to diagnose and treat in a timely manner.

Again coverage can be a very significant issue. Most pediatricians practice in groups so they can have coverage of their practice for days off, vacations, etc. Communication between associates must be formalized enough to assure patient coverage. In hospitalized patients, this communication must be direct and in detail. Weekends and holidays are particularly dangerous times for some significant knowledge to "slip through the cracks."

Another area that is sometimes a problem is that of monitoring the level and effect of drugs known to possess toxicity potential. If a child on one of these medications needs to have liver function studies, or any other test, at periodic intervals, it is not enough to tell the mother, "Bring him back in about three months for us to do the tests again." Rather, it must be, "Stop by the front desk and make an appointment for June 25 so we can look at these tests again."

Pediatricians are a unique and invaluable group of physicians. It seems to hurt them more than most of us when medical legal issues arise.

98.   WITHOUT A QUARTERBACK—YOU LOSE!

Allegation—Delay in treatment of drug reaction (Steven-Johnson's Syndrome)
Physician Issues—Failure of group physician communication; oversight of continuation of offending medication
Patient Issue—Prolonged hospitalization
Outcome—Modest six-figure settlement

CASE STUDY

An 8-year-old boy was admitted to the hospital by the senior member of a pediatric group with fever, headache, and rash. The child had a previous work-up one month earlier for a grand mal seizure disorder. At that time studies were normal, including skull and sinus x-rays, CBC, urine profile, glucose tolerance test, CT scan, and EEG. The child was given phenobarbital 60 mg twice a day until this admission. He had been followed in the clinic and was doing well, with his seizure disorder controlled on phenobarbital.

On admission, his temperature was 103°F with a generalized maculopapular rash. There was no history of tick bite. His admitting diagnosis was febrile illness, probably viral. Following admission, the patient was placed on a clear liquid diet, given antipyretics for his fever, and his phenobarbital was continued at 60 mg twice a day.

By the second hospital day, the patient had anterior and posterior cervical node enlargement, and the erythema multi-forme type rash persisted, but he had no liver or spleen enlargement nor were his febrile agglutinins elevated. At this point, it was suspected that the child possibly had Stevens-Johnson syndrome due to phenobarbital therapy.

On the third hospital day the child was still febrile, with a sore throat, and the rash had become confluent on his extremities; his liver had enlarged and was slightly tender. He was begun on steroids at 20 mg three times a day, and by the fourth day the child had less fever and felt better, and his liver was smaller. At that time it was again noted that Stevens-Johnson syndrome was the best diagnosis, as the patient had developed edema on his feet and hands, and anterior and posterior cervical nodes and his rash persisted. By the ninth hospital day the examination of the child revealed generalized lymphadeno-phathy, a sore mouth, and persistent fever.

On the 11th hospital day, with the persistence of the fever and rash, the phenobarbital, which had been continued because of the history of grand mal seizures, was stopped. By the 13th hospital day, the patient looked much better; his desquamation was superficial, he seemed more alert, and his temperature was normal.

The patient remained hospitalized for a total of 47 days. By the end of this time his rash had cleared and he progressed to a full recovery.

LOSS PREVENTION COMMENTS

The "system failure" in this case was the lack of communication among members of this pediatric group practice about a seriously ill patient. It was a pure oversight that the phenobarbital was continued for 11 days after admission to the hospital. Had all the physicians making rounds on this patient really taken personal interest in him, carefully reviewing the record, including his medications, it is inconceivable that this could have happened. The "system" of communication between colleagues fell apart here and produced this very large loss.

An additional problem here seems to be the failure to inform the patient's family about possible complications of phenobarbital therapy. The record did not indicate that the patient's family had been made aware that a rash could occur with phenobarbital and been instructed to stop the medicine in that event. Here the AMA's PMI (Patient Medication Instruction) sheets are very useful. These sheets are available on order directly from the AMA.

99.   A SLOW WALK ON A WEEKEND

Allegations—Delay in diagnosis and treatment of encephalitis (brain abscess); failure to consult neurosurgeon in timely manner

Physician Issues—Failure to act on evidence of bacterial infection; fragmented physician coverage (weekend)
Patient Issues—Prolonged pain and suffering; severe neurological deficits (blindness/hemiparesis)
Outcome—Six-figure settlement

CASE STUDY

The patient is a male adolescent with a past history of migraine headaches and sinusitis. He had not had a bad headache in over a year, and his mother thought that what had been suggested when the problem started was taking place: that her son would probably "grow out" of this problem as he matured. On the Monday that school started back after the Christmas break, a right-sided headache began. It was no different from previous episodes. After seeing some spots before his eyes, he very quickly developed a severe headache. His mother treated him symptomatically as she had many times in the past. She gave him aspirin, put him at rest in a darkened room, and waited for the pain to subside. He vomited within an hour of the onset but this was not a prominent symptom.

When the pain did not subside by the third day, Wednesday, she made a drop-in visit to the pediatrician who had been her son's doctor since birth. The patient had vomited again that morning and there was some nasal congestion and rhinorrhea that had developed about the same time the headache started. The examination did not reveal any neurologic findings, and the vital signs were normal. The throat was thought to be somewhat reddened, the nasal mucous membrane was boggy and swollen, and the WBC count was found to be 11,000/cu mm with 86 percent lymphocytes. The pediatrician thought that the patient had both one of his migraine headaches and some allergic sinusitis aggravating the condition. An antihistamine was prescribed and an injection was given for the continued vomiting.

Two days following the office visit, the mother called her doctor's office as instructed, reporting that the headache was no better. She talked to the office nurse, and in response to the nurse's question, reported that her son had not had any fever that she had detected. She was advised to continue the treatment prescribed at the office visit and to call if the symptoms did not improve. On the following day, Friday, she reported that her son's condition had not improved and asked the physician about the possibility of encephalitis. The pediatrician instructed that the patient be taken to the hospital for admission and that orders would be called in.

The young man was taken to the hospital and admitted about

mid-morning. The admitting diagnosis was probable viremia with dehydration. Orders for intravenous fluids were given, along with instructions to do CBC, urinalysis, electrolytes, blood cultures, capillary blood gases, and give IV Vistaril for headache and vomiting. The physician was to be called when the blood work was reported. Thirty minutes after admission the Vistaril was given for headache. Three hours after admission the nurses noted, "Continues to complain of headache." A "late entry" nurse's note reported, "Lab results reported." The WBC count was 16,400/cu mm with 88 percent segmented neutrophils.

Four hours after admission the physician called in orders for a throat culture and IV Ampicillin, and seven hours after admission he came to the hospital and repeated the physical examination. There were no new findings. There was a specific notation that the neck was "supple." The attending physician's impression remained, "Viremia; rule out sinusitis." X-rays of the sinuses were ordered for the following morning and Tylenol with codeine for pain. Progress notes by the pediatrician were made again at eight and ten hours after admission, confirming the persistence of the severe headache.

Every nurse's note from the time of admission recorded that the headache persisted and that every time he was aroused from the drowsiness induced by the medication, he reported severe headache. Vomiting continued, and the patient was unable to retain any food or fluids taken by mouth. The condition continued essentially unchanged during the night. The notes by the nurses included neurologic assessments which document that the pupils consistently reacted normally to light and accommodation.

About 24 hours after admission, Saturday, the attending physician made rounds, and after assessing the patient's condition, wrote, "No signs or symptoms of CNS other than headache. Will ask neurologist to see. Sinus x-rays negative." The orders written at that time instructed the nurse to call the neurology group for consultation. Two hours later, about noon, the neurologist came, took a detailed history, and did a physical examination. His consultation note is as follows: "History obtained from the mother. Six days ago developed right-sided headache with spots in vision. Improved. Able to go to school the day after onset, but in evening, developed more severe bifrontal headache, persistent to present. Headache associated with nausea and vomiting. Some somnolence and mild confusion. Not complaining of diplopia, weakness, or numbness. At onset, complained of some dizziness but none since. History of minor headache about once a week and more severe once a month for the last four to five years. Family history of migraine. Physical examination:

sleepy, easily arousable; not particularly cooperative. Follows simple directions. Fundi benign. EOM conjugate. Pupils 6/6 to 4/4 with light. Face symmetrical. Tongue midline without dysarthria. Grip symmetrical. Extremity movement symmetrical. DTR's 1+ and symmetrical through-out. Plantar response clearly extensor on right and flexor on the left. Sensory grossly normal. Neck movable without meningismus. Impression: Probable basilar migraine." The consultant continues, "Somnolence and mild confusion may be directly due to headache syndrome in addition to Vistaril. Because of the up-going toe, should schedule CT of head. No other evidence of CNS abnormality with current level of somnolence."

The CT of the head was ordered for the following morning. The attending physician called in to order a STAT serum ammonia. The patient became incontinent of urine. The attending physician called about 8:00 PM to inquire of the status of his patient and ordered liver enzymes in the morning.

About 10:00 PM, 36 hours after admission, the nurses notified the neurologist's "exchange" of a decided change in the status of the patient. About 15 minutes later the neurologist called in to learn that the "right pupil was sluggish to react. Left brisk. The patient was incoherent and had no grip on the right. There was no response to the mother's voice." Orders were received to do the CT of the head STAT.

The CT revealed what was thought to be "areas of early abscess formation or focal areas of encephalitis." The attending physician and the neurologist both agreed that a neurosurgeon should be consulted. The patient was moved to the ICU. The nurse's notes reflected that the patient's blood pressure "continues to rise" and documented increasing somnolence and unresponsiveness throughout the night. The neurosurgeon was notified about 5:20 AM. He arrived in the ICU after respiratory arrest had occurred and resuscitation was in progress. The patient had been intubated and was on a respirator. Within two hours of the arrival of the neurosurgeon, an emergency craniotomy was being done. The surgeon's note indicated that bilateral occipital abscesses were found, drained, and excised.

There followed a long hospitalization, severe neurologic impairment, including blindness, right hemiparesis, and marked cognitive deficit. A lawsuit was filed charging both the pediatrician and the neurologist with failure to diagnose and treat in a timely manner and a failure to consult a neurosurgeon in a timely manner.

LOSS PREVENTION COMMENTS

One of the most frequent allegations made in litigation against a physician when there has been a bad or unexpected result is that of failure to diagnose or treat the patient in a timely manner and alleging that the delay caused the patient's injury. One reason that it is difficult to defend against this charge is that even when we are relatively sure that the apparent delay has not affected the course of the condition, the lay jury can easily be led to the conclusion that since a certain recommended treatment was not employed early in the particular case, we cannot be certain that it would not have favorably altered the outcome.

It has been pointed out many times that weekends and holidays are fraught with danger in the medical malpractice arena. We have attributed this to the staffing patterns in the hospitals, the confusion of on-call arrangements and, sometimes, that being on call for a number of physicians over the weekend is overwhelming. All of these factors may well have played a significant role in this case. Headache is a confusing and complicated subject! It is a subject with which most of us would like never to deal! Yet, headache ranks high on the list of reasons that people come to see the doctor. In this case, we have a patient who had a well established history of a reoccurring syndrome. The story was the same every time this young man had a headache. It began on the right side of the head. It was preceded by scotomata most of the time. It was associated with nausea and vomiting. It responded to rest in a dark room and other simple remedies. It was self-limiting and consistent.

Here we have a headache that began as usual but did not progress and resolve as expected. By the time the pediatrician saw the patient for the second time, the headache was no longer right-sided. It was frontal and bilateral. It was different from the pattern that was familiar to the family and the physician. When first seen, there were indeed signs of an allergic or viral upper respiratory condition. The WBC count was 11,000/cu mm and there were 86 percent lymphocytes. When he was admitted to the hospital, his WBC count was 16,400/cu mm and there were 88 percent segmented neutrophils.

There was patient contact with his doctor on the third day of symptoms. There was another contact with his office two days later. The advice was to continue treatment and call back if there was no improvement. The physician's office record would strongly suggest that this encounter was between the mother and a nurse who spoke for the doctor.

By the time hospitalization was required, the somnolence that was attributed to the Vistaril was not thought of in the context of a headache that had changed. Nurses' notes consistently showed continued headache, sometimes described as severe, deepening somnolence, and slowly rising blood pressure. Vomiting continued. These signs were not taken together as possibly indicating increasing intracranial pressure.

When the attending physician recognized early the signs of possible neurologic problems, he ordered the CT for the following morning. When he thought that a neurologist was needed it was into the second hospital day, and he did not communicate directly with the neurologist but ordered the consultation by a member of a group, not knowing which member would respond. Direct communication between the two physicians might well have brought things to a head more quickly.

The neurologist responded quickly but even in the face of localizing neurologic findings did not change the order for the CT to STAT. He did this only after the patient had deteriorated significantly. The abnormal CT was reported and "probable abscess" was strongly suspected about midnight. It was hours later when the neurosurgeon was summoned, after respiratory arrest had occurred and the patient was on a ventilator. Stat craniotomy followed.

The damages here were catastrophic! An adolescent with severe lifelong neurologic impairment requiring constant attention and therapy. Fortunately, a settlement was negotiated.

The hazards of the weekend, an overburdened on-call physician, and less than adequate nursing support in the hospital are all possible players in this tragedy. The lack of prompt attention to a young patient with rapidly developing signs of neurologic deterioration was, the picture painted by the facts. It is almost always an error not to proceed rapidly and aggressively in such cases.

100.   ANOTHER PEDIATRIC NIGHTMARE

Allegations—Delay in diagnosis of meningitis; delay in CFS examination

Physician Issues—Office system failure (telephone calls not documented); continued treatment without examination

Patient Issues—Brain damage; deafness; seizures; retardation

Outcome—Seven-figure jury award

CASE STUDY

During the first year of life, this infant had endured more than most children have to endure in a lifetime! He was a double footling presentation at 38 weeks' gestation that terminated in an emergency C-section. At birth he weighed just under 5 lb. A mass was felt in the baby's abdomen extending from the right costal margin to the right pelvis. Postnatal evaluation revealed a cystic mass thought to be a duplication cyst of the GI tract. During the first week of life, an abdominal operation revealed the cyst, which was removed along with a necessary portion of the small bowel, followed by an end-to-end anastomosis. Postoperatively, the infant had intestinal obstruction requiring re-exploration with lysis of adhesions and revision of the anastomosis.

Although he was a low-birth-weight baby he seemed to survive this and begin to thrive. At 4 months of age, he fell out of a moving vehicle and sustained a cerebral concussion. CT of the head on this admission revealed a prominent subarachnoid space and prominent lateral ventricles that were seen by a number of physicians and thought to be a variant of normal. At 5 months of age, he was thought to have some delayed neurologic development but was improving.

At 1 year of age, the patient was seen with an upper respiratory infection and pain in the ears. Examination revealed a bilateral otitis media, for which an antibiotic was prescribed, and an appointment was made for a return visit in ten days. However, the mother brought her child back six days later with a fever of 102.8°F axillary. The ears seemed to be improved, so the antibiotic was continued and instructions were given to "return when the fever is over." Nine days after onset the child was again brought in with a history of a questionable seizure. The fever was 104°F rectal and the ears had cleared. The laboratory reported a normal urine and a normal WBC count. The examiner concluded that the infant had not had a seizure and that he had a "viral infection."

The mother stated that on day 8 and 10 of the illness she had called the office to report on her baby, but neither of her calls had been returned. The office record showed no phone calls during this time. The child was sent home on symptomatic treatment. The day following this office visit the physician said that he called and was told that there was no change in the child's condition. This call was not recorded in the office record. Three days after this last office visit, the child was brought to the ED with a history of seizures and somnolence. Examination revealed an almost obtunded child. A CT of the head revealed a generalized hydrocephalus, and a ventriculostomy revealed cloudy fluid that showed Haemophilus influenzae on culture.

During the month of hospitalization the baby remained very ill despite appropriate treatment. Sequelae included deafness, persistent seizure activity, and profound retardation.

A lawsuit was filed charging negligence due to the delayed diagnosis of the meningitis. Specifically, the physician was charged with negligence in not performing the CSF examination earlier. The trial resulted in a very large jury verdict against two of the physicians who had seen the patient during his acute illness.

LOSS PREVENTION COMMENTS

We again have an illness that in retrospect should have been suspected and diagnosed sooner that it was. However, being honest, would most of us have done a CSF examination earlier? Our experience with this disease would indicate that "experts" come out of the woodwork to criticize our physicians. They point to the rather waxing and waning course of the complaints, which should have triggered earlier suspicion of meningitis. Otitis media is a common precursor of this type of meningitis, and although it seemed to have cleared, the baby remained ill. This should, they say, have led to an earlier examination of the CSF. Then there were the unrecorded calls from the mother during the illness that were not returned, and the call from the physician after the last office visit, during which he was told that things were "unchanged." This call was also not recorded. This raised the cloud of doubt in the minds of the jury as to where the truth was in all of this.

Expert testimony for our physician was very strong and refuted every charge that the physicians could reasonably have reacted any sooner, given the information that they had to work with.

We are left with good expert testimony on both sides of this tragic case. Assuming that this testimony cancels out both defense and plaintiff experts, what should we conclude? We have a very damaged baby, the lifetime care of whom would cost hundreds of thousands of dollars. Who was going to pay for this care that all of us believe should be rendered? Is this an example of the tort system doubling for the social welfare needs of an individual? How could one look at such a child and deny that there should be a source of funds to assure his proper treatment and care? All of us would take that position. But should it be the physician!?

101. DELAY IS DEADLY

Allegation—Delay in diagnosis of meningitis (ER physician and on-call pediatrician)

Physician Issues—Admitted by ER physician without pediatrician examination; on-call pediatrician did not notify attending

Patient Issues—Severe CNS damage; prolonged rehabilitation service

Outcome—Seven-figure settlement

CASE STUDY

A 2-year-old girl was brought to the emergency department of a rural community hospital with a history of fever 102°F to 103°F (axillary) for the past ten hours. The fever was controlled to some extent by "suppositories," the last one about one and a half hours prior to arrival in the ED. The mother reported the child pulling at her ears. Evaluation by the ED physician within five minutes of arrival noted moderate nasal secretions (character not described), and rhonchi were noted in both lung fields on auscultation. It was noted that the child's tetanus immunizations were not up to date. The temperature was recorded at 100.3°F, pulse 104/min, respirations 35/min, and weight 30 lb. The remaining physical examination was within normal limits except for the "runny crusty nose," a dull red right tympanic membrane, and a croupy cough. She was discharged from the ED in "satisfactory" condition about 25 minutes after admission receiving a broad-spectrum antibiotic. The mother was instructed to "push fluids, give Tylenol for fever, and make arrangements to see her primary care physician (PCP) in three to four weeks" to check on the ear.

The following day, the mother brought her little girl back to the ED. The same physician that the patient had seen the day before was on duty, and he saw her about 40 minutes after her arrival. The admission note recorded that the patient was taking the antibiotic prescribed 24 hours before, but other symptoms had developed. The baby had had some kind of "fit" about one hour before her return visit. The mother said that the child's eyes "rolled back," she was "walking funny," and looked "strange out of her eyes." She described a decreased level of consciousness or an outright loss of consciousness for about five minutes. At that time her temperature was 103°F axillary.

The ED physician believed that if there had indeed been a true seizure, it was likely due to the fever unless it was a "shaking chill." The physical examination again showed the red ear. The note said, "Supple neck, heart, lungs, and abdomen negative. Skin—no rash, generally pale." The chest x-ray was negative and the CBC revealed a WBC count of 23,200/cu mm with 93 percent neutrophils, 23 percent of which were band cells. Two and a half hours after arrival in the ED the temperature was recorded at 100.2°F and the laboratory/x-ray studies were complete.

The ED physician reported to PCP #2 who was on call for PCP #1, and was instructed to admit the child for observation. The ED physician discharged the child from the ED and wrote admitting orders for admission to observation status. These orders included diet, an increased dose of the same antibiotic that had been started the day before, neurologic checks every two hours, Tylenol for fever, and

CBC/urinalysis in AM. The observations on the ED record were repeated as the admission note with the added fact that the physician had consulted with on-call PCP #2.

The nursing assessment on admission was that the child responded to her name, was agitated and unable to be still, and showed no current seizure activity, though the assessment was made about seven hours after the patient's arrival in the ED. An hour later the fever was again up to 102.3°F rectal, with a pulse of 138/min, and respirations 28/min. The laboratory findings were reported to PCP #2 and additional orders were given for blood cultures and IV fluids, and the broad-spectrum antibiotic was changed to IV ceftriaxone 500 mg every 12 hours. Forty-five minutes later the nurse noted seizure activity. The pupils were unequal, the right eye deviating inward, and the left pupil reacted to light while the right was nonreactive. The doctor was called.

PCP #1 (the child's regular physician) was in the hospital making rounds about 10:00 PM and was notified about his patient. PCP #2 apparently had failed to notify PCP #1 of his patient's admission. Seizure activity continued, and control was difficult. A lumbar puncture yielded cloudy fluid, with a markedly elevated spinal fluid protein and decreased glucose, and both white and red blood cells were present in the fluid. Gram stain showed numerous gram-positive cocci compatible with *Streptococcus pneumoniae*, and cultures of both CSF and blood were positive for the same organism.

The patient was transferred to a medical center's children's hospital, where the infection and the seizure activity were controlled with difficulty. Severe CNS damage was confirmed, and months in a rehabilitation facility gave little CNS improvement.

A lawsuit was filed charging the ED physician and PCP #2 with negligence in the delay in diagnosing the meningitis, failure to recognize the emergency nature of the condition, and failing to follow the accepted procedures to rule in or rule out meningitis. It was alleged that this failure was the cause of the resulting brain damage.

LOSS PREVENTION COMMENTS

Since the advent of antibiotic therapy, it has been recognized and reported that the earlier the diagnosis of meningitis is made the greater the chance that CNS damage can be mitigated. It is also well recognized that in some cases there is significant CNS damage even when the diagnosis is made early and treatment begun promptly. The experience coming from medical malpractice action across the country indicates that when an aggressive approach to the diagnosis and treatment of this condition is documented in the clinical record, the physicians have a good chance of being defended successfully regardless of the sequelae. It is of course true that in these cases, particularly those involving infants and children, there is a great "sympathy factor" to be considered when deciding how to manage the defense of the physicians involved.

In this case, the physicians exposed themselves to criticism in a number of ways. The ED physician took it upon himself to write the admission orders for this child, which, in effect, took him out of the strict emergency role and placed him in the role of patient management, It is seldom if ever a good idea for the ED physician to write the admission orders. If the attending physician, or, as in this case, the physician on call, orders admission without actually coming into the ED to deal directly with the patient, the ED physician probably should ask the attending physician to dictate the admission orders to a nurse. This is not always easy to do. Where the relationship between the attending physician and the ED physician is one of long duration and trust, the attending physician recognizes that his colleague is at the bedside making direct observations, and from that perspective might be more able to write the appropriate orders than the attending physician who is not at the bedside. Still, in any event the ED physician should be very careful about writing admission orders. In this case, apart from the admitting orders and the responsibilities that go with it, there is considerable doubt that the ED physician would have been sued.

What are the consequences of writing the admission orders in this case? The most glaring deficiency is the failure of the ED physician to make sure that the attending physician was promptly notified and assumed the responsibility of hands-on patient management from the outset. Because that was not done in this case, the ED physician became responsible along with the doctor on call.

Here, in addition, the physician on call failed to promptly notify the attending physician. Even when he was in the hospital making rounds there is doubt that he was aware of the patient's admission. In this case, PCP #2 should have been more in evidence in the management of this child from the time of the second ED visit until care was turned over to PCP #1.

It should be noted that less than 48 hours elapsed between the initial ED examination and the intractable seizure activity that led to the spinal tap and the true diagnosis. It should be further noted that the documented ED admission clearly included the thought of possible meningitis. Neurologic checks were ordered, and there was the specific note that "neck was supple." It was the delay in the notification of PCP #1 by PCP #2 and the written orders of the ED physician that brought on the lawsuit involving only those two doctors. This case had to be settled because of these deviations from good practice and because of the tremendous sympathy factor that is always present when within a short time a previously healthy child becomes permanently disabled.

102.   THERE AIN'T NO JUSTICE

Allegation—Delay in diagnosis of meningitis
Physician Issue—No negligence on review
Patient Issue—Deafness
Outcome—Large six-figure jury award

CASE STUDY

A 16-month-old male infant, who had had the usual upper respiratory infections of babies—otitis media, red throat, bronchitis—and who had responded to treatment with antibiotics, was brought to his doctor on the 10th of the month for sudden onset of fever, rhinorrhea, anorexia, and malaise. Examination revealed a red throat, no significant adenopathy, a negative chest examination, and a fever of 103.2°F. An injection of benzathine penicillin was given and aceto-minophen was prescribed for the fever.

Three days later the child had not improved, and office notes describe a "very irritable" little boy who still had a red throat and was still somewhat lethargic and febrile. There were no other positive physical findings. At this point, the attending physician added to the treatment cephalexin, a cephalosporin, by mouth.

The following day the mother brought the child to the emergency room with continued fever, anorexia and irritability; the fever again was recorded as 103.2°F and again the examination showed only a "red throat." A specific reference in the record stated that there was "no stiff neck." The mother was advised to continue the cephalexin and ASA for fever. Laboratory studies revealed a WBC count of 13,400/cu mm with 45 percent segmented neutrophils, 3 percent bands, and 52 percent lymphocytes.

Two days later, six days after the onset of fever, with the child still very sick, the examination showed a stiff neck. CSF studies showed 267 WBCs, mostly segmented neutrophils, and an elevated protein; cultures grew Hemophilus influenzae, type B. Amoxicillin was begun immediately after the spinal fluid was obtained. The child was afebrile in four days and recovered within a week. The amoxicillin was continued for a total of 10 days.

As the patient improved, it became apparent that his hearing was severely impaired. After a thorough evaluation by a speech and hearing center, it was determined that the deafness, in all probability due to the Hemophilus, was very probably going to be permanent. Shortly afterward, a lawsuit was filed charging the attending physician with negligence because of the delay in diagnosis of the true nature of the child's illness. It was charged that this delay in diagnosis caused the little boy's deafness.

LOSS PREVENTION COMMENTS

In the development of this case, expert witnesses gave testimony on both sides of this issue. Very credible physicians took opposite views on the relationship of the delay in diagnosis to the complication of deafness. The expert for the plaintiff stated that the probability was that if the antibiotic had been started earlier, the deafness would not have occurred. The defense expert pointed out that at least half the time deafness would have developed in a situation like this regardless of when appropriate treatment had been started. The defense further pointed out that on the first day that any evidence of meningeal irritation (stiff neck) developed appropriate treatment was begun.

The claims review committee of SVMIC thoroughly reviewed this case on two occasions and considered that there had been no significant deviation from an acceptable standard of care. Both the attending physician and the emergency room physician were sued and the jury found against both. The very large award was in the high six figures.

While there was no deviation from the standard of care in this case, can we learn anything from this case that might prevent this type of litigation? Yes. We can learn that a jury faced with a situation of this type is likely to award lots of money because of the expenses incurred and the likelihood of future costs related to the child's deafness. We can also learn to examine the CSF early in the patient with a febrile illness where there is no apparent cause and there has been no response to the usual treatment. For the physician caught up in this kind of situation there truly "ain't no justice."

103.   WHO SAID IT WOULD BE FAIR?

Allegations—Medication error (Theophylline)
Physician Issues—Unauthorized comment by physician at receiving hospital; no negligence on repeated review
Patient Issue—Sick baby not treated with acceptable standard
Outcome—Modest six-figure settlement

The truth is that the caliber of medical practice is almost always very good and meets any test of reasonableness that could be applied. In the "Case of the Month," where we are pointing out the ways that loss could have been prevented in cases where the care did not meet an acceptable standard, it is easy to lose sight of that fact. Occasionally it is necessary to demonstrate the uncertainties of the medical-legal environment by presenting a case where the management was thought to be good and the loss occurred anyway. The case that follows is one of those.

CASE STUDY

The patient was the product of a difficult labor and delivery three months before the case in question begins. The mother was a 16-year-old smoker. After attempts by the obstetrician to deliver this baby by first applying Kielland forceps, then trying Simpson-DeLee outlet forceps, the patient was taken for cesarean section. The baby had very poor Apgar scores and was cyanotic, requiring oxygen support. About four hours after delivery the baby's rectal temperature was recorded as 96.9°F and the blood sugar was recorded as 32 mg/dl. This was promptly corrected and the child left the nursery at 6 days of age, nursing well.

This little patient was doing well at 2 months of age, when seen in the office of the attending physician. The weight and height were within normal range, and it was recorded that the immunizations were being given by the county health department.

Two months later, at 1:24 AM, the patient was seen in the hospital emergency room with cough and diarrhea. On physical examination, the baby was wheezing and grunting on respiration. The rectal temperature was 97.9°F, pulse 160/min, and respirations 60/min. There was typical thrush in the mouth. The chest x-ray was suspicious of an infiltrative process, and the child was admitted with a diagnosis of thrush and "rule out pneumonitis."

The attending physician, who practiced in a group of three pediatricians, was called and agreed with the ER physician's orders of Amoxicillin, Mycostatin, routine formula, mist tent, and throat culture. The nurse carried out the orders and noted that the child was pale, had audible wheezes, and did not appear to "focus on anything" visually. The admitting physician, on call for his group the night of admission, came in to see the baby early the next morning and gave an order to discontinue the mist tent since the patient appeared so very fretful in it. Again, it was observed that the eyes did not appear to focus on anything.

The child did not improve during the first few hours in the

hospital and the tent was restarted. Another one of the group of pediatricians saw the baby and ordered intramuscular steroids, and an increase in the antibiotic coverage. The bronchial dilator Isuprel had been ordered on admission. An ophthalmologist who was consulted thought that the optic nerves were hypoplastic. He placed great weight on the history of "blindness since birth" in one of the grandmothers. He asked to see the patient in his office after discharge from the hospital.

The baby continued to have respiratory difficulties, and about 24 hours after admission, another one of the attending physician's associates changed the bronchial dilator to theophylline (Marax) 2 cc every four hours. The child continued to be fretful and cried almost constantly, becoming increasingly irritable and requiring some sedation. The attending physician visited the second morning after admission and detected no significant change in the patient's condition. Later in that day, the attending physician ordered Phenergan suppositories 12.5 mg every four hours as needed for restlessness. These were given three times in the eight hours after they were ordered.

The baby continued to be extremely fretful, crying almost constantly, and eating and drinking almost nothing. The wheezing continued unchecked. About 22 hours after admission, a nurse found the child lying on his stomach and not breathing. CPR was begun immediately; the attending physician came in promptly. With "bag breathing" the infant regained spontaneous respirations, but within the hour, the patient vomited, aspirated, and arrested again. The attending physician intubated the child without difficulty and a transfer to a children's hospital was promptly made.

In the children's hospital, the patient was put on a ventilator and given phenobarbital. Sodium bicarbonate was given to correct the respiratory acidosis and the patient slowly improved. A blood level for theophylline was obtained on admission to the receiving hospital and was found to be 20.5 μg. The baby was described to have "twitching of seizures" shortly after admission, for which Dilantin was prescribed later in the stay. Liver studies were negative for any evidence of hepatitis in the face of an admission SGOT of 600 U/L.

One of the treating physicians in the receiving hospital responded directly to an inquiry from an attorney representing the patient, and in the letter speculated that the level of theophylline may have been in the "toxic range" in the referring hospital.

The lawsuit filed alleged that the improper treatment in the community hospital caused the blindness and the mental retardation. The case was first filed in the circuit court of Tennessee, subsequently nonsuited and refiled in the federal district court where the first trial ended in a hung jury. Codefendants, the hospital and the manufacturer of the theophylline, settled with the plaintiff, leaving our pediatricians as the sole defendants.

There was sufficient expert testimony regarding the theophylline level and the chances of a filing against the obstetrician, who was not sued in this case, to justify a compromise settlement.

LOSS PREVENTION COMMENTS

This case was reviewed on two occasions by the SVMIC Physicians' Claims Review Committee, and each time, while the dangers of the letter from the receiving hospital were apparent and the involvement of all three of the physicians in this group might give rise to the claim during trial that the care of this baby was fragmented and uncoordinated, there was the unanimous opinion that there was no deviation from an acceptable level of care.

In this kind of case, where there is no detectable medical error and we still lose, the area of management that we need to scrupulously examine is the area of the physician/patient relationship. A failure in this area will not make itself readily discernible from a study of the medical record. Questions that we must ask are: Was the family kept constantly aware of our attention to the patient? Did we take the time to communicate to them our real concern for the one we were treating? Did the individual members of the treatment team communicate with each other to give our patient the benefit of our collective wisdom? Each time we raise these questions with ourselves, we become more conscious of the very real personal elements of our daily work.

104.   FAILURE TO MONITOR

Allegations—Failure to give informed consent for medication; failure to follow for evidence of toxicity from the medication

Physician Issue—Failure to recognize that both nortriptyline and Cylert were not being monitored

Patient Issue—Hepatic damage leading to death

Outcome—Large six-figure settlement

CASE STUDY

A 6-year-old girl who began seeing her pediatrician with a diagnosis of attention deficit hyperactive disorder (ADHD) was already taking Ritalin, and her mother brought with her an evaluation by the school psychologist. The testing showed performance abilities to be average to high. Attention and impulse control problems were confirmed by testing and the child was referred to this pediatrician for evaluation and perhaps further medication. On further testing, the child scored within the clinical range of being socially withdrawn with anxious obsessive behaviors. She also scored in the clinical range for hyperactive and aggressive behavior. Nortriptyline was added to the treatment regimen at this time at a dose of 25 mg at bedtime for one week then 50 mg at bedtime.

The child's teacher performed an evaluation monthly for the next two months. She was said to be loud, making noise constantly; she was unable to be still, and had a very short attention span. The second month's evaluation showed minimal improvement, but the child continued to be loud, easily upset, and occasionally showed aggressive actions toward other children, such as throwing rocks at them.

Two months after the nortriptyline was started a blood level showed the medication to be low, though within the acceptable range. The patient seemed to be a little better, and the nortriptyline was increased to 50 mg in the morning and 25 mg at night. A note was added to the record, "If cannot perform at school will add pemoline (Cylert). Recheck in a month."

A month later the mother complained that the child's stools were very hard and that she had difficulty in defecating. Pemoline 37.5 mg was added to the regimen, with instructions to check drug levels in one month and to return for a visit in two months. When the drug levels were checked a month later the nortriptyline level was at 154, which was in the high acceptable range. The liver enzymes were normal. About a month later, with the ADHD showing some improvement the medications were continued with the same dosage, pemoline a 37.5 mg tablet in morning and a half tablet at night. Nortriptyline was continued at the same dosage, 50 mg in the morning and 25 mg in the evening.

In April, three months later, she appeared to be better at home, but the school performance was still poor, though she was more manageable. She continued to be very constipated.

In July the patient's complaints were essentially unchanged. The medical record showed that instructions were given to have the nortriptyline level checked in one month and to return for a visit in four months. There was no mention in the record that the liver enzymes were to be rechecked at that time

Three months later the child was brought in jaundiced and

complaining of weakness and loss of energy. Pemoline was stopped. The blood work showed the nortriptyline still in the high acceptable range, but the liver enzymes very high, with the SGOT at 2,688 U/L and the SGPT 2,616 U/L. The serum bilirubin was 13.4 mg dl. She was admitted to the hospital, where further liver evaluations all showed marked deterioration. Consultants confirmed the liver problems and the consensus was that the child had severe necrosis, probably due to the pemoline. She was transferred to a transplant center for evaluation for a liver transplant, but she continued to deteriorate, and died before a liver became available.

A lawsuit was filed charging the pediatrician with failure to allow the parents to give a truly informed consent and the failure to properly monitor the child for evidence of toxicity. There were no experts willing to testify on behalf of this physician in the management of this patient, and a large settlement was required to end this litigation.

LOSS PREVENTION COMMENTS

Careful study of this record indicated that the physician did not clearly indicate whether both of the drugs this child was taking were to be checked each time he ordered blood levels on nortriptyline. I am led to believe that the doctor intended that both the level of the nortriptyline and the liver enzymes for pemoline were to be done each time she was sent to the laboratory, but this was not done, and the fact that it was not done was overlooked.

Nortriptyline is not recommended by the FDA for pediatric use and that is so stated in the Physician's Desk Reference. Drugs not recommended for a specific use are frequently used with good results, but when that appears necessary the patient should be made aware that it is clinical experience that dictates that the drug is beneficial even though it is not yet recommended for that purpose by the FDA. Adequate precautions were taken with this drug, and blood levels were correctly obtained to monitor it.

Pemoline has been known to be hepatotoxic from the beginning of its use in clinical medicine and liver function studies have been strongly recommended before it is begun and periodically during its use. How often is "periodically"? The literature leaves that to the judgment of the clinician, but certainly the frequency of monitoring in this case was inadequate. Over the period of 11 months during which this drug was used, the clinician had only one report of liver enzymes in the record before the child came to the office jaundiced. The literature seems to indicate that if enzyme levels are evaluated this effect is reversed on discontinuing the drug. Caution is also recommended in the combined use of pemoline and other drugs with CNS activity.

What should we do in a case like this? Clearly we must make the patient, or the patient's parents in this case, aware that pemoline could cause liver problems and that monitoring is of utmost importance, because these signs usually clear if the drug is stopped. We should adopt a reasonable schedule for checking the blood for levels, as in the case of nortriptyline, or the liver function for any signs of toxicity due to pemoline. I believe this clinician intended to monitor this patient more closely for signs of liver toxicity but failed to recognize that the appropriate tests were not being done. This kind of "system" can be handled by office employees if they are properly trained and motivated. Without informed consent and proper monitoring of potentially dangerous drugs, this outcome is unacceptable.

105.   EARLY SUCCESS—LATER FAILURE

> *Allegation—Failure to diagnose and treat small bowel*
>   *obstruction*
> *Physician Issues—Failure to respond to worsening condition*
>   *by telephone; failure to attend patient in emergency*
>   *department*
> *Patient Issues—Pain and suffering; death*
> *Outcome—Large six-figure settlement*

CASE STUDY

A 6-lb 3-oz male infant with a large omphalocele was delivered vaginally at 41 weeks. Within a few hours after delivery he was transferred as an emergency to the medical center's intensive care nursery for definitive surgical treatment. On the first day of life the surgical repair of the omphalocele was accomplished, but during the first week feedings were difficult to establish. A large right inguinal hernia and a smaller left inguinal hernia and hydrocele were identified and repaired.

After about six weeks in the hospital the infant was discharged home. He took formula, cereal, and fruit by 3 months of age. At 4 months, he weighed 12 lb and seemed to be doing well from a nutritional standpoint. The mother was worried about a deep pilonidal dimple with an area of firmness that the pediatrician believed was the coccyx. On this visit, the physician commented on some asymmetry of the head, with the left ear protruding remarkably while the right one lay fairly flat against the head. The doctor believed the baby was a "little slow" to hold up his head, but commented that he was very active, squealing and smiling. At about 6 months of age an ultrasound examination of the spinal cord showed no tethering of the cord or other abnormality.

The baby was being followed both by the hometown pediatrician and the medical center physicians. An MRI done in the community hospital showed that the pilonidal dimple area was normal. At the six-month visit the baby was "not sitting well," and was felt to be "lagging" a little neurologically, but was said to be quite "active." An early development program was begun on the occasion of his examination by physicians in the development and genetic center of the university. Chromosome evaluation revealed the child to be a normal XY male. While there was good bulk and strength at this examination, there was still some delay in sitting even when propped. There was mild motor delay in this 7-month-old infant, and the comment was made that while the child was very socially interactive, there seemed to be some lack of tone in the trunk and hyperactivity of the deep tendon reflexes of the lower extremities.

From 7 months to about 9 months of age there was a series of upper respiratory infections, principally bilateral otitis media, which cleared on antibiotic therapy. At 11 months of age the infant was "doing great." Motor skills appeared to be normal, and he was saying several single words. He seemed to have turned the corner neurologically.

At 14 months of age he was seen with a 24-hour illness, with vomiting but no diarrhea, and a temperature of 100.6°F. He had a wet diaper, but his skin was a "little dry." The throat was hyperemic with some exudate on the tonsils. Bowel sounds were hyperactive, a sort of "drippy cave" sound, and the child was thought to have a viral infection involving the throat and the intestinal tract. A throat culture was done and further treatment was delayed. The mother was instructed to call the pediatrician later that day and report the patient's condition. It was documented in the record that the doctor did not think the symptoms were related to the previous surgery and that there had been several cases of what appeared to be viral gastroenteritis in the area, although there had been more diarrhea than vomiting associated with them.

The mother called the pediatrician at 2:00 AM and 6:00 AM reporting continued vomiting, hardness of the abdomen, and continued crying. At 7:00 AM, the child was brought into the community hospital's emergency department in full cardiac arrest. Resuscitation was unsuccessful. Autopsy revealed small bowel obstruction.

A lawsuit was brought charging failure to timely diagnose intestinal obstruction. Physician reviewers believed that the pediatrician did not deviate from an acceptable standard of care. The doctor responded appropriately when the patient was examined within 24 hours of the onset of the condition, however there were weaknesses in the management of the infant that made settlement the wise option.

LOSS PREVENTION COMMENTS

The physician made the comment in the record that she took into account in her evaluation the history of the patient's massive abdominal surgery as a neonate. The examination revealed hyperactive bowel sounds, but no laboratory studies were done that might have revealed electrolyte problems and more dehydration than was apparent. A judgment was made to proceed with close observation, and it appears that the facts justified that disposition. The mother was appropriately instructed to call the doctor and report on the child's progress, and she did call twice, reporting continued vomiting, crying, and inability to retain fluids. In retrospect, we could find fault with the doctor for not getting the child into the ED for examination.

This child's illness progressed very rapidly! In less than 48 hours after onset, the baby died. It was less than 12 hours after the physician's examination that the patient was dead on arrival to the ED. Small bowel obstruction progresses rapidly in adults and even faster in children. Severe electrolyte problems develop quickly. Such rapid development apparently occurred in this case and the child died.

The parents of this baby must have felt cheated! They had followed their child through the critical times of massive surgery. They had watched their infant grow and develop even in the face of some delay and anxiety over the eventual outcome. It must have seemed from about 11 months of age until the terminal illness began that all the effort on their part and the dedication and skill of the physicians and other care givers was being rewarded in the growth and development of their little boy. All gone in such a short period of time!

This is a difficult call and yet, on balance, with the death of a child and the problems with management, it did not seem prudent to proceed to trial.

XI

Obstetrics

In the management of the routine obstetrical case, there are two individuals at risk, the mother and the fetus. More and more, we are learning how to assess the condition of both. It is in the areas of assessment and surveillance that so much progress has been, and is being made. With the development of the Electronic Fetal Monitor (EFM) came the ability to assess the condition of the baby during labor. While this technology has been put in general use, the ultrasound has added to the capabilities of the physician to follow the development of the fetus, gauge its size, discover abnormalities of development and rarely intervene in the pregnancy to correct them.

With the technology, there has come the expectation that nothing can go wrong. Both mother and baby will have a happy experience. While this happens the majority of the time, it doesn't happen all the time. When it does not happen somebody has to be at fault! The obstetrician should, during her contact with the mother during gestation, bring some reality to the experience. In almost every pregnancy, there will be the opportunity for the patient to ask about progress, development, etc. At these times the physician can bring reality to the table with a discussion of the limitations of technology and just how much that we still do not know. This can be done in a way that is reassuring to the patient that her doctor is knowledgeable about the known and the unknown in her specialty.

The EFM has been a life saver for both mother and baby. It requires skilled interpretation and the obstetrician must be supported by personnel able to keep her informed with reliable data during the labor process. This requires the doctor to respond to this support in the labor room by being present when needed or called for. The "bad" baby usually is one with neurological deficits that could be due to an unrecognized event during labor. This is one of the most frequent charges brought against obstetricians and the most expensive. Even when there is no real element of physician negligence, the jury looks at the damaged child, and the doctor and her colleagues become the social service agency that will support and care for the infant.

Gestational diabetes is a very real danger to the successful outcome of pregnancy. When there is any evidence that this condition might be present, the monitoring of blood sugar becomes essential. When the medical record does not support the fact that there has been this aggressive monitoring and there is some developmental problem or a stillbirth occurs defense is difficult and most of the time impossible. A timely cesarean section is frequently indicated.

When the development of hypertension, proteinuria, edema, or any of the signs of toxemia occur, they must be treated, and close monitoring is required. If these symptoms continue or worsen, the physician is frequently called upon to empty the uterus by C-section. Again, when the medical record does not support this aggressive approach and mother or baby is compromised, defense is problematic if a lawsuit develops.

With the development of any of these warning signs the patient must be thoroughly made aware of the possible consequences of surgery or problems with the fetus. When this is done, most of the time there is no legal action. When these events come as a surprise to the patient or spouse, we can expect to hear from an attorney. Of course, every bad result cannot be anticipated, but when it is reasonable to expect, the patient and her spouse must be informed.

Obstetrics is practiced in groups. Serious problems can and have arisen when all the members of the group, any one of whom may, on a given day or night, be called upon to attend the patient of an associate, do not know the plans for that patient or the significant facts regarding the prenatal course. Internal systems in the place of practice must be worked out so that this does not occur. The threat of legal action in this specialty is greater than in any other and must be taken into consideration by the practitioner with every patient.

106.   THE PERSONAL APPEARANCE

Allegation—Negligence in failing to examine patient on first emergency room visit
Physician Issues—Marked hypertension should have triggered examination; allowed patient to go home; aggressive and appropriate treatment on second admission to ER
Patient Issues—Seizure secondary to eclampsia; prolonged hospitalization
Outcome—Six-figure settlement

CASE STUDY

A 31-year-old primagravida was first seen by her obstetrician in December and found to be 16 to 18 weeks pregnant. The prenatal course was completely uneventful. Blood pressure ranged between 110-120/70-80 mm Hg. Urines were consistently negative for protein, and no edema was present. At 39 weeks, the blood pressure was 140/100 and a trace of albumin was present. Ultrasound showed the fetus in a breech position.

Three days after this last visit, the patient went to the emergency room of the hospital complaining of shortness of breath and muscle spasms in the neck and back. When her blood pressure was found to be 210/110, her physician was notified; he gave a phone order for hydroxyzine (Vistaril), 50 mg intramuscularly. Five minutes after the injection, the blood pressure was found to be 180/110, but five minutes later it was 210/130. Voided urine tested by dip stick was read as negative for albumin. Two hours later, while still under observation in the ER, the patient continued to complain of back pain, and a phone order was obtained from her physician to give her 8 mg of morphine sulfate and to discharge her from the ER. After the patient admitted to "feeling some better," she expressed some reluctance to going home. Reassured by the ER personnel, she left the ER and was instructed to call if further problems developed.

Two hours later she was returned to the ER in a comatose state, following what was described as a typical grand mal seizure. After arrival at the hospital, a second seizure occurred. Her obstetrician was called and on arrival he noted 1+ edema and 3+ albumin in the urine. With the diagnosis of eclampsia, an emergency cesarean section was scheduled, and an 8-lb 2-oz baby was delivered with Apgar scores of 6 and 8.

Her postoperative course was complicated by disseminated intravascular coagulation with blood loss, partial renal shutdown requiring dialysis, a pulmonary embolus confirmed by lung scans, and protracted coma. The patient awakened 12 days after her section, and after a prolonged hospital stay was discharged with no apparent residual damage.

A suit was filed against the physician charging negligence for failure to attend his patient in the ER and for treating her without benefit of his own personal examination and evaluation. A large cash settlement was paid.

LOSS PREVENTION COMMENTS

Without question aggressive and heroic treatment by the attending physician saved the life of this patient and her baby, but unfortunately this was not enough to prevent a successful lawsuit! The patient's attorney was able to find all the expert testimony he needed to prove a deviation from an acceptable standard of care. In retrospect, the doctor could be criticized for not interpreting the visit at 39 weeks, which revealed a blood pressure of 140/110 and a trace of albumin, as a sign of toxemia requiring bed rest and daily office visits or hospitalization. This was not the legal problem. Even the treatment given in the ER and the period of observation, although suspect, were not the underlying legal problem. We would agree that sending a patient like this home from the ER was a gross clinical error. Even this was not the legal problem.

The primary deviation from an acceptable standard of care in this case was the failure of the attending physician to personally come to the ER, examine his patient, and, with the benefit of his own personal evaluation, institute treatment. This behavior on the part of the physician could in no way be defended, and settlement was required.

The law does not require us always to be right, but it does require us always to be careful and reasonable. When we fail to personally attend outpatients in the ER and a catastrophe follows, we will find that defending ourselves against the charge of malpractice will be extremely difficult, if not impossible.

107. TECHNOLOGY! GOOD NEWS—BAD NEWS

*Allegation—Delay in diagnosis and treatment of
     compromised fetus
Physician Issues—Judgment call to allow labor to continue;
     abnormal fetal monitor tracing
Patient Issue—Brain-damaged infant
Outcome—Large six-figure settlement*

CASE STUDY

A 27-year-old female, gravida 2, para 0, abortus 1, was admitted to labor and delivery at 12:30 PM on May 27, 1980, with expected date of confinement of May 9, 1980, and with a history of her membranes having ruptured four hours earlier. There was slight meconium staining. Fetal heart tones were recorded by the nurse at 134/min with mild contractions every five to six minutes lasting 45 seconds, cervix 80 percent effaced and dilated to 3 to 4 cm. The head was presenting at -1 station. Following the preparation and enema, the patient's fetal heart tones and contractions were monitored externally and intravenous fluids were begun.

The patient's obstetrician examined her at 2:30 PM and applied the scalp electrode for internal monitoring of fetal heart tones; baseline was 140-150/min with normal variability. Epidural anesthesia was administered by a certified registered nurse anesthetist with bupivacaine (Marcaine) 0.25 percent without difficulty. No change in variability was noted following administration, but following it, though the contractions continued every three to four minutes, they were of only mild intensity. At 4:00 PM the cervix was 4 to 5 cm dilated and 90 percent effaced; the vertex presentation was -1 station. Following examination by the physician, a 1:1000 oxytocin (Pitocin) drip in 5 percent dextrose Ringer's lactate solution was begun at two drops per minute. Shortly afterwards the patient began to experience variable decelerations with return to baseline, indicating that the fetus was tolerating the variable decelerations. The oxytocin drip was increased as per protocol and the patient was placed on her left side, but she continued to have variable decelerations with each contraction and the variability was only minimal prior to the next dose of bupivacaine.

The patient's physician examined her again at 5:30 PM, noting the cervix to be 7 to 8 cm dilated, +1 station. At 5:35 PM, the patient experienced an episode of bradycardia of 60/min which lasted five to six minutes. The oxytocin drip was immediately discontinued, patient was turned on her left side, oxygen administered at 10 liters/min, and IV fluids were increased. The baseline returned to 140-150/min but she began having severe decelerations and variability was noted to be absent. The attending physician again examined the patient, finding cervix completely dilated and +1 station. She was allowed to continue labor since delivery would be soon. The patient continued to have severe decelerations with slow recovery to the baseline and absent variability. At 6:30 PM when a second episode of bradycardia of 60/min occurred, emergency delivery was performed by the physician with low forceps. The umbilical cord was wrapped tightly twice around the infant's neck. A 6-lb 3-oz male was delivered with Apgar scores of 0 at one minute, 2 at five minutes. The infant was unresponsive to positive pressure and oxygen mask resuscitation at two minutes and the pediatrician took over resuscitation, which required intubation followed by slow increase in heart rate and improvement of color. The infant began having seizures at 12 hours of age. Final diagnosis was hypoxic encephalopathy; the infant now has severe brain damage.

LOSS PREVENTION COMMENTS

Fetal monitoring has greatly added to the physician's ability to determine the intrauterine condition of the baby with some precision. While ultimate fetal outcome cannot always be predicted, there has emerged broad agreement that emergency intervention is indicated where certain patterns are observed on fetal monitoring.

Here we have a fetal monitoring strip showing "variable decelerations with minimal beat-to-beat variability" at least two hours prior to delivery. A five- to six-minute episode of bradycardia (60/min) occurred one hour prior to delivery. Since delivery was considered imminent, labor continued. An hour later another episode of bradycardia occurred and an emergency forceps delivery was accomplished. The baby was severely depressed and sustained severe brain damage.

Although expert witnesses for the defendant doctor testified that their colleague had made a judgment within the standard of care, other academicians were eager to swear that intervention by cesarean section should have been carried out at most two hours, and at the least one hour prior to delivery.

A brain-damaged baby has a strong appeal to a jury. From past experience in court, a six-figure settlement seemed very advisable.

108.   WHERE IS THAT PRENATAL RECORD?

*Allegations—Contraindicated use of progestational hormones
to induce menses x2; no pregnancy test
Physician Issues—Confusing menstrual history; examination
not conclusive for pregnancy
Patient Issue—Brain-damaged baby
Outcome—Six-figure settlement*

CASE STUDY

An established family physician who had previously delivered two babies for his patient saw her on December 19 with a history of amenorrhea. The LMP was said to be either August 25 or September 15. When pelvic examination revealed no evidence of pregnancy, Norlutate was given, but no menses resulted. On January 9, the patient returned, and again the uterus was normal in size and consistency. Provera was prescribed, but again, no menses resulted.

When the patient was seen again on April 1, no menses had occurred and the uterus was enlarged consistent with a four-month pregnancy. Ultrasound estimated the fetal age to be 21 weeks. Based on this information, the physician wrote in his record an EDC of August 15. The routine prenatal examination was within normal limits. On May 8, another ultrasound examination revealed the fetus in the breech position and the fetal age to be approximately 26 weeks with an accuracy range ±1.3 weeks. No other office visits were recorded in the medical record.

On July 4, the patient came to the hospital complaining of back pain. Examination by the nurse found the fetus in the breech position, BOW intact. The presenting part was at 0 station, and the patient was thought to be in labor. Cesarean section was scheduled for one hour later. Demerol was given as preoperative medication. Under general anesthesia, the C-section was done and a 3-lb 3-oz infant was delivered. Apgars were recorded as 3 in one minute and 1 in five minutes. Narcan was given, and the infant survived, brain-damaged and blind.

When the child was 6 years of age, a lawsuit was filed charging the attending family physician with negligence. The complaint listed, among other things, the prescribing of a progestational agent in the early weeks of pregnancy, failure to appreciate the degree of prematurity, accepting the nurse's diagnosis of active labor, the scheduling of a C-section based on that evaluation, and the use of a narcotic (Demerol) as preoperative medication in this premature delivery. All of these actions were said to be below an acceptable standard of care.

Loss Prevention Comments

Despite clear warnings in the *PDR* and other literature, the physician prescribed a progestational agent on two occasions for amenorrhea without having done a pregnancy test; the latter of the two prescriptions could have been in the first week or two of this pregnancy. Although there was some confusion as to the EDC, the attending physician had estimated it to be approximately August 15 after the first ultrasound examination, and recorded this in the patient's record. Six weeks before the EDC, the patient arrived at the hospital with back pain, the BOW intact, and the breech presenting. Although there were some uterine contractions, active labor was questionable from the medical record.

The physician apparently did not consult his office records as to the EDC and accepted the nurse's evaluation of active labor. He ordered the preoperative narcotic for the C-section, apparently having lost sight of the prematurity, without making any attempt to abort labor at that point.

The physician had a good relationship with his patient, but the financial demands on the parents for care of this severely handicapped child undoubtedly precipitated this lawsuit.

Unlike what so often happens, there was no lack of knowledge or skill on the part of the attending physician, nor in this case was there even the problem of sloppy record keeping that so frequently makes the lawsuit impossible to defend. Instead, though the facts were known, they were not acted upon, and the medical record was not reviewed. What was the physician's responsibility he apparently delegated to the nurse. This mismanaged case resulted in a severely compromised baby.

109. HINDSIGHT 20/20

Allegations—Delay in treatment (C-section)
Physician Issue—Physician judgment to continue labor
Patient Issues—Brain-damaged baby; (NICU) two months on
*   ventilator*
Outcome—Five-figure settlement

CASE STUDY

A 23-year-old gravida 2, para I came to the emergency department of her local medical center hospital at 37 weeks' gestation after an uneventful prenatal course. Uterine contractions had begun about an hour earlier. She was in no distress, her blood pressure was slightly elevated with a diastolic of 98 mm Hg, the fetal heart tones were heard best in the right lower quadrant at a rate of 140, and there was some bloody show. Her contractions were irregular but were of good quality. The cervix was said to be 2 cm dilated and the bag of waters was intact. There were no significant risk factors. She was admitted to the labor and delivery area for further evaluation prior to actual admission.

The external fetal monitor (EFM) was placed, and the nurse observed late decelerations on the first tracing; the physician was notified. One hour after admission the nurse again noted late decelerations and again notified the physician. Oxygen was started and the patient was turned on her side.

Two hours after admission, the attending physician placed a scalp electrode, and the tracing continued to exhibit variable and late decelerations. Two hours after placement of the scalp electrode the nurses reported a decreased variability to the physician. Cesarean section was discussed with the patient, and she was prepared for the operation. About six hours after admission the patient was delivered by cesarean section of an 8-lb baby in profound distress. The infant was sent to the neonatal intensive care unit in another city, where he died after two months on the respirator.

Within a few months, a lawsuit was filed charging the physician with the wrongful death of the infant due to a delay in performing the cesarean section.

LOSS PREVENTION COMMENTS

The mother was healthy, and the physician was one of the most respected in the community. The outcome of her second pregnancy was tragic. The expenses were enormous, especially in view of the two months on the respirator with "flat" EEGs.

In retrospect, would the result have been better if an emergency cesarean section had been done? There were indeed well-documented late decelerations on admission to the labor and delivery suite. These continued throughout the labor. There was some waxing and waning of the decelerations, but they never quite went away. After the scalp electrode was applied, the variability was in question, with the nurses consistently feeling that there was a loss of normal variability and the physician reporting on one occasion that the "variability" seemed to be improving. If a cesarean section had been done on admission, and if the infant had been severely compromised, there would have been no question that the intrauterine accident occurred prior to the time when any intervention could have made any difference. As it happened, however, our physician had to deliver a healthy baby or face the charge of negligence.

While the EFM tracings were not "abnormal" enough to prompt our obstetrician to do an emergency section, the experts on both sides of the case believed cesarean section was indicated. The experts of the plaintiff contended that the section was demanded, while the defendant experts believed that it was indicated but that the obstetrician made a judgment that was within an acceptable standard of care.

This was by no means an "open-and-shut" case for the plaintiff, but given the circumstances, a "modest" five-figure settlement was negotiated.

110. WATCH CLOSELY

Allegations—Delay in performing C-section; delay in transfer to NICU
Physician Issues—Delay in appreciating level of respiratory distress; delay by nursery in notification of baby's status
Patient Issue—Severely brain-damaged baby
Outcome—Large six-figure settlement

CASE STUDY

A healthy 20-year-old woman near term came to the hospital about mid-morning complaining of some cramping and low back pain. Since she was at about 38 weeks' gestation, she was observed in the emergency department for a short while before being admitted to the labor and delivery suite (L&D) in early labor. Her family physician knew from the initial prenatal examination that she had a marginal pelvis, but a trial of labor was thought to be a prudent course at that time.

Over a period of about five hours labor did not progress and she was sent for an x-ray of the pelvis to determine more precisely the cephalopelvic measurements. The baby appeared to be normal in size, but the radiologist's opinion was that delivery from below would be very difficult and dangerous. The need for cesarean section was discussed with the patient and her family. They agreed with the plan. Another five hours elapsed before the patient was taken to the operating room, where the operation was done by the patient's doctor. The baby was delivered and appeared to be normal, with Apgar scores of 8 and 9, and the baby was said to have a vigorous cry immediately after delivery.

In the nursery the baby's weight was 5-lb 13-oz, temperature 100°F (rectal), pulse 148/min, and respirations 36/min. "Some retraction" of the chest was noted on the initial nursery room note, but no nasal flaring was documented. The physician checked the baby on two occasions in the nursery during the first two hours of life. It is noteworthy that the respirations were recorded at 56/min on the second note. An x-ray of the chest done at this point reported, "Lungs still have a ground glass appearance. Heart somewhat indistinct and may be enlarged. There are prominent air bronchograms in the lateral projections." The impression of the radiologist was, "Respiratory distress without other definite abnormalities." The nurses in the nursery continued to record retractions, and about five hours after delivery, the nurses recorded respirations at 80/min and "cyanosis about the mouth." The attending physician came to the hospital to see the baby and wrote as order, "Just watch the baby closely." At 6 hours of age the respirations were still recorded at 80/min and the physician was notified by phone. He ordered Flo-bi O_2 and it was given with some recorded improvement in the baby's color. Again two hours later the infant was said to be "dusky" in appearance. There is no mention in the record of the O_2 being discontinued, so one must assume that it was going continuously.

The dusky color continued, with rapid respirations, and retraction was recorded that seemed to be more pronounced as time went on. At 10 hours of age the infant's heart rate was recorded at 100/min, there was nasal flaring, more cyanosis, and loss of muscle tone. The decision was made at that time to transfer the baby to a neonatal intensive care unit in a nearby medical center. The first blood gases were done after the transfer team arrived and reported pH 6.7, PCO_2 44.6, PO_2 53.2, O_2 saturation 50.5. The transfer was accomplished without incident and the child survived, but with severe brain damage.

A lawsuit was filed charging the physician with negligence in the delay in diagnosis of respiratory distress in the infant, and failure to effect a timely transfer of the baby to an appropriate facility.

LOSS PREVENTION COMMENTS

This case raises questions that must be asked. With a definitive diagnosis of a contracted pelvis and pelvic measurements that would not accommodate delivery from below, why the delay of more than five hours before doing the operation? The record would suggest that labor was going on all that time. With a 38 weeks' gestation history and the apparent need for operative delivery, why wait and chance other unforeseen complications?

When did the attending physician see the x-ray report? This was a rural hospital, and the time of day that the picture was taken would suggest that it was not until the next day when the written report so definitely suggested respiratory distress. This may have been an occasion when the attending physician needed the help of the radiologist at the time the film was taken. If the physician was relying on his own interpretation of the chest x-ray, then one must wonder whether or not his interpretation was adequate to help in the treatment of this baby.

It is curious that the early and consistent finding of "retraction" by the nursery staff seemed to arouse little suspicion. The respiratory rate was suspect from early in the life of this baby, arising from the initial 36/min to 56/min in the first hour of life. True, it did moderate somewhat with oxygen therapy, but the general trend was not reassuring. Why did not the attending physician write a definitive order for oxygen? How long was it given? Why was not a blood gas analysis ordered? Surely, with what we see here, the blood gas values could have prompted an early transfer.

While the nursery staff were "watching closely," there was a period of about six hours when the attending physician was not present to observe his patient. While the nurses were "watching closely," this baby became progressively hypoxic and acidotic. Certainly there was much evidence in the record that the nursing staff was not competent to care for a sick baby. This attending physician surely had to know that they were in over their head!

The questions of competence in this case were apparent. Competence of both the physician and the nursing staff is in question from this record. The conclusion here must be that, with a neonatal intensive care unit only an hour away, neither the physician of record nor the hospital staff knew where they were with this sick baby. Settlement of this lawsuit was necessary.

111.   THE LONG TAIL

Allegations—Failure to appropriately manage eclampsia (suit thirteen years after delivery); delay in performing C-section

Physician Issues—Did not manage toxemia aggressively and do timely C-section

Patient Issue—Child with spastic quadriplegia

Outcome—Six-figure settlement

CASE STUDY

Medical malpractice insurance is looked upon as a business in which the claims have a "long tail." The following is a "tail," which is perhaps not a record, but is certainly long enough to justify the reputation. The acts in this case that the plaintiff described as negligent occurred about a month after your company wrote its first policies.

A 32-year-old woman reported to her private Ob/Gyn early in 1976. She gave a history of having had her last menstrual period in November 1975. Her physical findings were compatible with that history and an EDC was assigned of mid-August of 1976. Blood pressure was 140/80 mm Hg, pulse 80/min, and her usual weight 140 lb. She was said to be 5 ft 2 in tall. Her weight on this first visit was 152 lb. All her blood studies were normal with the PCV 33 percent, and the urine was negative for protein. She gave a history of a G6PD deficiency and the record notes that certain drugs were to be avoided.

She was seen regularly every month, the only remarkable finding being weight gain. By 28 weeks she had gained almost 40 lb over her usual reported weight of 140 lb. At this visit she was put on a low-calorie and low-salt diet, and she was cautioned that she must lose some weight. Two weeks later she had lost 1 lb, but on this visit her urine protein was reported as 2+. Two weeks later, at about 32 weeks' gestation, her weight was stable, and she had no edema, but her blood pressure was 150/100 mm Hg and her urine showed 4+ protein. There was no documentation of any discussion of rest, medication, or any other intervention for her findings. Two weeks later she had gained an additional 4 lb, her blood pressure was 140/100 mm Hg, and her urine was 3+ for protein. Eclampsia was mentioned in the record and hospitalization was discussed, but the patient was sent home on a regimen of rest, diet, diuretics, and mild sedation with phenobarbital. Two days later, at about 35 weeks' gestation, the patient had a convulsion and was brought to the hospital.

At this time the FHT was said to be "good," and her blood

pressure 170/130 mm Hg. Treatment was begun with MgSO₄ IV, with intravenous hydralazine given for the elevated blood pressure, and she was prepared for surgery. Within four hours of the convulsion the uterus was emptied by C-section. Prior to that time, on EFM tracing there had been noted some "decelerations."

The infant was delivered with amniotic fluid grossly stained with meconium. There was no spontaneous respiration at delivery, but with stimulation respirations started and the Apgar scores were reported at 3 and 6. The baby appeared to do fairly well after a shaky start but developed increasing respiratory problems and was transferred to the NICU about 18 hours after birth.

The baby was discharged from the hospital with spastic quadriplegia and has been followed in a multi-disciplinary clinic all his life. At 9 years of age the child could walk with the aid of a walker and could feed but not dress himself. At 13 years of age, a lawsuit was filed on behalf of the child against the obstetrician alleging the failure to appropriately manage the mother's toxemia. The lawsuit further charged that there was a delay in performing the C-section once eclampsia had developed. This negligence was said to be the cause of the baby's disabilities.

LOSS PREVENTION COMMENTS

For a month before this pregnancy was terminated there were signs of preeclampsia. The blood pressure was up and there was significant proteinuria. One wishes there had been more documentation in the record of the physician's thoughts about these abnormal findings. Did he strongly urge hospitalization and the patient refuse? Did he talk with her about the danger to herself and the baby that could result from this condition? Should the doctor have admitted his patient as an emergency two weeks before the convulsion when her blood pressure was 150/100 mm Hg and her urine was 4+? There is no doubt that the latter would have been the safer course. Rest could have been enforced, the hypertension could have been more vigorously treated, and the convulsion possibly avoided.

This lawsuit could have been handled differently from a legal perspective if all the things mentioned had been done. Would the more vigorous handling of the clinical manifestations of preeclampsia have prevented the disability in the baby? That is certainly open to question. Serious questions are being successfully raised about cerebral palsy and its relation to an antepartum event rather that something that happened during labor and delivery. Cord blood examinations frequently help to determine the condition of the baby at the time of delivery. Placental examinations are being done with increasing frequency to attempt to relate the infant's problems to conditions that can be present in utero.

Currently, this case would have been handled differently! Obstetricians are much more alert to the consequences of proteinuria and hypertension now than they were 19 years ago. Not only are the clinical consequences better understood and the management more aggressive, but the legal consequences are certainly more apparent. The case was filed at age 13 of the child. It was settled at age 16 for a large amount of money.

Medical malpractice insurance— a long-tail business? Yes, medical malpractice insurance is a Long-Tail Business!

112.   HE SAID—THEY SAID

> *Allegations—Failure to diagnose early labor; failure to use*
> *   agents to delay/stop labor*
> *Physician Issues—No documentation of visit day before*
> *   delivery; physician testified to examination that day;*
> *   both patient and husband denied examination had*
> *   been done*
> *Patient Issues—Twin pregnancy; one died in first 24 hours,*
> *   other baby survived after stormy course in NICU with*
> *   extensive brain damage*
> *Outcome—Seven-figure settlement*

CASE STUDY

A young woman in her late 20s had a history of unprotected sexual intercourse for seven years. Convinced that she could not get pregnant, she and her husband appeared in the physician's office for an infertility work-up. The history further revealed irregular vaginal bleeding for three months, which was not unusual for this woman. On this visit, however, she had not had any vaginal bleeding for the past six weeks. She had had one previous pregnancy that terminated in a spontaneous miscarriage at seven months.

She was 5 ft 3 in tall and weighed 114 lb. The blood pressure was recorded at 120/60 mm Hg. The pelvic examination revealed the uterus to be softened and somewhat enlarged, and the left adnexa were enlarged in the region of the left ovary, which felt about 4x4 cm in size and cystic. The ultrasound was compatible with an intrauterine pregnancy, and the cystic left ovary was thought to be a corpus luteum cyst.

She was counseled as to diet and the results of the ultrasound examination, and was given routine prenatal vitamins. At about 12 weeks the uterus was the size of a 15-week gestation and the ultrasound revealed a twin intrauterine pregnancy. At 24 weeks' gestation the hemoglobin and WBC count were within expected ranges. An ultrasound examination was done and she was told to return in about two weeks.

On this last visit the patient later reported that she complained of abdominal pressure and that she was sent home and told to stay off her feet and rest more in bed. There was no mention of this in the OB record. The following day the patient called in to complain of vaginal itching and was sent some suppositories of Monostat by the attending physician's partner.

Later that same day the patient was visiting in the hospital when she began to complain of some significant vaginal pressure and the OB service was called. Attendants responded and arrived with a wheelchair and an emergency tray. They found that the patient had left the hospital and gone to her car in the parking lot. They found her in the back seat of her car with BOW bulging from the vaginal orifice. She stated that she felt like she was having her babies. The attending physician was called and the partner on call responded promptly. She was moved to a stretcher and taken to the OB department. The BOW was ruptured artificially. Ultrasound revealed the twin pregnancy but no heart action was observed. Within 20 minutes after her arrival in the OB department, she was delivered of twin male infants, both of whom appeared to be in good condition considering their prematurity. The record states, "We were all delighted when two male infants with good heart action and respiratory effort were delivered and taken to the ICU." In the ICU, Apgar scores were not reported on the first twin, and on the second were recorded as 2 at one minute, 5 at five minutes, and 7 at ten minutes.

The delivering physician thought that the placenta showed evidence of significant abruption, but the pathologic examination did not confirm the delivering physician's impression. In his post-delivery progress note, the delivering physician recorded Apgar scores of 2,5,7 on twin #1 and 2,5,7 on twin #2.

Twin #2 died within the first 24 hours after delivery. There was no record available on this baby. Twin #1 had a stormy course, with severe hyaline membrane disease, evidence of bilateral intraventricular bleeding, a bout of *staphylococcal* sepsis at three weeks, retinopathy of prematurity, and severe cholestatic jaundice. The child survived but had extensive brain disease which would require multi-specialty support for the rest of his life.

A lawsuit was filed charging the attending obstetrician (not the delivering doctor) with negligence for failure to diagnose early labor on the day before delivery in his office, and for failure to attempt to stop the labor with tocolytic therapy. The damages demanded amounted to $10 million.

LOSS PREVENTION COMMENTS

This tragic case was one of a young couple who had been desiring a baby for years and who had given up only to find that the wife was pregnant when she came to the Ob/Gyn's office to explore therapy for their inability. The history of a previous pregnancy that ended in a spontaneous miscarriage at seven months might have been a clue of possible complications with this pregnancy.

The case was lost when on the day before delivery, the patient appeared in the physician's office complaining of pressure sensations in the vagina. There was no office record of this encounter. The physician's recollection of the encounter was of complaints of pressure. The patient's and her husband's testimony was that she revealed to her doctor that she was having the feelings of pressure, but also was experiencing intermittent pains in the abdomen. The physician remembers a pelvic examination showing a thick, long cervix with no dilatation. Both the patient and her husband testified that no pelvic examination was done on that visit.

Based on the physician's deposition, this case was reviewed and although there was no patient record to corroborate the physician's testimony, his peers felt that though the case was indeed dangerous, based on the record there had been no deviation from an acceptable standard of care.

Expert testimony for the patient postulated that if a pelvic examination had truly been done on the day before this tragic delivery the attending physician would have found a softened and partially dilated cervix. This expert thought that the record did not reveal an indicated response to the first late miscarriage which, again, he speculated was due to an incompetent cervix.

The lawyers on the side of the patient were left with the question, "Which of the principals in this case were to be believed?" The questions regarding the unrecorded visit and the undocumented pelvic examination were thought to be too dangerous to place before a jury, where there would be a large sympathy factor pushing the facts toward the couple who had lost one twin and were attending to the demands of a severely brain damaged but surviving child.

A settlement in seven figures was worked out, with almost half of that amount placed in a structured instrument dedicated to the care of the surviving baby.

113.   DID THE TEAM KNOW THE GAME PLAN?

*Allegations—Negligence in allowing gestational diabetic to go
    to 41 weeks; failure to perform C-section in timely
    manner (38 weeks)*
*Physician Issues—Lack of coordination in practice; delay in
    diagnosis of gestational diabetes; inducing labor at 41
    weeks (two attempts over 48 hours)*
Patient Issues—Brain-damaged baby; spastic quadriplegia
Outcome—Seven-figure settlement

CASE STUDY

The patient first went to the Ob/Gyn group for prenatal care
when, according to the physician's examination, she was about 12
weeks into her first pregnancy. She gave her doctor a history of
nausea since her last menstrual period and one previous episode of
pelvic inflammatory disease two years before this visit. She related a
family history of hypertension and heart disease.

Her initial examination revealed a short, obese (height 5 ft 1
in, weight 180 lb) young woman whose blood pressure was recorded
at 100/80 mm Hg. The complete physical examination revealed only
the enlarged uterus compatible with the menstrual history at 12
weeks' gestation. The laboratory findings were all considered to be
normal. The urine showed a "trace" of protein, thought to be due to
vaginal mucous contamination. The blood glucose was recorded at 73
mg/dl. The CBC, including platelets, was normal. RPR, Sickledex,
rubella immune, hepatitis B, and Rh antibody screen were all normal.

The routine visits occurred each month as scheduled, and at
the 24th week of gestation the urine showed "large ketones." Glucola
done that day was reported at 156 mg/dl. She was to return in four
weeks to see her attending physician, and at the 28-week visit showed
only a "trace of ketones." At 30 weeks there were no abnormal
findings. The patient had gained only 11 lb since her first visit, her
blood pressure had remained normal, and she had no complaints.

At 33 weeks the findings were "some swelling," and the AFM
was positive. It was noted that because of the positive Glucola
reported two months earlier, a glucose tolerance test (GTT) was
needed as soon as possible. A week later she returned to the laboratory for the GTT, the results of which were: fasting 91, one hour 147,
two hours 150, and three hours 151. The results were signed by a
member of the three-physician group who was not her primary
doctor. The following day she was seen by the office nurse and placed
on a diabetic diet and given a one-hour consultation by a nutritionist.

Blood tests were done weekly for the following two weeks, and the glucose levels were normal. On visits at 37, 38, and 39 weeks' gestation the blood glucose levels were normal. At 40 weeks by dates an ultrasonogram was reported as showing a fetal age of 36.2 weeks, and the further suggestion that the findings were compatible with intrauterine growth retardation (IGR). Again at 40.5 weeks ultrasound suggested IGR. There was a comment in the record, "Induce when favorable." A week later, with a blood glucose of 56 mg/dl, she was sent to the hospital for a non-stress test. Fetal heart monitor tracing was on file at the hospital, but without a comment as to any non-stress test.

Another member of the group admitted the patient to the hospital for induction, commented that she was at 41+ weeks' gestation, and wrote appropriate induction orders. Pitocin was begun at 8:00 AM. Three and a half hours into the induction the fetal heart tone (FHT) was found to be between 80-100. When the patient was turned on her side, the FHT gradually returned to 130. The O_2 set-up was put in readiness for use. Labor was maintained with Pitocin, and five hours after induction was started, the note "late deceler-ations to 80" appeared in the record. With a position change the rate rose to the 130 baseline. Six hours into labor "late decels noted." "Not in good labor yet. O_2 not in use." By this time the cervix was softening some and a fingertip could be inserted into the Os. Eight hours into the induced labor, consideration was given to stopping the Pitocin and planning a two-day induction. The Pitocin was discontinued and orders for a diet were given. After stopping the induction, the contractions continued but were ineffective. The patient was given medicine for pain and returned to the floor. Throughout this attempted induction the observation of "accels" was made several times.

The following morning Pitocin was restarted, with irregular contractions reported. About one hour after beginning again the note "FHT unreactive" appeared in the record. The obstetrician was present, AROM carried out, and an internal monitor applied. A STAT blood glucose was ordered and the report 15 minutes later was 39 mg/dl. Glucose was ordered STAT. The FHT returned to 120-130 but BTB variability was much less than it had been throughout the labor. This seemed to return to normal and the induction continued. Eight hours into the second attempt to induce labor the BTB variability was reported as "minimal to moderate." Two hours later "late decels" began to occur and continued. Although the patient was pushing with contractions, no progress was being made. Delivery by outlet forceps was attempted without success and a C-section was done.

The infant required intubation. Apgar scores were 1 at one

minute, and 4 at five and 10 minutes. Cord blood pH was 6.6. Although the baby survived, he was a spastic quadriplegic, micro-cephalic, and had seizures.

A lawsuit was filed charging all three of the members of this Ob/Gyn group with negligence in permitting a gestational diabetic to go to 41 weeks without operative intervention and for failing to perform the C-section earlier in the course of the induction.

LOSS PREVENTION COMMENTS

How could a gestational diabetic patient be allowed to go to 41.5 weeks without intervention? Was there confusion about the significance of the ultrasonography suggesting a fetal age of at least two weeks less than the history would indicate and the possibility of IGR? What happened to the non-stress test that was ordered? Did all three members of this team know the plan for this patient? Several factors in this record suggest that the major problem in this case was the lack of communication between the physicians involved.

This was a three-member group. The patient was seen by all three at one time or another during the prenatal course. In some such groups this is routine, and the patient is informed that she will meet all of the members during the course of her pregnancy. There was a two-month delay between the abnormal Glucola test and the definitive GTT. This would suggest that the "left hand did not know what the right hand was doing." Nowhere does the record indicate that early intervention was planned. We would expect a note recognizing the gestational diabetes and commenting on the possible time that intervention would be done. At a critical time in the pregnancy, about 35 weeks, after the diagnosis had been made, the patient was seen by the office nurse to begin her diabetic diet. She was not seen again for two weeks. Again, we would have expected the documentation of some discussion with the patient about the possible need for a C-section. A good office nurse could have reminded the primary physician that the record was lacking a management plan.

Finally, in this very compromised patient, induction was begun by a member of the team who was not the attending physician; failing the first day, the second member of the team, again not the attending physician, continued the induction. The attending physician was the decision-maker in proceeding with the C-section.

The signs of a stressed fetus were suggested on the first day of attempted induction. They were unmistakable on the second day, hours before the operation was done. Were the two members of the team who were following the induction reluctant to commit to the operation with the active presence of the attending physician?

Something about this tragic case involving three adequately trained specialists was confusing to them, and appropriate decisions were not made in a timely fashion. There were warning signs all around, and they were not seen and acted upon. From the record, it would seem that failure to plan together for the appropriate management of this young woman with gestational diabetes during her first pregnancy played a large part in this outcome. The group practice of obstetrics demands no less.

114. NEGLIGENT DELAY OR JUDGMENT GONE BAD

Allegations—Negligent delay in management of labor (C-section); failure in early management of postpartum bleeding
Physician Issues—No compelling reason to do C-section earlier; judgment to correct DIC before hysterectomy
Patient Issue—Wrongful death of mother
Outcome—Mid six-figure settlement

CASE STUDY

A 24-year-old primipara with a normal prenatal course had an expected date of confinement two days prior to her admission to the hospital in active labor with the bag of waters spontaneously ruptured, the cervix 3 cm dilated, and 80 percent effaced. Her contractions were five minutes apart and lasted about 90 seconds. Four days prior to this admission she had been observed overnight, and it was determined that she was not in active labor. She was monitored and sent home.

Her amniotic fluid was clear and the nitrazine test was positive. Her blood pressure was 124/86 mm Hg. She had been followed regularly during her pregnancy and the only risk factor that appeared in her medical record was excessive smoking. Orders taken over the phone included Pitocin according to protocol. The uterine contractions increased in frequency and intensity, and two hours after admission decelerations were noted and epidural anesthesia was begun. Following the injection of the anesthetic agent Nescarine her blood pressure dropped and bradycardia appeared on the fetal monitor; both returned to baseline after the patient was turned on her left side. It was two and a half hours after admission before the Pitocin drip was started, with 2 cc in 250 cc to run at 2 mic/min. Twenty minutes later the Pitocin was increased to 4 mic/min, which produced contractions every four to five minutes and lasted for 60 to 70 seconds. Fifteen minutes later the Pitocin was increased again to 6 mic/min. Shortly thereafter, whereas three consecutive late decelerations occurred, the Pitocin was stopped and O_2 was started.

With the contractions at four to five minutes and lasting for 60 to 80 seconds, the Pitocin was restarted at 2 mic/min, and the order was to "augment slowly." Again, some five hours after admission late decelerations were noted, but these cleared when the patient was placed on her left side. The Pitocin was stopped by a phone order. Six hours after admission, with the patient not progressing despite contractions, the Pitocin was restarted at 1 cc IV every five minutes.

The attending physician came to the labor-and-delivery area and because no progress was being made ordered the crew to set up for a C-section because of "C-P disproportion." The surgery began about seven hours after admission, and without apparent complication the patient was delivered of a 6-lb girl with Apgar scores of 8 and 9. While in the operating room (OR), some excessive vaginal bleeding was noted and the uterus was somewhat boggy. With uterine massage and IV Pitocin this seemed to be corrected.

One hour after the surgery, while the patient was in the recovery room, massive clots were expelled and her blood pressure fell. Fluids and blood were ordered and administered, Methergine was administered IV, and the bleeding seemed to slow. Replacement treatment was vigorously pursued with blood and blood products, but vaginal bleeding continued. Thirty minutes after the C-section, the patient's blood pressure was recorded at 66/42 mm Hg. Vigorous bleeding continued. The attending physician, who had left the hospital, was called on his beeper. Telephone orders were given, and both IV Pitocin and Methergine were given, but without benefit.

With blood and blood products being given aggressively, the bleeding continued. The blood pressure remained low. When the attending physician was called and informed that his presence was needed, he said he was "on my way." Blood, packed red blood cells, albumin, and cryoprecipitate were "pushed"! When the bleeding continued, the attending physician decided to take his patient to the OR and examine the uterus under anesthesia. This was done, more oxytoxics given, and with vigorous massage the uterus contracted and the bleeding stopped, but resumed promptly after the patient returned to the ICU.

The patient was supported the next eight hours with more blood and blood products. A consultant was called for possible bleeding disorder, but he thought that there was no coagulopathy and suggested Swanz-Ganz catheterization, which showed that the patient was in fluid deficit. Emergency hysterectomy was delayed to correct the "DIC." The blood pressure remained low and continued to drop.

Ten hours after delivery, the patient was taken to the OR for an emergency hysterectomy.

Blood and fluid resuscitation were continued vigorously, but bleeding continued, and the patient died about 20 hours after her admission and 12 hours after the C-section. Autopsy was refused by the family.

A lawsuit was filed charging the attending physician with negligent management of the labor and failure to treat the postpartum hemorrhage in a timely manner.

LOSS PREVENTION COMMENTS

This 24-year-old woman died following a C-section because she bled to death and nobody could stop the bleeding. The attending physician tried to replace the blood and fluids. He gave massive amounts of Pitocin and Methergine after delivery in an effort to stop the bleeding. He even took the patient to the OR where he examined her under anesthesia, thinking that there might have been some intrauterine problem that he could correct. Doubtless he would have done an emergency C-section at that time, but the bleeding seemed to respond to massage and drugs. Both he and the consultants made the decision to correct what appeared to be the onset of DIC before doing the inevitable hysterectomy.

Throughout heroic attempts to stop and correct the bleeding, nothing seemed to work. Hypotension persisted after hysterectomy and the patient died.

It is always easy to second-guess the physician after a bad result. Monday morning quarterbacking is a sport that all of us play well! However, in the pretrial investigation and discovery depositions, very legitimate questions were raised. Was the use of Pitocin managed properly? Did the drug contribute to or cause the uterine atony after C-section? Was fluid resuscitation done properly? The S-G data seemed to support that contention. Should the hysterectomy have been done earlier? After the fact, that is a question easily answered. But at the bedside was there a good clinical reason to delay? It was obvious that expert testimony by the plaintiff was going to answer all these questions negatively. Was the Pitocin used and managed properly? No! Was fluid resuscitation pursued in a proper manner? No! Was the hysterectomy done in a timely manner? No! Was the attending physician on top of the management of this case? No! It was easy to challenge the record and almost impossible to defend it in the face of the death of a 24-year-old mother. A large settlement was thought to be the best way to close this case.

115.   FUNDAMENTALS ARE FUNDAMENTAL

Allegations—Failure to monitor FHTs (hospital and
physician); failure to supervise labor (physician)
Physician Issue—Visited the patient in the labor and delivery
room only one time in 24 hours
Patient Issue—Neurologically damaged baby probably due to
hypoxia in last stages of labor
Outcome—Large six-figure settlement

CASE STUDY

A 24-year-old woman was admitted at term to a rural hospital after an uneventful prenatal course; she was having irregular but painful uterine contractions. On admission at 3:30 PM, examination by the labor-and-delivery (L&D) nurse revealed a 3-cm dilation, 75 percent effacement, and the presenting part at 0 station. When the attending family physician was notified, he ordered the routine enema and preparation, which were accomplished.

The patient continued to have some irregular contractions, but she was ambulatory and slept at intervals until active labor began at about 5:30 AM, approximately 14 hours after admission. Vital signs reported at half-hour intervals continued to be normal; fetal heart tones (FHTs) reported at intervals of 30 minutes to one hour ranged between 130 and 150/min.

The bag of waters spontaneously ruptured at 12:00 noon, some 21 hours after admission, and the attending family physician saw his patient in the L&D suite for the first time. His examination revealed normal vital signs. with contractions occurring every five minutes with a duration of 40 to 60 seconds; FHTs continued to range between 130 and 150/min.

There was a gradual increase in the intensity of contractions for the next few hours, and at about 5:00 PM the cervix was completely dilated and the head was at a +2 station.

The patient was brought to the delivery room at 6:00 PM. At 6:10 the FHTs were discovered to be absent and the attending physician was summoned STAT; the patient was delivered promptly of a male infant with Apgars of 2 and 5. Spontaneous respiration was delayed for 20 minutes and the infant developed seizures at 12 hours of age; at six weeks the infant had ample physical evidence of a severe neurological deficit. Within eight months of delivery, a lawsuit was filed against the attending family physician for negligence in his management of the patient's labor and the hospital for negligence in not providing external fetal monitoring (EFM) for the obstetrical patients.

Examination of the medical record revealed that the last re-corded FHT was at 5:05 PM, when the rate was documented as being 144/min. As the legal positions of the defendant hospital and the physician were fully explored, it became apparent that an early settlement on the part of both was the wisest course to follow.

LOSS PREVENTION COMMENTS

The indefensible position of the hospital was not due to its failure to provide external fetal monitors, since ample proof was available that EFM is not the standard of care for all patients in labor, and the current guidelines of the American College of Obstetrics and Gynecology (ACOG) do not mandate universal EFM. The lack of regular monitoring of FHT by competent observers, however, cannot be defended. This failure militated against defending both the hospital and the physician. The absence of recorded FHTs at reasonable intervals (15 to 30 minutes) indicated that neither the nursing staff nor the physician was acting within an acceptable standard of care.

It was also decided that attendance by the family physician only once during the patient's 24 hours in the L&D area of the hospital indicated an indefensible attitude of indifference, and would never have been understood by a jury.

In most medical malpractice lawsuits, it is neither the presence or absence of sophisticated technology nor its function or malfunction that causes the problem. It is the behavior of the treatment team that is critical to preventing, or prevailing in the event of, a bad result.

116.   WHO'S TO SAY?

Allegations—Failure to manage preeclampsia; failure to attend and treat patient;failure to monitor patient and fetus (hospital and physician)
Physician Issues—Failure to attend patient in labor; treatment by telephone until C-section ordered
Patient Issues—Preeclampsia; stillbirth
Outcome—Large six-figure settlement

CASE STUDY

A 30-year-old mother of two began prenatal care with a family physician at 12 weeks of gestation and had regular prenatal visits. She experienced moderate weight gain but no other recorded problems through the first four months of pregnancy. Her blood pressure was noted to be somewhat labile beginning in the fifth month, and she also had a trace of edema. Fetal heart tones (FHT) were present and easily auscultated.

Late in the fifth month of pregnancy the patient developed 2+ edema, hypertension, with blood pressure ranging between 160/90 and 170/100 mm Hg, and 1+ albuminuria. She was admitted to the hospital with a diagnosis of possible preeclampsia. Toxemia monitoring, strict bed rest, and daily weights were ordered in addition to an appropriate diet and laboratory tests. She improved promptly and required only four days of hospitalization.

Following discharge, despite bed rest, the signs of toxemia gradually reappeared with the same symptoms, until at 38 weeks of gestation she was seen in the emergency room at 9:00 PM with a blood pressure of 150/80 mm Hg, fetal heart rate 156/min, 2+ edema, and in possible early labor. Hospital admission followed at 9:45 PM.

Following admission toxemia monitoring was again ordered. The fetal monitor was applied for 30 minutes and was to be continued if the patient was indeed in active labor. Vital signs were ordered on an hourly basis. The OB nurses applied the electronic fetal monitor, and determining that the patient was in active labor, continued its use. No abnormalities of FHT were noted.

The patient remained hypertensive, continued to have edema, and continued to spill protein and albumin in her urine. At 11:45 PM she began to complain of severe backache. The doctor was contacted by phone and, without examination, ordered the patient to receive hydroxyzine hydrochloride 25 mg orally. This was repeated at 1:00 AM for continued complaints of pain. It was noted about 2:00 AM that the fetal heart rate suddenly dropped to a rate of 80/min for one and a half minutes then spontaneously returned to a rate of 155 to 160/min, but no other abnormalities were noted. The patient continued to complain of pain; again the doctor was contacted by phone. This time he ordered the patient to receive 25 mg of meperidine hydrochloride intramuscularly. According to the nurses' notes, this order was carried out at 2:30 AM. Following this last injection and despite orders to the contrary, the patient's vital signs were not monitored for two hours. At that time the fetal heart rate could not be located. In addition, the patient was found to have 4+ albuminuria along with a significant increase in her hypertension. After an additional 30 minutes of attempting to locate the fetal heart rate by the nursing staff, the physician was contacted. In response to this, he ordered the patient placed on oxygen by nasal cannula and given an additional 50 mg of hydroxyzine hydrochloride.

Finally, one hour later, the physician arrived and a cesarean section was done delivering a stillborn male. The subsequent lawsuit was settled, with both hospital and physician contributing a large amount.

LOSS PREVENTION COMMENTS

It looks as if both the doctor and the hospital were doing their best to neglect this toxemic patient. This very sick mother was in the L&D suite for six hours without being seen by her physician. Not only were the patient's vital signs not monitored at all for at least two hours, but the L&D nursing staff did not specifically record that they had notified the attending physician about the one-and-a-half-minute episode of bradycardia, thinking everything was all right since the rate spontaneously returned to levels of 150 to 160/min, where it had been before. The L&D nurses had not been adequately trained in interpreting EFM tracings, and this physician "knew or should have known" this, according to the plaintiff. Furthermore, since the physician was dealing with a staff marginally trained, he should all the more have been in attendance with his patient during her labor. The stillbirth might have occurred anyway, but who's to say? If the hospital had provided its staff with adequate training, and if the patient had been adequately monitored, and if the physician had been present to assess the condition of both the mother and baby at a moment's notice, the cesarean section might have been done in a more timely fashion and the baby might have had a chance to survive. Who's to say?

117. MISSING DATA

> *Allegations—Failure to diagnose and treat pyelonephritis complicating pregnancy; system failure in failure to report/react to appropriate laboratory data*
> *Physician Issues—Denied getting health department data; failure to treat acute pyelonephritis*
> *Patient Issues—Prolonged hospitalization and treatment for renal failure; sepsis resulting in amputation and renal dialysis; required aortic valve replacement secondary to sepsis*
> *Outcome—Very large, six-figure settlement*

CASE STUDY

The patient, an 18-year-old Medicaid patient presented herself to the county department of public health (DPH) on August 3 with a positive pregnancy test and was seen by the nurse practitioner. She was a gravida 2, para 0, abortus 1, with an LMP of April 17 and the EDC January 22. Her blood pressure was 122/68 mm Hg and her weight 134 lb. Her normal weight was about 125 lb. Fetal heart tones (FHT) were 160/min and the uterine size was compatible with 16 weeks' gestation. The physical examination was otherwise unremarkable. She smoked more than a pack of cigarettes daily which put her at risk. The laboratory tests showed a hematocrit of 38 percent, blood type A, negative antibodies, and a negative urinalysis. The patient was counseled about the DPH program, which consisted of affiliating with a private Ob/Gyn group for evaluation at about 35 weeks' gestation and delivery at a local community hospital. The patient's records were sent to the private physician and his orders were made a part of the record.

She was seen in a month with negative findings and the uterine size was thought to be 20 weeks, compatible with the history. One month later the patient was seen with no complaints but with nitrites in the urine. Because this sometimes points to a urinary tract infection, the nurse in the DPH referred her to the Ob/Gyn in the chosen group for evaluation. All of the DPH records were sent to the physician in advance of her scheduled appointment. On this examination by the physician, she had gained about 25 lb, her blood pressure was 90/60 mm Hg, and a sonogram suggested the baby was about 26 weeks' gestation. The EDC was correspondingly changed. The urine glucose and protein were negative, but no microscopic examination of the urine was done for infection. Rh antibodies were checked and found to be negative, and the physician ordered RhoGAM to be given at 28 weeks in the DPH. The patient returned to the nurse for the injection at the appointed time and a week later all the patient's records were forwarded to the physician who was to deliver her.

On November 8 the patient presented to the community hospital with complaints of back pain and fever of 103°F at home. Bilateral costovertebral angle tenderness was present. She was diffusely tender over the abdomen. The FHT were heard in the left lower quadrant at 140/min. The cervix was found to be long and thick. The head was thought to be the presenting part though high and floating. The impression in the ED was that this young woman who was thought to be about 31 weeks pregnant had acute pyelonephritis and was admitted to the hospital for IV antibiotics. Complete laboratory studies were ordered by the attending physician including blood and urine cultures. Ampicillin was started as the antibiotic at 2 gm every six hours. A clean catch urine was positive for occult blood, showed 810 RBC and 8-10 WBC per HPF and 3+ bacteria.

In the nurse's notes on admission, there was the note that the patient had been experiencing the chills and fever for four days prior to coming to the hospital.

After her admission to the obstetric department the fetal monitor was connected externally. The nurse documents that she could not be sure that FHT were present. By 7:00 AM the morning after admission occasional contractions were noted. A chest x-ray was done, which showed "dense pneumonia" in the posterior gutter on the left. She was febrile and tachypneic having occasional contractions, which she did not feel. $MgSO_4$ was begun IV in an attempt to abort labor. Contractions continued and the FHT were located and counted at 158/min. The patient became progressively tachypneic (50/min) and blood gas determination revealed a pH of 7.32, CO_2 27, and PO_2 57. Oxygen was increased to 8 L/min in the early evening. The next morning early she was noted to be edematous and the respirations had become more labored. IV diuresis was begun with good results. Arterial blood gas revealed pH of 7.15, CO_2 49, and PO_2 60.

An internist was consulted to assist in the management of this critically ill patient. The chest x-ray was repeated and was said to show an "alveolar filling" in the right base and perihilar regions, thought to be fluid overload superimposed on pneumonia. His opinion was sepsis due to pyelonephritis complicated by ARDS. The patient was transferred to the coronary care unit, and Tobramycin was added to the antibiotic regimen. Respirations became more labored, and the patient began to be lethargic and poorly responsive. A Swan-Ganz catheter was inserted and the patient was intubated to support respirations. Labor began during this time, and PEEP was begun because of hypoxia. A repeat chest x-ray showed the alveolar filling process to involve both lungs.

In the early evening of that day, the second day of hospitalization, the patient spontaneously delivered a male infant with Apgar scores of 7 and 7. The infant was transferred to the neonatal intensive care unit in the medical center.

Though the chest x-ray showed some improvement, the patient continued hypoxic and moderately obtunded, the blood platelet count dropped, and some peripheral cyanosis developed. No obstructive uropathy was present on x-ray, but the patient was transferred to the medical center for amputation of the left forearm, and aortic valve replacement because of massive vegetations from the sepsis. She required dialysis because of renal failure. Over the succeeding months, she was in and out of the medical center five times for procedures related to her pregnancy and its complications. The baby required a ventriculoperitoneal shunt for hydrocephalus and continues to require extensive medical management.

A lawsuit was filed charging a host of physicians with failure to diagnose the pyelonephritis complicating this pregnancy and failure to treat the patient in an appropriate manner after admission to the hospital. After exhaustive negotiations the matter was finally settled requiring a very high six-figure amount.

Loss Prevention Comments

No one can question the terrible outcome of this case, beginning as a more or less routine Medicaid pregnancy in an otherwise healthy young woman who had had a previous abortion and smoked over a pack of cigarettes a day. Because of this, the nurse in the DPH classified her as "at risk."

The practice here is that the DPH nurses evaluate the patient, send the record to the physician who had agreed to deliver the patient, and continue to follow her, with the physician being available during the prenatal course to advise and to treat if necessary. Normally the physician sees the patient at about 28 to 30 weeks for evaluation, and then assumes sole responsibility for the patient during the last four to six weeks of pregnancy. This routine is fairly well established in Tennessee, especially in the rural areas where there are no public hospitals to support the indigent. It works extremely well because of the dedication of DPH professionals and the willingness of private physicians to support the program.

The dipstick test for nitrites as a screen for urinary tract infection (UTI) is an old test of questionable reliability. In pregnancy, the classical symptoms of lower UTI, i.e., frequency, dysuria, and burning, are not as reliable as in the non-pregnant patient. There is frequency due to the enlarging uterus, and mild dysuria and burning are likely to be misinterpreted by the patient. About 15 percent of pregnant women have asymptomatic bacteriuria. In some cases this progresses to overt infection of the bladder and can also involve the upper urinary system. In this case, however, the nurses in the DPH noted the positive test for nitrites and acted on it to send the patient to the obstetrician for evaluation. The record in the DPH indicated that the findings on urinalysis were sent to the physician's office. The record of the physician, however, did not appear to document that he had evaluated the patient for possible UTI. Did the DPH record get to the physician's office? Did the personnel in the doctor's office misplace the report? Did the physician ignore this screening test? These questions cannot be answered with accuracy in this case.

This case should prompt a review of the systems in our offices that support us, and, if functioning properly, protect us from events like this. As we have observed in many cases, the failure to handle reports appropriately has been key to our inability to defend ourselves when an unfortunate outcome occurs. In this case, the systems in the DPH must be reviewed as well as those in the physician's office. There simply must be communication beyond the report itself that prompts the physician to act in the way the ancillary personnel intend. Both have responsibility in situations like this and must recognize the support they offer to each other. What is an example of the cooperative management of an indigent population between the DPH and the private physician cannot be taken for granted, but must be constantly scrutinized.

XII

Obstetrics and Maternal Disease

      The following cases focus on the maternal side of the obstetrical practice. Some of these conditions develop during the pregnancy and, indeed, may be a consequence of it. Some, however, are conditions that the expectant mother brings to her doctor with the pregnancy. It is in these situations that system breakdowns in the practice can lead to delay or failure to diagnose and treat a problem.

      One of the system problems already mentioned in the previous chapter is the system in the practice to keep the entire team informed about what is going on in a pregnancy which could forecast possible problems later on or during labor and delivery. One such problem is the gestational diabetic who is seen by different associates during the last weeks of her pregnancy and who is allowed to proceed beyond the expected due date not knowing that the attending had planned to do a C-section at or near week 38. Another such problem is the patient who has had some elevation of blood pressure, perhaps more than expected edema, or minimal proteinuria and is seen by other physicians without the record in hand who must put together an emergency plan of treatment without knowing what has been done and, probably most important, without a real physician/patient relationship.

      On occasion the routine prenatal examination will reveal pathology that will have a bearing on the conduct of the pregnancy and plans for delivery. Such an instance could be the assessment of the size of the pelvis in a patient who is nulliparous. The conduct of labor might well be planned with this in mind. The patient may have diabetes type I requiring the assistance of the internist or endocrinologist who has been managing the condition. In the case of some heart problem the cardiologist would need to provide input to management. Chronic disease, i.e., rheumatoid arthritis, asthmatic states, gastrointestinal diseases all would require detailed plans of management or consultation with regard to labor, delivery, and postpartum care. The effectiveness of the system used by the members of the group to communicate with each other is crucial and must be relied upon to appropriately care for the pregnant female.

Inordinate delay in the diagnosis and treatment of post-operative complications is a hazard that must be taken into account in the post-C-section patient. Perforation of the bowel usually from injury with the use of electrocautery during the operation can be difficult to diagnose. When it is not looked for by the attending or the associate who performed the operation, the delay can be life threatening.

In the preoccupation with the "bad baby" issues, not enough attention has been paid to these very real maternal hazards.

118.   ELECTIVE STERILIZATION—NO GUARANTEES

Allegations—Negligent performance of sterilization
procedure; breach of warranty
Physician Issues—Physician relied on booklet for informed
consent; booklet: "Applied properly, device will not
fail"; physician had not read book he gave patient
Patient Issues—Patient couldn't read; no suggestion by
physician that procedure could fail
Outcome—Five-figure settlement

CASE STUDY

A 32-year-old, para 3, gravida 3 presented herself to her gynecologist requesting a tubal ligation. A thorough examination at that time revealed no contraindications for surgery or general anesthesia. The patient and the doctor discussed various methods of sterilization. The patient elected a method designed to occlude the fallopian tubes. Admission was arranged for one month later and the patient was given a booklet written by the manufacturer of the occlusion device to read in the interim. The booklet described the procedure and its risks and benefits.

The patient was admitted as previously arranged. During evening rounds, the physician asked if she had read the booklet to which the patient replied, "Yes." She was asked if she had any questions and she answered, "No." The doctor then had the patient sign a standard consent form, and the patient was taken to the operating room the next morning. Following routine skin preparation and drape, the abdominal cavity was inflated and the laparoscope inserted. The occluding device was placed over the loop of each tube. There were no anatomical abnormalities and visibility was good.

The patient was seen for follow-up visits as instructed and continued to see the doctor on a regular basis for annual check-ups. When it was discovered on one of the routine visits that the patient was pregnant, she filed suit for alleged negligence in performing the tube occlusion surgery and for breach of warranty.

The physician testified at the trial that he had never personally read the booklet that he gave his patients but had assumed it explained the procedure better than he could. The patient testified that the doctor had asked if she had read the booklet but denied saying she had. In fact, although she could sign her name, she could not read. In addition, she stated that the doctor had said this procedure was intended to be permanent. Her attorney further relied on the booklet that the doctor had given the patient, which stated, "If applied properly, this device will not fail."

LOSS PREVENTION COMMENTS

The real issue in this case is informed consent. The patient, surprised by an unexpected result, claimed her doctor was negligent. The facts do not point to negligence in his performing the procedure, but there is no record or documentation of informed consent. Not only did the doctor rely on a written booklet prepared by the manufacturer of the occlusion device, he had not read the booklet and did not follow up with his own comments to be certain the patient understood. Informed consent is a process. It requires that the patient receive enough information to make an informed decision about what the doctor will do. Without sufficient information, the patient may be surprised at the outcome and might sue the doctor, claiming that if only she had known of the risk, she would not have consented to that procedure or might have opted for another course of action.

Doctors can also find themselves with legal problems if they make statements that the patient construes as warranties or guarantees. Apparently the doctor did not explain to the patient that, although sterility was the intended result of the procedure, there is absolutely no guarantee that this will be the case. The doctor should have explained that although the failure rate is less than 1 percent, there is always the chance of pregnancy, even after the surgery is properly performed. The patient should also be told that the body itself will attempt to repair any injury to its reproductive system, so that she understands that future pregnancy does not automatically mean her doctor improperly performed the procedure. Here the doctor allowed a booklet, which he had never read, to speak for him that "if applied properly, this device will not fail." No surgical procedure should ever be guaranteed.

Once the doctor has fully discussed the procedure and its benefits and risks with the patient, the discussion should be documented. Many doctors have their patients sign a form indicating that such a discussion has taken place, that the patient understands what will be happening, and agrees to the procedure. Certainly, this documentation would be acceptable if it specifically covers the discussion with this particular patient. The preferred informed consent documentation is a note in the patient's chart stating that the doctor discussed the procedure, its benefits, the risks of having or not having the procedure, and any alternatives with the patient, and that she understood and agreed to go ahead. A note made by the doctor shortly after such a discussion cannot be later undermined by the plaintiff's attorney, whose witness testifies that, yes, she signed the informed consent form, but did not read it and/or did not understand what she was signing.

119.   TIGHTEN UP YOUR OFFICE PROTOCOL

Allegation—Progestational agent given without prior pregnancy test
Physician Issues—Confusing menstrual history; normal examination
Patient Issues—Operative procedure; no pregnancy test
Outcome—Five-figure settlement

CASE STUDY

Early in the fall, a 17-year-old unmarried gravida 0, para 0 went to her board eligible Ob/Gyn for her annual checkup. Her history included irregular menstrual periods associated with increased cramping. She also complained of slightly painful intercourse and recurrent urinary tract infections. Her birth control method was "the pill." Examination revealed the uterus to be slightly retroverted but otherwise within normal limits, and a change in the birth control pills, along with a lubricant prior to intercourse, were recommended.

The patient returned some two months later for a routine check, which was apparently conducted by the Ob/Gyn's employed office nurse. When several weeks later through a phone call the patient complained of burning on urination along with a yellow discharge, over the phone she was given a prescription for antibiotics and instructed to come to the office if the symptoms persisted.

One week later the patient came to the office complaining of itching and burning, along with continued yellow discharge. The pelvis was too tender to examine. Antibiotics were continued.

The patient was not seen for several months, nor was she heard from until she phoned the physician's office in the early spring stating she had not had a menstrual period in three months. The patient was instructed to come into the office for an examination, and when she was seen four days later, history confirmed no menstrual period for three months. There were no complaints of nausea or breast tenderness, though she did give a history of one or two missed pills. On examination the pelvis was within normal limits. Treatment was begun with medroxyprogesterone acetate (Provera) for five days, followed by regular ingestion of birth control pills after her menstrual period.

Two weeks later the patient phoned complaining that she had still had no menstrual period, and in addition she complained of abdominal pain localized in the right side that had been there for some two months. The patient was given some pain medication over the phone and instructed to come in for an examination, but instead she repeatedly contacted the office during the next three weeks by telephone, each time complaining of lower abdominal pain, a jelly-like, blood-tinged discharge, and a low-grade fever. Each call was handled by office personnel, and pain medications were refilled over the telephone.

After approximately three weeks without improvement, the patient returned to the Ob/Gyn's office. Examination revealed the abdomen and pelvis to be exquisitely tender. The patient gave a history of a menstrual period some three weeks earlier, but bleeding continued. The possibility of dilation and curettage was discussed with the patient, but she refused.

The patient returned one week later with the same complaints. Dilation and curettage was again recommended and this time accepted. She was consequently admitted to the hospital the next day, where she underwent a pelvic examination under general endotracheal anesthesia. This examination revealed a uterus that was approximately the size of a 12- to 14-week pregnancy, with the cervix open 1.5 cm. A suction curettage revealed umbilical cord fragments, and re-examination of the uterus revealed small fetal parts. When a uterus compatible in size with approximately four months' gestation was found, the uterus was emptied in a conventional manner.

The patient recovered well from her hospitalization, but filed suit alleging negligence in prescribing medroxyprogesterone before the doctor took steps to determine whether she was pregnant. The case was settled out of court.

LOSS PREVENTION COMMENTS

Even with the highly efficient methods of birth control now available, any woman who gives a history of missing a menstrual period must be considered pregnant until proven otherwise. In this case the failure to at least get a pregnancy test was deemed negligent and below an acceptable standard of care.

The error here was perhaps caused by sloppy practice habits. On numerous occasions treatment was prescribed over the phone without giving the patient an appointment to return for an examination. The standard entry in the chart, "return prn," is unacceptable when something goes wrong. "Sloppy" habits on the part of office personnel probably indicate sloppy habits on the part of the physician employer.

120.   POST-CESAREAN-SECTION DEATH

*Allegations—Delay in diagnosing perforated colon; negligent
     post-C-section management*
*Physician Issues—Operating Ob/Gyn did not see patient after
     surgery; weekend on-call physician saw patient post-
     C-section; fragmented care; poor progress notes;
     discharged home prematurely*
Patient Issues—Severe pain and suffering; wrongful death
Outcome—Large six-figure settlement

CASE STUDY

The patient was a 31-year-old mother of one who had an uneventful pregnancy except for some slight vaginal bleeding at 5 months gestation. The patient was observed in the labor and delivery area of the hospital, and the bleeding stopped spontaneously. No subsequent bleeding occurred. Her first baby was delivered by cesarean section and was known to be a normal child, now 5 years of age.

The patient came into the hospital at the expected time of delivery in early labor. She declined an opportunity to deliver vaginally and was taken to the operating room within two hours of her admission. It was Friday, and her regular attending obstetrician was not on call. His associate performed an uneventful cesarean section under epidural analgesia. The operative note did not describe any intraoperative problems. The development of the bladder flap was accomplished easily, and the uterus was entered through a low cervical incision. A healthy female infant was delivered with Apgar scores of 9/10. The remainder of the surgery proceeded without the slightest problem. The blood loss was estimated to be 500 cc.

The surgery was completed about 4:00 PM, and the patient went to the floor about two hours later. The nurse's note at 4:45 PM described a "soft abdomen with normal bowel sounds." The first night after the surgery the patient was medicated five times for abdominal pain.

The first day after the surgery, another one of the associates in the group made rounds on this patient. The patient was medicated five times for pain and one time for "gas." The blood counts that morning were normal, and the abdomen was said to be "soft" and the bowel sounds "hypoactive" by the nurses. The next day, Sunday, the same associate made rounds and ordered "Magnesium Citrate—one-half bottle now." The patient had been able to walk very little because of pain. The doctor noted the abdomen to be "distended but soft." Bowel sounds were described as "occasional."

The following day, Monday, the patient's regular attending physician returned and made rounds in the hospital. The nurse's notes during the night described the abdomen as "distended and firm" and the bowel sounds as "hypoactive." Again, "firm, distended, and tender" was the descriptive phrase used with reference to the abdomen. The patient had a small bowel movement during the night and "good results" in response to an enema at 8:00 AM. The attending physician discharged the patient, noting that the abdomen was "distended, soft, and the bowel sounds normal." In the discharge summary, the attending physician recorded the abdominal pain and distension with the comment that these complaints had responded to "cathartics, colon tube, and enemas."

The patient was readmitted to the hospital the same night because of "severe abdominal pain and distension." After discussion with the attending physician, the emergency room physician began NG suction, started IV fluids, and ordered abdominal x-rays and a CBC/urine. The CBC was remarkable in that there were reported 33 percent segmented neutrophils and 46 percent band forms in the smear. The films of the abdomen showed "a massive amount of free air in the abdomen" which was deemed "consistent with the recent cesarean section." The suspected diagnosis was intestinal obstruction.

The following day at 9:00 AM the attending physician felt that the abdomen was "distended, tender but not tense." Through the day the patient's urinary output was very low, and she was thought to be dehydrated. IV fluids were increased. A CBC was ordered for the night and was to be repeated the following morning. X-rays of the abdomen were also to be repeated in the morning. On both CBCs the band forms were reported to be 70 percent and 60 percent respectively.

Vital signs through the night continued to show tachycardia of 120 to 140. The x-rays of the abdomen again showed free air which seemed not to have changed from previous films. A CT scan of the abdomen reported, "the amount of free air is inordinate for the surgery done and a perforated hollow low viscus is suspected."

The patient was returned to the operating room, where a perforation of the cecum was found, along with massive peritonitis. Cardiac arrest occurred during surgery. The patient was temporarily resuscitated, but arrest occurred again, and ultimately she died during the operation.

A lawsuit was filed, charging the attending physician and all his associates with negligence in the delay in diagnosing and treating the perforation of the colon. A negotiated settlement was the ultimate outcome of the lawsuit.

LOSS PREVENTION COMMENTS

The evaluation of abdominal distension in the post cesarean section patient is not an easy problem. Several factors could have contributed to the delay in diagnosis. The patient seemed to require an unusual amount of narcotics following her surgery. There was an apparent lack of continuity of care in that the patient was operated on by an associate, seen the first two days after surgery by another associate, and discharged from the hospital by the attending physician who had not seen her in the hospital.

The readmission was the critical piece in this puzzle. This patient's distension continued and worsened, as did her pain and tenderness. With different physicians seeing her almost daily, these very important findings were hard to evaluate. It is worth noting that the attending physician did not come into the emergency room and examine his patient.

Certainly one would expect free air in the abdomen on the fourth postoperative day following a cesarean section, but "massive" free air? The unusually high percentage of band forms in the differential could have been due to intestinal obstruction, persistent acidosis, and dehydration, but it would not be expected to persist in the absence of infection. The "free air" did not change significantly in 48 hours as one would expect, and clinically the patient continued to deteriorate.

Would the result have been any different if the patient had been reoperated upon as an emergency on readmission? Or, if the possibility of bowel perforation had been entertained, would antibiotics have helped? What was the cause of the perforation in the first place? Certainly, in the absence of underlying pathology, the first consideration would have to be bowel injury at the first operation. Every decision made in the management of this patient could be explained and defended. However, the above circumstances taken as a whole made settlement the best option.

121. HELLP!

Allegations—Failure to make diagnosis and treat in timely manner; fluid overload in postoperative period

Physician Issues—Extremely poor records (no documentation of critical events); no system of recording phone calls and complaints received; continued proteinuria and weight gain without intervention

Patient Issues—Bout of nosebleeds and bruising reported; sent home from office day of admission "feeling bad all over"

Outcome—Death post-C-section

CASE STUDY

A 33-year-old deaf woman reported to the Ob/Gyn specialist. She was gravida 1, para 0, and gave a history of last menstrual period on May 10, 1990. There were no significant factors on history that were alarming. She was told that the expected date of confinement was about February 20, 1991. Physical examination revealed blood pressure 110/62 min Hg, weight 134 lb. The uterus was enlarged compatible with the history, and the urine showed a trace of protein.

She was seen at the usual intervals. The urine consistently showed a trace of protein, and the patient's weight gain was about 5 lb per month. Her blood pressure remained in the normal range. At about 20 weeks she had gained almost 40 lb, had 2+ edema, and the urine continued to show protein. Shortly after this visit, her husband called in to report nosebleeds, hemoptysis, and bruising. She was told to come to the office, but she did not return until her regular visit two weeks later. There was no office record of her husband's call or of the advice he had been given.

There was no documentation of nosebleed, hemoptysis, or bruising at that next visit. She continued to show protein in the urine and this time the edema was graded at 1+. The weight gain continued to be about 2 lb a week. On this visit she was told to take Epsom Salts in orange juice each morning. After this visit, the patient called in stating that she had been "sick" during the night.

At about 36 weeks she came in for a routine appointment. Her examination showed that she had gained over 50 lb. She had 2+ protein and her reflexes were described as 2+ with no clonus. She was told "if you feel bad again, you should come into the hospital." The urine was to have been sent to the laboratory for a complete urinalysis on order of the attending physician, but it was not sent. She was given a prescription for compazine suppositories, but the prescription was not recorded in the office record. The patient came to the hospital within a few hours of the office visit.

The routine hospital admission permit was signed by the patient, which stated in part, "Attending physician and the physician of his choice will perform delivery, therapeutic operations, or procedures as his judgment may dictate on the basis of findings during the course of said surgery. The attending physician has discussed with and explained nature and purpose of operation, complications, no warranty or guarantee, etc., etc." The admitting nurse recorded that her prenatal history was "negative." The fetal heart tones were recorded 180/min and the patient complained that she "felt bad all over." She had fever to 100.1°F, pulse 100/min, and blood pressure 160/100 mm Hg. She did not void, and on catheterization she had no urine in the bladder. The attending physician was notified of her admission. The physician who had consistently done her prenatal examinations was not on call, so she was seen by one of his associates who had seen her for the first time during the office visit that immediately preceded her admission.

One hour after admission, the patient had fever of 102.4°F. There was some urine in the bag which was tested 4+ for protein. Her blood pressure was recorded at 190/90 mm Hg. The attending physician was notified by phone and stated that he would be there "in 15 to 20 minutes"; he arrived in about 30 minutes. Before he arrived, he had ordered that the $MgSO_4$ protocol be started. The intravenous fluids that had been running at 200 ml/hr were ordered reduced.

When the attending physician arrived, he immediately ordered the standard orders for labor and delivery preeclampsia/eclampsia protocol. The laboratory work that had been drawn on admission showed an elevated PTT, platelet count of 72,000/cu mm, and a bleeding time of 6.5 minutes. The attending physician's note stated, "No problems since last recorded office visit; no complications of pregnancy (see note)"—apparently referring to the admission note by the nurse.

Two hours after admission the patient was being prepared for cesarean section. She was receiving $MgSO_4$ IV by perfusion pump. Since admission she had received 1,400 ml of fluid and her output was measured at 28 ml. She continued to remain anuric with reflexes said to be 3+ hyperactive. She received some IV antihypertensives, and at the time the surgery began her blood pressure was 168/96 mm Hg.

Three hours after admission the patient was delivered by cesarean section of a 4-lb 14-oz male infant with Apgar scores of 8 and 9. The postoperative progress note referred to "severe preeclampsia/HELLP syndrome." It was thought that she had either pneumonia or pulmonary edema accounting for her respiratory difficulty, which had been noted during anesthesia and continued to the degree that it was necessary to leave the ETT in place and support her on a ventilator postoperatively. Consultation with a pulmonologist supported the diagnosis of the HELLP syndrome; he suggested a CVP line. The CVP was recorded at 3 mm H_2O .

Her liver function progressively deteriorated, as her anemia worsened. She became intensely jaundiced and the serum bilirubin determination suggested intravascular hemolysis. The platelet count continued to drop, and she developed abdominal ascites, which on paracentesis showed to be hemorrhagic.

According to another consultant, the postoperative course had been "complicated by profound hypertension, intervals of pulmonary edema, and hypovolemia." It was thought that she might have developed acute tubular necrosis during the postoperative period.

The patient received a large amount of packed red blood cells, platelets, and clotting factors in the form of fresh frozen plasma. She continued a febrile course and developed more ascites, which proved to be old blood. Despite the efforts of many consultants, and what appeared to be aggressive treatment, the patient died on the 10th day after surgery. A lawsuit was filed about six months after the patient's death, charging the attending physician and his group with negligence. The allegations included failure to timely diagnose and treat this patient's condition, negligent postoperative care, and fluid overload.

Loss Prevention Comments

This syndrome of severe preeclampsia/eclampsia characterized by hemolysis, elevated liver enzymes, and low platelet counts (HELLP) has been described in the literature for about 12 to 15 years. In the last three years, many articles have been written to more clearly describe the syndrome and to more precisely define the biochemical abnormalities associated with this disease. It appears to occur in the setting of preeclampsia, usually in the last six weeks of pregnancy. The treatment of this condition is not within the scope of this article, but prompt delivery of the baby seems to be its cardinal principle.

There were a number of factors in this case that made defense virtually impossible. There was no documentation of the "nosebleeds, hemoptysis, and bruising" in the office record, and there was no recorded effort to follow up on this significant development. This may well have been due to a failure on the part of office personnel to inform the physician of this call. Office systems should be in place to record all calls, the caller, the nature of the complaint, and its appropriate disposition. The patient continued to show protein in the urine and a rather massive weight gain without any reference to its possible significance.

There was no documentation in this prenatal record that any member of the group other than the doctor who did her original examination had seen this woman until she was seen by the member who was called upon to manage her admission and all its complications. It is particularly important in a group Ob/Gyn practice that the record show that the patient has been allowed some opportunity to interact with other members of the group who might have to deliver her baby. It is particularly important for each member of the group to have some knowledge of the individual record of all the patients for whom he might become responsible.

During the last two weeks of her pregnancy she became more edematous and the protein in the urine increased. On the day of her admission to the hospital, she complained for at least the second time of "feeling bad all over." She was advised to go home and "if you feel bad again, come to the hospital." She reported to the hospital within a few hours.

After her admission to the hospital and the demonstration of near anuria, increasing hypertension, and proteinuria, some aggressive measures were begun. Some expert testimony contended that she suffered from profound hypovolemia on admission despite the tissue edema and supported that contention by the low CVP of 3 mm H_2O when that line was established. Perhaps earlier efforts at correcting this condition would have prevented the cascade of symptoms that eventually led to her death. Further, experts suggested that immediate measures aimed at correcting the coagulation problems that were evident on the initial laboratory reports might have provided some stabilization for the impending surgery. One must wonder whether or not some hemolysis occurred earlier in the course of this complication of pregnancy.

It is only speculation on the part of experts that earlier diagnosis and more vigorous treatment would have reversed this process. HELLP is a devastating condition, and even the earliest recognition and the most vigorous treatment might well have met with failure. However, in this case the critical clinical facts that were not recorded and seemed to be ignored, the lack of any attention to the proteinuria and edema that had been recorded several times, and the apparent failure to address the complaints of this patient all combined to make defense very hazardous.

122. PHYSICIAN-TO-PHYSICIAN COMMUNICATION

Allegations—Delay in diagnosis of breast cancer
Physician Issues—Screening mammogram "benign cysts"; no
  repeat suggested
Patient Issues—Changed physicians; breast mass; cancer; death
Outcome—Six-figure settlement

CASE STUDY

A 46-year-old woman with an eight-year history of ulcerative colitis under good control on conservative therapy had considered hysterectomy because of the presence of uterine fibroids and excessive bleeding. On at least one occasion the patient had been scheduled for the operation but had decided to wait for a while to see if symptoms would subside. During these examinations there had been no mention of breast abnormalities. Two years earlier, a screening mammogram in an examination by her regular physician, a board certified Ob/Gyn, had recorded, "Breasts normal." One month before reporting for this examination, there was no mention of the breasts on a visit to this same physician.

She went to have the screening examination, asking that the report be sent to her regular Ob/Gyn. She reported having a predominant mass in the upper outer quadrant of the right breast. She was given the screening examination although the policy of this specialty service stated that women who were symptomatic would be given the regular diagnostic mammogram. She got two views of each breast followed by ultrasound examination of the right breast showing two "cysts" corresponding to the "mass" which she had discovered and because of which she had come for the examination. The examination was done by a technician and read by the radiologist before he left for the day. Although the policy of the department called for an exami-nation by the radiologist (at his discretion), her breasts were not examined. The report was, "benign cysts right breast—return for repeat examination in one year."

This patient was also being followed by the "Bone Center" because of recent laboratory findings suggesting calcium loss. Two months after the screening mammography she was seen at this Bone Center, where the note was made that the patient "has developed cysts in the right breast and is being followed by her regular physician." Again, six weeks later, she was seen by the Bone Center where CT scan was done for bone densitometry.

It was six months after the screening mammography before she was seen by her regular physician. His examination revealed the "lump in the breast—cystic mastitis." Again she was scheduled for TAH to be done about a month later. She called in stating that she wanted an abdominal ultrasound prior to surgery and would like to delay the surgery for about a month.

The ultrasound revealed the "multiple discrete fibroids, five in number." She did not report for the TAH but went to another Ob/Gyn for evaluation of the breast lesion. This physician confirmed the presence of the fibroids, but because of the mass which had replaced about one half the breast, a mammogram was ordered and a surgeon consulted. The surgeon noted a firm 8-cm mass, some nipple retraction, and no axillary nodes. The mammogram revealed a significant change in the lesion, suggesting malignancy.

At operation, frozen section revealed malignancy confirmed by permanent sections after a modified radical mastectomy. Seven of 15 nodes were positive, and the chest x-ray showed multiple nodules, which proved to be metastases. With both radiation and chemotherapy, the patient survived only a year.

A lawsuit was filed charging both the regular Ob/Gyn and the radiologist with negligence in the delay in diagnosis, failure to advise that the mammogram was not diagnostic, and the failure to recommend more frequent follow-up examinations. A large settlement was necessary, as successful defense of this suit was not believed to be possible.

LOSS PREVENTION COMMENTS

This case is particularly troublesome. How could good physicians become distracted and fail to communicate with each other, so that errors like this happen? How could good physicians fail to communicate with their patients so that proper care is not given? It happens a lot!

The radiologist in this case certainly called this screening mammogram in such a manner as to raise a question as to his competence. Retrospective examination of the films would not have determined that the only possible diagnosis was benign cysts. Was he in a hurry that day? The technician did the examination, and although it was a "screening" test, proceeded to do the ultrasound examination that protocol indicated was to follow the diagnostic mammogram at the discretion of the radiologist. Again, protocol would have suggested an examination of the breast in this instance, but one was not done. The radiologist should have suggested a follow-up examination sooner than a year, and the regular physician should have examined his patient regardless of the radiologist's recommendation. He saw his patient six months after the mammography with only the comment, "breast lump—cystic mastitis."

Perhaps the regular physician was distracted by the repeated consideration of a TAH for her uterine fibroids. If the Ob/Gyn specialist was not going to follow the patient more closely, he should have consulted a surgeon to assume the responsibility of definitive treatment of this presenting complaint. Many nonsurgeons would have aspirated these "cysts" after the mammogram and followed closely the results of this procedure. Although all patients present unique situations, the nonsurgeon should have a protocol, in his head at least, as to the step-by-step management of breast problems.

In the office of both the radiologist and the Ob/Gyn, systems should be in place so that medical assistants could ensure the appropriate follow-up in cases of this type. This kind of scrutiny is certainly in the best interest of our patients, and no less is expected of us by the public at large. Laxity of this degree in the protection of our patients is not tolerable when bad results occur. We pay dearly, both emotionally and financially!

123.   MATERNAL/FETAL DEATH

Allegations—Negligence in management of pregnancy, labor, and delivery; maternal and fetal death
Physician Issues—Failure to follow gestational diabetes; failure to address hypertension and proteinuria-preeclampsia; failure to aggressively address hypotension (epidural)
Patient Issues—Death of both mother and baby
Outcome—High six-figure settlement

CASE STUDY

The patient was a 36-year-old woman who saw her physician because of having missed a third menstrual period and presuming she was about 12 weeks pregnant. She was obese at 190 lb and had a blood pressure of 120/70 mm Hg. On her initial examination the urine showed a trace of protein, and her serum glucose was reported as 117 mg/dl (normal 65 to 115). Her first pregnancy ten years earlier had ended in the birth of a male infant weighing 7-lb 14-oz, and a second had ended in a spontaneous abortion at about ten weeks' gestation.

She was seen at regular intervals of one month through the 28th week of pregnancy, after which she was seen every two weeks. She gained 24 lb, up to 217 lb by the 33rd week. At this time ultrasonography revealed a single fetus in the cephalic position at about 38 weeks' gestation. The "expected" fetal weight was 9.24 lb.

One week after this examination she was admitted to the hospital with contractions occurring irregularly and lasting for about a minute. The blood pressure was 174/107 mm Hg, pulse 110/min, and deep tendon reflexes were 2+. The membranes were intact and the cervix was only 1 cm dilated, with 30 percent effacement. The fetal weight was estimated at 8 lb and no fetal problems were identified. An external fetal monitor (EFM) was placed, revealing a fetal heart rate (FHR) of 140, with normal accelerations. Contractions had begun about three hours earlier, occurring at about three- to four-minute intervals and lasting 60 to 70 seconds. She was said to be in "true labor." She "had a cold."

One hour after admission the attending physician was notified of the presence of a "deceleration." She was repositioned and the blood pressure of 158/98 mm Hg was recorded. The attending physician informed the L&D staff that the patient was to have an epidural block. Contractions continued, and when the cervix was about 5 cm dilated, the anesthetic was administered. This was about four hours after admission. The preanesthetic note by the CRNA recorded a 1+ protein in the urine, normal serum electrolytes, and a normal EKG. The chest was said to be clear.

One-half hour after the first attempt at the epidural block the FHR was recorded at 150, with 9 cm cervical dilatation and blood pressure of 180/120 mm Hg. The attending physician was made aware of the blood pressure, which, when retaken, was recorded at 180/100 mm Hg. Oxygen was administered by mask. The epidural was then administered using standard technique and medication. Within 15 minutes the blood pressure was recorded at 92/60 mm Hg. Fetal heart tones (FHT) were very difficult to hear, but one observer thought that there was a deceleration. The resident was called to the bedside, but was unsure about the FHR. The contractions were said to be irregular at this time, the FHR was 120, and the blood pressure remained low at 82/55 mm Hg. The IV flow was increased. The resident examined the patient, ruptured the membranes, and placed the scalp electrode for monitoring.

With the increased flow of IV fluids, the blood pressure came up to 112/58 mm Hg after having remained below 100 for about one hour. Decelerations were noted and the patient was informed that a C-section might be necessary. She stated that she did not want the operation and was allowed to progress further. The cervix was fully dilated within 30 minutes. With the head (caput) at 3+ and the FHR showing decelerations, a note was entered into the chart, "Previous history of borderline diabetes. Estimated weight of fetus 9 lb. In order to avoid shoulder dystocia, a C-section will be performed secondary to macrosomia." The order for "C-section this AM" was written.

Decelerations were noted throughout the interval between the order and the transport to the delivery room. The EFM was discontinued before the transfer to the operating room.

Twenty minutes before delivery, the patient complained to the CRNA of shortness of breath. The oxygen flow was increased, and the baby was delivered. When her dyspnea became worse, the mother was intubated within 15 minutes of delivery and respirations were controlled. Almost simultaneously she had cardiac arrest and CPR was begun. The baby was stillborn, weighing 10 lb 10 oz. CPR of the mother continued for about one hour without any response. She was pronounced dead one hour and fifteen minutes after delivery. The impression by the physicians present was that the mother had suffered a pulmonary embolism. An autopsy was done on both the mother and the infant.

The pathologist's report of the autopsy stated the patient had died as a result of "toxemia of pregnancy" and that the infant's death had been due to "hypoxia secondary to maternal demise." A lawsuit was filed charging negligence in the management of pregnancy, labor, and delivery, leading to the death of the mother and the baby.

LOSS PREVENTION COMMENTS

The defense of a maternal/fetal death in this day and time is difficult in the extreme! This tragic outcome occurs so seldom that the presumption of negligence is almost automatic in the mind of everybody! In the review of this case, however, there were some very significant findings that took the attending physician outside of an acceptable standard of care.

The mention of a previous history of "borderline diabetes" in the preoperative note, when there had been no monitoring of blood sugar throughout the pregnancy after the initial determination, suggested that this very important aspect of the history had been overlooked. The persistent hypertension and proteinuria throughout the last eight to ten weeks of gestation also had not been addressed in the management of the patient. Indeed, there was no documentation of the possibility of preeclampsia in the medical record.

Perhaps the most significant occurrence was the persistent hypotension that began immediately after the epidural injection and was not corrected for over an hour. Should there have been a more aggressive treatment of the hypotension than only increasing the flow of IV fluids? That seemed to work, but did the low blood pressure, lasting for over an hour, compromise the fetus?

What was the etiology of the mother's shortness of breath and cardiac arrest? The autopsy report would support the diagnosis of acute congestive heart failure on the basis of preeclampsia. In the absence of another possibility for fetal death, the pathologist's opinion that the baby's death resulted from the mother's death seems accurate.

Why was the C-section delayed for over an hour after the decision was made? During that time the EFM showed a pattern of decelerations indicative of fetal distress. It is easy to conjecture that if the section had been done in a timely manner the cascade of events leading to the death of both mother and baby would have been avoided.

The standard of care was not followed in (1) not addressing the possibility of gestational diabetes during the pregnancy; (2) not addressing the preeclampsia that developed late in the pregnancy; and (3) the delay in performing the C-section after signs of fetal distress had developed and persisted. These sentinel events in the pregnancy of this "elderly multipara" demanded recognition and attention!

124.   DIFFICULT DIAGNOSIS

> *Allegation—Delay in diagnosis and treatment of surgical*
> *abdomen*
> *Physician Issues—Repeated treatment of pain with narcotics;*
> *failure to appreciate patient's evaluation that pain*
> *was not Crohn's; failure to carefully examine*
> *Patient Issues—Prolonged abdominal pain; postoperative*
> *death*
> *Outcome—Large six-figure settlement*

CASE STUDY

A 34-year-old woman had a long history of Crohn's disease involving the colon, with fistula formation. Two years before the present illness, the patient was under the care of a gastroenterologist for an exacerbation of her illness. With her disease improved for about 18 months after a regimen that included oral prednisone and IM methotrexate, she became pregnant and reported to her obstetrician for routine prenatal care in early December.

Her last menstrual period was reported to have been in mid-April. The urinary chorionic gonadotropin test was positive and her EDC was calculated to be July 20. On her prenatal record the history of Crohn's disease was recorded, along with the name of her gastroenterologist. She had had a low-grade urinary tract infection, which had been treated successfully by another physician. She had no nausea or vomiting, and her abdomen was reported as normal. The course of her pregnancy progressed without incident. The OB ultrasound about six weeks after her first OB visit and a repeat at 24 weeks' gestation were reported as entirely normal.

Two weeks after that visit to her obstetrician, she reported to the community hospital with right lower quadrant pain that had started about 12 hours earlier. Her vital signs were not remarkable and the fetal heart tones (FHTs) were heard and recorded at 120/min. The pain continued in the emergency department and she volunteered her history of Crohn's disease but stated that her "pain does not feel like that." She was having difficulty moving on the stretcher and stated that it felt like "muscle spasm." The obstetrician on call for her OB group ordered some routine laboratory work and authorized Stadol to be given in the IV that was running at a "keep open" rate.

The laboratory report, which included electrolytes, liver function studies, and blood counts only, showed a WBC count of 12,500/cu mm, with 85 percent segmented neutrophils. Her blood pressure remained at 115-120/72-78 mm Hg while she was in the ED, and she reported that she "felt better after the medicine." Reexamination of the abdomen at this time revealed no tenderness. Both she and her husband were reassured and were allowed to go home. She had been observed in the ED for almost five hours. Four days later she was seen in her obstetrician's office complaining of "severe abdominal pain." Again the patient and the physician thought the pain was musculoskeletal in nature. A urinalysis was done, some codeine given for pain, and the patient was sent home to be examined in a week by her obstetrician.

She was seen by her obstetrician at the regular appointment one week later. There were apparently no abdominal symptoms, the urine showed a 1+ protein, and the examination was negative. The patient was to return for her regular visit in two weeks, but five days later her obstetrician refilled by phone the codeine prescription for abdominal pain.

Three days later, at about 28 weeks' gestation, she was taken to the ED by ambulance complaining of severe "sharp" pain in the abdomen. She had a fever of 100.4°F and some vaginal spotting. She was nauseated but had not vomited. She gave a history of pain in her abdomen for about a month, but since early morning the pain had been occurring about every 15 minutes.

She was sent to the labor-and-delivery suite, where her abdominal pain continued and she began complaining of pain in the right chest, with difficulty breathing. Three hours after this admission to the ED her fever was 102.4°F. The FHTs were 120/min but there was thought to be some variable decrease. Believing that the patient was having some emergency associated with her pregnancy, her obstetrician ordered a cesarean section.

When the abdomen was opened about a "quart of pus came out." The uterus was opened, and a 2-lb 8-oz male infant, who seemed to be healthy in spite of the prematurity, was delivered. The abdomen was full of pus, with very heavy adhesion formation throughout. A blown-out appendiceal stump was identified, and the surgeon speculated that it had been ruptured for 10 days to two weeks. She was noted to be bleeding from every surface, and there was a noted lack of clotting of the blood. Laboratory studies confirmed the diagnosis of disseminated intravascular coagulation. She was transfused with quantities of fresh frozen plasma and whole blood. The operation was completed with the closure of the skin incision, and the patient, who "looked more stable," was transferred to the intensive care unit.

The patient's condition remained critical with hypotension, tachycardia, and fever, and she was thought to be in septic shock. Antibiotic coverage, begun in the operating room, was continued, but the WBC count rose to 87,000/cu mm, and a maculopapular rash appeared. The sequence of events was thought to be acute appendicitis with rupture and gram-negative sepsis. Blood culture confirmed this impression. She seemed to remain neurologically alert but developed purulent pleural effusions bilaterally. CT of the abdomen showed a very large collection of fluid extending from the left lateral subdiaphragmatic area down to the pelvis. Drainage of this fluid yielded 400 cc of purulent material followed by a comparable amount of frank blood. The surgeon believed that in attempting to remove what appeared to be a pleural effusion, the diaphragm had been opened and that the fluid came from the abdomen.

The patient began to develop multiple organ failure, with the heart becoming enlarged, the lungs showing evidence of congestive failure, the urinary output falling, and the BUN/creatinine rising. Renal dialysis was considered, but the patient was thought not to be a suitable candidate. She continued to go downhill and died some three weeks following the operation.

Despite some evidence of hyaline membrane disease, the infant was able to leave the hospital in good condition at 20 days of age.

LOSS PREVENTION COMMENTS

It is obvious that a deadly delay in diagnosis of acute appendicitis occurred in this case, but to make such an error in judgment is not medical malpractice! With the history of Crohn's disease, the physicians who cared for this lady were led away from the real diagnosis. There was a willingness to attribute the pain to "musculoskeletal" origins rather than to look further. She was given narcotics on her first visit to the ED at a time when she had an elevated WBC count and a shift to the left on differential count. There is no mention in the ED records of a thorough abdominal examination except for references to the pregnancy, and the statement after narcotics had been given that the abdomen appeared "normal." On the second visit to the ED, she was said to be having "severe abdominal pain," but again with no mention of an abdominal examination except for the pregnancy. No blood was drawn for a WBC count and differential. Codeine, which had been prescribed shortly after the first ED visit, was continued. There was a telephone refill of the codeine without a visit after the second ED evaluation. Obviously, the narcotics masked the pain in the abdomen which could have led to earlier intervention.

It looks very bad for our physicians, but given the history of Crohn's disease and some treatment of that condition with methotrexate and prednisone (we have no information as to how long before the pregnancy these drugs were stopped), there was plenty of room for confusion as to the real problem. It is hard enough to make an early diagnosis of acute appendicitis at this stage of pregnancy without the complication of a history of Crohn's disease.

However, the patient said all along that her pain did not feel like the pain she had experienced with the acute stage of her Crohn's disease, and in retrospect this statement should have played a greater role in the consideration of acute appendicitis as a primary diagnosis. The failure to listen to the patient, to consider as important the elevated temperature and WBC count, and the masking of the abdominal pain with narcotics were thought to be sufficiently serious deviations from the accepted standard of care to warrant a settlement in this case. There was also a very large medical expense bill, and a father left with a small baby to care for. All of this pushed hard for settlement rather than a trial and the risk of a jury verdict.

125.　REMEMBER THE PHYSICAL?

Allegations—Failure to do C-section in face of "borderline pelvis"; use of mid-forceps in compromised pelvis
Physician Issues—Initial diagnosis of "borderline pelvis"; negligent use of mid-forceps in small pelvis
Patient Issues—Birth injury with brain damage
Outcome—Modest six-figure settlement

CASE STUDY

A 19-year-old woman reported to her obstetrician giving a history of an LMP of October 22; EDC was calculated to be July 29. Findings on examination of the uterus were consistent with her history of about 6+ weeks' gestation. The history was unremarkable except for smoking 20 cigarettes a day. The pelvic examination further was recorded in the office record: BI—WNL; DC—10 cm; arch—<90°; sacrum—flat; coccyx—rigid; impression—borderline pelvis.

The patient was seen at the expected intervals of one month through the 28th week. The blood pressure and FHT were considered normal. An occasional trace of albumin appeared in the urine. In the last 10 weeks of pregnancy the blood pressure rose to levels of 138-156/90-94 mm Hg. At about 39 weeks a biophysical profile was done. There was no report of fetal activity, but the gestational age was determined to be 38 to 39 weeks with an estimated fetal birth weight of about 3,500 gm. Three weeks later the patient was examined and the cervix was said to be soft and about 3 cm dilated and 75 percent effaced; she was thought to be in early labor.

The patient was admitted to the labor room, and after two and a half hours of observation it was noted that there were "insufficient uterine contractions." Augmentation with Pitocin was ordered.

After five hours of gradually increasing intravenous Pitocin, "minimal variability" was noted and the Pitocin was stopped. Uterine contractions continued for the next three hours and the dilatation was noted to increase to 8 cm. Ten hours after admission, with no further progress, the Pitocin was restarted.

The augmentation continued, keeping the contractions at 2- to 3-minute intervals. The dilatation was noted to be complete 19 hours after admission. "Minimal variability" was noted on two other occasions during this period, and the patient was taken to the delivery room. Examination revealed some caput to be present, and low forceps were applied. Again the cervix was said to be completely dilated, but the station was reported to be +1.

Tucker forceps were applied and the head was brought to +2 to +3 station and the forceps were removed. With "minimal fundal pressure" the head was delivered. There was considerable caput, and some "cephalhematoma" was described over the left temporal area of the skull. The muscle tone of the infant was not described, but a pediatrician was called to evaluate the baby.

About one hour after delivery, the infant was examined by the pediatrician, who found a lethargic infant who cried only when stimulated and had a large caput/hematoma above the left ear. X-rays of the skull showed a definite depressed right parietal skull fracture with the noted cephalhematoma on the left side of the head. An emergency transfer to the medical center was accomplished.

In the medical center hospital, a CT scan of the head revealed the above-described fracture, some blood in the subgaleal area, with subdural and subarachnoid blood as well. Seizures were observed, and were brought under control by medication. The CT abnormalities resolved during the hospitalization and the baby was discharged after two weeks to go home with her parents.

A complete neurologic evaluation at 22 months of age revealed that there had been no more seizures since discharge from the medical center hospital at 3 weeks of age, and an EEG was found to be normal. The neurologist thought that speech would be slow to develop, and it was his opinion that the seizures and the delayed speech development were the direct result of injury at birth.

A lawsuit was filed, charging the obstetrician with negligence because he did not do a cesarean section in a timely fashion, and attempted to deliver the child vaginally by applying midforceps in a situation where he had already identified a "borderline pelvis." A defense could not be developed, making a settlement mandatory.

LOSS PREVENTION COMMENTS

When this case is examined retrospectively with all the records available to the reviewer, it is very difficult to understand how the physician could manage this patient's case in the way he did! Did he not take cognizance of the small pelvis after he had described it in the initial examination? Did he not wonder why, after augmenting the labor for more than 12 hours, the head did not descend into the pelvis as one would expect? Even after this experience, and with the patient under anesthesia, the head was still found at a +1 level. One would think that he would have surely related the failure of the head to descend into the pelvis to a cephalo-pelvic disproportion as a result of the "small pelvis." Had he processed the management of this patient with all the facts in mind, he would certainly not have tried to do a forceps extraction through this compromised pelvis.

Why did this attending physician not recognize the difficulties presented by this labor and proceed to do the cesarean section avoiding this traumatic delivery? Only the attending physician can really answer this question. We are left to conclude that he did not look at his initial physical examination after he had done it, and proceeded to manage this patient as if she had a normal pelvis. The reason for a medical record in the first place is to cause us to keep in mind important facts about the patient that will help us to better evaluate and treat. Here our physician ignored his own good record, and almost certainly caused patient injury.

126.   POSTPARTUM BACK PAIN—SO WHAT?

*Allegations—Failure to diagnose and treat post-epidural
            infection (paraspinal abscesses)*
*Physician Issues—Failure to react appropriately to patient's
            complaints; failure to obtain appropriate diagnostic
            tests in timely manner*
*Patient Issues—Pain and suffering; neurological deficit;
            months of rehabilitation and recuperation; residual
            neurological deficit*
Outcome—Very large six-figure settlement

CASE STUDY

A 30-year-old gravida 1 para 0 delivered a healthy male infant under epidural anesthesia after a normal labor. She was up and ambulating as expected on the first postpartum day. She voided and was able to be discharged home the following day. On the third day home she called the physician's office twice complaining of constipation and backache. The next day she made a call and was sent Darvocet N 100 for pain. (This phone call was not recorded by the office staff as the others had been.) She complained that the back pain had been getting worse every day and that she was intermittently feverish. On postpartum day 9 she called the physician's office and again complained of increasingly severe back pain, but this time the pain seemed to be involving her legs, worse on the left. She was advised to go the emergency department of the hospital for examination and further treatment.

The history given in the ED was a repeat of what she had given the physician on call for the Ob/Gyn group. She said again that she had delivered nine days earlier and had had an epidural anesthetic that "has been giving me problems ever since." The back pain now involved both legs and was getting worse. There was no swelling, tenderness, or redness at the injection site. Routine laboratory tests were done, and the WBC count was 18,000/cu mm with a shift to the left.

The urine showed some blood, WBCs 10 to 15/cu mm, 1+ albumin, and 3+ bacteria. On culture group D *Streptococcus* was identified which was reported as "usually susceptible to nitrofurantoin." An hour or more later in the patient's ED stay another physician, the "on-call" doctor for the Ob/Gyn group, re-examined the

patient and reported some tenderness over the epidural site and
questionable swelling in the area of L2-3. A neurologic examination
revealed no neck stiffness, but on straight-leg raising of both legs her
low back pain became severe at about 35 to 40 degrees. The evaluation
was somewhat confused by her severe constipation. Digital removal of
the impaction was accomplished on her admission to the outpatient
department.

A neurologist consulted by phone gave a telephone order for a
CT scan of the lumbar spine area, which showed a "density which
appears to displace the cauda equina posteriorly and is separate from
the annulus fibrosus." It suggested the presence of a "localized
hematoma or area of local infection." The neurologist examined the
patient on Friday, and believed transfer to a tertiary facility was not
needed at the time, but did order an MRI for Monday. She continued to
be febrile. Nitrofurantoin was ordered, and if the temperature went to
102°F the neurologist was to be called.

Over the next day she could not void, and an indwelling
catheter became a necessity. She continued to complain of back and
leg pain. She stated that her right leg now felt "dead." She could move
the leg with effort. She continued to complain of being unable to have
a bowel movement.

On Sunday, with the difficulty getting worse, she was
transferred to the center where more definitive measures could be
taken. By noon a laminectomy had been done, with a bilateral
paraspinal abscess found and evacuated. Aggressive antibiotic
treatment led to improvement, but there was a residual neurologic
deficit involving predominantly the left leg.

A lawsuit was filed charging negligent delay in diagnosis and
treatment of the post-epidural infection that led to the permanent
neurologic deficit in this young mother.

LOSS PREVENTION COMMENTS

On admission to the ED nine days after delivery, she stated, "I
had an epidural and have been having trouble with it ever since." She
had called the obstetrician's office three times, one of them not
documented, complaining of constipation, not an unusual postpartum
complaint, and pain that was centered in the low back, again not an
unusual complaint a few days after delivery. At the time of the ED
examination, she complained that the pain was involving both legs,
one worse than the other.

The obstetrician found some "swelling and tenderness" over
the epidural injection site, and discovered that on attempting to do
straight-leg raising the back pain became severe. The CT scan ordered

while she was in the outpatient department of the facility showed evidence of "hematoma or infection" in the area of the epidural.

The patient was febrile and the urine showed some infection, which, at the worst, was unimpressive even with the culture and sensitivity showing a group D *Streptococcus* sensitive to nitrofurantoin. The chemotherapy was begun, and one has to wonder if the epidural infection could have been resolved with more aggressive antibiotic therapy at that time.

It was Friday, and in retrospect the decision to delay transfer to the tertiary care facility in the face of these findings is confusing. It was a Sunday when symptoms, including fever, forced the transfer to the center with emergency definitive care.

It is always of fundamental importance to listen to the patient! "I had an epidural and it has been giving me trouble ever since," she said in the ED. One cannot escape the hint that, because it was a weekend, this management of the patient led to the delay in the correct diagnosis and treatment.

A very large settlement was required to close this case. Both the obstetrician, his group, and the neurologist and his group were found negligent, and contributed to the settlement.

127. LOST IN THE SHUFFLE OF A BUSY PRACTICE

Allegations—Negligence in diagnosis and treatment of ovarian cancer

Physician Issues—Very busy practice; staff shielded physician from patients; failure to follow up on known "complex mass" in left ovary

Patient Issues—Loss of chance; could not get in to see attending; metastatic disease; death

Outcome—Six-to-seven-figure confidential settlement

CASE STUDY

A 28-year-old asymptomatic gravida 2 para 1, eight weeks pregnant by dates, who had been a patient of a very busy obstetrician for about seven years, returned looking forward to his delivery of her second baby. Her first is now a healthy and active 3-year-old girl. A routine ultrasound examination at about 24 weeks' gestation showed a "complex mass" in the left ovary. The patient was informed about the findings and was assured that "we" would "watch it," although it was probably some ovarian enlargement associated with her pregnancy. The second routine ultrasound showed the same mass, but no increase in size.

The patient progressed to term uneventfully, delivered a healthy female infant, and at four weeks postpartum seemed to be doing well. The pelvic examination was recorded as being "within normal limits." No mention was made of the ovarian mass. At five months postpartum the patient was still breast-feeding. On this visit the history of breast cancer in the family was recorded. The pelvic examination again was reported as "within normal limits," with no mention of the ovarian mass.

When the baby was 10 months old, the patient called her obstetrician's office with a history of having "pulled her back" while playing with her older daughter. She complained of pain in the right chest and was sent tablets of a synthetic codeine for relief. Two weeks later the patient again contacted the office with a history of intermittent vaginal bleeding for ten days. Birth control pills were prescribed, but when a week later she made another phone call to the office complaining that the pills made her very nervous, the prescription was changed.

The next day she went to an urgent care center complaining of the severe right-sided chest pain on movement, deep breathing, and cough. Examination revealed some tenderness over the painful area and a chest x-ray revealed two fractured ribs, for which she was given a codeine preparation and a rib belt. A week later she called the urgent care center stating that the pain was still very troublesome and the rib belt was changed at no charge.

A week later, after making two calls to the urgent care center requesting narcotics for pain and being denied a call-in prescription, she came in bitterly complaining of the chest pain. At this visit, the examination was documented to show "clear lungs" and no tenderness over the chest cage.

It was now eight weeks after the injury and six weeks since her last contact with her obstetrician. She called in requesting to be seen and was placed on the "cancellation list." She was seen within a few days and complained of continued pain in her chest, some frequency of urination, and vaginal discharge. Nitrobid was prescribed, and the pain prescription was refilled. An ultrasound of the pelvis again showed the "complex mass" of the left ovary suggesting a hemorrhagic cyst, cyst abscess, or endometrioma. The mass was thought to be slightly larger than on previous examinations.

At this time in the illness, her husband became involved and called the obstetrician's office to report that he had taken his wife to an orthopedist who had sent her to a lung specialist. He had found fluid on her chest, for which a thoracentesis was done. Cytology on the fluid disclosed some "atypical" cells. A CT of the abdomen showed the ovarian mass and findings suggesting carcinoma, with metastases to the peritoneum. A biopsy of the ovary showed an ovarian carcinoma. Radical pelvic surgery was done following a course of chemotherapy. The prognosis was very grave, and indeed the patient died about six months later. Her last baby was 2 years old at the time of her mother's death.

A lawsuit was filed charging the obstetrician with negligence in the management of ovarian carcinoma.

LOSS PREVENTION COMMENTS

It is well known that the earlier the diagnosis and treatment of ovarian carcinoma, the better the prognosis. The treating physician in this case failed to follow up on the initial ultrasound report with definitive confirmation of the findings and tissue diagnosis of the lesion. The urgency of this situation demanded no less, even during the pregnancy. Multiple contacts with the office were made. There were two more ultrasound examinations showing the same ovarian mass. The "fractures" of the ribs in the absence of a history of a blow of some sort to the chest is suspicious. The visits to the urgent care center were clearly made because nothing definitive was done by her primary physician. The multiple refills of narcotic prescriptions over the telephone without investigation and the general laxity of the telephone management of this long-time patient's complaints are suggestive of a practice that is too busy to attend to the patients being seen. Is it possible for a physician to be so busy that he fails to follow acceptable standards of practice? I believe it is! As managed care proliferates, the temptation to see more and more patients could expose more and more of us to this danger. Running faster and faster on the treadmill in order to stay in the same place is truly a temptation, but it is also a danger.

In this case, no expert testimony could be developed to assist in the defense of the defendant physician. The sympathy factor in this case of a young woman with two small children is such that, in this medicolegal environment, settlement seemed mandatory. Although confidential as to amounts, high six-/seven-figure sums are routine.

128.   PRIMARY CARE EQUALS PRIMARY RESPONSIBILITY

Allegations—Failure to diagnose and treat breast cancer in a timely manner
Physician Issues—Casual approach to breast findings; failure to follow breast findings closely

> *Patient Issues—Loss of chance; went through pregnancy*
> *without definitive diagnosis of breast mass; metastatic*
> *when definitively treated*
> *Outcome—Large six-figure settlement*

CASE STUDY

A 32-year-old gravida 2, para 2 reported to her obstetrician/ gynecologist, whom she considered her primary care physician, with a complaint of some fullness in the left breast, which she had discovered about two months before while taking a bath. Six months previously, when the patient had had a complete physical examination, she had no complaints and the physical examination was completely normal.

The breasts were examined and the physician recorded in the office record "an area of diffuse nodularity in the left breast typical of fibrocystic disease." Nevertheless, he ordered a mammogram as a baseline procedure. The radiologist reported "no definite abnormalities noted." He added that "no calcifications were seen" and "no evidence of neoplastic disease." The report concluded with a statement, "certain neoplasms are not detectable on mammography" and "repeat mammogram should be considered in three months." This was reported to the patient by her primary care physician.

The next visit to her physician was about six months later. She had not menstruated in about ten weeks, and after examination was said to be eight weeks pregnant. The EDC was determined to be seven months later. Routine prenatal care was begun with this visit. The course was uneventful and the patient was seen at the expected intervals. There was no mention of the breast on the initial examination, but the prenatal record at 20 and 32 weeks contained the notation "no change left breast." An uneventful delivery occurred at the expected time and the patient did well postpartum. She did not breast-feed the baby.

When her baby was 3 months old, the patient again visited her physician, this time reporting some "soreness in the left breast." Examination revealed what her doctor thought was an area of increased nodularity with some evidence of inflammation. Repeat mammogram reported "significant change since last exam" and suggested biopsy. A careful review of the earlier films revealed some suggestion of a mass.

The primary care physician then called the patient's surgeon into consultation. His examination revealed a 5-cm mass with a palpable axillary node. Excisional biopsy was followed by a modified radical mastectomy. Pathology reported a large carcinoma of the left breast, and 15 of 23 nodes were positive.

A lawsuit was filed charging both the Ob/Gyn and the

radiologist with negligence. The complaint alleged that the Ob/Gyn was negligent for not more aggressively following the patient. The radiologist was charged because he had not followed up on the management of the patient since he had recommended "repeat examination should be considered in three months." During the litigation, the radiologist was dismissed on summary judgment. The jury found for the patient, with a large monetary award.

Loss Prevention Comments

Though two physicians were involved in the management of this patient, the court considered that there was no negligence in the radiologist's initial interpretation of the mammogram even though a subsequent mammogram revealed a suggestion of a mass, and this physician was dismissed from the litigation on summary judgment.

The Ob/Gyn's medical record revealed an almost casual approach to the management of his patient, whom he found to have an area of "diffuse nodularity" in her left breast. He saw the patient repeatedly without focusing his strict attention on the left breast and recording a careful examination. The record seemed to suggest that the physician shifted the responsibility of carefully watching the left breast to the patient and did not take his own responsibility seriously enough. More than a year had elapsed since the recommendation of "repeat examination in three months," and still the primary care physician had taken no positive action.

Perhaps the most important error made by the Ob/Gyn was that he did not involve in this case a specialist who would definitively manage the breast mass. It is very doubtful that a primary care physician should ever assume the responsibility for following a patient of this type without the input of the physician who will do surgery if it becomes the treatment of choice.

129. OUTPATIENT RISK—INPATIENT INJURY

Allegations—Negligence in management of gestational
diabetes; negligence in management of toxemia;
negligence in management of shoulder dystocia
Physician Issues—Failure to take into account elevated blood
sugar (health department); system failure
physician's office/health department)
Patient Issues—Severe hypoxic brain damage in baby
Outcome—Demand large seven figures; settlement for a
six-figure amount

CASE STUDY

Our colleague had agreed to assist in the management of medically indigent patients who were pregnant. He cooperated with the local health department (HD) in this most commendable effort. Many times the physician would initially examine a pregnant woman referred to him from the HD, calculate the EDC, refer her back to the HD for regular prenatal visits, re-examine her again at about 28 weeks, and, if the pregnancy progressed normally, weekly visits would be resumed about two weeks before the calculated due date. This kind of protocol has been acceptable to the prenatal clinics of local HDs, the medically indigent patients, and many Ob/Gyns and FPs all over the state for about ten years. Many thousands of babies have been given a good start in life by this kind of concern for the care of the indigent pregnant patient. Under this kind of arrangement, the laboratory work necessary to properly monitor the patient was done by the state laboratory.

The patient is a 25-year-old HD patient who was seen in July with a history of an LMP of March 15. She was a gravida 3 para 2 who had been toxic with her first pregnancy, with high blood pressures and a 9-lb baby. The second pregnancy had ended in the delivery of a 7-lb 10-oz baby who was transferred to an NICU with seizures. She had normal blood pressures on the initial examination but was more than 15 percent overweight (5 ft 5 in, 210 lb). The remainder of the examination was within normal limits. The physician made the necessary arrangements for his patient to be followed in the HD clinic and, on the proper prenatal record form sent his findings to that facility. A month after her initial evaluation she weighed 213 lb and continued to gain about 3 to 5 lb per month. The HD visits had not shown any problems except the weight. Her urine examinations had not revealed any protein or glucose and her blood pressure had not gone above the levels of the first examination (136/80). A fasting blood sugar was done at about 28 weeks' gestation and was reported as 125 with a normal range of 60 to 115. The HD record contained the note, "Yellow copy to attending physician's office."

On the following visit to the HD, at about 32 weeks, there was a 1+ protein and the blood pressure was not changed. On that visit, the weight was 226, a 36-lb weight gain since onset of pregnancy. Two weeks later, at about 34 weeks, she weighed 231 lb, had a blood pressure of 150/100 mm Hg, and again had a 1+ protein. She was sent to see the Ob/Gyn that same day. On his record the findings were about the same except the protein was 2+. She was sent home for bed rest. One week later, the blood pressure was improved at 152/90 mm Hg, the weight was unchanged, her protein was still 2+, and she was to stay in bed and return in one week.

When she returned, she was about 37 weeks' gestation, and her weight was 231 lb, blood pressure 146/90 mm Hg, protein 2+ with "large" ketones. She continued on bed rest with the protein showing 2+ to 4+; her weight increased slowly, with a blood pressure 90 to 100 diastolic, but she complained of no headache or dizziness. At 39+ weeks she was admitted for probable induction.

The hospital record does not show any significant differences from the prenatal findings. After observation for about 18 hours, and with a planned induction scheduled for the following morning, the membranes spontaneously ruptured at 6:30. The fluid showed thin meconium staining and a scalp electrode was applied. Labor progressed uneventfully with an epidural analgesia. The FMT did not show any significant abnormality, and after about 12 hours the patient was 9.5 cm dilated with the baby "moving down." She began to push, and after 14 hours of good labor vaginal delivery was attempted with the aid of vacuum extraction.

The head was delivered without difficulty, but it soon became apparent that there was shoulder dystocia, and the anterior shoulder could not be delivered. The appropriate maneuvers were attempted to no avail. The posterior clavicle had to be fractured in order to get the baby delivered. It was about 8 minutes between the delivery of the head and the delivery of the rest of the baby. The infant weighed 13 lb 13 oz. With Apgar scores of 0-0, intubation and vigorous resuscitation were carried out. Transfer to the NICU took place promptly and the baby was found to have sustained severe brain damage.

A lawsuit was filed demanding $2 million in damages and charging negligence in the management of the toxic pregnant patient with gestational diabetes.

LOSS PREVENTION COMMENTS

When physicians in our state cooperate with the state health department for the delivery of the indigent patient, it is indeed a public service of great importance, and those physicians should be commended for it. While there might have been areas of management in this case that could be criticized, the real problem was not taking into account the finding of an elevated blood sugar that was found in the laboratory work done in the HD, and according to their record mailed to the attending physician. In fact, the report was received by the physician's office but not correctly added to the patient's record.

Again and again in these case reports we have found that there is a breakdown in the physician's office management that is the key to his liability. Here again we see it. The management of this case would have been entirely different had the doctor known he was dealing with gestational diabetes. Certainly, with the history of toxicity in the past two pregnancies, there would have been a heightened sensitivity to the likelihood of trouble that would require aggressive management in the form of earlier delivery of this patient by cesarean section. While experts were ready to be critical of management of the toxemia independent of the diabetes, there was no question that a different approach would have been taken had the HD's blood glucose been taken into account. What can we do? First of all, in our offices we can employ good help with the appropriate training and motivation to be a participating partner in the management of our patients. Such training is available for your staff. They can make all the difference in the world in our practice, in our patients' outcomes and confidence, and in the prevention of patient injury. This is another example of our office practices being the key to loss prevention.

XIII

Conclusion

What started out to be a collaborative educational
effort for the physician owners of State Volunteer Mutual Insurance
Company and the members of the Tennessee Medical Association has
become a much larger effort that has continued for fifteen years.
Regular inclusions of these cases in the *Journal of the Tennessee
Medical Association* has met with solid readership interest. Now,
there appears one of these cases in the Medical Journal of the Medical
Association of Arkansas, and I am told that the same kind of interest is
apparent. I am extremely gratified that physicians read the cases and
express their own interest in the subject matter. That was and is the
intent with every case.

Scrutiny of the cases will show that while the situations vary,
the principles of loss prevention for the doctor are simple but, by no
means, easy. There must be the recognition by the physicians that the
medical record is either the greatest ally or the greatest enemy if
litigation occurs. For it to be the ally needed in litigation it must
contain certain elements that tell a story.

The story begins with a relationship between the physician
and the patient that allows for a careful history of the complaint to be
recorded. There must follow a careful physical examination that
highlights the specific complaints brought to the doctor that appears
in the record. Based on this data, the physician must gather what
corroborative information needed to make a reasonable and probable
diagnosis and fashion a logical plan of treatment. This evidence can
consist of information from the clinical laboratory, the x-ray (imaging
department), consulting physicians, the clinical record of physicians
that have treated the patient in the past, or any other source of
information that bears on the complaint being studied.

In order for this story to be complete, these corroborating
pieces of evidence must be a part of the record. This requires a
system in the physician's practice that ensures that these reports from

the ancillary areas mentioned become known to the physician, get acted upon by him or her, and get in the record. While this system sounds simple, it breaks down frequently and becomes the center-piece of litigation. Examples are the repeat mammogram that never gets done because the report of the previous one never makes it to the record with evidence that the physician has seen and acted on the report. Another all, too, common occurrence is the x-ray study that is read and acted on by the physician when there follows a report from the radiologist that differs in a material way from the reading of the physician and requires a different response. The implementation of this system can take many different forms that are successful, but it must be present and functional and accurate to assist the physician in any challenge, legally or professionally.

By far the most frequent error in the medical record is the failure on the part of the caregivers to document appropriately the elements of the story that show that there has been a logical approach to diagnosis and treatment. When the documentation is lacking it is assumed that whatever part of the record that is missing was never done regardless of the testimony of the physician. Sloppy documentation is interpreted many times as evidence of sloppy patient care.

It is the hope of all of us who have had any part in the production of this book that those who read it will use it in their encounters with patients.

Glossary

1,2, or 3+
Measurement of the descent of the fetal head into the pelvis during labor

2L
Two liters/min

A
Indicates temperature has been taken in the Axilla

AAA
Abdominal Aortic Aneurysm

ABG
Arterial blood gas

Acetabulum
The socket of the hip joint

ACOG
American College of Obstetrics and Gynecology

AFB
Acid Fast Bacillus (Tuberculosis)

AFC
A marker for malignancy found by testing blood

AMA
American Medical Association

APGAR score
A numerical expression of a newborn infants condition one minute after birth(1-10;10 best)

Arch
Less than 90 degrees—A manual pelvic measurement

AROM
Artificial rupture of membranes

Arthroplasty
Hip replacement surgery

Arthroscopic surgery
Surgery done through a small instrument that allows the surgeon to operate in the interior of a joint

ASA
American Society of Anesthesiologists (Risk Assessment before surgery)

AVM
Arteriovenous Malformation

Bells palsy
Paralysis of facial nerve

BI
Bi-ischeal—A manual pelvic measurement

BOW
Bag of waters

BP
Blood pressure

BTB
Beat to beat

C-spine
Cervical spine (neck)

CABG-6
Coronary artery bypass graft X 6

CBC
Complete Blood Count

CCU
Coronary Care Unit

CFS
Cerebrospinal fluid

Chemoneucleolysis
Dissolution of the disc by the
injection of a chemolytic agent

Circumflex
A coronary artery

CO₂
Blood carbon dioxide level

Coccyx
Rigid—A manual pelvic
measurement—An intravaginal
description of the Coccyx

Comminution
A break of a bone that is
fragmented

CPR
Cardiopulmonary Resuscitation

CRNA
Certified registered nurse
anesthetist

CT
Imaging by use of compurterized
tomography technology

Cul-de-sac
Area behind the uterus

CVF
Cerebrospinal fluid

CVP
Central venous pressure

CXR
Chest x-ray

CYA
Cover your ass

Cylert
A drug recommended for Attention
Deficit Disorder

Cytology
Microscopic examination of cells

D&C
Dilatation and Curettage of the cervix

D5
5% glucose solution

DC
Diagonal conjugant—a manual
pelvic measurement

Demerol
A commonly used narcotic

Diastasis
Separation

DIC
Disseminated Intravascular
coagulopathy

DKA
Diabetic ketoacidosis

DSRL
Dextrose (glucose) 5% in solution
of Ringer's Lactate

DTR
Deep tendon reflexes

ED
Emergency Department

EDC
Expected date of confinement
(delivery)

EDP
Emergency department physician

ERP
Emergency room physician

EEG
Electroencephalogram

EFM
Electronic fetal monitoring

EGD
Examination of the stomach and
the duodenum using an endoscope

EKG
Electrocardiogram—a recording of
the electric impulses generated by
the beating of the heart

EMG
Electromyography—the recording of the electrical activity of nerves/muscles

EMS
Emergency medical system (or service)

EOM
External ocular movements

ER
Emergency Room

ETOH
Alcohol

ETT
Endotracheal tube

FHR
Fetal heart rate

FHT
Fetal heart tones

Fiorinal # 3
A pain reliever containing codeine, a narcotic

Fx
Fracture

GI
Gastrointestinal

Gr2,Pa1
Two pregnancies, one live birth

GTT
Glucose tolerance test

Guillain Barré
Febrile polyneuritis

H$_2$ blockers
Drugs that inhibit the secretion of acid in the stomach

Hct
Hemotocrit

HEENT
Head, eyes, ears, nose, throat

Heimlich maneuver
Squeezing of the chest in order to express any obstruction in the trachea (windpipe)

HELLP
Hemolysis, elevated liver enzymes, low platelet count

Hematoma
Collection of blood in the tissues creating swelling

Hgb
Hemoglobin

Hired gun
An expert witness paid for testimony in a lawsuit

HMO
Health maintenance organization

HNP
Herniated nucleus pulposus (ruptured intervertebral disc)

Hyperostosis
Overgrowth of bone usually at the joint margin

IT&O (I&O)
Fluid intake and output

ID
Infectious disease physician

ICU
Intensive care unit

IGR
Intrauterine growth retardation

IM
Intramuscular

IV
Intravenous

IVP
Intravenous pyelogram (Visualizing the kidneys using an intravenous dye)

Jousting
One physician blaming another for a bad result

KUB
Plain x-ray of the abdomen showing the kidney, ureter, and bladder area

L&D
Labor and delivery

L5
Lumbar 5

LAD
Left anterior descending coronary artery

Leucocytosis
High white blood cell count

LMP
Last menstrual period

LP
Lumbar puncture

Lytes
Electrolytes (sodium, chlorides)

Mastectomy
Surgical removal of the breast

Menarche
Onset of menstrual periods

Menometrorrhagia
Irregular and excessive menstrual periods

Met
A measurement of muscular exercise

Mgm
milligrams

MgSO$_4$
Magnesium sulfate

MRI
Magnetic resonance imaging

MS
Multiple sclerosis

MVA
Motor vehicle accident

Myelogram
A diagnostic test for which a dye is injected into the spinal canal to visualize the space and demonstrate any protrusion into that space.

Narcan
A drug to counteract the opiate analgesics

NG
Naso-gastric

NICU
Neonatal intensive care unit

NPH insulin
Intermediate acting insulin

NPO
Nothing by mouth

NS
Normal Saline Solution

O$_2$
Oxygen

Omphalocele
Herniation of abdominal contents through the umbilicus

OR
Operating room

ORIF
Open reduction internal fixation

Osteophytes
Bone spurs

P
Pulse

Pamelor Nortryptoline—An antidepressant not recommended for children

PARR
Postanesthesia recovery room

PCP
Primary care physician

PCV
Packed cell volume—a measure of the red cell mass

PDR
Physicians' Desk Reference

PE
Pulmonary embolus

PEEP
Positive end—expiratory pressure

PHD
Public health department

Phenergan
A drug for suppression of nausea

PO$_2$
Blood oxygen level

Popliteal fossa
Space behind the knee

PPT
Prothrombin time—a measure of blood coagulability

PRN
As needed

PT
Physical therapy

Quadriplegia
Paralysis of all four extremities

R
Respiratory rate

RCA
Right coronary artery

RUL
Right upper lobe

RUQ
Right upper quadrant

Rx
Treatment or prescription

S1
Sacral 1

Sacrum
Flat—A manual pelvic measurement (an intravaginal description of the sacrum)

Salpingo-oophorectomy
The surgical removal of the Fallopian tubes and ovaries

Scotomata
Spots before the eyes

Serum Lipids
Fats in the blood (cholesterol and triglycerides)

S-G
Swanz-Ganz

SGOT
A blood test for liver function

SGPT
A blood test for liver function

SICU
Surgical Intensive Care Unit

SLWC
Short-leg walking case

SOB
Shortness of breath

STAT
Do immediately!

Subluxation
The slipping of one vertebra on another

Supp
Rectal suppository

SVMIC
State Volunteer Mutual Insurance Company (Tennessee's physician owned medical malpractice company)

T
Temperature

T&A
Surgical removal of tonsils and
adenoids

T3
Third thoracic vertebra

Tachycardia
Rapid heart rate

Tachypnia
Rapid breathing

TAH
Total abdominal hysterectomy

Talwin
A narcotic

Tardive dyskinesia
A late developing complication of
antipsychotic drugs characterized
by uncontrolled, purposeless
movements.

TBC
Tuberculosis

TM
Tympanic membrane (Ear drum)

TNTC
Too numerous to count

Toradol
A nonnarcotic pain reliever

Ureter
The tube that leads from the
kidney to the urinary bladder

VS
Vital signs

WBC
White blood cell count

Acknowledgments

I would like to express my appreciation to the following:

To my long-time friends, Dr. and Mrs. Bob Taylor, who live in Salem, Oregon, and work in risk management for the Northwest Physicians Mutual Insurance Company. For their support and encouragement I am forever grateful.

To Bob Brittain, Colorado surgeon, risk manager (retired) for both the Colorado and the Arizona physician liability insurance companies, who was in the forefront of professionals, who believed in and promoted the teaching of loss prevention to physicians in an effort to prevent medical legal action against them. I am thankful for his example in my efforts to follow him in this pursuit.

To C. J. Gideon, trial attorney, senior in the firm Gideon and Wiseman in Nashville, who has the reputation of being a brilliant and effective defense counsel throughout Tennessee and contiguous states, I express my profound thanks.

To Theo J. (Jim) Emison, in Alamo, Tennessee, an eminently successful and honored trial attorney principally in the field of medical malpractice litigation, for his encouragement in the idea to put the "Cases of the Month" into book form and to the continuation of the work that resulted in this book.

To John Gilbert, senior vice president for marketing in State Volunteer Mutual Insurance Company, for his careful review of most of the "cases" and promoting them for reprint in the *Journal of the Arkansas Medical Association*.

To Clifton Meador, MD, Vanderbilt University, my former director of medical affairs at Saint Thomas Hospital, Nashville, for his encouragement all along the way.

To Jean Wishnick, assistant to the editor of the *Journal of the Tennessee Medical Association* for teaching me repeatedly how to "attach" a document to e-mail.

To Charla Honea, an invaluable consultant on this project, and to her crew for their good work for us both.

To Dee Dee Evans for her continuing support and her keen eye in reading the proof.

To many other friends and colleagues for their encouragemeny throughout the process of *Let the Record Show.*

J. KELLEY AVERY, MD